Neo-Fascism in Europe

Edited by
Luciano Cheles
Ronnie Ferguson
Michalina Vaughan

LONGMAN
London and New York

Longman Group UK Limited,
Longman House, Burnt Mill, Harlow,
Essex CM20 2JE, England
and Associated Companies throughout the world.

Published in the United States of America
by Longman Publishing, New York

© Longman Group UK Limited 1991

First published 1991
Second impression 1992

British Library Cataloguing in Publication Data
Neo-fascism in Europe
1. Europe. Neo-fascism
I. Ferguson, Ronald II. Cheles, Luciano III. Vaughan, Michalina
320.533094

ISBN 0–582–03951–7 pbk
ISBN 0–582–03950–9

Library of Congress Cataloging in Publication Data
Neo-Fascism in Europe edited by Luciano Cheles, Ronnie Ferguson,
Michalina Vaughan.
p. cm.
Includes bibliographical references.
ISBN 0-582-03950-9 -- ISBN 0-582-03951-7 (pbk.)
1. Europe--Politics and government--20th century. 2. Fascism –
Europe--History--20th century. I. Cheles, Luciano. II. Ferguson,
Ronnie III. Vaughan, Michalina.
D726.5.N46 1991
320.5'33'094--dc20
90 – 5866
CIP

Set in 10/12 pt Bembo

Produced by Longman Singapore Publishers (Pte) Ltd
Printed in Singapore

Contents

List of contributors   v

List of illustrations   viii

Acknowledgements   x

Foreword   xi

1 Introduction: concepts of right and left   1
    Jaroslav Krejčí

2 The 'Movimento Sociale Italiano': A historical profile   19
    Roberto Chiarini

3 'Nostalgia dell'avvenire'. The new propaganda of the MSI   43
    between tradition and innovation *Luciano Cheles*

4 The far right in Germany since 1945 *David Childs*   66

5 Militant neo-nazism in the Federal Republic of   86
    Germany in the 1980s *Christopher T. Husbands*

6 The Holocaust denial: a study in propaganda technique   120
    Roger Eatwell

7 The extreme right in Spain: a dying species?   147
    Sheelagh Ellwood

8 The radical right in contemporary Portugal   167
    António Costa Pinto

9 Neo-fascism in modern Greece   191
    Vassilis Kapetanyannis

iii

Contents

10 The extreme right in France : 'Lepenisme' or the   211
    politics of fear *Michalina Vaughan*

11 The new right in France *Douglas Johnson*   234

12 The far right in contemporary Britain   245
    Gerry Gable

13 Women and the National Front   264
    Martin Durham

    Select Bibliography   284

    Index   289

List of contributors

Luciano Cheles lectures in Italian Studies at Lancaster University. He is especially interested in the relations between visual arts and politics. He has published *The Studiolo of Urbino. An Iconographic Investigation* (Reichert Verlag and Penn State Press, 1986), and essays on Renaissance political frescos and the propaganda of contemporary Italian parties.

Roberto Chiarini teaches in the Faculty of Political Sciences of Milan University. He has worked on liberalism, fascism and neo-fascism, and his publications include *Da Salò a Piazza della Loggia* (Franco Angeli, 1983), *L'armonia e l 'ardimento. L'ascesa del fascismo nella Brescia di Augusto Turati* (Franco Angeli, 1988) and *Fini e fine della politica* (Franco Angeli, 1990).

David Childs is Professor of Politics at Nottingham University, and Director of its Institute of German, Austrian and Swiss affairs. His recent publications include: *East Germany to the 1990s : Can it resist Glasnost?* (Economist Intelligence Unit ,1988) and (co-editor with T. A. Baylis and M. Ruschemeyer), *East Germany in Comparative Perspective* (Routledge, 1989).

António Costa Pinto lectures in Modern European and Portuguese History in the Department of Sociology of the *Instituto Superior de Ciências do Trabalho e da Empresa*, Lisbon. He has been a researcher at the European University Institute, Florence since 1986, and is currently Visiting Fellow at the Center for European Studies, Stanford University.

Martin Durham is a lecturer in Politics at Wolverhampton Polytechnic. His research centres on British Fascism and sexual politics. He has written essays on women and the British Union of Fascists, and on the New Right's 'pro-family' politics. He is currently completing a book on the latter topic.

Roger Eatwell lectures in Politics in the School of Social Sciences at the University of Bath. He is General Editor of Pinter Publishers' series *Themes in Right-Wing Ideology and Politics*, and recent publications include (co-editor with N. O'Sullivan), *The Nature of the Right* (Pinter, 1989).

Sheelagh Ellwood is Visiting Fellow at the Centre for Contemporary Spanish Studies, Queen Mary – Westfield College (University of London). She is the author of *Spanish Fascism in the Franco Era: 'Falange Española de las JONS', 1936–1986* (Macmillan, 1987).

Ronnie Ferguson is Head of Italian Studies at Lancaster University. He was educated at the Universities of Glasgow and St Andrews, and has published on the Italian Renaissance, and on language and society in Italy. He has co-organised (with Luciano Cheles) exhibitions on Fascist art and propaganda, and on the 1984 Euro-elections.

Gerry Gable is the publisher of *Searchlight* magazine and a television producer. He writes, broadcasts and lectures internationally on the subjects of fascism and racism. He holds an American Adjunct Professorship in journalism.

Christopher T. Husbands is Reader in Sociology at the London School of Economics and Political Science. He has done extensive research in political sociology, and during recent years he has produced numerous publications on British voting behaviour, and on racism and right-wing political extremism in several European countries.

Douglas Johnson was educated at the Royal Grammar School, Lancaster; Worcester College, Oxford; and the Ecole Normale Supérieure, Paris. He was Professor of Modern History at the University of Birmingham before becoming Professor of French History at University College, London, in 1968. He is author of several books on French history.

Vassilis Kapetanyannis is Press Officer at the Greek Ministry of Information. He lived in London for fifteen years where he worked for the BBC, and at the Embassy of Greece as Press Attaché. He holds a Ph.D. in politics from Birkbeck College (University of London), and writes on Greek politics and international affairs.

Jaroslav Krejčí was born in Czechoslovakia. He specialised initially in macroeconomics, but his life experience led him towards the path of integrated social science, for which he eventually found the institutional base at the University of Lancaster, where he is now Emeritus Professor. His recent books include: *Great Revolutions Compared* (Harvester Press –

St. Martin's Press, 1987); *The Civilizations of Asia and the Middle East, Before the European Challenge* (Macmillan – State University of New York Press, 1990), and *Czechoslovakia at the Crossroads of European History* (Tauris, 1990).

Michalina Vaughan, *Docteur en Droit (d'Etat)*, read law, politics and sociology at Paris University. She taught sociology at LSE (1959–72) and at Lancaster University (1972–87), where she is Emeritus Professor.

List of illustrations

1. MSI poster produced for the 1970 elections.
2. Fascist poster, c.1935, urging Italians to buy Italian goods.
3. MSI poster produced for the 1970 elections.
4. Poster produced by the Fascist Party in 1922 to celebrate the near-failure of the general strike of July–August.
5. Recruitment poster of the youth league of the MSI, 1983.
6. Cuban poster, late 1960s.
7. MSI poster protesting against the State's 'repression' of right-wing activists.
8. May 1968 poster.
9. MSI poster celebrating 1 May, 1985.
10. May 1968 poster.
11. MSI poster calling for the introduction of death penalty for drug traffickers.
12. Michelangelo, *Pietá* (Vatican). Reproduced by kind permission of Plurigraf Terni.
13. MSI poster produced shortly after the terrorist attack in *Piazza della Loggia* in Brescia, 1974.
14. Titian, *Ecce Homo* (National Gallery of Ireland, Dublin).
15. Auxiliary of the Salò Republic being exposed to public insult at the fall of the regime, 1945.
16. MSI poster produced for the 1970 elections.
17. Propaganda postcard of the Salò Republic, 1943–45.
18. MSI poster showing Almirante talking at a party rally in Rome, 1983.
19. Mussolini addressing a crowd from a public building in Venice, 1938.
20. MSI poster urging people to vote 'YES', i.e. in favour of the abolition of the divorce law, in the referendum of 1974.
21. Fascist billboard on Palazzo Braschi, Rome, urging people to vote 'YES', i.e. in favour of the list of parliamentary candidates proposed by the regime, in the plebiscite of 1934.

22. Fascist poster announcing triumphantly the results of the plebiscite of 1934.
23. Anti-divorce poster produced for the referendum of 1974.
24. Goose-stepping soldiers.
25. MSI poster denouncing 'Communist' terrorist attacks against the police forces.
26. Wartime official portrait of Mussolini.
27. Poster produced by the women's caucus of the MSI, professing an anti-terrorist stance, 1979.
28. Film poster for Salvatore Samperi's *Cuore di mamma*, 1969.
29. Poster produced by the youth league of the MSI, 1986.
30. Cover design of Adolfo Mignemi's volume *Immagine coordinata per un impero. Etiopia 1935–1936* (published in 1984), which critically investigates the nature of Fascist propaganda during the Ethiopian campaign.
31. MSI poster commemorating the centenary of Mussolini's birth, 1983.
32. Poster produced by a self-styled 'Centre de Propagande anti-Bolscévique [sic], Genève', c.1983.

Acknowledgements

We are grateful to the following for permission to reproduce copyright material: The National Gallery of Ireland for the painting *Ecce Homo* by Titian and the picture of *Pietà* courtesy of Plurigraf S.p.A.

Foreword

This book stems from a conference on neo-fascism held at the University of Lancaster in November 1987. It was organised by the Italian Studies Section of that University. Support – both material and intellectual – was gratefully received from the French Studies Section, the German Studies Section, and the Departments of History, Linguistics, Politics and Sociology. We are also indebted, for help and intellectual stimulation, to Gill Seidel of Bradford University and to our late and much-regretted colleague Max Adereth. Finally, we should like to thank Mavis Connolly, Bridget Cook, Pat Kitchen and Sylvia Walmsley for the care with which they typed various parts/versions of the manuscript.

Nine of the chapters in this volume were presented by their authors as papers at the Lancaster conference. They have been revised in the light of participants' comments and brought up to date. The remaining three – by António Costa Pinto on Portugal, by Vassilis Kapetanyannis on Greece, and by Martin Durham on 'Women and the National Front' – were commissioned to cover areas which discussion had shown to arouse keen interest, such as the connection between neo-fascism and economic underdevelopment on the one hand, and the political exploitation of gender on the other.

Professor Krejčí's wide-ranging introductory chapter highlights the relevance of our theme to current trends and events. It would be superfluous to go over the same ground again. However, it might be worth commenting on the shift which has occurred since 1987 in the political landscape. The far right is no longer an exclusively Western European phenomenon; its presence in Central and Eastern Europe is by now a fact. Once more nationalism is an ideology of world-wide scale and its potential for disrupting the balance of power cannot be ignored. Conversely, the left – in particular its communist variant – has lost a great deal of credibility in Western Europe. In this volatile context, the threat of extremism is increasingly likely to come from the far right rather than from its polar opposite. In making this statement we do not only mean to insist on the topicality of neo-fascism as an ideology with a considerable – probably a growing – potential for mass mobilisation. We also wish to convey our awareness that the privilege of living in times of rapid historical change entails a corresponding responsibility for enforcing strict standards of political morality. To paraphrase Auden, to have 'lived by honest dreams cannot be an excuse for backing the bad against the worst'.

Luciano Cheles
Ronnie Ferguson
Michalina Vaughan
August 1990

CHAPTER ONE

Introduction: Concepts of Right and Left

Jaroslav Krejčí

As an introduction to our theme I would like to raise two points which are partly methodological and partly analytical in nature. First, that the appearance of Fascism, in conjuction with Soviet-type communism, has undermined the established concepts of right and left in politics. Second, that the existence of powerful Fascist-type movements and regimes was an ephemeral phenomenon in European history. Their rise was due to a specific type of relative deprivation caused by disorder, economic calamity and national humiliation, and they won power because of the direct or indirect support of all those who were afraid of expropriation in the event of a Communist or Socialist victory. At present, no such combination of factors exists in Europe, but a new configuration of conditions conducive to the rise of similar movements has emerged in various parts of the world.

The terms Fascism and neo-Fascism are classic ideal-type concepts derived from the proper name of one political movement and one political party, a name chosen by the founders of the party themselves. Since then, they have become generic terms applicable to all similar movements or parties throughout the world, irrespective of the name or colours under which they act. Understandably, the generic usage of any term cannot take into account all variations which necessarily appear both between countries and over time.

For a more differentiated evaluation, a more systematic terminology is preferable to such ideal-type concepts. Unfortunately, apart from the time-honoured Aristotelian criteria, there is only one system for arranging individual political phenomena into a conceptual spectrum. This system was taken from the sitting order which developed in the French parliament after Revolution (from what other source could a Cartesian-type

1

geometry appear in political nomenclature?): namely from the right to the left, from one extreme to another with a wide range of nuances in between. With respect to the complex nature of social issues which political groupings have to tackle more or less simultaneously, the practical application of such a scheme has to take into account several dimensions.

In the historical context of political differentiation which emerged in the French Revolution and which, to a greater or lesser extent, was followed by other European countries, the criteria of the right–left spectrum were basically defined by the degree to which individual groupings wanted to move away from the status quo. The possibility of a cyclic return was not, as a rule, envisaged.

The stance was projected into specific fields of social action. In political decision-making the right–left range was perceived as follows: (1) absolute monarch; (2) representative body of aristocracy; (3) representative body of propertied people elected by a limited suffrage (dependent on property census); (4) representative body of citizens elected by universal but unequal suffrage; (5) representative body elected by universal and equal suffrage.

In economic matters, the main concern was for the economic regulator and property rights; the spectrum from the right to the left was: (1) market regulated by guilds, and limited in its effects by the existence of government monopolies and feudal-type claims on the peasants' work and property; (2) unlimited free market and full private property rights, with a ban on associations which sought to curb market forces; (3) free market subject to government regulation aiming at the protection of the poor, with wage earners' associations permitted, and private property operation within these limits.

In cultural matters, the move towards the left was marked by extending the range of personal liberties especially with respect to religious and political views, artistic expression and life-style.

However, though in all these matters the range was seen initially as unilinear, as time went on some cyclical elements could be distinguished. Yet in most instances, such as with respect to the contrasting aims of economic regulation (whether in favour of the propertied people classified as of the right, or in favour of the have-nots classified as of the left), this cyclic feature can be better understood as a spiral-type development. Another cyclic element emerged with respect to the limitations of universal and equal suffrage and freedom of political association.

According to Rousseau's theory, favoured by the Jacobins, the citizens were to accept the general will of the free, fraternal society of equals. This is not the place to discuss the intricacies of Rousseau's thought, but a quotation may illuminate the extent to which the philosopher's reasoning affected the views of rank and file soldiers in the revolutionary army. One of them, serving in the Charante battalion, expressed it in the following verses:

> La liberté n'est donc que dans la loi;
> La loi, de tous la volonté suprême,
> C'est mon ouvrage, elle est faite par moi,
> Soumis aux lois, j'obéis a moi-même,[1]
>
> [Liberty is only found under the law;
> A law that springs from the supreme will,
> It is my work, I did it,
> Subject to laws, I obey myself.]

As long as the views of individuals coincided with the policy of the revolutionary establishment, the general will was really there, but once the two were separated, there was a clash of loyalties which could be overcome only by balloting or by a new kind of absolutism. Thus, a tendency emerged for the extremes on the right and left, to meet.

It was under the two Napoleons that the criteria of right and left in politics became particularly blurred. In the mid-nineteenth century, equal universal suffrage in France proved to be the gateway to a protracted period of absolutism. In several ways, this solution foreshadowed those political philosophies which form the subject matter of this volume. Yet, eventually, the Bonapartist phenomenon proved to be an *extempore*, a kind of deviation from the trend which in post–1870 France returned to the pre-Napoleonic pattern, though with a significant shift to what had been understood as the political left.

Meanwhile, spectacular but uneven, and often interrupted, economic growth strengthened the belief in the beneficial functioning of the free market and, on the other hand, gave rise to serious doubts about the social usefulness of this economic regulator. The left became more than ever identified with the opposition pitted against the free market and private property. The idea of a socialised and centrally planned economy became an integral part of its political programmes. The question of how to harmonise this kind of economic regulator with decision-making by ballot was scarcely asked. Some simply believed that the majority vote of equal citizens would find the right way to resolve the issue. Others, distrusting the goodwill of those whose privileges would of necessity be abolished as a result of majority voting, looked for a kind of authoritarian rule which could pursue, unopposed, a socialist policy. Thus, the idea of the dictatorship of the proletariat was born. A move to the right was intended to help impose a left-wing solution. Rousseau's general will turned out to be the will of the suppressed class, on behalf of which its vanguard, the Communist Party, was to act. The ballot and universal suffrage, even of those who were supposed to be the beneficiaries of the revolution, lost any practical meaning.

The story which started in Russia in 1917 is too well-known to be repeated here. However, what has not always been fully appreciated is that this spiral-like switch towards a new type of absolutism, a switch which brought Soviet-type communism out of the traditional right–left political spectrum, had a mirror-image. The right was transposed to the left in the conceptually less comprehensive and articulate movements of Italian Fascism and German National Socialism.

These two movements, generally classified as the radical right, moved, in several respects, closer to the radical left, though as time went on this became more a matter of rhetoric, of occasional ostentatious measures and, above all, of methods which could hardly have any significant effect on social structure. Furthermore, the co-operation between the conservatives of a traditional brand and the populist radical right represented by Fascism and National Socialism was a shot-gun wedding rather than a genuine love-match. Only with respect to ethnic and racial minorities was the policy of structural change pursued with the utmost determination. There was no question of a Fascist or National Socialist Internationale, only a tactical co-operation of Nations with similar regimes and interests in expansion which, at least for the time being, could be co-ordinated.

In this context we should stress one substantial difference between Italian Fascism and German National Socialism. Fascist nationalism aimed at absorption, not extermination, of ethnic minorities and, above all, did not share the anti-Semitic fury of the Nazis. As racial policy was in fact the cornerstone of what was hailed as the National Socialist revolution there was, in matters of domestic policy, less common ground between the Fascists and the Nazis than is widely believed.

Let us now turn to the two extremes—the communist left and the Fascist-type right—and look at them from the point of view of the traditional political spectrum. When in power, both rejected decision-making by ballot, thus behaving as the radical right, while in their vocabulary they preserved the image of the radical left. Both suppressed free political and artistic expression. Both did not hesitate to terrorise their opponents. Both were led by people who did not recognise the privilege of property and education but considered ideological conformity and full dedication to the party as legitimation for ruling others. Yet there were also significant differences: Communist Ideology was more rational, articulate and coherent. On the other hand, Fascist-type ideology with its irrational, exhortative type of nationalism was better suited to overcoming, at least *temporarily*, the contrasting interests within the particular society.

The main systemic difference, however, were in the degree of concentration of power and, consequently, also in the range of power. Under Soviet-type Communism the concentration of power was comprehensive. As all means of production were socialised and the whole economy became centrally planned and managed, economic power was merged with or rather subordinated to political power. In addition, the all embracing ideology became the exclusive philosophy of the state, and religious education was banned from the schools and churches.

The Fascist-type regimes were satisfied with the absolute concentration of political power alone. Private property was to be preserved and, subject to ethnic or racial limitations and occasional political interference, protected. Economic planning was envisaged only for the duration of the war. Churches, though not always treated with respect, were allowed to carry on all their main activities. Thus, private property and churches represented two significant loopholes in the would-be totalitarian grip of the Fascist-type regimes. (Those who experienced Nazi rule from the position of a subject nation and are able to compare it with the subsequent Soviet-type rule can best appreciate this particular difference.)

Both Soviet Communism and Fascist-type movements envisaged a society freed from class antagonism. The Communists believed they had achieved it by the abolition of private property, the Fascist-type regimes by propaganda. In fact the radical right preserved the classes intact, whereas the Soviet regime created a new ruling class – the apparatchiks – who, to borrow Ossowski's terms, ruled over all means of production, education and compulsion.[2]

As far as the working class is concerned, the classic proletariat of the Marxists did not enjoy any genuine protection in either instance. In Russia, trade unions became, to use Stalin's expression, transmission belts for party policy. However, in contrast to Fascist Italy and Nazi Germany, the apparatchiks in the Soviet Union were largely recruited from industrial workers, (especially in the first generation of the regime). A significant channel of upward social mobility was opened for the activists from the working class. On the other hand, those who remained on the lower echelons of social stratification were treated, in some important respects, less favourably than under Nazi rule. The rationing of consumer goods in time of war illustrates the point. Whereas the Germans (apart from privileges for their military and political elite) provided manual workers with additional rations, graded according to the arduous nature of their work, soviet rationing was differentiated according to position on the scale of the institutional hierarchy, and those at the bottom of the pyramid had often to be satisfied with less than their due.

Under all these circumstances, even the term socialism – conceived in various ways on the two sides of the war-front – could be taken only with a very large pinch of salt. As has been shown with respect to almost all criteria, neither the Soviet socialist nor the National Socialist regimes could be assessed in terms of the traditional scheme of right–left political differentiation, thus making it virtually obsolete.

In the general perception, however, the unilinear imagery survived. In spite of many affinities between them, the Communists continued to be viewed as the extreme left and the Nazis as the extreme right. Only later, when the split within the Communist fold – a split between the 'reform' or 'euro' Communists on the one hand, and the 'orthodox' or 'conservative' Communists on the other – created a situation in which each side saw the other as being on the right, did the unsuitability of the traditional left–right spectrum become obvious to a wider public.

Experience with Fascist-type movements in Europe may serve as an example of difficulties with too abstract a scheme of political differentiations. The emergence of these movements was due to a combination of particular circumstances in which economic deprivation and frustration of national pride and aspirations played dominant roles.

As far as the social basis of the Fascist-type movement is concerned, it is obvious that its core was in the lower middle class, both urban and rural, and usually among people of a lower level of education. However, in the ranks of the most successful Fascist-type movements, the Italian and German, students and university-educated people were strongly represented.[3]

Occasionally, philosophers such as Giovanni Gentile[4] brought the otherwise simplistic ideology, amalgamating elements of contradictory tendencies, to a more sophisticated level and gave it some reputation among intellectual circles. German philosophy, in particular, tended to erect theoretical constructions on foundations of sand. Logic based on empirical evidence had difficulty in asserting itself in such a climate.

Obvious nonsense may crop up and thrive in any society, but the belief that the Jews were the cause of all evil, a belief which took root even among the educated, testifies to there having been something very peculiar in the German society of that period. Anti-Semitism had been known in many countries and in earlier times it used to peak in occasional outbursts of ugly violence. Nowhere, however, did it reach such a pitch of frenzy, nowhere was its brutishness pursued so systematically, with the aim of a 'final solution', as in Nazi Germany.

The German proclivity to take everything in life seriously and to carry things to extremes, together with an extraordinary capacity for discipline, made German National Socialism the most formidable specimen of a Fascist-type movement.[5] The fact that the Italian Fascists made an earlier political break-through and in several respects set an example, is less important. The Germans brought the idea to perfection and eventually created the leading Fascist-type establishment, the 'Big Brother' so to speak, of all the others.

In the international setting after the First World War, the position of Germany was also more dramatic than that of Italy. Defeat in war, lost territories, long-lasting reparation payments, inflation running into astronomic figures: all this did not affect Italy which, on the contrary, was numbered among the victors. But her victory in war (due, incidentally, more to her allies than to her own performance) did not bring her the territorial gains to which she aspired, and her irritation at this failure was increased by the considerable acquisitions made by her allies, Britain and France. On the other hand, unlike Germany, Italy entered that war in a state of wide-spread disorder, indeed almost of anarchy, and victory in war did not make the situation any better. Thus, Italy was confronted with the continuation of an old problem and this may have been why she moved faster on the road to a Fascist take-over.

In spite of these differences, the general pattern of the struggle was similar. In Italy, as in Germany, the Fascist victory emerged from a three-cornered contest. Supporters of parliamentary democracy were squeezed from two sides, in traditional terms: from the left and the right. Fear of one extreme, which after its triumph in Russia appeared to be more menacing, pushed many democrats into the arms of the Fascists. Big business was alarmed by the prospect of socialisation. The failure of the democrats to withstand Fascist pressure was more conspicuous in Italy where even the centre-right Liberals allied themselves with the Fascists and realised their blunder only when it was too late. In Germany the democratic centre was more cautious. But eventually its calculation which was based on a lesser evil, i.e. a strong president in the person of a renowned general as a barrier against the Nazi tide, proved equally wrong.

It is also important to realise that both the Fascists in Italy and the Nazis in Germany came to power by their own efforts, which involved both electioneering and terrorism. Furthermore, in neither case did this happen without the connivance, or indeed the support, of some segments of the pluralistic establishment, such as part of the police or the military.

Everywhere else in Europe, Fascist-type movements were less prominent and less successful. They either : (a) played second fiddle to the army in founding the Fascist-type regime — this was the case with the Spanish Falange; or (b) did not gain wider popular appeal or military support, as with the Finnish Lapua movement, the Hungarian Scythe Cross or the Romanian Iron Guard; or (c) appeared as a more or less ephemeral movement of opportunist nature, due to the situation during the Second World War, such as the Croatian Ustasha (a belated response to the originally pluralistic Yugoslavia), the Vlaamsch National Verbond and the Rexists in Belgium, and the Slovak People's party or (d) lacking both popular and intellectual appeal, lingered on the fringes of political life, such as the British or Czech Fascists (both used that borrowed label); or (e) as in France, cropped up, petered out and again reappeared in another form and with a new leader without making a serious impact on the general course of political development; or, finally, (f) appeared as a hybrid such as the Austrian combination of the conservative Patriotic Front with the paramilitary Heimwehr.[6]

The three most clearly identifiable common denominators of all these movements were fierce nationalism, anti-Communism and rejection of what was considered as weakness, indecision and licence. We may say that there were two underlying psychological attitudes: the cult of martial virtues and *horror libertatis*.

When we turn to the achievements of the Fascist-type regimes, we are struck by their ephemeral nature. They were extremely successful in the short run. They destroyed a pluralistic establishment in a few years and built up a war machinery which, in the German case, was formidable indeed. They managed to impose their images of order on the whole of society and, by concentrated propaganda and terror, created the impression that the whole nation was behind them. And who can truly guess how many did not succumb, at least for a while, to this skilfully aroused and maintained enthusiasm bolstered by resounding military victories?

The Fascist-type restructuring of society was focused on other than socio-economic aims. Hitler and his companions were obsessed with racial purity and with extending the German *Lebensraum* to the east at the expense of Slavic peoples. Otherwise, they had little idea of how to strengthen German-ness other than by exhortation and discipline; it was these methods in the main which were destined to harmonise or trivialise the contrasting interests within society.

The Italian Fascists were more inventive. Their corporatist System appeared to be a more systematic solution to, or rather cosmetic feature cover for, the class struggle. In contrast to Germany, there were at least some tokens of the conflict-regulation which is an essential systemic feature of modern democracies. On the other hand, the military build-up in Italy was something of a flop. Italy could win against the weak and under-developed Ethiopia or Albania, but everywhere else, as the experience of the Second World War showed, her armies could not do without German help.

In the end, Hitler's primitive mind, the effects of which remained for many years concealed by the pusillanimity and blunders of his opponents, brought forth its unavoidable fruits. The terror which he unleashed against so many could only end in the complete destruction of his machinery and in the occupation of the whole of Germany. The country thus paid dearly for having so long obeyed a demagogue who let himself be carried away by the initial successes of his gambles. In the end, German National Socialism proved to be wholly counter-productive for the great-power aspirations of the German nation.

Italian Fascism having allied itself for life and death with its German counterpart, met the same fate. Yet it seems that, for many, it was this alliance and not its inherent insufficiency which caused the demise of Italian Fascism. This may be the reason why some nostalgia for the Fascist past still survives in Italy.

On the other hand, a conservative leader like General Franco, who did not allow the Falange to escape his mastery, was prudent enough (even if the exhaustion caused by the prolonged and bitter Civil War was also a contributing factor) not to let himself be enticed into the Second World War, and provided Germany with only token help: one division of volunteers was specifically destined for the war against the USSR. Furthermore, Franco also made the thoughtful provision that after his death the Falange would not take over, and opted for what he expected to be a conservative monarchy.[7]

To sum up: whether by war or by evolution, the most successful Fascist-type movements disappeared as serious factors from the political landscape of Europe.

Ironically, the main 'achievement' of the most powerful Fascist-type movement was the extension of Communist rule in central and south-eastern Europe. What had been intended as a drive towards the East ended with the opposite move, in which a substantial part of Germany also became the victim. In the other part of Europe, it is a liberal, parliamentary democracy combined with various types of mix involving capitalism with the welfare state, which has become the norm.

Military dictatorships which for some time survived or reappeared on the southern fringe, in Spain, Portugal and Greece, have gone within one generation of Germany's collapse in 1945.

With the exception of Spain, where the transition was extraordinarily smooth (a compensation, so to speak, for the horrors of the Civil War which had brought Franco to power), the military dictatorships (in Portugal and Greece) fell as a result of failure in a military adventure: protracted, exhausting and inconclusive colonial war in the case of Portugal, and the instigation of the unfortunate Greek-Cypriot venture in the case of Greece. In a way, both Portugal and Greece followed the path of Italy and West Germany in commuting their particular types of dictatorship into liberal, parliamentary democracies. It has to be added, however, that in Portugal this happened only after a period of flirtation with a dictatorship of a leftist ideological complexion.[8]

Everywhere in Europe the remnants of Fascist-type groupings have been dwindling. This, however, does not mean that their appeal has been forgotten. significant Fascist-type parties still exist in Spain and Italy and a new one has emerged in France. Small and splintered Fascist-type groupings vegetate in many more countries. To appreciate the possibility of a revival of a Fascist-type movement on a larger scale, we have to enquire whether there are conditions propitious to their revival in the respective countries – whether there are, so to speak, any Fascist breeding-grounds in parts of Europe.

Even at first glance, we can see a substantial difference between conditions now and those which obtained after the First World War. The economic deprivation which can at present be found throughout Western Europe, is either less widespread or less intense than at the time of the economic crises of the early 1920s or mid-1930s. Contemporary unemployment has resulted, in the main, from structural shifts in overall demand. It hits particular areas and branches of industrial production, leaving others unscathed or even prosperous. The dole and other social security benefits may, in some countries, be less than satisfactory, but in most they are far higher and more widespread than before the war; together with moonlighting (the underground economy), they provide a cushion against the worst consequences of unemployment. And the main sufferers, the old and sick, one-parent families and also the unemployed, do not have muscle to enter the arena of industrial or any other organised strife.

The scope for ethnic conflict was considerably reduced by the huge transfers of population and changes of boundaries after the Second World War. The idea of separating peoples of different ethnic and/or religious affiliation who, because of acute communal hatred, cannot live peacefully together was followed on an unprecedented scale in Central Europe.

Apart from the nationalities which were on the index of Stalinist purges in the USSR, it was mainly the Germans who were subject to such transfers in very large numbers. More than ten million of them were driven westwards. Though most of these transfers were performed under very harsh conditions, the fact that they happened in the wake of a still worse war and also that, eventually, most of the German expellees have attained a higher standard of living than they might have enjoyed if they had been allowed to stay at home, created a situation which, as time went on, defused a good deal of the tension created by the expulsion of so many people. The new generations have integrated well into a society with the same language and cultural tradition and do not seem (at least as far as opinion polls indicate) to be interested in a return to the country of their ancestors. On the contrary, the lure of Western prosperity resulted in such a large-scale exodus in 1989 from East Germany that it virtually toppled its Communist regime.

As the Germans and Slavs no longer rub shoulders in the same area, where they might be exposed to contradictory patriotic propaganda and in addition compete for scarce jobs (a situation which provided the seedbed for Hitler's propaganda), this particular type of communal hatred has disappeared from the historical scene. Furthermore, in the war, German military machinery was crushed with particular thoroughness and the economy had to start again from scratch. By way of compensation for suffering and humiliation, the Germans were offered new prospects. As is well known, the Federal Republic was helped, by Marshall Aid and other measures, to start a quick, vigorous economic revival which eventually made her one of the leading economic powers of the world, fully integrated as an equal partner in the political, economic and military alliances of the West. On the other hand, the East Germans were driven to bring to an end the merciless drain on their resources by the USSR in a most dramatic way: only after the desperate uprising in 1953 were themselves allowed to enjoy some fruits of their workaholic virtues.[9]

However, the very success of the West German economy created a new source of ethnic tension. After having recruited millions of guest-workers from abroad (mainly from Turkey), the Federal Republic of Germany became a haven of political and economic refugees from various parts of the world. These, however, came at the time when a discomforting level of unemployment made their absorption into West German society increasingly difficult. Ironically, it was also the influx of ethnic Germans from Eastern Europe that aggravated the situation to such an extent that, again, a fascist-type party, *Die Republikaner*, entered the

German political stage. It remains to be seen whether the upsurge of this party will be short-lived, as was the case with the extreme right-wing parties in the 1950s and 1960s (such as *Deutsche Reichspartei* and *National Demokratische Partei Deutschlands* respectively), or whether, in conjunction with what is going on in East Germany, its appearance heralds a new phase in the political culture of German society.

Paradoxically, the Italians did better after the war which they lost than after that which they won. It seems that the shock of Fascism led them to be more appreciative of the advantages of a pluralistic society. Furthermore, economic growth, which has lasted for an unprecedented length of time, has helped to make the appeal of the Fascist past less likely. It is significant that the main strength of the neo-Fascist movement is amongst the poorer, less-educated population of the *Mezzogiorno* rather than elsewhere.

Apart from the ethnic transfers and creation of new boundaries, the general trend after the Second World War was towards greater self-determination of ethnic minorities. Though there may still be some dissatisfaction with the respective arrangements, there are in Western Europe only three 'hotspots' where substantial segments of the population feel that their ethnic or religious communities had not been given an adequate institutional framework for the assertion of their identity: Ulster, the Basque country and, up to a point, Corsica. Though in all these instances economic hardships underscore the bitterness, the divide is not economic (class-bound) but ethnic, whether explicitly as in most cases, or implicitly as in the case of Ulster, where it parades under the banner of religious affiliation.

Unfortunately, in several countries (we have already mentioned West Germany) the abolition of most hotbeds of national discord has been matched by the emergence of new ones: refugees and migrant workers. Among the different peoples concerned, only those who come in great numbers and are in same way conspicuous by their appearance and/or behaviour, are liable to provoke occasional Fascist-type reactions. It does not matter whether the host country received them because of her legal or moral obligations towards the subjects of her former colonies, or whether she invited them in order to perform those kinds of work which the natives themselves did not want to do. What matters is how numerous and how different the newcomers are and, last but not least, to what extent, under changed economic circumstances, they compete with the natives for scarce jobs.

Understandably, this is the new ground on which various National Fronts (a term used in the West not East European sense) can feed. It is a situation which also brings to the surface more or less apparent forms of racist feelings and attitudes. But can we see in these movements and attitudes a tendency to a Fascist revival on a large scale?

In my opinion, the danger, at least as far as Western Europe is concerned, is not imminent for the following reasons. As noted already, economic deprivation has assumed a different and less acute form. In most West European countries, the wave of exaggerated nationalism has abated. Religious and cultural pluralism has been widely accepted as a natural condition of life. Big business is not afraid of a Communist take-over as it was after the First World War. On the contrary, it is keen to make commercial deals with the USSR, and this policy is reciprocated. With respect to the situation in the world at large, a further progressive *rapprochement* between the super powers and an easing of international tension has followed Gorbachev's *perestroika* in the USSR and the rapid transformation of all the Eastern bloc regimes in the late 1980s.

Frustration brought on by the narrowing of a sympathetic social base or, in some cases, its total disappearance, has driven a handful of radicals, the ultras, on both sides of the traditional political spectrum, to desperation. Irrespective of whether they consider themselves to be on the right or on the left, they have embarked on desperate and reckless acts of terrorism. Their logic is wholly out of touch with common sense. They want to provoke the 'establishment' to use excessive means of repression, in the hope of inciting the masses, at the time either contented or apathetic, to opposition. The ultras imagine that, in such a climate, they will get their chance. Another novel aspect of post-war developments is the fact that the ultras, not only those under the red banner but also those calling themselves neo-Nazis or neo-Fascists, have succeeded in establishing international contacts and in helping each other in terrorist undertakings.

Turning to more relevant phenomena in wider geographical perspectives, we discover in Latin America a perplexing mix of 'rightist' and 'leftist' tendencies in various populist movements which succeeded in winning power and establishing in their countries more or less repressive dictatorial regimes. In the pre-war period, the *Peronistas* in Argentina and, to a certain extent (until recently), the *Partido Revolucionario Institucional* in Mexico, may illustrate the point. (In contrast to these movements the traditional type of military dictatorship, endemic in Latin America, is based more on co-operation with the *latifundistas* and big business than on the mass political parties, and thus constitutes an element which can be interpreted as a mere survival of a bygone era).[10]

On the other hand, the European impact on Asia was directly responsible in some areas for the rise of nationalistic movements aiming at a more vigorous assertion of national identity in a more or less Fascist vein. Their means were the combination of a selective Westernisation with a revitalisation of traditional domestic value. This was the case with the State Shinto in Japan and up to a point with the Guomindang Party in China. By contrast, however, Kemal Atatürk and his movement opted for a straightforward and comprehensive Westernisation of Turkey.[11] Although in all these instances a certain affinity with European Fascism, especially its Italian paradigm, can be perceived, the inherent potential for further adaptations made of them a particular species of nationalism with ideological reinforcement. Furthermore, the Kemalists allowed a flexible framework for pluralism and democratisation to develop. The difficulties, which in Turkey continue to hamper the full implementation of these principles, lie more in traditional authoritarianism than in an ideological commitment to enforce uniformity of opinion. Yet, with respect to the ethnic minorities, especially the Kurds, Turkish policy does not differ from that of Mussolini or Franco.

After the Second World War, the struggle for the emancipation of colonial peoples from the domination of the West European powers, which was eventually brought to a successful end, was often either carried through by nationalist-populist movements or else by such movements which took over power later, after the respective country had won its independence by means of a peaceful arrangement with the former colonial power. In many instances, it was the idea of socialism which coloured the ideology of these movements. After it had been utterly discredited by Hitler, the concept of National Socialism was refurbished and became, under various titles, a common feature of the most energetic populist movements in the Arab countries. The best known are: the Arab Socialist Renaissance (*Ba'ath*) Party which, at the time of writing, rules in Syria and in Iraq (a fact which however does not dispose these two countries to friendship), the *Front de Libération Nationale* in Algeria, the *Parti Socialiste Destourien* in Tunisia, and, the most colourful specimen in this group, the Socialist People's Libyan Arab *Jamahiriya* (state of masses). However, the reference to socialism in these labels may correspond to very different degrees and intensities of socialist measures in the respective countries. Paradoxically, Algeria, whose leading party does not even contain the term 'socialist' in its name, has been in practice (up to the time of writing) the most socialist of them all. A similar National Socialist type of one-party rule has been established in what has been since 1974, the Socialist Republic of the Union of Burma.

In contrast to the one-party regimes in the above-mentioned countries, the individual political parties of the ethno-religious communities in Lebanon are conveniently assigned either to the 'right' in the case of the Maronite-Christian groupings, or to the 'left', in the case of the Druzes and the Shi'ites; the Sunnites seem to have taken the middle ground. However, what makes individual political groupings appear more to the left or to the right is more a matter of their economic strength or weakness than of a specific policy or of social arrangement within the respective communities. Otherwise, in all these ethno-religious groupings, it is a type of authoritarian, patriarchal regime, upheld by the strength of armed militias, which prevails. [12]

The one-party states of various parts of Africa also reveal features which can be classified either as rightist or even Fascist (e.g. Kenya, ruled by the Kenya African National Union), or leftist, even communist (e.g. Ethiopia, rules by the Mengistu's Workers Party of Ethiopia). The difference rests mainly with the type of ownership and economic management which, together with international alignments, reflects the ideological colouring of the respective regimes. In most African states, however, the position is unstable and shifts in either direction frequently occur.

A special case is South Africa, where the political regime consists of two tiers: a pluralistic, democratic regime for the whites at the top, and an authoritarian domination of the whites over the black and other races at the bottom. Racial discrimination here appears more as an anachronism than a manifestation of Fascist ideology. Some Afrikaaner political parties, however, show an explicit affinity with Nazi ideology. In some other parts of Africa, hatred exacerbated by the traditional contrast between racially different rulers and their subjects, (a hatred which occasionally erupts into large-scale massacres such as happened between the Hutu and Tutsi in Burundi in 1972) has to be considered as a survival of bygone ages rather than as a parallel to the Nazi or Young Turks' actions towards hated minorities, Jews and Armenians respectively.

Oddly enough, the European Communist regimes in place until 1989 were also not immune to the use of Fascist practices. The Zhivkov regime in Bulgaria, like the Italian Fascists before the Second World War, forced its ethnic minorities to use the Bulgarian language and to Bulgarise their names or else leave the country. The late Communist *conductor* of Romania, Ceausescu, surpassed Stalin in his social engineering by taking a leaf from the manual of Fascist practice: he had embarked on a policy which aimed to 'systematise' (i.e. homogenise) Romania's population not only politically and ideologically, but also ethnically. And who knows what might happen in the USSR if Gorbachev fails in civilising his multi-ethnic empire? Bellicose tribalism, endemic in the Caucasus and Central

Asia, on the one hand, and the resurgent Great Russian chauvinism on the other hand, pose a serious threat of a new brand of Fascism.

The extraordinary excesses of some Communist governments in Asia, such as that of the Chinese regime during Mao's Cultural Revolution or, above all, the genocide of their own people practised by the Khmers Rouges in Cambodia, appear, in this context, to be beyond any framework of reference.

Finally, there is yet another new element on the political map of the contemparary world which should not be left unnoticed in this context. This is the Islamic Republic of Iran with its revolutionary offshoots amongst the Shi'ites in other Islamic countries. Although the revolution which has brought the Shi'ite clerics to absolute power in Iran has not yet run its full course, and substantial modifications may be expected before that happens, some features of the present regime reveal a striking similarity with what, in European conditions, has been described as clero-Fascism; its pro-Iranian Shi'ite specimen, active especially in the Lebanon, is particularly virulent.

The acrimony of the clerical regime in Iran, however, has been matched and even perhaps surpassed, by the ethnic policy of its main foe, the Ba'athist regime (in fact personal dictatorship) in Iraq. To quote the London-based Minority Rights Group, the Iraqi government 'seems to be intent on destroying its Kurdish community by deliberately inflicting [. . .]conditions calculated to bring about its physical destruction, in whole or on part'.[13] Hitler's or Stalin's recipe? No matter; merely another example of how, *in extremis,* the concept of right and left in policy loses any sense.

To conclude: before the Second World War, the most determined Fascist-type regimes were concentrated in Central and Southern Europe. Although, at that time, the distinction between right and left in politics was not always unambiguous, in the public view the straightforward right–left spectrum was widely accepted.

After the Second World War, in which the Fascist Big Brother was utterly defeated, the Fascist-type elements in politics became more diffuse. This happened both with respect to their geographical spread and to their frequency, or intensity, in individual movements. Furthermore, not only nationality but also religious affiliation became more often a rallying point for Fascist-type feelings and practices. The affinity of the extreme right with the extreme left became more conspicuous. This has been demonstrated, mainly, in various authoritarian regimes in the Third World, which have claimed to be at the same time nationalistic and socialistic.

There has also been some give-and-take and even some co-operation between the two extremes.

In the left–right classification, only the issue of private *versus* public ownership remains as a clear-cut yardstick. In the final analysis, however, various degrees of concentration of societal power and also various ranges of that power, tend to overshadow the importance of the role of formal ownership in societal life.

NOTES

1. Quoted from A. Soboul, *Paysans, Sans-cullottes et Jacobins. Etudes d'histoire révolutionnaire*, Claureuil, Paris, 1966, p. 218.

2. S. Ossowski, *Class Structure in the Social Consciousness*, Routledge & Kegan Paul, London, 1963, pp. 185–86.

3. D. Schoenbaum, *Hitler's Social Revolution, Class and Status in Nazi Germany 1933–39*, Weidenfeld & Nicolson, London, 1967, p. 72.

4. For an account of how and why an old Liberal philosopher and politician, Giovanni Gentile, became a Fascist, see H. S. Harris, *The Social Philosophy of Giovanni Gentile*, University of Illinois Press, Urban, 1960.

5. For a recent assessment see J. Hiden and J. Farquharson, *Explaining Hitler's Germany, Historians and the Third Reich*, Batsford Academic & Educational, London, 1989 (2nd edn).

6. For a general and comparative outline of various Fascist movements in Europe, see esp. F. L. Carsten, *The Rise of Fascism*, B. T. Batsford, London, 1967; G. L. Mosse, *International Fascism: New Thoughts and New Approaches*, Sage, London and Beverly Hills, 1979; and S. J. Woolf (ed.), *Fascism in Europe*, Methuen, London, 1981.

7. The story of Fascist Spain is well told in M. Gallo, *Spain under Franco*, Allen & Unwin, London, 1973, For the brighter aftermath, see R. Graham, *Spain, Change of a Nation*, Michael Joseph, London, 1984.

8. Cf. H. G. Ferreira and M. W. Marshall, *Portugal's Revolution. Ten Years On*, Cambridge University Press, Cambridge, 1986.

9. For a detailed comparison of the situation in the two Germanies, see J. Krejčí, *Social Structure in Divided Germany*, Croom Helm, London, 1976.

10. For a concise account of various forms of Fascism and of similar movements in Latin America, see A. Hennesy, 'Fascism and Populism in Latin America', in W. Laqueur (ed.), *Fascism, a Reader's Guide*, Wildwood House, Aldershot, 1976, pp. 255–94. Still valid is the analysis of the background given in S. Andreski, *Parastism and Subversion, The Case of Latin America*, Weidenfeld & Nicolson, London, 1966.

11. The contrast between the selective and comprehensive Westernisation is discussed in J. Krejčí, *Great Revolutions Compared. The Search for a Theory*,

Wheatsheaf Books–Harvester Press, Brighton, 1987 (reprint), esp. pp. 207–11.

12. The complicated situation in Lebanon is reviewed in M. Gilsenan, *Lords of the Lebanese Marches. Violence, Power and Culture in an Arab Society*, Tauris, London, 1989.

13. Quoted from *The Economist*, 15 April 1989, p.84.

CHAPTER TWO

The 'Movimento Sociale Italiano': A Historical Profile

Roberto Chiarini

Forty years on from the fall of Italian Fascism, the MSI remains a stable, if isolated, presence on the Italian political scene. Indeed, the continuous, albeit marginalised, parliamentary presence of a neo-Fascist party distinguishes the Italian political system from those of other Western European countries. In the last four decades the MSI has averaged 4–5 per cent in elections, with a low of 1.9 per cent in 1948 and a high of 8.7 per cent in 1972. Its impact is not much greater than these scores suggest, if we consider that the party is virtually the sole representative of the undemocratic right, i.e. of that part of the right which does not fully accept the constitutional framework of the Italian Republic, which was established in 1946. Taken together, the parties of the far right, including the various Monarchist groups active in the 1950s and 1960s (Alfredo Covelli's National Monarchist Party [*Partito Nazionale Monarchico, PNM*], and Achille Lauro's Popular Monarchist Party [*Partito Popolare Monarchico, PPM*], later known as the Democratic Party of Monarchist Unity [*Partito Democratico di Unità Monarchica, PDUM*]) have never scored more than a modest 12 to 13 per cent in elections.[1]

Table 2.1. Votes obtained by the MSI in the elections for the Chamber of Deputies, 1948-87. The 1989 figures refers to the European Parliamentary elections.

Year	Votes	%	Year	Votes	%
1948	526,670	1.9	1972	2,894,722	8.7
1953	1,582,567	5.9	1976	2,238,339	6.1
1958	1,407,550	4.8	1979	1,930,639	5.3
1963	1,570,232	5.1	1983	2,511,487	6.8
1968	1,414,036	4.5	1987	2,282,212	5.9
			1989	1,915,596	5.5

WHY THE MSI SURVIVES BUT IS MARGINALISED

Both the persistence of the neo-Fascist phenomenon and its limited importance need to be explained. The reasons are to be sought in both national and international factors linked to the post-war political settlement.

A first, general point is that the allied victory against Nazism and Fascism was, above all, an ideological one. While it brought into being a new set of international power relationships, the war also bankrupted Nazism and Fascism as viable ideologies. The two great powers, the USA and the USSR, in spite of the cold war, were united in their determination not to allow any renewal of the far right in Europe. At most, in the short term, they could be occasionally accommodating (e.g. with the Colonels in Greece), but in the long term they stuck to a hard line. What happened to right-wing regimes already in power was, in this context, symptomatic. The Salazar dictatorship in Portugal and the Franco regime in Spain failed to survive the death of their founders, despite their apparently deep roots.

All this meant that the extreme right's strongholds were wiped out and suggested that right-wing radicalism had no future. The unconditional surrender of Hitler's Germany and of the Italian Social Republic [*Repubblica Sociale Italiana*, RSI] – the puppet regime set up by Mussolini in Northern Italy after he had been deposed by the Monarchy in 1943 – is what undermined the future of the extreme right. The deaths of the *Führer* and the *Duce* also had a symbolic impact. Military defeat made the association of right-wing extremism with blood, death and destruction inevitable. The myths held dear by the right (nationalism, colonialism and racism) as well as its political and ideological heritage (elitism, authoritarianism, corporatism and anti-parliamentarianism) were totally discredited. The extraordinary appeal of the right between the wars seemed impossible to recapture.[2] The extreme right could only stand by, powerless, as moderates were drawn irresistibly towards the centre. The unification of the middle classes, carried out by the totalitarian regimes of the right, survived but was no longer available to form the right's social backbone.

The prospect of an irreversible decline in capitalist society and the liberal state, which loomed on the horizon of the immediate post-war period, was soon dispelled, and economic growth became the foundation on which a consumer society was built and on which political democracy was consolidated. The parties of the far right which had staked everything on the hope of crisis and conflict were thus drained of their sustenance. This went to the parties of the centre or of the moderate left which aimed at maintaining the favourable economic trend by shrewdly managing political and social conflict.[3]

There were two further factors which handicapped any grouping associated with the totalitarian/authoritarian tendencies of the right. First of all, in reaction to the repression exercised by Fascism against political parties and trade unions, there was now a deeply-felt appreciation of the rights and freedoms guaranteed by the State to both individuals and associations. As Juan Linz recently observed, 'everybody understood that an authoritarian government not only meant the removal of rights from left-wing politicians, trade unions and peasant protest movements; it also meant they were taken away from large sections of the middle classes and even from the upper classes'.[4] Democratic governments and organisations derived strong legitimation from this public realisation. Secondly, the credibility of right-wing radicalism was undermined in the post-war period by the absence of any authoritarian model. There was no country able to provide an example like Fascist Italy in the 1920s and Nazi Germany in the 1930s. Franco's Spain, Salazar's Portugal and even the Greece of the Colonels were museum specimens rather than credible models of an endangered species. If moderate Western public opinion tolerated them it was because they seemed the most suitable type of regime for smoothing the way of these late-joiner countries towards democracy. Even regimes with greater ideological pretensions, like Pinochet's Chile, could not be viewed as permanent solutions to a country's problems, but only as a stop-gap bulwark against communism.

In Italy's case there were additional factors which discouraged a revival of neo-Fascism. To begin with, whereas Mussolini's regime could count on having a monopoly of all the political resources of a totalitarian state (from press, radio and education, right down to leisure organisations), neo-Fascism had to learn to compete, on equal terms, for the electorate's support.

Secondly, the right discovered that it lacked a social base. While it had never enjoyed a natural relationship with any class or social group, it had, now, even lost the capacity to represent the middle classes which had supported Mussolini. This unifying and protective function was taken over by political Catholicism. The Catholic lay organisation *Azione Cattolica* had been the only non-Fascist organisation able to operate legally in Mussolini's Italy, so that, after the war, the newly-formed Christian Democrat Party [*Democrazia Cristiana,* DC] was able to take advantage of the vast network of branches that had been set up over the years. Ultimately, political Catholicism had two great advantages. The Church–State rift which, since Italian unification (1860–70), had excluded Catholics from political life had been healed. In addition, the Church benefited from being perceived as the only true representative of institutional continuity in the country. This was especially the case since the monarchy had been largely discredited (after the king fled Rome in the wake of the Armistice signed with the Allies on 8 September 1943) and the country had suffered a constitutional crisis, one that was not resolved fully even when the referendum of 2 June, 1946 established the Republic.[5]

What contributed most to curtailing the extreme right's capacity to make an impact – while, paradoxically, helping to strengthen its Fascist identity – were the discriminatory measures taken against it by the Italian State. The Republic came into being as a system explicitly hostile to, and hence incompatible with, any survival of Fascism. The Constitution left no political space for any successor to Mussolini's National Fascist Party [*Partito Nazionale Fascista, PNF*]. The democratic parties formed the so-called *arco costituzionale* (constitutional spectrum), which was intended as an alliance guaranteeing the anti-Fascist nature of the State. The corollary was that the shadow of suspicion also fell over the political area adjacent to neo-Fascism so that the rigid equation right = Fascist was born and, with it, two implications. As far as the party system was concerned, it meant that no conservative party could win office. It also led, inevitably, to right-wing groupings identifying themselves more strongly with Fascism. Pride in being different brought them to look upon the Fascist experience as the fundamental ingredient of what it meant to be right-wing. At the same time, it supplied the moral strength to withstand the onslaught of anti-Fascist measures in the immediate post-war period, and to resist the temptation, when these ceased, to become integrated within the democratic system.

However, while this constant backward glance towards Fascism undoubtedly benefited the Italian extreme right after the war, it also cost it dear. The nostalgia for the rural and provincial Italy of the 1920s and 1930s prevented it from noticing how the country was being transformed by the 'economic miracle' of the 1950s and 1960s. While it talked of 'moral' and 'spiritual' values, the country at large was adopting the materialistic language of the consumer society. While neo-Fascism proclaimed the failure of the free-enterprise economy (and the need to overcome individual and sectional interests for the sake of the national interest) and that of tolerant democracy (in the name of a hierarchical system), mass, democratic society was thriving all around it. The right's inability to understand, at the deepest level, the social and economic mainsprings of Western capitalist society led to its exclusion, to all intents and purposes, from the most influential collective experiences in contemporary society, such as trade unions, the education system, the mass media and culture.

But these considerations bring us back to our original query: how is it that the right's cultural and political exclusion did not lead to its withering away or even to its complete disappearance from the political scene? Undoubtedly, it had deep roots, but a further factor needs to be taken into account, i.e. the Italian electoral system. The Italian system of outright proportional representation which came into effect in 1946, and which has not been modified since, has encouraged a proliferation of parties – even allowing parties like the MSI, with fairly low-level electoral support, to survive.

THE BEGINNINGS OF NEO-FASCISM IN ITALY

The most difficult years for the extreme right were, obviously, those immediately after the war. It was ostracised not only morally and politically, but legally too. Those young people caught carrying arms at the fall of the Salò Republic ended up in internment camps. The most important Fascist officials were arrested, or took refuge abroad, or lay low in Italy (thanks, in some cases, to a blind eye being turned by the authorities). People suspected of having belonged to the defunct PNF were handed over to the *tribunale dell'epurazione* (de-fascistisation tribunal), set up to try those who abetted Fascism in a major way.

Therefore the problem for ex-Fascists, in the short term, was not how to make a political mark again, but how to survive. There were numerous abortive attempts on the right to bring together its depleted forces,[6] but there were clearly only two ways forward and each had serious drawbacks. It could either set up a full-blown neo-Fascist organisation which would fall foul of the law or, more prudently, it could adopt a convenient cover within a legitimate political party and wait for better days. This was the situation which obtained until 28 June 1946 when a political amnesty was granted, as a symbol of reconciliation, upon the proclamation of the Republic. Both options were explored. Some underground groups were formed, the most important being the Revolutionary Action Fasces [*Fasci di Azione Rivoluzionaria*, FAR], which was openly faithful to Fascism. The main strategy, though, was to operate in a more limited fashion, under the umbrella of the *Uomo Qualunque* (UQ) party.

The *Uomo Qualunque*, literally 'man in the street', was an organisation founded by an oddball character, Guglielmo Giannini, a political outsider with an extraordinary flair for understanding and expressing the average

Italian's frustration with the State. The UQ's main targets were the parties, held up as perverse power structures whose only purpose was to perpetuate the rule of the politicians over the people. UQ's initial popularity derived from that of its eponymous newspaper, cleverly used by Giannini to attack, in trenchant and often vulgar language, the credibility of the new, post-Fascist Italy. After the Liberation, UQ decided to face the voters, and changed from a movement to a party. In the elections for the Constituent Assembly in June 1946, it obtained 5.3 per cent of the vote. Four months later, in the local elections, it improved its position significantly. It performed sensationally in the main cities of Southern Italy, achieving 20.7 per cent in Rome, 19.7 per cent in Naples, 46 per cent in Bari (in alliance with the Monarchists and the conservatives of the Italian Liberal Party [*Partito Liberale Italiano*, PLI]), 34.6 per cent in Foggia, 47 per cent in Lecce, 34.6 per cent in Catania (with the Liberals) and 24.5 per cent in Palermo.[7]

Two main features have characterised the Italian extreme right since these earliest elections: a mostly Southern base and a predominantly clientelistic nature. The deep-rooted presence of a Catholic sub-culture in the North-East, and of a left-wing one in the Centre, together with the country's ready adoption of democratic values brought about, first of all, by the Resistance to Nazism and Fascism and, secondly, by the activities of the major parties, jeopardised the chances of the right in these parts of Italy. The right-wing vote cannot therefore be treated as a reaction to a strong swing to the left. The areas where Socialists and Communists were strongest (notably in Emilia-Romagna) did not correspond to those where the extreme right achieved its best results. Similarly, in the industrial, mostly working-class areas of the North, modern social conflicts did not spark off a bourgeois mobilisation of an anti-democratic nature. It is, on the contrary, from the very heart of the South that the extreme right drew its votes. Here, limited industrialisation kept political relations dependent mostly on basic social ties – i.e. the family and the 'clan'.[8] This society was reluctant to be represented by parties such as the Communists and Socialists, which derived (and still derive) their support directly from the work-place or, indirectly, through class-based loyalties. At the same time, it could identify only in part with the DC which did not have, here, the sort of network of associations which the Catholic movement established in the North. It is the extreme right which took advantage of the clientelistic character of political relations that prevailed in the South. Its continuous polemic against *partitocrazia*, the domination of political parties in national life, made it especially appealing to local notables envious of the competition of the big parties. In other words, the future of the extreme right was tied to the aspirations of a largely pre-modern society. In the long run, however, its electoral base was likely to decrease, with the advance of capitalism and consumerism – these being factors which de-personalise human relations and so undermine the clientelistic structure of political relations. Its chance of reversing the downward slide was not subject to its willingness to play the rules of modern mass democracy and represent a specific class; it depended on its ability to exploit the sporadic discontent of the classes most exposed to the effects of the unbalanced modernisation which had taken place in southern Italy since the 1950s. This modernisation led to the traumatic overthrow of the old rural world, the loss of the young through emigration, chaotic urbanisation (e.g. in Naples, Palermo, Catania), the growth of an 'underground economy' and of jobs of a precarious and marginal nature, and to the huge and unjustified rise of a commercial and white-collar middle class which relied on the protection and favours handed out by the political powers that be. Simplifying a little, it could be said that, in the early

Table 2.2 Distribution of MSI voters by geographical-political areas

	1948	1953	1958	1963	1968	1972	1976	1979	1983	1987
Industrial area	12.7	16.3	17.9	18.6	19.3	18.9	18.4	19.8	21.4	23.0
Traditionally Christian Democrat ('White') area	6.4	8.2	10.8	8.8	8.6	6.8	7.2	7.4	7.6	9.9
Traditionally Socialist-Communist ('red') area	11.3	14.2	15.5	14.8	14.2	11.0	11.0	11.7	12.3	14.0
Southern area	53.1	41.1	41.2	43.8	47.7	46.7	46.5	46.6	44.8	39.6
Islands	16.5	20.3	14.6	14.0	13.2	16.9	16.9	14.5	13.9	13.5

Source: P.Ignazi, Il pollo escluso. Profilo del Movimento Sociale Italiano, Il Mulino, Bologna, 1989.

N.B. The geographic-political area named here include the following regions:
 – Industrial area: Piedmont, Lombardy, Liguria
 – 'White' area: Trentino, Alto Adige, Veneto, Friuli Venezia Giulia
 – 'Red' area: Emilia-Romagna, Tuscany, Umbria, Marches
 – Southern area: Latium, Abtuzzi, Molise, Campania, Calabria
 – Island: Sicily, Sardinia

1950s, the MSI's mostly southern electoral base appealed to the economically as well as culturally deprived classes and to factory workers, tended to represent the urban middle classes employed in tertiary activities in the 1960s,[9] and was closely associated with the phenomena of urbanisation and underdevelopment, and in particular with those seeking employment for the first time, in the 1970s.[10]

THE BIRTH OF THE MSI

The Southern base and the clientelistic nature of the UQ vote, in essence, are the structural features that the neo-Fascists inherited when they decided to start an autonomous party. Soon after being given freedom of political action by the general amnesty, they officially entered the political arena. Though the UQ provided a useful screen to shelter them from the storm of de-fascistisation measures, it could not become their permanent home. It suited the neo-Fascists while it refused to distinguish between Fascism and anti-Fascism, but was no longer acceptable when it claimed that 'the anti-Fascists of today are yesterday's Fascists'. Besides, UQ and neo-Fascists held different conceptions of politics and the State.[11] With the slogan the 'administrative state', the UQ advocated – without actually formalising it – a watered-down version of the 'minimal state', i.e. the liberal conception of the state that makes its presence felt as little as possible and makes way for civil society, which it considers to be the only force capable of achieving progress. The neo-Fascists, on the other hand, wanted to exhume the 'ethical state', i.e. a state capable of determining not only political and economic objectives, but the moral ones of the individual and of society as well. Clearly, the 'partnership' could not last very long.

The *Movimento Sociale Italiano* was started on 26 December 1946. All its founding-fathers – starting from Giorgio Almirante – were figures in one way or another associated with the RSI. They all felt, therefore, an absolute need to refer to Fascism, and in particular to its most intransigent sides. Even the party's programme echoed, explicitly, themes dear to historical Fascism: the fundamental role of the nation (a role that was not supposed to be superseded by that of the individual, as the liberals advocated, nor by that of class as the Socialists insisted); the workers' state intended as the promoter of a complete partnership between employees and employers; Catholicism as the state religion; foreign policy as a form of nationalist ostentation or even as a civilising mission for the Italian nation.[12]

The first move the party made was to refute the Peace Treaty and the institutional and political set-up which came out of the war. Its intention was, in the first place, to de-legitimise the new republican state. It also helped to preserve a collective identity for the MSI, by distinguishing it from all the parties of the 'constitutional spectrum', and by turning it into a magnet for the clandestine neo-Fascist groupuscules scattered about the country. The rejection of the conditions imposed on Italy by the Allies, and the attacks on *partitocrazia* stem from the MSI's conception of the nation as a superior political value, overriding all other interests – be they those of the individual, of the unions and even of the parties – in order to establish the only true interest, that of the national Community. The colonial losses and the failure to retain the disputed territories around Trieste were considered to have damaged the political unity of the nation just as much as the intrusion of the parties in the daily life of the citizen.

The MSI's attacks on the post-war political settlement reflected its intention of discrediting the ruling class of the new State, and was thus intended to invalidate the anti-Fascist arguments on which it was based. The rejection of the guiding role which the two victorious super-powers had taken upon themselves offered the chance to argue in favour of an unlikely 'third way' – a way that was allegedly different from, and superior to, both capitalism and Communism, because it was capable of avoiding their shortcomings: extreme individualism in one case, and out-and-out State control in the other.

A strong ideology was, after all, an essential resource for a movement that was discredited in the eyes of the outside world and was searching for an uneasy internal unity. The MSI had, in fact, to fight two battles: one for its own survival, against the Committee for National Liberation [*Comitato di Liberazione Nazionale,* CLN]; the other to convince the scattered neo-Fascist forces that they should abandon the temptation to go underground, and should organise into a party. These were the two fronts on which battle was engaged, and from which the MSI emerged victorious. The out-and-out appeal to the Fascist idea was not enough for the FAR to survive the political stranglehold that was suffocating it. The stigmatisation of the MSI by the anti-Fascist parties succeeded in marginalising it but not in eliminating it altogether. In the parliamentary elections of 1948, the MSI secured 1.9 per cent of the vote – a modest result if we set it against the high ambitions the party had nurtured, but an encouraging one if we consider the polarisation (DC *vs* Socialist/Communist alliance) that characterised the election campaign, the modest organisational resources of the party, and the left's attacks on it. The very fact of entering Parliament and local councils forced the MSI to moderate its ideology, which conflicted too markedly with that of other parties. Besides, its arrival on the public political stage occurred precisely when the anti-Fascist discrimination was being succeeded in Italy by an anti-Communist one which led, in the spring of 1947, to the expulsion of the Socialists and Communists from the government, and to the establishment of a DC-dominated centre government. The credentials which the neo-Fascist right could boast of with regard to the defence of 'Christian Civilisation' and the fight against Bolshevism were not inferior to those of the centre. The MSI was thus offered the chance to overcome the isolation to which it has been condemned, provided it underplayed the much-vaunted 'difference' that opposed it to its potential allies (DC and Monarchists). The growing southern base also worked to the party's advantage. Suffice it to say that the six deputies and the one senator who were elected in 1948 all represented southern constituencies. The outlook was encouraging, but risky. The creation of a broad anti-Communist front meant, in the short term, the achievement of ideological legitimation and, in the long term, the widening of its sphere of influence beyond the circle of former Fascists unable, or unwilling to, adapt to a mass democracy. The overtures to the monarchists and to the DC, had a price, though, one which the hard-liners were not prepared to pay, i.e. the watering-down of the party's ideology, in the name of a 'holy alliance'. The stormy debate on this question absorbed the MSI's energies throughout the early 1950s, and led it to seek an anti-Communist alliance encompassing Monarchists, Liberals and Christian Democrats.

MODERATES AND HARDLINERS

At first the MSI chose a compromise position. It supported the policy of dialogue and, soon after, one of overt co-operation with centre-right parties at local level. As early as the autumn of 1947, its Rome city councillors played a decisive role in the election of the Christian Democrat mayor Aldo Rebecchini. In the local elections of 1951–52, the MSI achieved reasonable results, and obtained seats on many city councils, including such major Southern centres as Naples, Salerno, Foggia, Bari and Lecce. In Sicily, it comfortably exceeded its national average of 1948, and its regional deputies were able to exercise a decisive influence over this important semi-autonomous region. On national issues, however, the MSI pursued a policy of uncompromising opposition. The event that best exemplifies this attitude is the party's vote against Italy's membership of NATO.[13] Behind the apparent intransigence, however, some changes were taking place. Almirante, whose leadership was viewed as an obstacle to a more effective policy of alliances with right-wing and centre parties, stepped down in 1951 and was succeeded by Augusto De Marsanich who was favourably disposed to the idea of a pact. Shortly afterwards, an agreement with the Monarchists was signed with the local elections of 1951–52 coming up. A shift in the MSI's attitude to NATO also took place at the end of 1951. Even the party's political *modus operandi* began to follow that of the other parties. The MSI shed, almost completely, its tendency to rely on anti-democratic and clandestine forms of political activism. A series of affiliated organisations was set up. These included the Italian Confederation of National Workers' Unions [*Confederazione Italiana Sindacati Nazionali Lavoratori*, CISNAL], the National Welfare Association [*Ente Nazionale di Assistenza*, ENAS] and the University Front for National Action [*Fronte Universitario di Azione Nazionale*, FUAN].

Strong internal opposition to the new line did not discourage the party from pursuing it. In fact, the appointment of Arturo Michelini to the leadership in 1954 confirmed and reinforced the victory of the moderate wing of the party. Moreover, the MSI was encouraged – in a way even forced – not to make a U-turn by the political situation of the time. At the end of the first parliamentary term, in fact, the DC prepared itself to deal with the growing strength of the right – a strength which emerged clearly after the local elections of 1951–52 – by means of two manoeuvres: firstly, by replacing the proportional representation system with one which apportioned two-thirds of the parliamentary seats to the party, or coalition of parties, that obtained more than 50 per cent of the vote, and secondly, by passing the so-called Scelba Law – named after the Home Affairs minister who championed it. This added a clause to the Constitution, which prevented the disbanded PNF from being re-formed. The new electoral system was intended to re-create conditions favourable to a political polarisation between centre and left: it warned conservative public opinion that a vote for the right was tantamount to a wasted vote which could indirectly benefit Socialists and Communists. The second manoeuvre threatened the very existence of the MSI in that it urged voters not to support a party on the fringes of the law. Faced with such measures, De Marsanich's party had no choice: it had to moderate its anti-system stance or fall foul of the law.

THE MSI AND THE UNSTABLE CENTRE GOVERNMENT

The DC's strategy turned out to be only partly successful. While it prevented a completely legitimated right-wing force from developing, the DC did not succeed in winning an outright majority for its centrist coalition with the Liberals, Republicans and Social Democrats. The period of *centrismo stabile* (stable centre-party government), gave way to that of *centrismo instabile*. Having trebled its vote since 1948 (it now stood at 5.9 per cent), the MSI, with its 29 deputies, was in a position to exert a pivotal influence on a governmental coalition. This was especially the case as the DC was unwilling – or unable – to choose between right and left and was therefore forced, willy-nilly, to construct governments dependent on the non-belligerence or even the complicity of part of the opposition. Besides, the DC's middle position between the extremes of left and right was not always self-evident. Whenever Communist pressure mounted, the Christian Democrats did not hesitate to rely on MSI and Monarchist support. They never went so far, though, as to disregard the underlying premise of the Italian political system: the central position of the DC between two de-legitimated extremes. While the central position was thus justified by the presence of the two opposing anti-system parties (MSI and Communists) it also, paradoxically, required the de-stabilising threat, which they posed, to continue. The most precarious moment for this balancing act was reached in 1953 when the DC openly discussed setting up a right-wing ticket in Rome to prevent the capital falling into the hands of the Socialists and Communists. This was the so-called 'Sturzo operation', named after the priest Don Sturzo who, in 1919, set up the first Catholic political party in Italy, the Italian Popular Party [*Partito Popolare Italiano*, PPI]. This move was supported by powerful Catholic lay groups such as the *Comitati Civici* (Civic Committees), an organisation with a widespread network which actively mobilised public opinion in defence of values and institutions like the family and the school, as well as by influential sections of the Church, e.g. the Roman Curia and many bishops. It was only stopped from embracing the rightist option by its coalition partners who threatened to bring down the government.

Collusion between the government and the right was a regular feature of the Republic's second parliamentary term. First the Pella government (1953), then that of Zoli (1957) took advantage of MSI support. Furthermore, the second President of the Republic, Giovanni Gronchi, was elected in 1955 with the help of MSI votes.[14] In order to take full advantage of this situation, the MSI silenced those within its ranks who wanted it to be an anti-system party (in 1956 the 'diehards' of Pino Rauti's New Order [*Ordine Nuovo*, ON] left the party). In every way possible it endeavoured to take on the mantle of the one and only true defender of the system. It took to the streets in 1953 and 1954 to defend the right of Trieste to be Italian. It entered the schools to take on young left-wingers, using an aggressive, no-holds-barred style. It went out of its way to seek violent confrontation with Socialist and Communist militants during election campaigns or strikes. In the South, especially, it strengthened its ties with Monarchists and Christian Democrats in local government. All it needed to complete its 'long march through the institutions' and achieve full legitimation was a foothold in government.[15]

THE TRIAL OF STRENGTH DURING THE TAMBRONI PREMIERSHIP

Its big opportunity came midway through 1960 when the Tambroni government was formed. To the disappointment of the DC, the 1958 general election had failed to solve the basic problem of stabilising the centre ground. The result was particularly bad for the right. Both Monarchist parties declined, as did the MSI (it only received 4.8 per cent of the vote). A centre-left government, which would draw the Socialists into the majority, was now on the agenda, in spite of residual resistance within the DC and in spite of the continuing attempts by the MSI leaders to minimise the importance of this shift. The Prime Ministerial mandate given to Fernando Tambroni – who was not one of the DC's top men – has to be seen as part of the normal Italian practice of putting off difficult political decisions; this involves setting up deliberately transitional governments, led by secondary figures, whose job is simply to keep government ticking over. However, a crisis was sparked off when the MSI vote in parliament was decisive in clinching the vote of confidence for the new government, and was officially accepted by the Prime Minister. The DC saw that its whole central position was being undermined. The country now appeared to identify with the left which was revitalised by the appeal to anti-Fascism. There were some ten deaths in street clashes. The political price of MSI support was too heavy. Tambroni fell and his demise showed that a right-wing solution to the problem of governmental instability could only compromise the DC's linchpin policy of mediation between the extremes. This gave the green light to a centre-left solution.

For the MSI, the failure of the Tambroni operation was not simply a setback. It meant that the Michelini policy, based on the party gradually integrating into government, was in ruins. After ten years of painfully slow progress towards full legitimation within the party system, the MSI stood isolated, excluded and also empty-handed. The commitment of the centre-left coalition partners (Christian Democrats, Socialists, Social Democrats and Republicans) to exclude the Communists on the left and the Monarchists, Liberals and MSI on the right from central and local government, destroyed, in the space of a few months, all the gains put together by the MSI since the early 1950s. Michelini survived but without a policy for the future, especially after the elections of 1963 (giving the MSI a meagre 5.2 per cent) confirmed his inability to channel the disgruntlement of moderate public opinion, whose votes went to the Liberals. In the subsequent period, the MSI stepped up the viciousness of its attacks but remained impotent. In fact, its hold on society appeared to be crumbling. Symptomatic of this was the fact that its student movement, the FUAN, lost its position of dominance at Rome University, a traditional neo-Fascist stronghold. For the right as a whole a difficult and uncertain period of policy re-thinking had opened up.

In the previous fifteen years the MSI had, in effect, come to represent all neo-Fascist opinion. Now, with the party drifting, new faces appeared[16] and its whole position was re-thought. It ceased looking exclusively back towards its Fascist past and became more sensitive to developments on the world stage. The parochial horizons of the extreme right were now broadened to take in the economic, technological and political struggle going on between East and West. (This confrontation was no longer the direct one of the cold war but the indirect one of 'peaceful co-existence', and its focus was de-colonisation.) The extreme right saw 'peaceful co-existence' as a Trojan horse, part of a Communist plot based both on supporting and, thereby, taking over national liberation struggles (from Algeria to Cuba and from Latin America to Vietnam) and on subtly undermining democracy by working quietly on the hearts and minds of Western public opinion.[17]

In this perspective, the centre-left in Italy seemed to be a national version of this world-wide Communist plot. Far from staunching the drift to the left, it was seen as surrendering to Communism. Under the umbrella of democracy, the Italian Communists appeared to be gaining important footholds everywhere: in the press, in schools and among intellectuals, not to mention trade unions. They were about to prepare a very gradual take-over under the gaze of a public opinion lulled into complacency by the rules of the democratic game. The extreme right's process of taking stock was complicated by its realisation of the profound changes brought about in Italian society by the post-war 'economic miracle'. A traditional agricultural and provincial society was disappearing, while consumerism was rampant. In this climate, the right's most clearly-held values (the defence of religion, love of country, attachment to the family and respect for authority) were drained of their potency. It could only appeal to what it called 'the Nation's vital forces', i.e. the upper echelons of the army, of the Civil Service and, in general, of the anti-Communist establishment.[18]

These new aspirations and, in parallel to them, the search for an audience sympathetic to the extreme right's new message meant appealing to sectors of the population not traditionally associated with neo-Fascism. This was the period, too, when the so-called 'invisible government' (*governo invisibile*), became a major factor in Italian politics. This term is used to describe all the power centres in the country (the various state agencies, the secret services, important elements in the economic and financial sectors) not operating in an openly democratic way, but trying, instead, to run the country in the absence of an official government able to safeguard their own vital interests.[19] The effect of all this was to alter the relationship between neo-Fascism and the world of anti-democratic subversion in general. Their aims were the same, i.e. attacking democratic institutions, but their methods differed. While the official extreme right was content to adopt a more hard-line opposition to the centre-left governments, the subversive groups were formulating a ruthless plan of attack on state institutions. They had recourse to covert actions (i.e. terrorist attacks which they did not claim responsibility for) in order to create a climate of fear in the country and, thus, build the foundations for a right-wing backlash. This was the so-called 'strategy of tension', (*strategia della tensione*). Above all, the relationship between the extreme right and the state was changed. Before this, there had indeed been a relationship of connivance and sometimes there had been cover-ups. For instance, the MSI's frequent attacks on symbols and institutions of the Resistance and even its thuggish attacks on trade union demonstrations had often been tolerated or even encouraged by the police. But now there was an unexpected shift of emphasis. Right-wing plots and coups were being hatched within the state itself, while the neo-Fascist forces were simply instruments. It is now known that, in the summer of 1964, during a trying period following the government's resignation, the doomsday scenario of a suspension of political and trade union freedoms was brought forward. This was based on a plan drawn up by General De Lorenzo, Commander of the *carabinieri*.

THE 'VITAL FORCES' OF THE NATION AGAINST THE 'COMMUNIST PLOT'

It later emerged during judicial enquiries that, within a year, the union between those elements in the secret services favourable to a *coup d'état* and those forces, both old and new, on the subversive right had focused on a plan of 'revolutionary war'. This was drawn up at a conference held on 3–5 May at the Parco dei Principi hotel by the 'Alberto Pollio' Institute for Historical and Military Studies. Its diagnosis of a Communist threat looming over the West called inevitably for a mobilisation of all the 'vital forces'. Two important points emerged from this response to the 'Communist threat'. First, the conference's call for a guerrilla counter-offensive left no room for an extreme-right party to operate above-board. Second, the need to respond effectively to the challenge meant acting ruthlessly, even if this entailed violating the basic tenets of democracy and having open recourse to political violence.[20]

The scenario outlined at the Parco dei Principi conference stands out as a disconcerting prelude to the strategy-of-tension years about to hit the country. The call to mobilise had the effect of revitalising the whole sector of groups and organisations which rejected the policy pursued by Michelini's MSI, and which were determined to go for a radical alternative to the system. *Ordine Nuovo* aimed to become the focal point for all those forces which were no longer willing 'to obey the orders of the MSI "moderates" '. National Vanguard [*Avanguardia Nazionale*], the group founded by Stefano Delle Chiaie in 1960, burned its bridges with the party and its 'sterile and purely backward-looking' policy, and launched into action on the basis of a plan of anti-democratic subversion.[21] The MSI itself, as the 1960s came to a close, was preparing itself to face up, in the appropriate way, to the convulsive period which began with student protests and which immediately descended into a spiral of political violence. The first bomb in the strategy of tension exploded in Milan on 12 December 1969.

GIORGIO ALMIRANTE'S 'STRATEGIA DEL DOPPIO BINARIO' (TWO-PRONGED STRATEGY)

In 1969, Michelini was succeeded by Giorgio Almirante. The change in leadership brought about the so-called *strategia del doppio binario*. The new party secretary put an end to the policy of dialogue with the DC: it had proved to be such a handicap to the MSI that, in the 1968 elections, it polled a mere 4.5 per cent of the vote. Instead of the accommodating approach of the previous years, Almirante advocated a grander and more vigorous one that might enable the party to take advantage of the troubled social and political situation of the early 1970s. His ambition was to turn the MSI into a truly autonomous right-wing force, free from the conditioning influences of the governing parties, and thus to abandon the tactic of offering tacit support to the latter in return for clientelistic favours. The aim now was to directly undermine the central role of the DC. This role was already under threat from the crisis of the centre-left coalition, and the ensuing political instability, from the mass demonstrations of the student, feminist and trade union movements (which were intent on taking over from the parties the function of representing the country) and from the accompanying radicalisation of the political struggle. Almirante attempted to exploit the country's quest both for law and order and for change. He aimed to bring together the conservative middle classes of the North (e.g. the 'silent majority' of Milan, tired of the student unrest and trade union mobilisation of 1970–71) and the lower classes of the South (the demonstrators of Reggio Calabria who rebelled against the authorities' decision not to grant the city regional-capital status in 1971).

The new strategy proved immediately successful. In the local elections of 1971, the MSI vote rose to 13.9 per cent. Even better scores were achieved in the South. In Sicily, support for the party grew from 6.6 per cent in 1967 to 16.3 per cent, and was particularly strong in Palermo (19.5 per cent) and Catania (27 per cent). In Rome, too, the MSI nearly doubled its vote (from 9.3 to 15.2 per cent). Once again, as had happened before with the rise of the *Uomo Qualunque* and the Monarchists, the DC ran the risk of having its traditional base eroded by the right, and its hegemonic role in the political system weakened.

To increase its impact as an opposition force, the MSI tried to rally under its wing the entire right. It merged with the Monarchist Party (new party was given the name MSI – National Right [*MSI – Destra Nazionale*, MSI-DN]) and, in 1972, drew to its ticket personalities potentially attractive to the conservative middle classes, such as the former general De Lorenzo and the former NATO admiral Birindelli, as well as the hardliners of *Ordine Nuovo*, who had earlier been re-admitted into the party fold. The outcome of the whole operation was very successful but not decisive. The MSI polled 8.7 per cent of the vote – its best general election result yet and one that placed the party neck-and-neck with the Socialists, in third position, after the DC and the Communists. However, it failed to unseat the DC from its central position. Another onslaught was attempted in 1974, by campaigning, together with the DC, and in competition with it, in favour of the abolition of the divorce law. This too ended in failure: the entire anti-divorce vote amounted to no more than 40.9 per cent. These results paved the way for the government's opening up to the Communists, which occurred after the early general election in 1976. The MSI vote dropped to 6.1 per cent (in the regional elections of 1975 it had already polled a mere 6.4 per cent). The MSI's hopes for a shift to the right brought about by years of political violence, terrorism and chronic political instability, vanished. Instead of acquiring full legitimacy through its own strength, the party found itself even more isolated. In this way, the tide turned against the MSI in the second half of the 1970s. The right-wing constellation could no longer identify solely with this party. A number of splinter groups jeopardised the party's very unity. The following parliamentary term saw a split in the party and the birth of a new group called National Democracy [*Democrazia Nazionale*, DN], which succeeded in halving the number of MSI deputies. This group accused Almirante of failing to turn his party into a democratic parliamentary one, and tried to establish in Italy a respectable right-wing party of the type found elsewhere in Western Europe. The attempt proved unsuccessful. The DC's unwillingness to respond to the overtures of DN led to the latter's total isolation. None of the breakaway deputies were re-elected in 1979.

The radical right's ambiguous relationship with the MSI – one which wavered between rivalry and complementarity – also went through a critical period. The years in question saw the establishment of the 'governments of national solidarity' – so called because they were intent on re-creating the spirit of solidarity with which the democratic parties had, together, first fought against Fascism, then founded the Republic. These governments were formed in 1976–78, with the PCI's decisive external support, the first time this had happened since the party was ousted from government in 1947. They marked the end of a phase that saw the secret services covering up plots and coups. Though the details are still unclear, these plots and coups involved blatantly neo-Fascist organisation such as Stefano Delle Chiaie's National Vanguard and Valerio Borghese's National Front [*Fronte Nazionale, FN*], militantly nationalistic organisations like Carlo Fumagalli's Revolutionary Action Movement [*Movimento di Azione Rivoluzionaria, MAR*], and Amos Spiazzi's Wind Rose [*Rosa dei Venti*].[22]

The State's offensive against what was left of the remaining radical right groups was countered by a strategy of violence devised by Franco Freda: this sought to attract those forces, of both right and left, which aspired to destroy the existing order. Judge Vittorio Occorsio, murdered in 1976, was one of the victims of this strategy. Political activism no longer aimed to overthrow the democratic regime. It now consisted of terrorist attacks devoid of any political aim, whose sole purpose was to strike at some of the hated symbols of the 'system' – a procedure known as 'armed spontaneism' (*spontaneismo armato*).

This strategy was based on two facts. Firstly, it was realised both that there was no hope of convincing the 'renegade' MSI to adopt a revolutionary stance and that the *coup d'état* scenario had led to the strengthening rather than the destabilisation of the system. Secondly, there was the arrival on the scene of a new generation of activists with no historical memories of Fascism. Their commitment tended to be personal and existential, rather than ideological or political. It grew, first and foremost, out of a need to assert themselves. They had an instinctive solidarity, on the ground, with anyone who was anti-system: from Italian left-wing terrorists operating as loners, to the Palestinian Fedayeen, and from the Argentinian Monteneros to the IRA. Their 'armed propaganda' which preached the slogan 'Let's build action' left the task of putting together a new consensus to the language of violence. The Armed Revolutionary Nuclei [*Nuclei armati rivoluzionari*, NAR] had no strategy, while Third Position [*Terza Posizione*, TP] hesitated between the 'armed spontaneism' option and a strong hierarchical structure.[23] In other words, the situation was a very fluid one reflecting the Italian right's crisis of political confidence.

A further warning light that the extreme right was in disarray was the setting up of the New Right [*Nuova Destra*, ND] movement, in the wake of the *movimento del '77* (a youth protest movement born in 1977, which transcended political ideologies and was mostly interested in the fulfilment of subjective aspirations). The ND shared with the French *Nouvelle Droite* a marked preference for ideological and cultural positions related to the idea of commitment within civil rather than political society. As a starting point, it wished to distance itself from all the right's previous stances – both illegal and legal. At the same time it set out to rethink the right's cultural paradigm in an attempt to free it from its sterile backward-looking position and to prepare it for the challenges of the future.[24]

THE MSI: A PROTEST PARTY OR A COMMUNITY PARTY?

The failure of the strategy of tension, the deradicalisation of the political

struggle and the growing tendency of the parties to contend for the political middle ground[25] led the MSI to look again at where it was going.
There seemed to be two basic strands in the strategy for the 1990s: winning democratic legitimacy once and for all, and finding a revitalised political programme. The first part seemed well on the way to being achieved
in spite of the flagrant ambivalence of the party's leaders (who claimed, at
one and the same time, that they were faithful to Fascism and loyal to
democracy), and despite bitter internal disputes (with the majority, supporting first Almirante and later Fini, opposed to the battle-hardened minority of Rauti). A number of symbolic gestures confirmed that, in the early
1980s, the MSI was being integrated into the system: in 1982, Mario
Pannella, the flamboyant leader of the Radical Party [*Partito Radicale*, PR],
attended the MSI's conference, while in 1984, official representatives of
the DC and PLI were present. More concretely, when Prime Minister
Bettino Craxi was forming his government in 1983 he also consulted the
MSI, with the express intention of bringing it in from the cold.

On the more important question of defining a party strategy for a
post-industrial society, the 1980s were marked by uncertainty and confusion. One thing which does emerge clearly is that the MSI has gradually
shifted from out-and-out opposition to the system as a whole towards a
concentration on particular issues (e.g. the excessive power of the parties,
the lack of legislation limiting the right to strike or the weakness of the
country's executive power). Its traditional style of clashing physically with
opponents was gradually losing its attractiveness. Even young party
members showed themselves increasingly at ease with the techniques of
peaceful political persuasion such as collecting signatures in the street or
passive resistance to the security forces. As regards the general direction of
the party, there was a clear desire to achieve legitimation, especially
within Europe. Following contacts with the Spanish *Fuerza Nueva* and the
French *Parti des Forces Nouvelles*, Almirante set up the Euro-Right. Internally, the MSI's unflagging attacks on the Republican institutions which
had emerged from the fight against Fascism gave way to a battle for the
'reform of the State', meaning, above all, that Italy's President (at present
elected by Parliament) should be directly elected by the voters and that
executive power should rest with him.[26] The same can be said of its
polemic against *partitocrazia*, which was aimed initially at discrediting
democracy. Now, however, it moved towards attacking a spoils' system
which encouraged parties to extend their power rather than to serve the
people. The party turned its attention increasingly to quality-of-life issues
such as pollution, social marginalisation and the condition of women.
Good examples are the Charter for the Handicapped, the call for house-

wives' wages, and the campaigns in support of pensioners. Nevertheless, the MSI was often tempted – when faced with the many, complex problems of a modern society – to go for hasty and simple solutions which pandered to the demand for 'law and order' from right-thinking voters. An instance of this was the party's campaign for the introduction of the death penalty in response to the violence of the 1970s.[27]

What is clear is that, after the turmoil of the strategy of tension and of terrorism, the MSI has returned to a political and electoral limbo. Its prospects of escaping from it seem slim.[28] Its electoral scores are now the same as they were in the 1950s and 1960s: 5.3, 6.8 and 5.9 per cent in the General Elections of 1979, 1983 and 1987 respectively, and 5.5 per cent in the Euro-elections of 1989. These are way below its high expectations following the 1972 result.[29] Above all, the death in 1988 of its founding leader Giorgio Almirante underlined the party's crisis. This came to a head in a bitter confrontation between the two main tendencies within the party (i.e. that led by Almirante's heir apparent Gianfranco Fini, and that led by the former leader of the extra-parliamentary right Pino Rauti), which took place against a background of internal disarray. The former is looking to be a party of protest and of institutional reform, while the latter wishes to be a movement of dissent, a 'community party'.[30] The two strategies are miles apart; neither is likely to meet with success. The prospects for a solution to this crisis did not appear to have been improved when the young but irresolute Fini was replaced as party leader, in January 1990, by the older but politically more foolhardy Rauti.

(Translated by Ronnie Ferguson
and Luciano Cheles)

LIST OF ABBREVIATIONS

CISNAL   *Confederazione Italiana Sindacati Nazionali Lavoratori* [Italian Confederation of National Workers' Unions]

CLN   *Comitato di Liberazione Nazionale* [Committee for National Liberation]

DC   *Democrazia Cristiana* [Christian-Democrat Party]

DN   *Democrazia Nazionale* [National Democracy]

ENAS   *Ente Nazionale di Assistenza* [National Welfare Association]

FAR   *Fasci di Azione Rivoluzionaria* [Fasces of Revolutionary Action]

FN   *Fronte Nazionale* [National Front]

FUAN   *Fronte Universitario di Azione Nazionale* [University Front for National Action]
MAR   *Movimento di Azione Rivoluzionaria* [Revolutionary Action Movement]
MSI   *Movimento Sociale Italiano* [Italian Social Movement]
MSI-DN *Movimento Sociale Italiano-Destra Nazionale* (Italian Social Movement - National Right)
NAR   *Nuclei Armati Rivoluzionari* [Armed Revolutionary Nuclei]
ND   *Nuova Destra* [New Right]
ON   *Ordine Nuovo* [New Order]
PDUM   *Partito Democratico di Unita Monarchicá* [Democratic Party of Monarchist Unity]
PLI   *Partito Liberale Italiano* [Italian Liberal Party]
PNF   *Partito Nazionale Fascista* [National Fascist Party]
PNM   *Partito Nazionale Monarchico* [National Monarchist Party]
PPI   *Partito Popolare Italiano* [Italian Popular Party]
PPM   *Partito Popolare Monarchico* [Popular Monarchist Party]
PR   *Partito Radicale* [Radical Party]
RSI   *Repubblica Sociale Italiana* [Italian Social Republic]
TP   *Terza Posizione* [Third Position]
UQ   *Uomo Qualunque* [Man-in-the-street Party]

NOTES

1. G. Galli, *Il difficile governo*, Il Mulino, Bologna, 1972.
2. K. V. Beyme, 'Right-wing extremism in post-war Europe', *West European Politics*, XI, 2, pp. 3–5.
3. P. Farneti, 'Partiti, stato e mercato: appunti per un'analisi comparata,' in L. Graziano and S. Tarrow eds, *La crisi italiana*, Einaudi, Turin, 1979, vol. I, p. 123.
4. J. Linz, 'Legittimazione ed efficacia di governo', *MondOperaio*, XLII, 1989, p. 116.
5. R. Chiarini, 'Neofascismo e destra eversiva in Italia nel secondo dopoguerra', in *Storia dell'età presente. I problemi del mondo dalla IIa Guerra Mondiale ad oggi*, Marzorati, Milan, 1984, vol. I, pp. 907–11.
6. P. G. Murgia, *Il vento di Nord. Storia e cronaca del fascismo dopo la Resistenza (1945–1950)*, Sugarco, Milan, 1975.
7. G. Almirante and F. Palamenghi Crispi, *Il Movimento Sociale Italiano*, Nuova Accademia Editrice, Milan, 1958, p. 25, and S. Setta, *L'Uomo Qualunque, 1944–1948*, Laterza, Bari, 1975, pp. 161–2.
8. L. Graziano, *Clientelismo e mutamento politico*, Franco Angeli, Milan, 1974.

9.   G. Galli (ed.), *Il comportamento elettorale in Italia. Un'analisi ecologica delle elezioni in Italia fra il 1946 e il 1963*, Il Mulino, Bologna, 1968, pp. 266 and 247–8.

10. B. Bartolini, 'Analisi ecologica del voto del MSI-DN alle elezioni politiche del 20 giugno 1976', *Rivista italiana di scienza politica*, IX, 1979, pp. 297–316.

11. E. Forcella, 'Dieci anni di neofascismo. La chioccia qualunquista', *Il Mondo*, 20 April 1954, pp. 13–14.

12. P. Rosenbaum, *Il nuovo fascismo. Da Salò ad Almirante*. Storia del MSI, Feltrinelli, Milan, 1975, pp. 55–60.

13. S. Finotti, 'Difesa occidentale e Patto Atlantico: la scelta internazionale del MSI (1948-1952)', *Storia delle relazioni internazionali*, I, 1968, pp. 85–124.

14. G. Mammarella, *L'Italia contemporanea (1943–1985)*, Il Mulino, Bologna, 1985, pp. 209–62.

15. G. De Luna, 'Neofascismo' in F. Levi, U. Levra and N. Tranfaglia, *Il mondo contemporaneo. Storia d'Italia*, vol. II, La Nuova Italia, Florence, 1978, pp. 780–4.

16. D. Barbieri, 'Notizie sulle nuove organizzazioni che animano il cosmo nero a partire dagli anni sessanta', in *Agenda nera. Trent'anni di neofascismo in Italia*, Coines, Rome, 1976.

17. Various Authors, *La guerra rivoluzionaria*, Proceedings of the conference organised by the *Istituto 'Alberto Pollio'*, Volpe, Rome, 1965, pp. 262–4.

18. R. Chiarini and P. Corsini, *Da Salò a Piazza della Loggia. Blocco d'ordine, neofascismo, radicalismo di destra (1945-1974)*, Franco Angeli, Milan, 1983, pp. 213 ff.

19. G. Galli, *La crisi italiana e la destra internazionale*, Mondadori, Milan, 1974, pp. 32 ff., and A. Del Boca and M. Giovana, *I 'figli del sole'. Mezzo secolo di nazifascismo nel mondo*, Feltrinelli, Milan, 1965, pp. 203–21.

20. For a detailed analysis of the connections between radical right and state institutions, see G. Flamini, *Il partito del golpe*, Bovolenta, Ferrara, 1981, vol. I, pp. 3 ff.

21. On *Avanguardia Nazionale* and other extra-parliamentary right-wing groups of this period, see, 'La destra eversiva', in F. Ferraresi (ed.), *La destra radicale*, Feltrinelli, Milan, 1984, pp. 62–71.

22. G. Flamini, *Il partito del golpe* cit., vols. II and III, *passim*.

23. F. Ferraresi, 'La destra eversiva', in F. Ferraresi (ed.), *La destra radicale*, cit., pp. 78–96.

24. M. Revelli, 'La nuova destra', in F. Ferraresi (ed.), *La destra radicale*, cit., pp. 119–214.

25. P. Farneti, *Il sistema dei partiti in Italia 1946-1979*, Il Mulino, Bologna, 1983, pp. 227–39.

26. Istituto di Studi Corporativi, *La rifondazione dello Stato*, Proceedings of the 2nd National Conference, Rome, 18-19 April 1980, undated.

27. P. Ignazi, 'Il MSI partito della protesta', *Il Mulino*, XXXVII, 1988,

pp. 633–51; L. Cheles, 'Le "new look" du néo-fascisme italien', *Mots*, No. 12, 1986 pp. 29–39; idem, '"Dolce stil nero"? Images of Women in the Graphic Propaganda of the Italian Neofascist Party', in Z. Barański and S. Vinall (eds)., *Women and Italy. Essays on Gender, Culture and History*, Macmillan, London, 1991, pp.64-94.

28.   Recent surveys also agree in underlining the MSI's static position, forced on it by its attempt to set itself up as an alternative government. See P. Ignazi, U. Mancini and G. Pasquino, 'Omogeneità e diversità nei quadri intermedi (DC, MSI, PDUP, PSDI)', *Biblioteca della Libertà*, XVII, 1979, p. 241.

29.   P. Corbetta, A. M. L. Parisi and H. M. A. Schadee, *Elezioni in Italia. Struttura e tipologia delle consultazioni politiche*, Il Mulino, Bologna, 1988, pp. 215–47.

30.   P. Ignazi, *Il polo escluso. Profilo del Movimento Sociale Italiano*, Il Mulino, Bologna, 1989, pp. 213–49.

CHAPTER THREE

'Nostalgia dell'Avvenire'. The New Propaganda of the MSI between Tradition and Innovation*

Luciano Cheles

In April 1970, not long after his election to the leadership of the *Movimento Sociale Italiano* (MSI),[1] Giorgio Almirante (1914–88) stressed at a party conference the need to change the image of his party: 'If the Communists have won the war of words, we have so far lost it. [...] We, of all people, must beware of representing Fascism in a grotesque way, or at any rate, in an outdated, anachronistic and stupidly nostalgic way.'[2] Almirante, who had been a close associate of Mussolini in the Italian Social Republic (*Repubblica Sociale Italiana*, the Nazi-backed state founded by the Duce in northern Italy, with headquarters in the resort of Salò, shortly after he was deposed by the king in 1943), aimed to make his party look modern, law-abiding and respectable in order to widen its appeal and end its isolation.

On becoming leader, Almirante attempted to unite the two main factions in the MSI: the intransigent one (of which he had been the main exponent in the 1950s and 1960s), and the moderate one, which cultivated a policy of *inserimento* (gradual integration).[3] In the early 1970s, he officially projected an image of non-violence, but in practice tolerated, and even encouraged, street agitation, in the hope that a climate of social disorder would lead to a right-wing backlash.

Almirante's preoccupation with party image and his ability in transforming it (as we shall see) will not seem surprising if we consider his past experience in the field of 'political persuasion'. He was in fact, in 1944–45, Cabinet Chief in the Ministry of Popular Culture (MIN-

CULPOP), whose activity was almost exclusively concerned with the organisation of the regime's propaganda machinery.[4]

The change in the party's image took various forms. Fascist trappings and rituals (e.g. the black shirts and the Roman salute) were eliminated, and the language updated. In the early 1980s, encouraged by the legitimation that other parties were beginning to bestow upon the MSI as a result of the deradicalisation of political conflict in Italy and of a more widespread attempt to 'historicise' Fascism, Almirante embarked on high-profile public-relations activities. He got himself invited to well-publicised social occasions (gala performances, exhibition openings, etc.), went on a visit of the United States (where he lectured at some universities), and arranged an audience with the Pope. Clearly, the purpose of all this was to persuade the general public that he was no different from any other political personality. In June 1984, he surprised everyone by visiting the headquarters of the Communist Party in Rome, where the party leader Enrico Berlinguer was lying in state, in order to pay his last respects.[5]

In this essay, I intend to consider the MSI's new image as expressed by one type of activity only: poster production. I shall examine the new images that the MSI has devised in order to appear respectable, and attempt to prove that frequently, beneath a veneer of modernity, lie hidden nostalgic themes.

It is worth noting at this point that, contrary to the practice of other political parties in Italy, the MSI produces its propaganda internally, instead of entrusting it to outside agencies: the graphic artists who design the posters are also party activists.[6] This means that the party can exercise total control over its publicity, and include whatever allusions to Fascism it thinks fit.[7]

Before looking at the new propaganda, it is worth considering two posters that well typify the old approach, and which Almirante would have described as 'outdated, anachronistic and stupidly nostalgic'. They were both produced for the regional elections of 1970. The first depicts in the foreground a man surrounded by Italian tricolours, his index finger pointed at the onlooker (Fig. 1). In the second, a man clutching the Italian flag rescues another man whose imploring hand we see in the foreground (Fig. 3). Both posters are strongly dependent, both stylistically and thematically, on the graphic propaganda of the Fascist period. The photographic realism – a style the general public was and is especially predisposed to respond to, since it is the one used by many of the popular media (e.g. cinema, television, photonovelettes, adventure comics)[8] – permits a more effective rendering of the men's athletic build, their foreshortened gestures, and their crumpled shirts and flags. The values that these posters evoke are those typical of Fascist ideology: the cult of virility, courage, action and patriotism.[9]

The first poster's direct source is quite likely to be one issued by the regime around 1935 as part of its campaign for economic self-sufficiency (Fig. 2). A number of similarities support such a view: the three-quarter leftward turning of the men's torsos, with their unusual left-handed pointing gestures; the peremptory, three-word slogans ('AIUTATECI A DIFENDERVI!' [Help us defend you!] and 'ACQUISTATE PRODOTTI ITALIANI' [Buy Italian goods]); and their italicised lettering – the latter being very uncommon in MSI propaganda. It is worth noting that the finger pointed at the observer is a motif which recurs especially in wartime recruitment propaganda (its early prototype is Alfred Leete's well-known Lord Kitchener poster of 1914), and lends the two posters militaristic overtones. Equally martial is the slogan 'AIUTATECI A DIFENDERVI'.

As for the second poster of the MSI, it too might have been inspired by a Fascist one: that featuring a *squadrista*-thug rescuing a drowning Italy from the perilous waters of Bolshevism, which was produced in 1922 to celebrate the near-failure of the general strike of July and August (Fig. 4). If this picture is not actually a direct source, the two posters undoubtedly share the typically Fascist fixation with heroic deeds.[10] The apocalyptic rather than rationally-argued slogan of the MSI poster – 'CON NOI PRIMA CHE SIA TROPPO TARDI' [Join us, before it's too late] – is an appropriate complement to the dramatic image, and recalls the desperate tone of the propaganda of the besieged Salò regime.[11]

Since 1970, posters so blatantly reminiscent of those of the Fascist period have rarely been produced.[12] The MSI has in fact gone out of its way to disguise its identity. To do so, it has not hesitated to plunder from the visual codes of ideological traditions quite different from its own, if it considered them capable of triggering positive associations. Hence the adoption of images drawn from Renaissance iconography and, paradoxically, from the visual propaganda of the radical left. We will begin by considering examples of the latter type of borrowing.

Left-wing images are copied frequently especially by the youth wing of the MSI, the *Fronte della Gioventù*. Let us take the recruitment poster of 1983 (Fig. 5). It depicts a group of young people demonstrating. The bottom section of the poster is a photograph, while the upper one is a stylised drawing featuring the outlines of six rows of people, together with a superimposed left-wing-sounding slogan: 'COSTRUIAMO NELLE SCUOLE L'ALTERNATIVA CULTURALE PER COSTRUIRE NEL PAESE L'ALTERNATIVA AL SISTEMA' [Let's build an alternative culture in the schools, in order to build an alternative system in the country]. The section of the poster that is of the greatest interest is the stylised image, for it is almost certainly based on a Cuban poster of the late 1960s (Fig. 6). Instead of the demonstrators, we see in the latter a tractor ploughing the earth from which words expressing the ideals of Castro's revolution sprout ('work ethics', 'worth', 'honesty', etc.), but the visual conception is the same, as the wavy strips and superimposed irregular lettering show. The idea of the outline of tightly-knit rows of people – suggesting unity and solidarity – is derived from a well-known May 1968 poster. It is worth remarking that the neo-Fascist poster looks at first more left-wing than its Cuban source, on account of the dominant use of red and the very presence of the demonstrators. Only on closer inspection do we notice in the photograph the tricolours and the black banners, one of which carries the slogan 'DALLE SCUOLE, DALLE CITTÀ, SPAZZIAMO VIA IL COMUNISMO' [Let's rid our schools and our cities of Communism].

Equally inspired by the left is the poster produced by the *Fronte della Gioventù* in 1979, which depicts the riot police clubbing a demonstrator, and carries the caption: '345 detenuti di destra per motivi ideologici. NO ALLA REPRESSIONE DI REGIME. VEGLIA PER LA LIBERTÀ' [345 right-wingers detained for political reasons. Say no to the repression of the regime. Guard your freedom] (Fig. 7). The image is strongly reminiscent of those which the radical left has been using since 1968, in its press and posters, to denounce the violence of the State against its militant activists, and which was featured in another celebrated May 1968 poster (Fig. 8). Red is again the dominant colour, and it is worth noting that 'NO ALLA REPRESSIONE DI REGIME' echoes the French students' slogan 'Non à la répression'.

Finally, let us briefly look at a poster brought out in 1985 by the Italian Confederation of National Unions of Workers [*Confederazione Italiana Sindacati Nazionali Lavoratori*, CISNAL], the trade union affiliated to the MSI, to celebrate May Day (Fig. 9). In this case, the left-wing imitation concerns, first of all, the very nature of the festivity. Its commemoration by the MSI, which began in 1970 (a year after Almirante became leader of the party), is all the more surprising if we consider that the Fascists had banned it from their calendar of celebrations in 1924, to replace it with the *Festa del Lavoro* (Labour Day). This was made to coincide with the date of the mythical foundation of Rome (21 April) to give the commemoration a 'constructive' and optimistic character rather than the polemical one of the socialist May Day.[13] As for the picture used, the motif of the factory whose chimney coincides with the number one of

May 1 is an adaptation of yet another May 1968 poster (Fig. 10)[14]

The aping of the visual language of the left is not entirely surprising. Cuban graphics and those of May 1968 enjoyed considerable popularity among young people, especially in the late 1960s and in the 1970s, partly because they were the product of movements which had fired their imagination, and partly on account of their originality. They became cult images, appreciated beyond the circles of those who shared their actual political messages.[15] The MSI's appropriation of these icons – as indeed of the jargon of the radical left, the so-called *sinistrese* (leftese),[16] and of such socialist festivities as May 1 and Women's Day – is essentially an attempt to project an up-to-date and youthful image.[17] It is worth adding that, in the past decade, the MSI has put itself forward as the interpreter of social protest (protest against *partitocrazia*, i.e. the excessive power of Italian political parties, consumerism, unemployment etc.). In particular, the *Fronte della Gioventù* has made some overtures to left-wing youth.[18] The adoption of leftist modes is clearly intended to ease such a dialogue.

However, the left-wing imitation can also serve a more negative function: that of making it difficult to distinguish between right-wing and left-wing propaganda, thus emptying the latter of its radical content.[19]

Let us now consider the MSI's use of Renaissance art as a source for its propaganda. The prestige enjoyed by this visual tradition makes it a code suitable for expressing, in an acceptable manner, unpalatable messages. The imagery chosen tends to be of a religious nature. Clearly, this enables the MSI to address itself to a wider audience – the type of audience which, consciously or unconsciously, reacts to it with awe, on account of its Catholic upbringing.

The first poster we shall examine was produced in 1980 as part of a campaign to introduce the death penalty for drug-trafficking (Fig. 11). It features the naked torso of a dead man lying on an unidentifiable object. His head is tilted backwards, while his right arm hangs down prominently across the lower half of the street. The slogan beneath it reads: 'CHI TI DÀ LA DROGA TI DA LÀ MORTE. FIRMA CON NOI PER LA VITA' [Those who give you drugs give you death. Sign our petition if you want life]. Now, it is not difficult to recognise in this figure the Christ of Michelangelo's Vatican *Pietà* (Fig. 12). The drawing is rudimentary (the right arm's connection to the torso and the torso itself are anatomically dubious), but it is clear that the author's intentions are 'artistic' rather than simply illustrative, as the use of hatching, its incompleteness (which gives it the appearance of a preparatory sketch), and the conspicuous presence of the author's signature indicate. The allusion to the *Pietà* has precise functions: it aims to hit the viewers both emotionally and 'artistically', to prevent them from considering lucidly the gravity of the proposal being put forward. The identification of the drug addict killed by an overdose with Christ also seems to imply that the enormity of the crime justifies a punishment as extreme as the death sentence.[20]

The slogan too needs to be commented upon, since, like the picture, it serves a mystificatory function. The text strikes one especially for its symmetrical structure, based on two equations linked to each other through a relation of opposition: drugs=death *versus* we (MSI)=life. This structure is emphasised by the spatial arrangement of the slogan. The two sentences are placed on different levels in the left-hand and right-hand sides respectively of the lower section of the poster. Each sentence is in turn split in two parts occupying two lines, in such a way as to draw attention to the key-words of the equations: 'drugs', 'death', 'we' and 'life'. The slogan also features a number of interrelated phonic effects: the alliteration of the 'd' in 'CHI TI DÀ LA DROGA', that of the 't' in 'MORTE' and 'VITA', that of the 'm' in 'MORTE' and 'FIRMA', and the anaphoric repetition 'TI DÀ'. Such rhetorical and structural virtuosities aim to solicit a consensus based on effect rather than argumentation.[21] The antithetical structure of the slogan also fulfils a euphemistic function. It idealistically opposes life to death, yet in actual fact demands that whoever causes death should be punished with death.

The iconography of the Passion occurs, in less obvious form, in a poster on the subject of terrorism, brought out in June 1974, just after the terrorist attack in *Piazza della Loggia* in Brescia, to refute accusations that the MSI was implicated (Fig. 13). It features a man in shirt sleeves, whose hands are crossed at the front and handcuffed, while his head is bowed. The colour of the plain background is red, no doubt to imply that it is because of Communist accusations that he had ended up in gaol. The caption reads: 'PUÒ ACCADERE ANCHE A TE!' [It can happen to you too!]. The posture of the figure is based on the traditional iconography of the *Ecce homo*, which in fact depicts Christ with his hands tied and his head tilted forward (Fig. 14).[22] The reference to this episode of the Passion serves to present the MSI as a defenceless victim of persecution. The religious metaphor ultimately fulfils a euphemistic function, since there is no doubt that the party's denial of all involvement in the massacre would hardly have appeared credible if stated explicitly. The *Ecce homo* image, like the *Pietà* one in the previous poster, is, finally, also an implicit celebration of sacrifice – a theme dear to Fascist rhetoric.[23]

The placard round the protagonist's neck, with the writing 'ANTI-COMUNISTA', is also worthy of comment. It confirms that the picture is not purely realistic, but includes a symbolic dimension, since wrongdoers are no longer pilloried. The detail is a likely reference to the way the supporters of the Salò regime were humiliated after its fall, i.e. to the ritual of exposing them to public insult with placards inscribed 'FAS-CISTA', 'AUSILIARIA', (i.e. member of the women's militia), etc. (Fig. 15). This reference to the past is probably intended to hint at the continuous persecution which, allegedly, the extreme right has been subjected to since the war.

The practice of including motifs which discreetly allude to the Fascist period, with the intention of establishing an ideal link with it, recurs frequently in the recent propaganda of the MSI, as the examples which follow will show.

We shall begin by considering a poster of 1970 depicting two men and a young woman walking arm in arm before a red, white and green rainbow (a less overtly patriotic version of the Italian flag) (Fig. 16). The subject matter of the poster is far from obvious. Umberto Eco has argued that the young woman represents her gender, while the two men stand for the middle class and the working class, and hint at the party's cross-class appeal and corporatism − hence their linked arms. Yet this explanation is unconvincing, because the two male figures' clothes do not denote specific professions or classes. The key to the interpretation of the poster is provided by the slogan 'NOSTALGIA DELL'AVVENIRE' [Nostalgia for the future], which asserts the MSI's intention of projecting itself into the future while drawing inspiration from the past,[24] as well as by the source of the composition. The latter is undoubtedly a propaganda post-card of the Salò Republic featuring two marines and an auxiliary of the submarine and motor-torpedo force 'X MAS' (as the badge with the Roman number "X" she wears indicates) (Fig. 17). We must conclude that the MSI poster was intended as a tribute to the last few months of the regime. Given Almirante's position in the MINCULPOP, it is likely that the idea of seeking inspiration from the war postcard originated from him. To him may also be ascribed the slogan 'NOSTALGIA DELL'AVVENIRE', since he used it in a party rally in April 1970.[25] The poster has a more overt meaning too. The figures probably represent two generations: the man in the middle stands for the older one, as his formal clothing indicates; while the young woman in a miniskirt and the man in jeans and sports-jacket stand for the younger one. In a word, the three-some, who walk cheerfully with linked arms, and whose composition has been modelled on the war postcard, are the very embodiment of the slogan: they stress the continuity with the past and the perennial relevance of Fascist ideals.

Before examining other posters incorporating allusions of a nostalgic nature, it should be remarked that, ever since its foundation in 1946 by veterans of the Salò Republic, and in spite of the fact that the Constitution forbids the reorganisation of a Fascist party and the apology of Fascism, the MSI has revered and mythologised the *Ventennio*. Indeed, this cult is at the core of the party's identity.[26] It is worth recalling that the very acronym 'MSI' was devised because the first letter, as well as standing for 'Movimento', corresponded to Mussolini's famous monogram, while the remaining two, 'SI', were the qualifying initials of the *Repubblica Sociale Italiana*.[27] More recently, in 1986, the MSI chose to begin the celebration of the fortieth anniversary of its foundation with a rally entitled 'Italia domani' [Italy tomorrow] which was held at the *Teatro Lirico* in Milan – the very premises where Mussolini made his last speech on 16 December 1944. In his keynote address, Almirante alluded to the 'historic' significance of the location and stressed his party's loyalty to its roots. 'The past', he remarked, 'is embodied in our present and projects us into the future.'[28]

The party acronym and the event at the *Teatro Lirico* provide irrefutable evidence that the MSI delights in referring to its origins.

However, unlike these two instances, and as the *Ecce homo* and *Nostalgia dell'Avvenire* posters suggest, the allusions to Fascism presented in the propaganda which is aimed at the general public tend to be covert, being intended mostly for the initiated. The posters we are about to consider confirm such a view.

The Fascist past is frequently evoked through the way the leaders are portrayed. A poster of 1983 features Almirante in the foreground before a large audience (Fig. 18). The aim is to recall one of the canonical images of the *Ventennio*: that of the Duce haranguing one of his *adunate oceaniche* (or 'ocean-like gatherings', as the cheering crowds were hyperbolically referred to by the media) from the balcony of *Palazzo Venezia* in Rome, or from other public buildings elsewhere (Fig. 19). It is an image which the Luce newsreels and the press (all of which was party-controlled) had popularised in the 1930s and 1940s.[29] Now, all parties like to show that their leaders are charismatic, and it is undoubtedly true that the most effective way of doing so is by photographing the political figure together with the crowd from the very place where he/she is standing. However, the iconography of the foregrounded leader addressing a mass audience is so charged with Fascist connotations that in Italy no party other than MSI would consider using it in a form of political communication as public as the poster. Similar representations of leaders occasionally appear in press and promotional publications of other parties, but when they do, care is always taken to differentiate them from their Fascist counterpart – for instance by portraying the figures in unusual or informal attitudes, rather than in severe, dignified and rhetorical poses, and also by making it quite clear that the leader is speaking from a platform.[30] In the poster under consideration, Almirante too is speaking from a platform, but the photograph has been taken or cropped so as to give the impression that he is addressing his audience from the more exalted heights of a balcony.

Just like the ceremony marking the fortieth anniversary of the MSI's foundation, held, as we have seen, in the very premises where Mussolini delivered his last speech, the party's printed publicity alludes at times to specific events of the Fascist period. Let us consider a *Fronte della Gioventù* poster of 1974 inviting the public to vote 'yes', i.e. in favour of the abolition of the divorce law, in a referendum held on 12 May (Fig. 20). It sports the reiterated phrase 'ALT AL COMUNISMO' [Stop Communism] printed in red, with a superimposed large, black 'SI' in the middle, complemented below by the explanatory phrase, printed in smaller characters: 'ALL'ABROGAZIONE DELLA LEGGE FORTUNA' [to the repeal of the Fortuna law].[31] This layout recalls that of a giant billboard which the Fascists erected in 1934, on the facade of *Palazzo Braschi*, the party's national headquarters in Rome, to urge people to vote 'yes' in a plebiscite for or against the list of new deputies proposed by the Great Council for the following parliamentary term (Fig. 21).[32] Here, it is the 'SI' that is reproduced in repeated form, while pride of place is ascribed to a stylised effigy of Mussolini. That the similarity between the two posters is not coincidental is shown by another poster produced by the MSI for the same occasion. It depicts a large 'SI' over which the following slogan has been printed: 'I COMUNISTI VOGLIONO FARE DEL REFERENDUM UN'ARMA PER IMPORRE IL LORO INGRESSO AL GOVERNO. GLI ITALIANI DEBBONO FARE DEL REFERENDUM UN PLEBISCITO CONTRO IL COMUNISMO'. [The Communists want to use the referendum as a weapon to impose their entry into the government. The Italians must use the referendum as a plebiscite against Communism] [33] Given that the word 'plebiscito' is no longer used in Italian in this sense, we must conclude that the aim was to establish a wishful parallel with the plebiscite of 1934, when the 'SI' amounted to 96.25 per cent of the total vote – a result achieved partly through vote-rigging and systematic intimidation. The parallel was also appropriate because in both 1934 and 1974 the Communists campaigned for a 'NO' vote (they could have advised people to abstain in 1934). The very fact that the referendum on divorce was taking place exactly forty years after the plebiscite must have been seen by the MSI, out of some kind of number mysticism, as a good omen. A final confirmation that the MSI poster just described contains a reference to Fascism is provided by the three-dimensional letters 'SI' with serifs: these have been copied from the poster produced by the Fascists to announce triumphantly the results of the plebiscite, and featuring a photomontage of Mussolini (Fig. 22).

An allusion to Fascism, albeit a generalised one, is also present in another anti-divorce poster. This features a young, modern and conventional family; the woman wears a miniskirt, while the man sports a beard (a sign of anti-conformism, at the time) and carries a little girl on his shoulders (Fig. 23). Clearly, he is presented as an affectionate father – a far cry from the Rambo-like man depicted in a poster only four years earlier, urging the onlooker 'Help us defend you!'. The couple walks with a playful, synchronised gait. Now, it is precisely this last detail which lends itself to a second interpretation: it is in fact tempting to suggest that it is a reference to the goose step (Fig. 24). It should also be noted that the criss-crossing of the legs evokes the letter 'M', Mussolini's monogram; and, if we combine the 'M' with the 'SI' we obtain the acronym MSI.[34]

The next two posters we shall examine deal with the issue of terrorism. The first, dated 1975, depicts a *carabiniere* standing to attention before the tricolour (Fig. 25) – a picture quite probably inspired by the standard armed forces recruitment posters of the 1950s and 1960s.[35] A gun is pointed at his head by a 'Communist' (as the hammer and sickle on his cuff indicates). We naturally sympathise with him, not only because he is the defender of the nation's law and order, but because he is being treacherously attacked by the terrorist. However, a detail strikes one as odd: the military helmet. It is unexpected because it is not generally worn in peace-time. Its martial overtones are confirmed by the facial features of the *carabiniere*, which, on closer inspection, look familiar: the fleshy lips and prominent jaws recall Mussolini's legendary profile. The portrait of the *carabiniere* is in fact a fairly accurate copy of one of the official war portraits of the *Duce* (Fig. 26). It is arguable that the aim was to establish an implicit parallel between the execution of Mussolini by the Partisans in 1945, and the murder of representatives of law and order perpetrated by left-wing terrorists in the 1970s. The parallel also suggests, perhaps, that the violence and social anarchy which shook Italy in that decade is the direct consequence of the termination of Mussolini's 'firm' leadership.

The second poster we will focus upon was produced in 1970. It depicts a mother sheltering her child from the menacing hand of a 'red' terrorist (as the colour of his hand indicates). The text reads: 'LA DONNA TI DÀ LA VITA, IL TERRORISMO LA TOGLIE. CON LE DONNE DEL MSI–DN, CONTRO IL TERRORISMO' [Women give you life, terrorism takes it away. Join the women of the MSI–DN to

1. MSI poster produced for the 1970 elections.
2. Fascist poster, *c*. 1935, urging Italians to buy Italian goods.

CHI HA SALVATO L'ITALIA?

Bolscevismo

IL FASCISMO !!

4. Poster produced by the Fascist Party in 1922 to celebrate the near-failure of the general strike of July–August.

CON NOI
PRIMA CHE SIA GIA TROPPO TARDI
MSI

3. MSI poster produced for the 1970 elections.

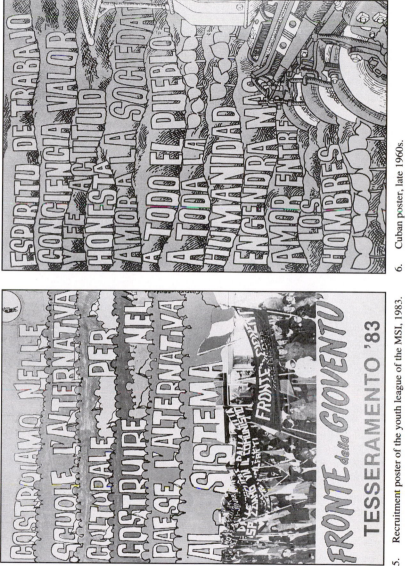

5. Recruitment poster of the youth league of the MSI, 1983.

6. Cuban poster, late 1960s.

7. MSI poster protesting against the State's 'repression' of right-wing activists.

8. May 1968 poster.

9. MSI poster celebrating 1 May, 1985.

10. May 1968 poster.

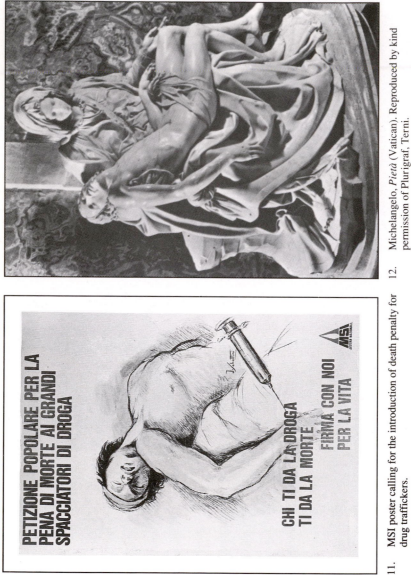

11. MSI poster calling for the introduction of death penalty for drug traffickers.

12. Michelangelo, *Pietà* (Vatican). Reproduced by kind permission of Plurigraf, Terni.

13. MSI poster produced shortly after the terrorist attack in *Piazza della Loggia* in Brescia, 1974.

14. Titian, *Ecce Homo* (National Gallery of Ireland, Dubin).

15. Auxiliary of the Salò Republic being exposed to public insult at the fall of the regime, 1945.

17. Propaganda postcard of the Salò Republic, 1943-45.

16. MSI poster produced for the 1970 elections.

18.   MSI poster showing Almirante talking at a party rally in Rome, 1983.

19.   Mussolini addressing a crowd from a public buiding in Venice, 1938.

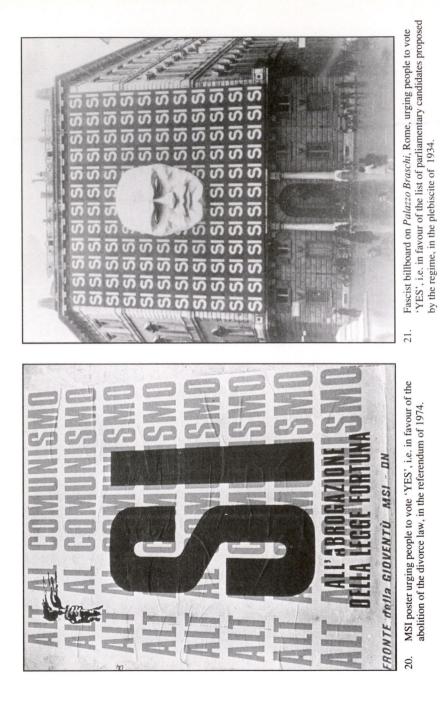

20. MSI poster urging people to vote 'YES', i.e. in favour of the abolition of the divorce law, in the referendum of 1974.

21. Fascist billboard on *Palazzo Braschi*, Rome, urging people to vote 'YES', i.e. in favour of the list of parliamentary candidates proposed by the regime, in the plebiscite of 1934.

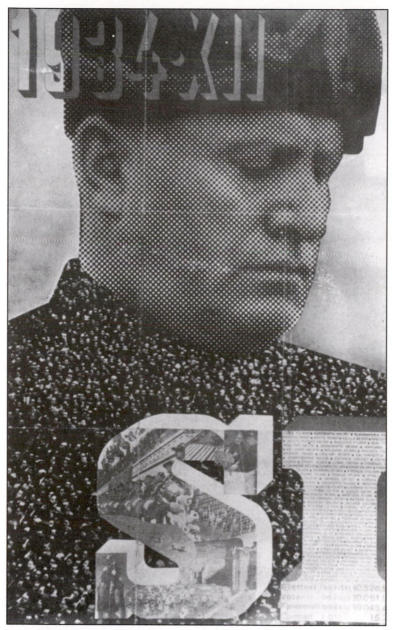

22.   Fascist poster announcing triumphantly the results of the plebiscite of 1934.

▲ 23. Anti-divorce poster produced for the referendum of 1974.

24. Goose-stepping soldiers

25. MSI poster denouncing 'Communist' terrorist attacks against the police forces.

26. Wartime official portrait of Mussolini.

27. Poster produced by the women's caucus of the MSI, professing an anti-terrorist stance, 1979.

28. Film poster for Salvatore Samperi's *Cuore di mamma*, 1969.

30. Cover design of Adolfo Mignemi's volume *Immagine coordinata per un impero. Etiopia 1935-1936* (published in 1984), which critically investigates the nature of Fascist propaganda during the Ethiopian campaign.

29. Poster produced by the youth league of the MSI, 1986.

"Dovete sopravvivere e mantenere nel cuore la fede. Il mondo, me scomparso, avrà bisogno ancora dell'idea che è stata e sarà la più audace, la più originale e la più mediterranea ed europea delle idee. La storia mi darà ragione".

32. Poster produced by a self-styled 'Centre de Propagande anti-Bolscévique (*sic*), Genève', c. 1983.

31. MSI poster commemorating the centenary of Mussolini's birth, 1983.

combat terrorism] (Fig. 27). Like the poster urging the introduction of the death penalty and featuring a *Pietà* – like image, examined earlier, this one has a Manichean structure that inevitably presents a distorted view of reality. Women, the life-givers, are contrasted to death-bringing terrorists. This opposition is underlined by the visual arrangement of the first sentence: the text has been split into two parts, and each placed at opposite ends of the picture, near the detail it refers to. The claim that left-wing terrorism kills innocent women and children is gratuitous and meant to elicit facile outrage: 'Red' terrorists, in fact, tend to aim at specific targets (e.g. members of the establishment). Just as false is the idea, implied in the opposition, that terrorists are always male, as indicated by the examples of the Red Brigade terrorists Barbara Balzarani and Natalia Ligas, and of the member of the Armed Revolutionary Nuclei [*Nuclei Armati Rivoluzionari*, NAR] Francesca Mambro, who was implicated in the Bologna station massacre of 1980. But it is the picture that interests us most; this is because it has been copied from the poster of Salvatore Samperi's film *Cuore di mamma*, a political parable on contemporary violence and the breakdown of all values, whose main characters are a woman fascinated by all sorts of terrorism, and her three children, two of whom, budding Nazis, play sadistic games (Fig. 28).[36] The film poster must have appealed to the graphic artist of the MSI because the younger child featured in it wears an SS helmet (for obvious reasons, this detail has been excluded from the political poster). It is likely that the film itself impressed him/her, on account of its apocalyptic message (and perhaps for its extreme violence too). That the MSI should choose to proclaim the firm anti-terrorist stance of its women's caucus by secretly quoting from the poster featuring Samperi's sadistic heroine is disconcerting. At best it will be assumed that the quotation was intended as a generic reference to the party's origins, and not as a celebration of Nazism and terrorism. It should be noted that a period of ten years separates the MSI poster from its source, so in this case too, the allusion could not have been recognised by the general public, but is likely to have been known only to the party hierarchy and their immediate entourage.

The above is not the only example of the technique of appropriating and adapting a picture originally devised to deal critically with the subject of Fascism, in order to cryptically celebrate the *Ventennio*. Another is provided by a recruitment poster of the *Fronte della Gioventù*, dating from 1986, which carries the slogan 'IL TUO FUTURO LO PUOI COSTRUIRE SUBITO. CON NOI.' [You can build your future *now*. With us] (Fig. 29). It depicts the group's logo (a black hand clutching a torch with a tri-coloured flame) repeatedly, and so arranged symmetrically as to produce, depending on how one looks at it, an alternating horizontal effect or a diagonal pattern. The idea is very likely to have been borrowed from the specially-designed cover of a book by Adolfo Mignemi, entitled *Immagine coordinata per un impero. Etiopia 1935–36*. [A Corporate Image for an Empire. Ethiopia 1935–36], published by Gruppo Editoriale Forma, Turin, in 1984 (Fig. 30). This work deals with the propaganda produced by the regime to justify and promote the Ethiopian campaign, and intersperses official images arguing that the Italians were bringing civilisation to a backward country, with pictures of massacres carried out by the invaders. The book's implicit aim is to explode the myth that Italian imperialism was more 'humane' than its British and French counterparts. The reiterated motif on the book's cover (a motif also featured full-page, once) is actually a blackshirt giving the Roman salute, rather than a torch; however, the general visual conception is the same. It should also be noted that the two motifs are not dissimilar: the man's black shirt is paralleled by the black, torch-clutching hand, and his outstretched arm is vaguely echoed by the rightwards-bending flame. The formal analogy with the youth group logo enables the latter to strengthen the poster's secret allusion to the book on the Ethiopian campaign – an allusion that points synecdochically to the Fascist period as a whole.

Not all the nostalgic references in the propaganda of the MSI are expressed in concealed form. Some posters unambiguously celebrate Fascism. However, these are intended for purely internal consumption: they are used to decorate the walls of party branches and, presumably, the homes of some of the activists. Two recent posters, both featuring Mussolini, provide good examples of this genre. The first, issued in 1983 to commemorate the centenary of the Duce's birth, carries the caption 'MUSSOLINI UOMO DI POPOLO' [Mussolini, man of the people] (Fig. 31). The second poster, dating from around the same time and officially produced by a self-styled 'Centre de Propagande anti-Bolscévique [*sic*], Genève' (as a credit in small print along the left-hand margin of the poster declares), has a quotation from one of Mussolini's speeches/writings: 'Dovete sopravvivere e mantenere nel cuore la fede. Il mondo, me scomparso, avrà bisogno ancora dell'idea che è stata e sarà la più audace, la più originale e la più mediterranea ed europea delle idee. La storia mi darà ragione.' [You must survive and keep faith alive in your heart. The world, after I have gone, will still need the idea that has been and will be the most daring, the most original, and the most Mediterranean and European of all ideas. History will prove me right] (Fig. 32).[37] It should be noted in passing that, though the poster commemorating Mussolini's centenary was not, as far as I am aware, posted up in public spaces, the actual commemorative events that were organised were given considerable visibility by the MSI. This proved feasible thanks to their 'cultural' nature. The main events were in fact a colloquium bearing the academic title of *L'Italia tra le due Guerre* [Italy between the Wars], which was held at *Castel Sant'Angelo*, one of the leading sights of Rome, and twenty smaller conferences, organised in several cities along an *itinerario mussoliniano*.[38]

Posters with fairly explicit allusions to Fascism, evidently directed at the converted, do occasionally make a public appearance, but only in carefully selected locations: usually in the immediate proximity of party branches, where the activists are able to cast a vigilant eye and to ensure that they are not torn or defaced by indignant passers-by.[39] A good example of this type of propaganda is the poster brought out by the *Fronte della Gioventù* in 1985, featuring two youths with their right arms raised (Fig. 33). Though the picture is far from sharp (it is based on a much-enlarged photographic detail), there is little doubt that the white, amorphous blot to the left is the open palm of a Roman salute. In order to temper the strong Fascist connotations of the picture, the graphic artist has superimposed on the youths' arms an extended text that could equally well have featured on a poster or tract of the radical left:

> FARE FRONTE:
> * Per una cultura aldilà dei vecchi schemi
> * per la sperimentazione e la creatività didattica
> * per la partecipazione studentesca diretta
> * per superare la burocrazia dei Decreti Delegati favorendo forme spontanee di rappresentanza
>
> [LET'S STAND TOGETHER:
> * for a truly innovative type of culture
> * for pedagogic experimentation and creativity
> * for direct student participation
> * to defeat the bureaucratised staff–student–parent committees, and replace them with spontaneous forms of representation]

In conclusion, in the last two decades, the propaganda of the MSI has undergone great transformations. The macho-militaristic images of direct Fascist inspiration has been replaced by others borrowed from a number of 'alien' sources, such as Renaissance iconography and the fashionable graphics of the radical left, principally in the hope that they may make the party more acceptable. When, as is frequently the case, Fascist images or images alluding to the Fascist period are used, they are manipulated and camouflaged so that they may look 'innocent' and contemporary to a

55

general audience. The MSI's urge to refer to its origins, and the practice of doing so in a coded, even esoteric, form, require some general comments.

The cult of the past is one of the features that best characterises the extreme right. Most parties – indeed most societies – consider the past as a model for the present, but their devotion to tradition tends to be accompanied by the awareness of a need for innovation and change. The right, on the other hand, obsessed as it is by its quest for stability and by its dissatisfaction with the present, clings to its roots resolutely.[40] The MSI's veneration of Fascism is also to be ascribed to the violent suppression of the movement and in particular to Mussolini's tragic end. 'Martyrdom' inevitably leads to mythologisation.

The realisation that the party needs to project a modern image if it is to survive, and the Italian Constitution's ban on the reorganisation of Fascism clearly frustrate the MSI's urge to declare its unwavering devotion to past ideals. Hence the creation of visual propaganda incorporating two levels of meaning: an overt one, aimed at the public at large, respectable and above board, and a hidden one, nostalgic in tone, intended essentially to fulfil an existential need (the proud self-declaration of the party's identity), but also to reassure the *cognoscenti* that, in spite of what appearances suggest, Fascism has not been repudiated.

Some of the nostalgic allusions are so outrageous (e.g. the goose step in the poster of 1974, and the portrait of Mussolini in that of 1975), that it is tempting to treat them as typically Fascist acts of bravado. They challenge the Constitution and attempt to prove that they can make a mockery of a mightier opponent on its own ground.[41]

As already noted, the references to Fascism present in the propaganda of the MSI are intended for very small audiences. Those in the *Nostalgia dell'Avvenire* poster, and in the poster featuring the *carabiniere* standing to attention may have been recognised by some war veterans, but the allusions to the plebiscite of 1934, incorporated in the anti-divorce poster (which, it should be recalled, was produced by the *Fronte della Gioventù*, and thus aimed at a generation born *after* the fall of Fascism), and to Samperi's film in the anti-terrorism poster, are esoteric to the point that only the party cadres could possibly have been aware of them.

The existential need to affirm one's identity and the bravado spirit can only in part account for this surprising approach to propaganda. Since some MSI posters also contain cryptic references of a non-political/controversial nature,[42] one could attribute it to an elitist attitude, i.e. a form of contempt for the unaware masses. The taste for 'secret' messages may equally be connected to the party's generally circumspect attitude to the 'outside world' – an attitude resulting from its past marginalisation.[43] It should also be pointed out, in all fairness, that political communication tends to be allusive and even cryptic in Italy – though no other propaganda is as esoteric as that of the MSI.[44]

The MSI is not unique in devising propaganda that addresses two distinct audiences: a general public, from which new votes must be conquered, and the converted, who merely need to be reassured.[45] What distinguishes this party from the others is the fact that its posters address the two audiences simultaneously, through a double level of meaning, one of which is secret. Another unusual feature is the fact that, by itself, the overt level tends to be unremarkable to the point of banality. The posters look ingenious only if their recondite meanings are identified. This emphasis on the message aimed at the initiated suggests that the MSI's attempt to appeal to a wider electorate is half-hearted, and that, in fact, the party prefers to talk to itself.

NOTES

*   I wish to express my gratitude to the Italian Institute in London, whose financial support made the research for this chapter possible. I must also thank the staff of the Library of the *Istituto Gramsci* of Bologna, and to Dr Fausto Sacchelli in particular, for their invaluable assistance.

1. On the MSI, as well as Roberto Chiarini's chapter herein, see: P. Rosenbaum, *Il nuovo fascismo, da Salò ad Almirante*, Feltrinelli, Milan, 1975; L. B. Weinberg, *After Mussolini. Italian Neo-Fascism and the Nature of Fascism*, University Press of America, Washington, D.C., 1979; R. Chiarini and P. Corsini, *Da Salò a Piazza della Loggia*, Franco Angeli, Milan, 1983; M. Caciagli, 'The Movimento Sociale Italiano – Destra Nazionale and Neo-Fascism in Italy', *West European Politics*, XI, 2, 1988, pp. 19–33; P. Ignazi, *Il polo escluso. Profilo del Movimento Sociale Italiano*, Il Mulino, Bologna, 1989.

2. The full text of the speech was published in the *Secolo d'Italia* (the party's official newspaper), on 7 April 1970, p. 3.

3. The MSI hoped to win power by making the ever-weaker governments of the Christian-Democrat Party dependent on its support.

4. Ph. Cannistraro, *La fabbrica del consenso. Fascismo e mass media*, Laterza, Bari, 1975, pp. 326–33.

5. On the MSI's recent attempts to modernise its image, see especially: G. Rossi, 'C'eravamo tanto odiati. Almirante spiega cosa è cambiato tra MSI e governo', *La Repubblica*, 11 November 1983, p. 4; P. Franchi, 'In fondo, a destra ...', *Panorama*, 17 February 1989, pp. 47–52; C. Incerti, 'Giovanni delle

bande nere', *Panorama*, 21 April 1985, pp. 62–3; S. Messina, 'MSI, la possibilità di essere normale', *La Repubblica*, 10 June 1987, p. 10. As far as the linguistic updating is concerned, see: M. Dardano, *Il linguaggio dei giornali italiani*, Laterza, Bari, 1981 (2nd edn), pp. 279–80; M. Revelli, 'Panorama editoriale e temi culturali della destra militante' and O. Calabrese, 'I linguaggi delle destre', in *Fascismo oggi. Nuova destra e cultura reazionaria negli anni ottanta*, special issue of the *Notiziario dell'Istituto Storico della Resistenza in Cuneo e Provincia*, No. 23, June 1983, pp. 51, 57–8, 63 and pp. 126–7 respectively. The party's modernisation also concerned its internal organisation. See Rosenbaum, *Il nuovo fascismo*, cit., pp. 67–9, 132–3, and Ignazi, *Il polo escluso*, cit., pp. 140–2.

6. I owe the information that the MSI relies on its activist artists to the kindness of Sigra Sala of the party's Propaganda Department in Rome, who also explained to me that the poster designs are often chosen from entries submitted to specially-organised competitions. The obvious danger of such a system is that of unprofessionalism. This is implicitly recognised by the official in charge of the publicity of the party, Domenico Mennitti, in an unpublished paper, 'Il Partito e la sua immagine', delivered at the 1986 conference of the MSI, held in Taormina. While calling for greater professionalism in the presentation of political messages, and drawing attention to the need for a 'corporate image', Mennitti also strongly argues against the dominant tendency to commission party publicity from commercial advertising agencies, on the ground that politics should not be sold to the public like a brand of washing powder. Such 'purist' views have a familiar ring, of course. They were shared by the Italian Left (the Communist Party in particular) until the mid–1970s, and by the British Labour Party till the early 1980s.

7. It is true that, as Dominique Memmi has shown in *Du récit en politique. L'affiche électorale italienne*, Presses de la Fondation Nationale des Sciences Politiques, Paris, 1986, pp. 96–7, 100–1, parties which rely on advertising agencies work closely with them anyway, and have the final say in the designs. However, a collaboration of this nature might prove problematic if attempted by the MSI. It is arguable that the party prefers to turn to its own propagandists because it might find it difficult, or at least embarrassing, to convince an 'outsider' to devise publicity that refers to Fascism and, as with one of the posters analysed below, even Nazism.

8. See A. C. Quintavalle, 'Il modello', in M. G. Lutzemberger and S. Bernardi (eds)., *Cultura, comunicazioni di massa, lotta di classe*, Savelli, Rome, 1976, p. 25.

9. A. C. Quintavalle (ed.), *Nero a strisce. La reazione a fumetti*, University of Parma, 1971; U. Eco, 'Fascio e fumetto ('Eja, Eja! Gulp!)', in *Il costume di casa*, Bompiani, Milan, 1973, pp. 183–93.

10. The MSI poster (as well as its possible source) lends itself to being analysed in the light of the scheme of standard narrative functions which Vladimir Propp identified in folktales. The sequence of events that are condensed in the picture may be expressed thus: There is a danger (Communism) and a

defenceless being (Italy) has fallen victim of it. However, a hero, whose special powers derive from his talisman-like flag (Fascist ideology), rescues him, thus triumphing over Evil. It is worth noting in passing that the Christian-Democrat propaganda of the cold-war period was similarly structured. See A. C. Quintavalle 'La fiaba 'manifesta'', in D. Audino and G. Vittori (eds.), *Via il regime della forchetta. Autobiografia del PCI nei primi anni '50 attraverso i manifesti elettorali*, Savelli, Rome, 1976 (unpaginated). Mythical stories of the type just outlined have an easy appeal. The general public is favourably predisposed to them not only through its familiarity with the fairy-tale tradition, but because much of the mass culture too (the popular weeklies, commercial cinema, comics, etc.) is constructed along the same lines. See A. C. Quintavalle (ed.), *La bella addormentata. Morfologia e struttura del settimanale italiano*, University of Parma, 1972.

11. On the propaganda of the Italian Social Republic, see: G. Vittori (ed.), *C'era una volta il Duce. Il regime in cartolina*, Savelli, Rome, 1975; R. Guerri, *Manifesti italiani della Seconda Guerra Mondiale*, Rusconi, Milan, 1982; Various Authors, *1943–45. L'immagine della RSI nella propaganda*, Mazzotta, Milan, 1985. Interestingly, the same apocalyptic approach has recently been used by the British extreme right. A National Front poster of 1983, featuring a map of Britain made up of a photo-montage of aggressive-looking black people, carried the slogan 'WHILE THERE'S TIME'. Clearly, the similarity with the MSI slogan is not due to direct influence, but to both parties' isolation – a condition that leads them to adopt a persuasive strategy based on hyperbole and doom-mongering in order to attract attention.

12. Macho imagery has more or less disappeared from the propaganda of the MSI. When it recurs, it is always tempered by graphic stylisation. See, for instance, the poster dated *c.* 1975 which accuses the government of 'stealing' and squandering tax-payers' money. It depicts a simply-drawn, literally square-chested 'hunk' pulling out his empty pockets to show that he has been fleeced by the State. For an illustration, see O. Calabrese (ed.), *Italia Moderna. IV, 1960–1980: La difficile democrazia*, Electa, Milan, 1985, p. 57.

Heroic and military themes are no longer featured in pictorial form in the posters, though they still recur in the slogans. See, for instance the following: 'PER LA TUA SALVEZZA, IL NOSTRO CORAGGIO' [For your salvation, you need our courage], 1972; 'IL VOTO DEL 15 GIUGNO È IL VOTO DELLA SALVEZZA' [The vote of 15 June is the vote of salvation], 1975; 'SALVARE LA SCUOLA DAL COMUNISMO' [Save the schools from Communism], 1976; 'ELETTORE ANTICOMUNISTA, LA DC TI TRADISCE. VOTA A DESTRA E GLIELO IMPEDIRAI' [Anti-Communist voter: the Christian-Democrat party is betraying you. Vote for the Right to prevent it.], 1976; 'LA DC SI ARRENDE AL COMUNISMO. LA DESTRA MAI!' [The Christian-Democrat Party is giving in to Communism. The Right will never do that!], 1979; 'CARLO ALBERTO DALLA CHIESA. ASSASSINATO DALLA MAFIA, TRADITO DAL REGIME. GLI ITALIANI TI VENDICHERANNO' [Carlo

Alberto Dalla Chiesa. Murdered by the Mafia, betrayed by the regime. The Italians will avenge you.], 1982. (Dalla Chiesa was the prefect of Palermo.)

Though Fascist-looking posters have virtually ceased to be produced by the MSI, I am convinced that the party hierarchy continues to favour, above all, the macho-martial aesthetic. The two 1970 posters discussed above were the only ones to be seen, attractively framed, in the meeting room of the main branch of the MSI in Padua, when I visited it in 1985. The poster featuring the man pointing his finger at us also hangs at the entrance of the Ferrara branch of the party, and was recently referred to me as 'one of our dearest possessions'.

13. M. Massara, C. Schirinzi and M. Sioli, *Storia del Primo Maggio*, Longanesi, Milan, 1978, pp. 119–214. In spite of its abolition by the Fascists, May 1 continued to be commemorated clandestinely. See L. Casali, 'Il Primo Maggio proibito, 1923–1943', paper presented to the conference on May Day held in Lecce in April 1988 (forthcoming in the proceedings).

14. For a few other examples of MSI posters inspired by left-wing graphics, see: L. Cheles, '"Dolce Stil Nero"? Images of Women in the Graphic Propaganda of the Italian Neo-Fascist Party', in Z. Barański and S. Vinall (eds.), *Women and Italy. Essays on Gender, Culture and History*, Macmillan, London, 1991, pp.75-79, 85-88. Plates 20-27.

15. On Cuban graphics and their cult, see esp.: D. Sterner (ed.), *The Art of Revolution*, Pall Mall Press, London, 1970 (with an excellent introduction by Susan Sontag); D. Kunzle, 'Uses of the Che Poster', *Art in America*, September–October 1975, pp. 66–72. On the graphics of May 1968, see M. Rohan, *Paris,' 68, Graffiti, Posters, newspapers and films of the events of May 1968*, Impact Books, London, 1988.

16. The widespread prestige enjoyed by *sinistrese* during the years of social unrest was due to its association with the student and trade union movements, considered at the time as the intellectual and political vanguards. On *sinistrese*, see esp.: P. Violi, *I giornali dell'estrema sinistra*, Garzanti, Milan, 1977; M. A. Cortellezzo, *Il linguaggio dei movimenti di contestazione*, Giunti-Marzocco, Florence, undated [1980]; A. Martin and M. A. Cortellazzo, *Il linguaggio politico-sindacale*, Giunti-Marzocco, Florence, undated [1980]. For the MSI's borrowings from the jargon of the left, see Dardano's, Revelli's and Calabrese's works, cited in note 5, above.

17. The need to modernise the party's image by imitating the left, whose language had achieved a hegemonic position, is implied in Almirante's statement of 1969, quoted at the beginning of this chapter. The term 'language' may be extended to cover all forms of political communication.

18. See P. Ignazi, 'Il MSI partito della protesta', *Il Mulino*, XXXVII, 1988, pp. 633–51, later incorporated in *idem, Il polo escluso*, cit., pp. 197–238.

19. In December 1975, the MSI's misappropriation of left-wing phrases prompted a students' organisation in Padua to denounce the practice and its mystificatory aims with a poster. See M. A. Cortellazzo, 'Note sulla lingua dei volantini', *Versus. Quaderni di studi semiotici*, X, 1975, p. 77. It is worth not-

ing that a similar manipulative technique had been used by Mussolini, who, originally a Socialist, was quite familiar with Marxist jargon. See P. Agosto, 'The Language of Mussolini', *The Italianist*, I, 1981, pp. 60–1. The appropriation of left-wing commemorations by the extreme right has a most notable precedent in Hitler's proclamation of May Day as a national festivity, in 1933. By obliging workers to take part in the spectacular parades stage-managed by Goebbels together with the Nazis, he effectively transformed a revolutionary day of class struggle into one of class collaboration. See U. Achten, *Illustrierte Geschichte des 1. Mai*, Asso Verlag, Oberhausen, 1985, pp. 262-77, and U. Achten, M. Reichert and R. Schultz, *Mein Vaterland ist international. Internationale illustrierte Geschichte des 1. Mai, 1886 bis Heute*, Asso Verlag, Oberhausen, 1986, pp. 57–8, which also reproduces (p. 57) a satirical photomontage by Heartfield showing Goebbels applying a false bushy beard to Hitler's face to make him look like Marx. To mention a more recent example of appropriation, it will be recalled that on the eve of the French presidential elections of 1988, Le Pen brought forward the *Front National's* traditional Joan of Arc festivities (23 April) by eight days in order to celebrate May 1 in competition with the left. See *Le Monde,* 2 May 1988, pp. 1,6,16.

20. Michelangelo's *Pietà* had been used before in Italian political propaganda, for equally manipulative ends. A Christian-Democrat poster of 1957 commemorating the anniversary of the Liberation (25 April) depicts a Madonna-like woman mourning the semi-naked body of a young partisan lying across her lap. An extended caption urges the public not to forget that it owes its liberty to her son's sacrifice, and calls for all-out opposition to 'Communist dictatorship'. The aim of this thinly disguised *Pietà* image and its complementary text is clearly to deny the Communist Party its hegemonic role in the anti-Fascist resistance struggles. For an illustration of the poster, see C. Dané (ed.), *Parole e immagini della Democrazia Cristiana*, Broadcasting & Background, Rome, 1985 (unpaginated). The Christian-Democrats have in the past relied fairly systematically on Christian iconography for propaganda purposes. They virtually abandoned this practice in the late 1950s, when they realised that the rapid secularisation of Italian society had considerably weakened the persuasive power of such images, and revived it briefly only during the campaigns for the referenda on divorce and abortion to give them a crusade-like character. See L. Cheles, 'L'uso delle immagini rinascimentali nell'iconografia del manifesto politico', in R. Varese (ed.), *Letture di storia dell'arte*, Il Lavoro Editoriale, Ancona–Bologna, 1988, pp. 49–50. Today, only the MSI continues to believe in the political effectiveness of religious imagery.

21. Inevitably, one is reminded the Mussolini's high-flown rhetorical style, about which see esp.: G. Lazzari, *Le parole del fascismo*, Argileto, Rome, 1975; A. Simonini, *Il linguaggio di Mussolini*, Bompiani, Milan, 1977; E. Leso, M. A. Cortellazzo, I. Paccagnella and F. Foresti, *La lingua italiana e il Fascismo*, Consorzio Provinciale di Pubblica Lettura, Bologna, 1977;

P. Agosto, *La semantica del potere*, Ph.D. thesis, Sheffield City Polytechnic, 1980; K. Ille, *Politische sprache im Dienst der Gewalt. Untersuchungen zu Production und Rezeption faschistischer und neofaschistische Texte*, Ph.D. thesis, University of Vienna, 1980.

It is interesting to note that, in his paper 'Il partito e la sua immagine' (see note 6 above), Mennitti states quite candidly that in political communication *impressione*, which is 'by its very nature tied to the emotional sphere of the unconscious', is just as important as *convincimento*, which is 'based on the rational logic of argumentation'. Mennitti's dichotomy seems to echo that expressed by Mussolini in a celebrated interview with Emil Ludwig, when he argued that, in addressing the masses, one should bear in mind that the 'mystical' element was as essential as the 'political' one. See E. Ludwig, *Colloqui con Mussolini*, Mondadori, Milan, 1965, p.131.

22. On the iconography of the *Ecce homo*, see L. Réau, *Iconographie de l'art chrétien*, Presses Universitaires de France, Paris, 1957, tome II, vol. II, pp. 459–60.

23. On the Fascist ethos of sacrifice, which derives precisely from the Christian dialectic of death and resurrection, see M. A. Ledeen, *The First Duce. D'Annunzio at Fiume*, The Johns Hopkins University Press, Baltimore, 1977, pp. 19–20, 202–3; G. L. Mosse, 'The Poet and the Exercise of Political Power: Gabriele D'Annunzio', in *Masses and Man. Nationalist and Fascist Perceptions of Reality*, Howard Fertig, New York, 1980, pp. 92-7. See also: U. Eco, 'La voglia di morte', in *Sette anni di desiderio. Cronache 1977–1983*, Bompiani, Milan, 1983, pp. 123–5. It should be noted that not all the Christian imagery the MSI uses is centred on the Passion; some of the posters aimed at a female audience rely on Renaissance representations of the Virgin. See L. Cheles, '"Dolce Stil Nero"?' cit., pp. 69-71, Plates 8-10,12,13.

24. This past–future dialectic parallels Mussolini's exaltation of the Roman past, and his call to imitate it in order to achieve future greatness. See: N. Tranfaglia, 'Il capo e le masse. L'esempio di Mussolini', in *Labirinto italiano. Il fascismo, l'antifascismo, gli storici*, La Nuova Italia, Florence, 1989, p. 51. For an exhaustive study of the Roman myth during Fascism, see D. Cofrancesco, 'Appunti per un'analisi del mito romano nell'ideologia fascista', *Storia contemporanea*, I, 3, 1980, pp. 383–441.

25. See *Il Secolo d'Italia*, 7 April 1970, p. 3.

26. The reverence I am talking about is of a general, mostly emotional nature. The question of the MSI's actual ideological and cultural debts to Fascism is in fact quite complex, because of the faction-riven nature of the party, and, of course, of Fascism itself. See D. Cofrancesco, 'Le destre radicali davanti al Fascismo', in P. Corsini and L. Novati (eds.), *L'eversione nera. Cronache di un decennio (1974–1984)*, Franco Angeli, Milan, 1985, pp. 57, 134; M. Revelli, 'La RSI e il neofascismo italiano', in P. P. Poggio (ed.), *La Repubblica Sociale Italiana, 1943–45* (proceedings of the Brescia conference, 4–5 October 1985), Brescia, 1986, pp. 417–30; P. Ignazi, 'La cultura politica del Movimento Sociale Italiano', in *Rivista di Scienza politica*, XIX,3,1989, pp. 431-65.

27. The genesis of the party's name was described by Alfredo Cucco, a former member of the National Directory of the Fascist Party and an under-secretary in the Salò Republic, in the preface to A. M. La Grua's *Lo Stato Nazionale del Lavoro nella vocazione del MSI*; the relevant passage is quoted in Revelli, 'La RSI e il neofascismo', cit., p. 424.

28. For Almirante's speech at the *Teatro Lirico*, see *Il Secolo d'Italia*, 28 Jan. 1986, pp. 1, 3. Mussolini's last speech was especially close to the MSI leader's heart. In a recent interview he described it as 'one of his most beautiful'. See F. Nirenstein, 'Almirante – una vita vista da destra', *Epoca*, 5 February 1987, p. 98.

29. On the ritual of the speech from the balcony, which originated from D'Annunzio, and its iconography, see: M. Isnenghi, 'Iconografia della stampa fascista', in *Intellettuali militanti e intellettuali funzionari. Appunti sulla cultura fascista*, Einaudi, Turin, 1979, pp. 176, 179; G. L. Mosse, 'Public Festivals: The Theatre and Mass Movements', in *The Nationalization of the Masses*, Howard Fertig, New York, 1975, pp. 109–10; M. A. Ledeen, *The First Duce* cit., pp. 3, 8; N. Tranfaglia, 'Il capo e le masse', cit., pp. 41–53.

30. It should be noted that not only are MSI leaders always represented formally in the party's propaganda, but their actual behaviour at party rallies tends to be stiff and solemn. See P. Leone, *Lo spettacolo della politica*, Editoriale Bios, Cosenza, 1987, p. 117.

31. Fortuna was the Socialist MP who introduced the divorce Bill. On the referendum, which the MSI fought alongside the Christian-Democrats (an opportunity it was eager to seize in order to come back to the political arena as a legitimate political force), see M. Clark, D. Hine and R. E. M. Irving, 'Divorce – Italian Style', *Parliamentary Affairs*, XXVII, 1974, pp. 333–58.

32. On the plebiscite of 1934, see R. De Felice, *Mussolini il duce. I. Gli anni del consenso, 1929–1936*, Einaudi, Turin, 1974, pp. 311–13.

33. For an illustration of this poster, see P. Mancini, *Il manifesto politico. Per una semiologia del consenso*, Edizioni Rai Radiotelevisione Italiana, Turin, 1980, Fig. 19.

34. It will be recalled that the 'M' in the party's acronym was chosen precisely because it coincided with Mussolini's initial. A pun not unlike that on the anti-divorce poster was featured on a poster produced for the local elections of 1972; here the 'M' in 'DESTRA NAZIONALE MSI' was coloured differently so that that party's name could be read as the slogan 'DESTRA NAZIONALE MSI, SI [say 'yes' to Destra Nazionale MSI]. (The phrase 'DESTRA NAZIONALE' was added to the name of the MSI in 1972, when the Monarchists were incorporated into the party.) The opposition too has exploited the punning possibilities afforded by the acronym: an alternative magazine of the early 1970s, *Ca Balà*, urged its readers to 'neutralise' neo-Fascist graffiti by modifying the letters 'MSI' daubed on walls into 'MNO'. See the illustration in R. Cirio and P. Favari (eds), *L'altra grafica*, Bompiani, Milan, 1972, p. 142.

35. By the early 1970s, the military-men-standing-to-attention motif looked

pathetically outdated on account of its unabashed patriotism; hence its replacement with pictures stressing the armed forces' high-tech equipment and training. Clearly, it is precisely this patriotic quality that made it so appealing to the MSI. On the theme of the serviceman standing before the flag and its 'lay' use, see Roland Barthes's *Mythologies*, Paladin, London, 1973, pp. 116 ff.

36. On this film, see G. Grazzini, *Eva dopo Eva. La donna nel cinema italiano*, Laterza, Bari, 1980, pp. 118–19.

37. Both types of posters were offered to me in a number of MSI branches I visited in 1985.

38. Giuseppe Ciarrapico's introduction to the proceedings claims that 'the *Castel Sant'Angelo* meeting was characterised by papers following a strictly historical approach', while the other conferences were 'dominated by the contributions of right-wing intellectuals and politicians, who wished to reconstruct the life and works of Mussolini motivated by scholarly rather than propaganda purposes'. See *Mussolini nel centenario della nascita*, Ciarrapico Editore, Rome, 1985, p. 9. However, apart from the contributions of two serious historians, Renzo de Felice and James Gregor, who were no doubt invited so that they could bring prestige and academic respectability to the events, the proceedings are totally apologetic and hagiographic.

39. The more remote the location of the party branch, the greater will be the density and 'hardness' of the posters that are on public display. In Bologna, for instance, such posters are to be found on the walls of *vicolo Posterla*, a long and narrow side-road, half-way along which are the offices of the MSI. In spite of its central location, the party exercises such a 'control' over it, that in the politically-troubled 1970s, it was practically a no-go area.

40. As the political philosopher Norberto Bobbio has put it:

> The sense and cult of tradition are [for the extreme right] a constant, passionate and emotionally-felt rather than rationally-justified reference to the past – a past that must be relived and in which one must mirror oneself. Little it matters if this is the kitsch Roman empire of the Fascists with their massed legions, the crude blood and soil communities of the Germanic peoples, or quite simply the *ancien régime*. Every reactionary right has its own past – a past more or less remote, mythical or historical, one that has to be recovered, restored, pointed out as a model, and to which one must remain loyal; loyalty to tradition is an unfailing element of the declarations of principle and the rhetoric of the ideologues and the propagandists of the radical right. [...] The revolutionary left, on the other hand, places its trust in great transformations, in rebirth and in renewal, not in the revival of ancient virtues, but in the creation of a new man. The former looks backwards to find its Golden Age, the latter forward. [...] Whoever seeks consolation and salvation in tradition starts from a ruthlessly critical analysis of the present, interpreted as an age of decadence.

('Per una definizione della destra reazionaria', in *Fascismo oggi* cit., p. 31.) For detailed accounts of the extreme right's attitudes of tradition, cf. esp. D. Cofrancesco, 'La tradizione come archetipo e i suoi usi politici', *Il politico*, XLI, 1976, pp. 209–36; *idem*, *Destra e sinistra*, Bertani, Verona, 1984, pp. 45–54. See also J. LeGoff, 'Il peso del passato nella coscienza collettiva degli italiani', in F. L. Cavazza and S. R. Graubard (eds.), *Il caso italiano*, Garzanti, Milan, 1979, pp. 534–52; *idem*, entry 'Passato/Presente', in *Enciclopedia*, Einaudi, Turin, 1980, X, pp. 502–8.

41. One is reminded of D'Annunzio's flight over the enemy capital of Vienna to drop Italian propaganda leaflets (Ledeen, *The First Duce*, cit., pp. 1–2), and of the much-publicised exploits of the *maiali*, the frogman-guided torpedoes that sank the British battleships *Valiant* and *Queen Elizabeth* in the port of Alexandria, in December 1941.

42. A Women's Day poster of 1986, for instance, depicts in slightly modified form a female portrait drawn from Caravaggio's painting *Judith and Holophernes* – presumably in order to celebrate both heroic womanhood and chastity, two features traditionally symbolised by Judith. See L. Cheles, '"Dolce Stil Nero"?' cit.

43. On the MSI's diffidence towards the outside world and its cult of secrecy, see Ignazi, *Il polo negato*, cit., p. 291, n. 51.

44. On the obscure nature of much political communication in Italy, and the reasons for it, see: U. Eco, 'Il linguaggio politico', in G. L. Beccaria (ed.), *I linguaggi settoriali*, Bompiani, Milan, 1973, pp. 94–102; J. Jacobelli (ed.), *La comunicazione politica in Italia*, Laterza, Bari, 1989; M. Baldini, *Parlar chiaro, parlare oscuro*, Laterza, Bari, 1989, ch. II. An example of allusive propaganda produced by a party other than the MSI is provided by a series of posters issued by the Socialist Party (PSI) for the general elections of 1983. They featured the Party's leader Bettino Craxi, together with the slogan 'PSI. l'ottimismo della volontà [PSI. The optimism of the will] – a phrase which hinted at Gramsci's far from universally known aphorism 'Pessimismo dell'intelligenza, ottimismo della volontà' [Pessimism of the intelligence, optimism of the will].

45. See G. Pasquino, 'Alto sgradimento: la comunicazione politica dei partiti', *Problemi dell' informazione*, XIII, 1988, pp. 480–4, who calls the two audiences *elettorato d'opinione* (floating voters) and *elettorato d'appartenenza* (hard-core voters). The MSI also devises visual propaganda intended exclusively for the latter category, as shown above.

CHAPTER FOUR

The Far Right in Germany since 1945

David Childs

Was the Nazi seizure of power in 1993 the culmination of long-term trends in German politics and society or was it the result of a series of avoidable accidents? The issue will continue to excite the passions of historians but can have no definitive conclusion. On the one hand, it can certainly be argued that the National Socialist German Workers' Party [*Nationalsozialistische Deutsche Arbeiterpartei*, NSDAP] drew on ideas and emotions – racism, anti-Semitism, imperialism, nationalism, anti-Marxism, opposition to Versailles, anti-capitalism, rejection of the old generation of politicians, acceptance of hierarchy, statism – which were widespread currency in Weimar Germany. On the other hand, support for the Nazis grew rapidly over the brief period 1929–33, which meant that many of its supporters, even members, did not have strong political convictions. In this they were different from the supporters of the Social Democratic Party of Germany [*Sozialdemokratische Partei Deutschlands*, SPD] and the Catholic Centre Party [*Zentrum*, Z], both pillars of the Weimar Republic.

The Nazis seemed to attract the politically inexperienced voters; their vote grew when turnout was high.[1] They achieved their best support in Protestant agricultural areas and areas where the frontier issue was important (Silesia and the Palatinate). Their support came from all social groups but the industrial workers were under-represented among their supporters and members, as were Catholics. If we wish to explain the Nazi rise to power, we must conclude that it was the result of certain ideas having widespread currency, but that it needed a particular set of circumstances to turn those holding such views into Nazi supporters. The explosion of support for the Nazis would not have heralded the death of Weimar democracy had not key elements of the bourgeois and aristocratic political and economic establishments lost their nerve and persuaded President

Hindenburg to appoint Hitler Chancellor in 1933. A new party like the Nazi Party needs instant success to maintain the loyalty of its weakly-motivated electorate.

After 1933, many foreign observers believed the Nazi regime had immense support. This was due to the tourist reports of a clean, well-organised Germany where poverty did not seem to exist.[2] Secondly, it was due to the efforts of Nazi film propaganda. Thirdly, it was the result of the Nazi regime thriving, in spite of the strain of war, unlike the Kaiser's regime, which collapsed in 1918. Finally, it was later convenient for the wartime allies to stress the support of the Germans for the Nazis because this gave them greater justification for the mass bombing and their plans to dismember Germany once victory was achieved. When one considers the matter more carefully, it becomes clear that this view of over-whelming support for the Nazi regime needs to be modified. Firstly, it is likely that the roughly 20 per cent of the electorate who were SPD supporters and the roughly 12 per cent who were centre party supporters did not change their views much after 1933. To a lesser extent, we can say the same for the more than 10 per cent of voters who had consistently opted for the communists.[3] Such a conclusion seems consistent with experience from other countries and with what happened in Germany after 1945. There figures allow for a weakening of support for these and other non-Nazi parties after 1933, as the regime appeared to be successful. But the outbreak of the war in 1939, predicted by the left, would have strengthened the scepticism of the non-Nazis. German patriotism, Allied mistakes, the Gestapo, the efficient rationing system and the exploitation of the occupied states explain how the Nazi regime survived until May 1945.

THE EARLY POST-WAR YEARS

At the end of the war, the Allies seriously expected substantial right-wing opposition in occupied Germany. Col. R. L. Frazier, who was then in charge of the investigation of all right and left-wing political, paramilitary and other subversive groups which might in some way threaten the occupation force in the American Zone, from early 1946 to mid-1949, and was also in close touch with British counter-intelligence authorities for all of this period, has described the situation as follows:

> The Americans always considered the possibility of post-war German resistance by right-wing elements as a definite danger.

This fear had an effect even on strategy in the last days of the war (e.g., the argument between Churchill, who wanted all effort directed towards Berlin, and Eisenhower, who insisted on moving south-east to prevent the 'National Redoubt' of the Alps being used as a base for long-term resistance). Much of the American (and British) counter-intelligence effort in Germany, from early 1945 onward, was taken up with the investigation of possible Nazi underground organisations which would lead a resistance against the occupation. Both the Gestapo and the *Hitler Jugend* planned such underground organisations, and some effort was made to put them into operation. Both were rolled up by mid–1947, and never really constituted a significant threat, although the *Hitler Jugend* group made a lot of money by turning itself into a haulage firm.[4]

By 1948 ultra right-wing organisations were appearing, ostensibly as embryo political parties. The occupation authorities in the British and American zones took this development seriously and devoted considerable effort to observing the new groups, particularly for indications of any paramilitary activity. Because there was no evidence of the latter, and because the various groups were small and fragmented, no charismatic leader having arisen, it was accepted that there was no real danger, but a watching brief was maintained, even after the Bundesrepublik came into existence.

Frazier's statement makes it clear that the Allies expected significant Nazi opposition after the war. Why did such opposition not appear? There can be no final answer to this question, but a number of factors can be mentioned which must have contributed to this situation. Firstly, there was the destruction of the NSDAP leadership and cadre. At the highest level, virtually all of the leading Nazis were either dead or interned. Even at the lower levels, many had either been killed, killed themselves, were interned or were seeking refuge abroad. On the automatic arrest list of the Americans were NSDAP functionaries down to the lowly level of the *Ortsgruppenführer* (local group leader). By December 1945, around 100,000 former members of the Nazi Party, of the SS, of the *Sicherheitsdienst* (the security service responsible for internal surveillance and the monitoring of opinion) and other beneficiaries of Hitler's regime were interned in the American Zone.[5] Similar policies were implemented with varying degrees of intens-ity by the other three occupying powers. Once released, many of the former Nazis were in no psychological or physical state to contemplate opposition and, in any case, had to find ways and means of earning their living. Some former Nazis, it is true, had found employment with their erstwhile foreign enemies, but they probably felt there was no future in biting the hand that fed them. All activity considered by the occupying power to be Nazi, militarist or anti-democratic was of course banned. But even without any ban it would have probably fallen on deaf ears. Germany's defeat was so obvious and total, and National Socialism so obviously a disaster, that few Germans would have been likely to give it a second chance. Germany lay in ruins, on the verge of starvation, had no friends in the international community and, unlike what happened in 1918, was totally occupied by powerful armies. All this represented a devastating psychological blow against Nazism. Michael Balfour, Chief of Information Services, Allied Military Government of Germany, 1945–47, has summed up the position as follow:

> The proportion of those professing to think Nazism 'a good thing badly carried out' never dropped below 42% between November 1945 and January 1946. There is good evidence that 10% of the adult male population remained convinced Nazis – 4 million people. Yet the incontrovertible evidence of total defeat was hard to overlook or excuse away by stories of treachery or corruption... Goebbels had left behind a deep scepticism about anything officials said. The Germans may have had a little more faith in us, because, after all, our wartime forecasts had come true.[6]

The occupying powers sought to convince the Germans by 're-education' programmes in the mass media and in the schools. Despite all of the above, it is something of a miracle that a nationalistic, if not directly Nazi, resistance movement of significant proportions did not appear after 1945. The Germans could easily have felt that, as after the 1914–18 war, they were being unjustly treated. Firstly, there was the dismemberment of their country. Germany lost 24.3 per cent of its territory to Poland and the Soviet Union. This territory had been the home of 13.9 per cent of the population of 1937 Germany.[7] Until January 1957, the important industrial region of the Saar was separated from Germany under a pro-French regime. In 1950. 16.7 per cent of the population of West Germany was classified as expellees from the lost territories and a further 3.3 per cent were refugees from the Soviet Zone.[8] These could have formed the basis for a dangerous revanchist movement. In fact, many of them supported the relatively moderate League of Expellees from the Homeland and of those without Rights [*Bund der Heimatvertriebenen und Entrechteten,*

BHE]. Founded in Kiel in 1950, the party gained 23.4 per cent of the vote in the regional (Land) election in Schleswig-Holstein in the same year. There, 38.2 per cent of the population were expellees or refugees. In the national (*Bundestag*) election of 1953, the BHE gained 5.9 per cent (1.6m votes) and joined the government coalition. Splits later destroyed the party. Other factors which could have fuelled a nationalist movement were the dismantling of important industrial plants for reparations, restrictions of the economy and unemployment. It is often forgotten that there was a general strike in the British Zone in 1948 against the policy of dismantling. Luckily, the trade unions were firmly in democratic hands. Unemployment stood at 5.5 per cent in the Western Zones in 1948. It rose to 8.2 per cent in 1950 and was still 6.4 per cent in 1952, four years after Ludwig Erhard, the economic director, introduced his famed currency reform. By 1956 it had fallen to 2.2 per cent and in 1960 it was as low as 0.5 per cent.[9] Another potential reserve for a new nationalist movement in the early years were the many displaced ex-officers, civil servants, teachers and others who had lost their jobs and status.

Konrad Adenauer, Chancellor 1949–63, attempted, successfully, to integrate these elements into the new Federal Republic of Germany. Thus, many servants of the Third Reich became servants of the democratic state. In 1952, a *Bundestag* investigation revealed that 184 senior officials out of 542 (34 per cent) in the Foreign Ministry were former members of the Nazi party.[10] The same was true in other parts of the public service such as the police and the judiciary.[11] Many medical practitioners were also former party members.

THE SRP AND THE DRP

The former members of the NSDAP and of the German National People's Party [*Deutsch-Nationale Volkspartei*, DNVP], who were the coalition partners of the Nazis in 1933, found it difficult to set up a new party. Their efforts to do so were rejected several times by the suspicious French and American occupation authorities. The German Rights Party [*Deutsche Rechtspartei*, DReP], set up in Northern Germany, North Rhine-Westphalia and Hesse in 1946, gained more than local significance. An amalgam of the German Conservatives [*Deutsche Konservative*, DK], the German construction Party [*Deutsche Aufbaupartei*, DAP], and the German Farmers and Peasants Party [*Deutsche Bauern- und Landvolk-partei*, DB-Lp], it propagated nationalistic and monarchical ideas and had five representatives in the first *Bundestag*.

In early 1949, the Fellowship of Independent Germany [*Gemeinschaft unabhängiger Deutscher*, GUD] was founded in Bad Godesberg and broke away from the older party. This had been an initiative of Dr Fritz Dorls, who was joined by the former general Otto Ernst Remer. Remer had been promoted by Hitler for his part in crushing the July plot of 1944. On 2 October 1949, Dorls went one step further and founded the Socialist Party of the Reich [*Sozialistische Reichspartei*, SRP], which was joined by a majority of members of the German Rights Party [*Deutsche Rechtspartei*, DReP], sometimes by entire local or district groups. This new party, in contrast to the DRP, had a rather positive attitude towards National Socialism, and made some considerable gains in former Nazi strongholds. In the Lower saxony Landtag elections in 1951 it even got 11 per cent of the vote. On the demand of the Federal Government, the Federal Constitutional Court banned the SRP in 1952.

After the ban on the SRP, the German Reich party [*Deutsche Reichspartei*, DRP], formerly DReP, was joined by most of its former supporters. The party's name was taken from a conservative party which existed in Germany between 1871 and the end of the *Kaiserreich*. The party chairman and his three deputies – Otto Hess, Wilhelm Meinberg and Hans Heinrich Kunstmann – had all been members of the NSDAP before 1933. Two others joined the Nazi party after 1933.[12] All in all, these parties of the 'national opposition' remained without significance during the period up to 1964. In the federal election of 1953, the DRP received 1.1 per cent of the vote; in 1957 its vote fell to 1 per cent and in 1961 its percentage fell to 0.8.[13] This was due mainly to three stabilising factors – the years of economic progress, the clear leadership of Konrad Adenauer and the reinstatement of so many potential extreme right-wing voters and activists. Along with this went the integration of the Federal Republic into the Western alliance and building of the German army, the *Bundeswehr*, which in itself was enough to relieve national inferiority complexes.

The success of the DRP in the *Land* election in the Rhineland Palatinate in April 1959 caused great attention. About 90,000 voters, including Catholic voters of the government party, had decided for a party with clear neo-Nazi tendencies. With 5.1 per cent of the vote, the DRP was able to jump the 5 per cent hurdle necessary to win seats in the regional parliament.[14] The DRP put on its last party congress in Bonn in June 1964. There it was decided to found a new union of all 'national democratic forces'. The DRP dissolved itself, thus providing the necessary preconditions for the setting up of the National Democratic Party of Germany [*Nationaldemokratische Partei Deutschlands*, NPD]. Consequently, former functionaries of the DRP provided the nucleus of the NPD.

THE 1960S: THE RISE OF THE NPD

The foundation of the NPD by Adolf von Thadden, Fritz Thielen and Waldemar Schütz in Hanover on 28 November 1964 as a magnet for all the nationalistic forces did not, at first, seem to bear more fruit than any of their previous efforts had done. Thielen was elected chairman of the new party. He had represented the Christian-Democratic Union [*Christlich-Demokratische Union*, CDU] in the Bremen *Landtag* for eleven years, but joined the conservative German Party [Deutsche Partei, DP] in 1958. Von Thadden had represented the DRP in the first *Bundestag* in 1949. He later became chairman of the DRP and was elected first deputy chairman of the NPD. Schütz was a former NSDAP member and *Waffen* SS officer. A publisher, he joined the NPD's presidium. One source has claimed that, of eighteen members of the first executive committee of the NPD, twelve had been active NAZIS before 1945.[15]

In its report for 1968, the West German *Verfassungsschutz*, a body similar to USA's Federal Bureau of Investigation, commented that 'a democratic formation of opinion from the basis to the leadership cannot be realised in the NPD'. Several NPD district chairmen left the party, claiming that any criticism of party members was being muted by the leadership. The deputy chairman of the Lubeck district of the NPD, Rektor Heinz Willner, said he left the party because 'the individual member is not regarded as a politically mature citizen, but is degraded and becomes a transmitter of party propaganda and opinion'. The speakers, candidates and functionaries were forced 'to publicly defend grotesque slogans coming from the leadership'.

The NPD looked to Salazar's Portugal and the Greece of the right-wing military dictatorship for its version of the German state.[16] The *Verfassungsschutz* characterised the NPD as a party of aggressive nationalism which was against the Bonn system.

At the beginning of 1968, the NPD had about 28,000 members, only 9 per cent of them women. There was a high turnover of members, especially among the young. The refugee community was over-represented among party members and voters. Members from the middle-class professions provided the backbone of the NPD. Within this group, the proportion of urban and rural self-employed had increased further. It rose from 25 per cent in 1966 to 29 per cent in 1968 of total membership.

Party members of this group are least inclined to leave the NPD. Against this, there was a high turnover of employees and workers in family/small- and middle-sized enterprises. The share of industrial workers was about 14 per cent in 1968. Public sector employees, including members of the armed services, made up about 6 per cent members in 1968. This corresponded to their share of the workforce as a whole.[17]

The 'national opposition' found fertile ground again when political and economic insecurity under Chancellor Erhard (1963–66) and obvious disagreement between Paris and Washington dominated the scene. General De Gaulle was demonstrating quite clearly how important and crucial it could be to a people to act out of nationalistic motives. The formation of the grand coalition of CDU and SPD in 1966 caused some right-wing voters to feel that their leader had sold out to the left. There was also the feeling that the big party bosses had ganged up against the 'little man' leaving virtually no opposition in Parliament. Some right-of-centre voters wanted to protest against the increasing student unrest, and some farmers wanted to protest against the European Community's agricultural policy. In the federal election of 1965, the NPD gained 664,000 votes (2 per cent). Given the newness of the party, this vote could not be seen as a total failure. The NPD's success in subsequent *Land* elections is given in Table 1.

The NPD failed to win seats in the Saar, Hamburg and North Rhine Westphalia.

In the federal election of 1969, the NPD gained 1.4m votes (4.3 per cent). Thus, it failed to reach the 5 per cent minimum required to gain seats in the *Bundestag*. This compared with the liberal FDP's 1.9m votes

Table 4.1 NPD's result in *Land* elections

Land	Seats in regional parliament		Election date
Baden-Württemberg	12 out of 127		20/4/68
Bavaria	14	204	20/11/66
Bremen	8	100	1/10/67
Hesse	8	96	6/11/66
Lower-Saxony	10	149	4/6/67
Rhineland-Palatinate	4	100	23/4/67
Schleswig-Holstein	4	73	23/4/67

Source: *Vetfassungsschutz* report for 1968, Bonn, 1969, pp. 29–30.

(5.8 per cent). The FDP has been in government continuously since 1969.

Why did the NPD fail? The *Verfassungsschutz* report for 1968 believed the reasons were as follows:

− the increasing isolation of the NPD
− factional fights within the party
− improved economic conditions
− the fact that there was a limited number of people responsive to the right-wing exploitation of prejudice and emotion
− the increasing radicalisation of the political style of the right-wing extremists, which was rejected in more moderate conservative circles
− the increasing understanding by the population of the relationship between right-wing radicalism and foreign policy
− the lack of charisma of the representatives of the 'national camp', its functionaries, candidates and (regional) parliamentarians
− the lack of tangible parliamentary successes by the representatives of the NPD in local and regional parliaments
− the worry of being identified with a party whose banning was demanded by wide sections of the population.

Undoubtedly, the perception that the NPD was harming the Federal Republic's credibility abroad helped to put off potential supporters and spur on its opponents to greater efforts to defeat it.

Table 4.2 Far-right organisation members, 1965–86

1965	1966	1967	1968	1969	1970	1971
26,100	34,500	38,500	36,800	36,300	29,500	27,700
1972	1973	1974	1975	1976	1977	1978
24,500	21,500	21,200	17,300	20,300	18,200	17,800
1979	1980	1981	1982	1983	1984	1985
17,600	19,800	20,300	19,000	20,300	22,100	22,100
1986						
22,100						

Source: *Verfassungsschutz* report for relevant years.

Like many new parties, the NPD fell to pieces after failing to achieve a quick success. The NPD and other far-right groups saw their membership decline after 1969.

FAILURE IN THE 1970S

The 1970s were a dismal period for the far right in Germany, as the membership figures in Table 2 indicate. Various opinion polls revealed changing attitudes to West Germany's political system and showed increasing, and overwhelming, support for it.[18] One indicator of public attitudes were the replies to a question about great Germans (see Table 3).

Table 4.3 Responses to question: 'Which great German, in your opinion, has done most for Germany?'

	1950 %	1956 %	1962 %	1967 %	1971 %	1977 %
Adenauer		24	28	60	47	42
Bismarck	35	27	23	17	21	13
Brandt					3	9
Frederick the Great	7	3	3	1	0	1
Hitler	10	8	4	2	2	3

Source: F. Neolle-Neumann ed. *The Germans: Public Opinion Polls 1967-1980*, Westport, Conn., 1981, p. 109.

MIGRANTS: A POLITICAL FACTOR

In the 1980s, a number of developments have helped to create an atmosphere in which far-right parties could be expected to thrive. These have been unemployment, especially youth unemployment, the continuing influx of foreigners seeking political asylum or simply work in West Germany, the migration of ethnic Germans and citizens of the German Democratic Republic to the Federal Republic. There has also been a renewal of the discussions about 'the German Question', the Nato alliance and, especially since the collapse of the Communist regimes in Eastern Europe in 1989, Germany's place in Europe.

Unemployment in the Federal Republic is not high by the standards of most of its West European neighbours, but at 7.9 per cent in February 1989 (UK: 6.8 per cent; France: 10.0 per cent; Italy: 16.4 per cent)[19] it causes great anxiety in Germany. It leads many to think that the government should find ways and means of stopping the influx from outside which aggravates the difficulties. In 1987, there were 4,630,200 officially recorded foreigners in the Federal Republic. In 1986, the reported figure was 4,512,700. By far the largest number came from Turkey (1,481,400), Yugoslavia (597,600), Italy (544,400) and Greece (279,900). Of these, 2,764,200 – including the majority of the Turks, Yugoslavs and Italians had lived in the Federal Republic for ten or more years.[20] Like many west European states, West Germany is faced with considerable numbers of foreigners seeking political asylum, as Table 4 shows.

Table 4.4 Influx of political refugees

1980	1981	1982	1983	1984	1985	1986	1987
107,818	49,391	37,423	19,737	35,278	73,832	99,650	57,379

Source: *Statistisches Jahrbuch für die Bundesrepublik Deutschland*, 1988, p. 69.

The largest number in each of the above years were as follows:[21]

1980: 57,913 Turks

1981: 9,901 Poles

1982: 6,630 Poles

1983: 2,645 Sri Lankans

1984: 8,063 Sri Lankans

1985: 17,380 Sri Lankans

1986: 21,700 Iranians

1987: 11,426 Turks

Thousands of ethnic Germans (*Aussiedler*) have also been arriving from Eastern Europe: 460,888 in 1968–80; 69,455 in 1981; 48,170 in 1982; 37,925 in 1983; 36,459 in 1984; 38,968 in 1985; 42,788 in 1986; 78,523 in 1987.[22] Finally, every year thousands migrate from the German Democratic Republic to the West (29,459 in 1986; net 26,834).[23] The net increase of German and foreign migrants to the Federal Republic in 1986 (the last year for which figures are available) appeared to be 188,383 of whom 130,559 were foreigners. Net migration in the 1980s was as follows: 311,900 in 1980; −117,100 in 1983; 151,100 in 1984; 83,400 in 1985.[24] The figures reveal that the Federal Republic has a considerable number of foreigners (like its neighbours), but that the scale of net migration into the Federal Republic is not as great as many Germans believe. The foreign ghettos in some German towns, and the belief that newcomers are a burden, do cause friction and irritation.

The feeling that the threat from the Soviet Union has lessened greatly since Mikhail Gorbachev took over as Soviet leader in 1985 has made Germans more aware that their country is still, 44 years after the Second World War, an occupied and divided land. As in other European Community member states, a minority of Germans fear that the development of the Community in the run-up to 1992 represents an intolerable loss of national identity and sovereignty.

THE 1980S: THE NPD AND THE DVU

Given the above-mentioned factors, it was not surprising that the NPD should have improved its position in the last federal elections (1987). In the election of 25 January, the NPD put up candidates in 172 of the 248 constituencies and in 10 state lists; it received 227,045 votes on the state lists (0.6 per cent). This was more than twice the number of votes it had in the federal election of 1983 (91,095 = 0.23 per cent). With more than 0.5 per cent of votes on the state lists, it was paid DM 1.3m reimbursements for campaign expenses from public funds.[25] In its campaign, the NPD demanded reunification of Germany and 'all-German neutrality'[26] Dr Gerhard Frey (see below) supported the NPD campaign through his leaflets.

Thus the National Democrats remained the most attractive party to far-right voters at that time. In 1987, they had a membership of around 6,200. With 2,500 members, the German People's Union [*Deutsche Volksunion*, DVU], under its chairman Dr Gerhard Frey, was the second biggest right-wing extremist grouping.[27] In 1987, however, it showed less activity than in previous years because Frey had shifted his activities to the newly-founded German People's Union (List D) [*Deutsche Volksunion (Liste D)*, DVU (List D)]. He endeavoured to extend his traditionally good contacts among nationalists in Austria and the South Tyrol to right-wing extremists in France, especially the *Front National* of Jean-Marie Le Pen. Le Pen gave several interviews in Dr Frey's newspapers.[28]

The NPD and DVU (List D) were the two most important of the 69 (1986: 73) right-wing extremist organisations in the Federal Republic in 1987. Allowing for double membership, all these bodies together had a net membership of around 25,200.[29]

The total electoral failure of the far right in West Germany between 1969 and 1988 disguised the fact that there is a far-right constituency which is larger than membership of the various right-wing organisations would indicate. This is, to some extent, revealed by the circulation of far-right publications. According to the report of the *Verfassungsschutz* for 1987, the NPD monthly *Deutsche Stimme* had a circulation of over 150,000. This appeared to be the most successful far-right publication. A survey carried out by the influential weekly *Der Spiegel* (No. 9, 1989), about attitudes to Adolf Hitler on the centenary of his birth in 1989, also revealed some disturbing tendencies. The first question, 'How is Hitler to be viewed in history?', produced an overall average of −2.7 on a scale between +5 ('absolutely positive') and −5 ('absolutely negative'). To the second question, 'Would you say that without the war and without the holocaust Hitler would have been one of the greatest German statesmen?' 60 per cent replied that 'no, he would not' and 38 per cent that 'yes, he would'. Asked about their view of the Third Reich, 16 per cent thought that it had only bad sides to it, 38 per cent that it had predominantly bad sides to it, 43 per cent thought that it had good and bad sides, and 3 per cent that it bad only good sides. In all responses throughout the survey, Green and Republican voters (see below) were at the opposite extremes, while the voters of the CDU and the Christian-Social Union [*Christlich-Soziale Union*, CSU] alliance, those of the SPD and of the Free Democratic Party [*Freie Demokratische Partei*, FDP] held somewhat differing views within the centre.

DIE REPUBLIKANER

It was also in 1989 that the far right got its biggest boost since the 1960s. This was the success of the Republicans [Die Republikaner, REP] in the West Berlin elections of 29 January (see Table 5).

Table 4.5 1989 and 1985 election results compared

Party	29 January 1989 Turnout: 1,220,524 (79.6%)		10 March 1985 Turnout: 1,259,788 (83.6%)	
	Votes	%	Votes	%
CDU	453.161	37.8	577,867	46.4
SPD	448,143	37.7	402,875	32.4
AL (Greens)	141,470	11.8	132,484	10.6
REP	90,140	7.5	−	−
FDP	47,129	3.9	105,209	8.5
Others	20,368	1.7	25,180	2.0

Source: *Das Parlament*, 3–10 Feb. 1989

The REP was set up by Franz Schönhuber in Munich in 1983. A butcher's son, Schönhuber is a native of Bavaria who served in the *Waffen* SS in the Second World War. He established himself as a journalist after the war, moving gradually from the far left to the CSU, Bavaria's leading party. Owing to the publication of his war memoirs in 1981, he was forced to give up his job as deputy chief editor of Bavarian television. He subsequently set up the REP with other disgruntled elements of the CSU who felt their leader, Bavarian Prime Minister Franz Josef Strauss,was going too far in his conciliatory policy towards the German Democratic Republic. So far, the public position of Schönhuber has been German nationalist, exploiting discontent about the alleged breakdown of law and order, and the influx of foreigners and ethnic Germans. It is fair to point out that, in an interview with *Der Spiegel* (No. 6, 1989), Schönhuber stated: 'I have no Nazi past, I regard the National Socialist state as absolutely incompatible with the rule of law. Racism and fascism led us into the most horrible catastrophe in our national history.' He further claimed he was not against foreigners, but wanted to introduce the Swiss system of rotation for foreign workers and an amendment to article 16 of the Basic Law, the article granting the right of political asylum. The editors of *Der Spiegel* were not convinced, pointing out that the Berlin REP used emotional anti-Turkish material in its television advertising campaign. Schönhuber, in the same interview, expressed his doubts about the present European Community, claiming it would cement the division of Germany and lead to the centre of Europe moving to the South-East and the South. Schönhuber went on to say: 'the main reason why I reject this EC is the impörtation of crime, drugs, the Mafia and Camorra'. He also advocated a united, neutral Germany with its own nuclear weapons.

That the influx of ethnic Germans and foreigners was a key issue in the Berlin Campaign is beyond doubt. In an opinion poll, 40 per cent of those asked thought it was 'not in order that there are so many foreigners in Berlin'. There are in fact 220,000 foreigners living in West Berlin out of total of 1.8m. In addition, there are thousands of ethnic Germans and Germans from the GDR. According to *Der Spiegel* (No. 6, 1989), some 20,000 ethnic Germans and Germans from the GDR took up residence in West Berlin in 1988.

One particular feature of the Berlin election which caused alarm was the relatively high number of members of the West Berlin police force who voted for the REP. The police trade union (*Gewerkschaft der Polizei*) is worried that its members in parts of West Germany are also joining the new party. It estimated that 20 per cent of members of the police supported it. In Bavaria, it was possibly over 50 per cent. In Berlin, Baden

Württemberg, Schleswig-Holstein and the Saar, the chairmen or the deputy chairman of the REP are policemen. The majority of West German policemen and women are dissatisfied over pay, the lack of promotion chances and the effect of police service on their life.[30] Many of them appear to believe that they have been neglected by the mainstream politicians.

The REP did better than expected in the elections to the European Parliament in June 1989. Franz Schönhuber succeeded in getting elected together with five of his colleagues. The party gained 7.1 per cent of the vote, which compared with 5.6 per cent for the FDP, 8.4 per cent for the Greens, 37.3 per cent for the SPD and 37.8 per cent for the CDU. The CDU vote had fallen from 45.9 per cent in 1984, the SPD vote remained static and the FDP and Greens slightly improved their position. It appeared therefore that the REP had gained mainly at the expense of the CDU. Their best result was in Bavaria where they won 14.6 per cent. Their worst result was in North-Rhine Westphalia where they reached only 4.1 per cent. It seems likely that the Bavarian result was influenced by the recent death of Franz Josef Strauss who had previously managed to attract the bulk of right-wing voters for his CSU. Its vote fell from 57.2 per cent in the 1984 Euro-election to 45.4 per cent. This was the highest percentage loss for the Christian Democrats in any region.

According to the psephologist Joachim Hofmann-Gottig, the REP appears to be attractive, above all, to young men. This is also true of the NPD. No other party draws such a small percentage of its voters from women. Hofmann-Gottig concludes that the REP is likely to be on the political landscape for some time because of its support among young voters.[31] Another feature of the REP which is causing alarm, are the large numbers of activists, candidates and executive committee members who have NPD backgrounds.

Meanwhile, Dr Frey has been building up support for his organisation. In the last year, Frey's DVU (List D) has grown from 6,000 to over 24,000 members. Frey recruited at least 5,500 of them through a nation-wide mailing campaign to 27 million households.[32]

Although the NPD and the DVU-Liste D were, up to 1989, the largest far-right groups, there exist many other, much smaller groups, which openly proclaim their support for Nazi ideas. Among the more significant are The Movement [*Die Bewegung*] and The Free German Workers' Party [*Die Freiheitliche Deutsche Arbeiterpartei*, FAP]. The Movement, which its around 500 members see more as a 'community of attitude' (*Gesinnungsgemeinschaft*), wants to re-establish the NSDAP as a political party in the Federal Republic. It was created by former activists, and draws the majority of its members from the Action Front of National Socialists/National Activists [*Aktionsfront Nationaler Sozialisten/National Aktivisten*, ANS/NA] which was banned in 1983. Since 1986, The Movement has been split into two roughly equal factions. The first is led by Michael Kühnen, a former ANS/NA organiser who was imprisoned until March 1988 and his deputy Thomas Brehl, the second group by the neo-Nazis Jurgen Mosler and Volker Heidel. Both groups debate polemically about the issues of homosexuality and leadership. Both publish a periodical called *Die Neue Front* and organise regional and national meetings in which sometimes more than 100 people participate. During imprisonment in 1978-88, Kühnen wrote a pamphlet, *Die Zweite Revolution*, of which volume one, *Glaube und Kampf*, appeared in spring 1987, and volume two, *Der Volksstaat*, in the autumn of the same year. He advocates an 'Aryan peoples' community', led by armed elite units of the NSDAP and the *Sturmabteilung* (the Nazi storm troup). There would be a European Reich under the domination of a Nazi Germany, ideologically based on anti-Zionism, anti-Communism and anti-capitalism. The 500-member strong FAP is largely controlled and led by The Movement, most of its members being activists of the latter. It is organised in North Rhine-Westphalia (which has the biggest group with 180 members), Hamburg, Hesse, Lower Saxony, Bremen and Baden-Württemberg; there are also several groupings on a regional level in Bavaria and Schleswig-Holstein. Often, these only consist of a few persons. There is no party manifesto, but in its activities the FAP rejects the democratic order in the Federal Republic. It fights against the supposed alienation of the German people by too many foreigners. Its activities range from daubing-campaigns and provocative marches to deliberate fights with opponents and violence against foreigners.

RIGHT-WING VIOLENCE

In 1987, FAP members broke the law in 266 cases; 26 of those involved violence (arson attacks, damages), the rest were related to propaganda and intimidation. In 1987, 327 persons were arrested in connection with FAP activities; 44 per cent of all the crimes were committed on North Rhine-Westphalia. In the 1987 federal election, the FAP had two direct candidates and one on a state list; it could not put up candidates in *Land* elections in Hesse and Schleswig-Holstein because it did not manage to collect the necessary number of signatures.

Table 4.6 Infringement of the law by right-wing extremists

	1986	1987
bomb attack	1	0
arson attack	4	8
bodily harm	41	38
damage to property involving serious violence	25	30
threats of violence	134	115
propaganda offences (daubing, graffiti, etc)	695	1,055
other infringements	381	201
total	1,281	1,447

Source: *Verfassungsschutzbericht, 1987*, p. 128.

Table 4.7 Legal measures against right-wing extremists in 1987

1. Sentence (in brackets figures for 1986):
   12 (20) imprisonment of more than a year, of which 6
   (14) not suspended
   19 (36) imprisonments of up to a year, of which 8 (8) not suspended
   31 (35) fines
   29 (22) other sentences
2. Charges:
   In 1987 143 (182) charges were preferred

Source: *Verfassungsschutzbericht, 1987*, p. 129.

Although disturbing, the figures of right-wing breaches of the law, including the use of violence, provided in Tables 6 and 7 should not be seen out of context. There have always been such incidents throughout the history of the Federal Republic. These are carefully recorded and open to public scrutiny in a way which is not possible in many other countries where extremist violence is a common occurrence. One other aspect of the extremist scene in Germany which is often neglected is that the number of foreign residents who are members of foreign right-wing extremist organisations far outweighs the number of Germans who are members of German extremist organisations.[33]

As we have seen above, there have been a number of issues in recent years which have provided, and do provide, ammunition for far-right parties. The death of Franz Josef Strauss in 1988 could also be regarded as helping the far right by removing a figure very popular in conservative circles in Germany. Without his commanding presence, Christian Democracy appears less attractive to the more right-wing voters. The decline of knowledge about the Second World War could also aid the far right as young voters feel no responsibility for what happened then, and perhaps have come to feel, with the aid of certain historians, that Germany was wronged by the victors. On the other hand, many young West Germans are concerned about ecological issues, Third World poverty and better relations with the Soviet Bloc, and are inclined towards the Greens. Up to now, the older generations of voters have not wanted to endanger the Federal Republic's prosperity and its respected place in the international community by voting for extremist parties.

Any open avowal of Nazism does not seem to have any prospect of success. As for the REP, it is as yet an enigma. It is not clear whether, in spite of its recent strong electoral showings, it can maintain enough support (5 per cent is required) to gain entry into the *Bundestag* in 1990. It is also not yet clear whether it will fall prey to extremist infiltration (as it attracts NPD activists and functionaries), or whether it will become merely a right-wing conservative party. Were it to gain entry into the national parliament, it could complicate West Germany's coalition politics, and it should never be forgotten that Hitler gained power through the respectability given him by right-wing conservative politicians. The REP could act as a ventilator for right-wing voter dissatisfaction with the two big 'people's parties' (CDU/CSU and SPD) thus helping to contain a revolt of the vaguely-alienated, harassed and underprivileged middle and lower public officials and lower-paid service employees who seem to form a considerable part of its following.[34] More dangerously, the REP could act as a bridge between mainstream conservatism and right-wing authoritarian elements, giving the latter entry into polite society.

LIST OF ABBREVIATIONS

ANS/NA   *Aktionsfront Nationaler Sozialisten/Nationale Aktivisten* [Action Front of National Socialists/National Activists]

BHE   *Bund der Heimatvertriebenen und Entrechteten* [League of Expellees from the Homeland and of those without Rights]

CDU   *Christlich-Demokratische Union* [Christian-Social Union]

DAP   *Deutsche Aufbaupartei* [German Construction Party]

DB-Lp   *Deutsche Bauern-und Landvolk-partei* [German Farmers and Peasants Party]

DK	*Deutsche Konservative* [German Conservatives]
DNVP	*Deutsch-Nationale Volkspartei* [German National People's Party]
DP	*Deutsche Partei* [German Party]
DReP	*Deutsche Rechtspartei* [German Rights Party]
DRP	*Deutsche Reichspartei* [German Reich Party]
DVU	*Deutsche Volksunion* [German People's Union]
DVU (List D)	*Deutsche Volksunion* (Liste D) [German People's Union (List D)]
FAP	*Freiheitliche Deutsche Arbeiterpartei* [Free German Worker's Party]
FDP	*Freie Demokratische Partei* [Free Democratic Party]
GUD	*Gemeinschaft unabhängiger Deutscher* [Fellowship of Independent German]
NPD	*Nationaldemokratische Partei Deutschlands* [National Democratic Party of Germany]
NSDAP	*Nationalsozialistische Deutsche Arbeiterpartei* [National Socialist German Workers' Party]
REP	*Die Republikaner* [The Republicans]
SPD	*Sozialdemokratische Partei Deutschlands* [Social Democratic Party of Germany]
SRP	*Sozialistische Reichspartei* [Socialist Party of the Reich]
Z	*Zentrum* [(Catholic) Centre Party]

NOTES

1. For an analysis of voting behaviour at the end of the Weimar Republic, see R. F. Hamilton, *Who voted for Hitler?*, Princeton University Press, Princeton, N. J., 1982.
2. See, for instance, the comments of W. L. Shirer, *The Rise and Fall of the Third Reich*, Book Club Associates, London 1971. Shirer was a correspondent in Germany at the time.
3. I. Kershaw, *Public Opinion and Political Dissent in the Third Reich. Bavaria 1933–45*, Clarendon, Oxford, 1983, esp. pp. 303, 304 and pp. 313–14. For a discussion on the meaning of National Socialism, see also P. Aycoberry, *The Nazi Question*, London, 1981.
4. Letter to the author.
5. C. Schick, 'Die Internierungslager', in M. Broszat, K. D. Henke and H. Woller (eds.), *Von Stalingrad zu Währungsreform*, Olderbourg, Munich, 1989, p. 306.

6. M. Balfour, 'In Retrospect: Britain's Policy of "Re-Education"', in N. Pronay and K. Wilson (eds.), *The Political Re-Education of Germany and Her Allies*, Croom Helm, London, 1985, p. 148.

7. Press and Information Office of the Federal Government, *Regierung Adenauer 1949–1963*, Wiesbaden, 1963, p. 190.

8. Ibid., p. 54.

9. Ibid., p. 386.

10. *The Times*, 15 July 1952, p. 4; 43 per cent of senior officials in The German Foreign Ministry were former NSDAP members, 28 per cent had belonged to the old Nazi Foreign Ministry and 16 per cent had suffered political persecution under the Nazis.

11. C. J. Friedrich, *Die Kalte Amnestie. NS Täter in der Bundesrepublik*, Fischer, Frankfurt, 1984.

12. K. Hirsch, *Kommen die Nazis wieder? Gefahren für die Bundesrepublik*, Dokumente zur Zeit in Verlag Kurt Desch, Munich, 1967, p. 54.

13. H.-H. Röhring and K. Sontheimer, *Handbuch des Deutschen Parlamentarismus*, Munich, 1970, p. 118.

14. Hirsch, *Kommen die Nazis wieder?* cit., p. 36.

15. R. Kühnl, R. Rilling and C. Sager, *Die NPD. Struktur, Ideologie und Funcktion einer Neo-Faschistischen Partei*, Suhrkamp, Frankfurt, 1969, p. 226.

16. Federal Ministry of Interior (*Bundesministerium des Innern*), *Zum Thema, hier: Verfassungsschutz 1968* (henceforth: *VSB*), Bonn, 1969, p. 11.

17. Ibid., p. 17.

18. S. Eisel, *Minimalkonsens und Freiheitliche Demokratie*, Paderborn, Munich-Vienna-Zurich, 1986, pp. 230–31.

19. *The Economist*, 1 April 1989, p. 139.

20. Statistisches Bundesamt, *Statistische Jahrbuch 1988 für die Bundesrepublik Deutschland*, Stuttgart, 1988, p. 82.

21. Ibid., p. 69.

22. Ibid., p. 84.

23. Ibid., p. 80.

24. Ibid., p. 80.

25. *VSB 1987*, p. 112.

26. Ibid., p. 112.

27. Ibid., p. 117.

28. Ibid., p. 117.

29. Ibid., p. 98.

30. ARD television programme 'Panorama', 16 May 1989.

31. *Die Welt*, 17 May 1989, p. 5.

32. *Die Welt*, 19 May 1989, p. 4.

33. *VSB 1987*, pp. 136–59.

34. *Der Spiegel*, 29 May 1989, contains a great deal of information and analysis on the REP. For an up-to-date analysis of *Die Republikaner*, see H.-G. Betz 'Post-Modern Anti-Modernism. The West German "Republikaner"' , in *Politics and Society in Germany, Austria and Switzerland*, Vol. 2,3, Summer 1990.

CHAPTER FIVE

Militant Neo-Nazism in the Federal Republic of Germany in the 1980s

Christopher T. Husbands

On 29 January 1989, to almost universal surprise, the party called The Republicans [*Die Republikaner,* REP][1] emerged from what had hitherto been increasing obscurity to take 7.5 per cent of votes cast and eleven seats in the election for the West Berlin House of Deputies. In the European Parliament election on 18 June 1989, The Republicans won 7.1 per cent of votes cast and six seats. The party is, self-confessedly, a right-wing conservative one, but its many critics have gone further in claiming that it should be regarded as a conventional component of the extreme right, along with groups like Dr Gerhard Frey's German People's Union [*Deutsche Volksunion,* DVU][2] and the National Democratic Party of Germany [*Nationaldemokratische Partei Deutschlands,* NPD], despite numerous disavowals by The Republicans of any association or comparability. Those arguing that The Republicans are really right-wing extremists have cited in support such issues as their alleged xenophobia and their indisputably explicit anti-immigrant stances (especially against Turks), the one-time membership of their leader, Franz Schönhuber, in the Waffen-SS, the presence among their leadership of at least one prominent and notorious former activist in the NPD, and (since June 1989) their membership of the European Right group in the European Parliament with the French National Front [*Front National,* FN] delegation led by Jean-Marie Le Pen, and with the Flemish nationalist from the Flemish Bloc [*Vlaams Blok,* VB], Karel Dillen.

Yet, despite the existence of The Republicans as a party since November 1983, they have never been officially monitored by the Federal Office for the Protection of the Constitution [*Bundesamt für Verfassungsschutz,*

BfV], the body within the Federal Ministry for the Interior [*Bundesminist-erium des Innern*, BMI] charged with monitoring both left- and right-wing extremism.[3] Their sudden emergence to prominence in early 1989 sparked a major debate about whether they should now be monitored by the BfV and about the criteria that determine which political groupings should qualify for such observation.[4]

For a long time the BfV has operated particular categorising principles for the right-wing extremist activities that it monitors, principles whose implementation has – it is true – been altered slightly over the years in the light of prevailing circumstances. At the beginning of the 1980s, as described in the 1981 annual report,[5] the BfV recognised five major categories of extreme right-wing organisation:

(a) that associated with groups that were explicitly terrorist, violent and/or militaristic;

(b) that associated with organisations and parties that the BfV explicitly labelled 'neo-Nazi';

(c) the NPD and its spin-off affiliates;

(d) the so-called 'national liberal right', a category apparently used solely to accommodate Frey's numerous initiatives, particularly the DVU; and

(e) a residual category for other extreme right-wing groups, especially various youth groups, nationalist cultural groups and an organisation for former soldiers in the Waffen-SS.

Further subsections of the section devoted to right-wing extremism discussed publications, links with right-wing extremist movements outside the Federal Republic, offences involving right-wing extremists, and measures taken by the state against such individuals.

In the 1987 annual report, most of the above-listed headings recurred, although there were some differences of nomenclature and order. The German state's successful moves against one of the major right-wing ter-rorist organisations of the early 1980s, the Hoffmann Defence and Sport-ing Group [*Wehrsportgruppe Hoffmann*, WSG Hoffmann],[6] changed the character of right-wing terrorist activity; it ceased to be so immediately identifiable with one or more particular groups and proliferated into ac-tivities such as arson attacks on asylum-seekers' hostels that were under-taken by individuals belonging to one or more of several groups, or to none. Thus, the section on right-wing terrorism in the 1987 report fol-lowed, and was subordinate to, those concentrating on descriptions of relevant organisations and parties. The 1981 section on 'neo-Nazism' was retitled 'New National Socialism/Neo-Nazism' in 1987, reflecting the enhanced importance at the latter date of a so-called Strasserite element in neo-Nazi circles.[7] The 1981 section on the NPD was in 1987 titled 'National Democrats', in line with the increased significance of some of the NPD's affiliates, not merely the party itself, as its fortunes improved during the previous several years. Frey's 'national liberals' then still merited their own subsection. By the 1988 annual report, however, Frey's initiatives and the NPD were subsectioned together, in the light of the electoral pact between him and the NPD that was finalised in June 1988.

The practices followed by the BfV in its annual reports in subsectioning and labelling right-wing extremism have, to an extent, become hallowed through long habituation and repetition in more or less the same form; however, they have not been uncontentious. To many, the reporting of Frey's 'national liberal' initiatives and of the NPD using the self-labelling of these groups rather than some more appropriate, attributed, adjective has seemed perverse. Thus, anyone who has observed the fixations in Frey's publications with the Hitler period, with the Second World War, with casting doubts upon conventional accounts of the concentration camps and with the general denial of German guilt, or who has noted the Nazi memorabilia that are offered to readers for purchase, may feel that withholding some epithet containing 'Nazi' – whether 'Nazi' or 'neo-Nazi' – is drawing a fine distinction, if ever there was one. However, in reserving the label 'neo-Nazi' for a more specialised collection of political groupings and organisations, the BfV claims that they are a quite specific category. In its 1981 annual report, this was expressed as follows:

> In contrast to other right-wing extremists, the neo-Nazis openly favour the perspective and programme of the old NSDAP [*Nationalsozialistische Deutsche Arbeiterpartei*, National Socialist German Workers' Party]. In their view a new NSDAP should be founded into which all contemporary neo-Nazi groups would have to be amalgamated. This NSDAP should as a single party lead the new National Socialist 'movement'.[8]

The 1988 annual report of the BfV described a similar ideological perspective but noted an important new development: Until 1982 Adolf Hitler and his 'Third Reich' were the undisputed models for all neo-Nazis. Since then, an increasing number of neo-Nazis see themselves as 'national revolutionaries' following in the steps of the Strasser brothers. They criticise Hitler and reproach him for having betrayed National Socialism.[9]

One may feel that at least some of the categorisation and/or labelling practices of the BfV are difficult to justify. However, whatever the merits or otherwise of any misgivings concerning the BfV's implicit exoneration of the DVU and the NPD from an attribution of neo-Nazism – not to mention its neglect hitherto of The Republicans – it is undeniable that the groups whom it does explicitly label as 'neo-Nazi'[10] are a phenomenon *sui generis* and are qualitatively different in several important respects that, taken together, do justify analysis as a separate extreme-right category.

Their distinctiveness is clear on several criteria. The first is especially important now that the DVU and NPD, as well as The Republicans, have broken out of their electoral backwater and have become mass voting movements: whereas these other parties have all achieved significant recent polling performances and now impinge seriously upon the calculations of the major political parties, none of the electoral forays by a 'neo-Nazi' group has managed more than a tiny fraction of the vote, 0.1 per cent being a typical figure; several attempts to offer candidates have failed through inability to secure sufficient nominating signatures. An eschewing of conventional electoral activity is not, then, the characteristic that distinguishes the BfV's 'neo-Nazis' from the remainder of the extreme right, although most of its 'neo-Nazi' movements have not wanted or been able to participate in elections. Still, it must be said that only in September 1987 did Frey, with his DVU (List D) in Bremen, test his support with the general public, after considerable preparation with a very well-financed campaign. A second criterion of distinctiveness is the number of activists involved and the degree of their activism. It is perhaps an exaggeration to describe the DVU as a mass movement but, according to the BfV, by 1988 it had more than 12,000 members, having grown steadily throughout the 1980s to become the largest extreme-right organisation in the Federal Republic.[11] It claimed a membership in early 1989 of just under 28,000 members.[12] The NPD itself was credited by the BfV with about 6400 members in 1988.[13] On the other hand, memberships of the individual 'neo-Nazi' groups were, and are, to be counted in tens or, at most, hundreds. The BfV estimated the existence of 1480 'neo-Nazis' in 1988, with 1320 belonging to 'neo-Nazi' groups.[14] A third criterion of distinctiveness: although there have, of course, been calls for the proscription of the NPD and DVU, these have not – except perhaps during one short period of the NPD's former strength in the late 1960s – ever been very seriously considered. The same cannot be said about the 'neo-Nazi' groups. As organisations, they often flirt with illegality and banning and there have been several actual proscriptions. Moreover, their memberships are known to have a drastically disproportionate record of involvement in criminal activity, sometimes of a very serious and violent sort, and indeed twenty-five deaths have been attributed to 'neo-Nazi' activity during the past ten years.[15] One is clearly therefore dealing with a fairly small and dedicated group of activists who, together, justify the epithet 'militant neo-Nazism'[16] used in the title of this chapter and who are thereupon its principal subsequent subject matter.[17]

MILITANT NEO-NAZISM – NUMBERS AND TRENDS

Quantitative data on militant neo-Nazism that are independent of those of the BfV are impossible to acquire and one is thus obliged to refer to this as a data source; presented in Table 5.1 are the figures of those classified as 'neo-Nazi' by the BfV since 1977.

These data merit several comments, both general and specific ones. Firstly, after the well-documented increase in the activism and numbers of activists of militant neo-Nazism from the late 1970s into the early 1980s, the period since 1982 has seen no clear continuation of this trend. In 1988 the number of members enrolled in militant neo-Nazi groups was barely above the *per annum* average since 1977; in 1988 the total number of individuals labelled by the BfV as 'neo-Nazi' was scarcely above the corresponding average since 1977. Similarly, the number of groups has, with a couple of exceptions, been quite stable. Although most of the publicity surrounding militant neo-Nazism focuses upon a small number of groupings whose membership numbers are in excess of a hundred, many groups attract little or no general publicity on their own account and – being often locally based – have only very small memberships. Also, some groups seem *de facto* to be small subgroups within larger organisations. The data on the mean number of members per group have therefore to be interpreted in the light of this skewness of their distribution. Variations in the numbers of non-enrolled activists in militant neo-Nazism are attributable to a series of factors. The proscription of the WSG Hoffmann in January 1980 produced a pool of unattached activists, particularly in 1981. However, by 1982 a large number of these had been persuaded, by continuing state attention to their activities, to retire from active involvement in militant neo-Nazism.[18] Thus, despite the proscription of two further groups in January 1982 for seeking the re-establishment of National Socialism – the Popular Socialist Movement of Germany/Labour Party [*Volkssozialistische Bewegung Deutschlands/Partei der*

Table 5.1 Numbers of militant neo-Nazi groups and activists in the Federal Republic of Germany, 1977–88

Year	Number of groups	Number of enrolled activists[a]	Mean number of enrolled activists per group	Number of non-enrolled activists[b]	Total number of activists
1977	17	900	52.9	–	900
1978	24	1000	41.7	–	1000
1979	23	1400	60.9	–	1400
1980	22	1800	81.8	–	1800
1981	18	1250	69.4	600	1850
1982	21	1050	50.0	250	1300
1983	16	1130	70.6	270	1400
1984	34	1150	33.8	200	1350
1985	29	1270	43.8	150	1420
1986	23	1210	52.6	250	1460
1987	20	1380	69.0	140	1520
1988	23	1320	57.4	160	1480
Mean:	23	1238	57.0	253	1407

Sources: BfV, *Annual Reports*, 1978 to 1988

a   This column includes those classified as participating activists within these groups and those who merely supported them financially.
b   This column includes those regarded as independent activists and also a few individuals who flirted with a number of groups. These data were not given separately for the 1977–80 period. Thus, the mean number of non-enrolled activists has been calculated using data only for the 1981–88 period.

Arbeit, VSBD/PdA] and its youth organisation, the Young Front [*Junge Front*, JF] – the number of unattached individuals declined to 250 in 1982. These further proscriptions might be expected to have enlarged the pool of the unattached, but that seems not to have happened, perhaps because the VSBD/PdA was an early example of the Strasserite tendency and, as we shall see, many of its members moved into new but similar organisations.

The major proscription of the 1980s, that promulgated by the BMI on 7 December 1983 against the Action Front of National Socialists/National Activists [*Aktionsfront Nationaler Sozialisten/Nationale Aktivisten*, ANS/NA] led by Michael Kühnen,[19] had a rather different outcome. The increase of the number of groups from sixteen in 1983 to thirty-four in 1984 was directly attributable to this proscription, which the BfV quixotically regarded as a fissiparous tendency that was to be welcomed.[20] Instead of retiring from militance, former ANS/NA members formed at least twelve new groupings under Kühnen's influence, with about half of these having five to ten members and the remainder fifteen to twenty-five. However, as we shall see, many of these former ANS/NA activists subsequently infiltrated a hitherto inconsequential militant neo-Nazi movement, the Free German Workers' Party [*Freiheitliche Deutsche Arbeiterpartei*, FAP], which by late-1986 had become the most significant contemporary example of militant neo-Nazism, although it has recently had a change of leadership and perhaps political direction. It has been suggested by the BfV in its 1988 annual report that the FAP suffered a loss of membership during that year.[21] However, any implications of this for the future are disputable since, as described below, the most recent proscriptive action by the BMI, the banning of Kühnen's National Assembly [*Nationale Sammlung*, NS] on 9 February 1989, seems likely merely to have strengthened the FAP in its emergent form under its new leadership.

PRINCIPAL TENDENCIES WITHIN MILITANT NEO-NAZISM IN THE 1980s

It has been noted already that the 1980s saw the increased prominence of a Strasserite wing within militant neo-Nazism in the Federal Republic, although this was not entirely new since the proscribed VSBD/PdA did take this tendency back into the 1970s. The BMI has even claimed that most contemporary militant neo-Nazis in the Federal Republic are Strasserite, this being the modish political orientation.[22] In any case, without being too gross in one's categorisation, one may still identify three major tendencies within the contemporary scene.

1. A 'traditional' political wing, which now consists of groups whose organisational origins may be traced back into the 1970s, especially to the predecessors of the ANS/NA. This tendency still has the conventional celebratory attitude to Hitler and the Third Reich. Its most visible recent embodiment has been the FAP. However, as we shall see, the recent change in direction and a continuing possibility of further schism have left the FAP less easy to label unambiguously and there are now indications that it, or some part of it, is tending in a more Strasserite direction. It is Kühnen's recent

initiatives that now most closely represent the 'traditional' type of militant neo-Nazism, although even he seems to have made some concessions to the new orthodoxy.

2. A Strasserite political wing, the purest contemporary example of which is perhaps a group called the Nationalist Front [*Nationalistische Front*, NF], which – like the FAP – lays claim to being a political party (albeit one that has not managed to run candidates in elections).

3. A number of cultural and support groups, the most celebrated being the Organisation for the Assistance of National Political Prisoners and Their Dependants [*Hilfsorganisation für nationale politische Gefangene und deren Angehörige*, HNG], which supports convicted right-wing extremists imprisoned in the Federal Republic and abroad.

THE 'TRADITIONAL' WING

In order to understand the contemporary nature of the 'traditional' wing of militant neo-Nazism, it is instructive to return to the mid-1970s; around 1974, there clearly emerged a new, younger and more aggressive activism within the German extreme right. Possible predisposing factors for this were the post-1973 economic recession and the demise and division of the NPD. Further, the surge in left-wing terrorism in the mid-1970s may have encouraged some on the extreme right to feel that they could sharpen their own challenge to the state, partly under the influence of the left-wing example but also taking advantage of the distraction of the state's policing activities that the latter was causing. Whatever the reasons for the emergence of this new extreme-right militance, it did have novel features, especially the unwonted willingness of some of those concerned not to shun publicity, sometimes even to court it, despite the consequent certainty of attention by the monitoring authorities of the state.

Although there were a number of groups and individuals who attracted the special attention of the BfV at that time, it was Kühnen and the group that he founded which had the greatest reputation for provocation and the most long-term influence. What became the ANS/NA had been formally founded by him as a party in November 1977, when he was only twenty-two years old, under the name of the Action Front of National Socialists [*Aktionsfront Nationaler Sozialisten*, ANS].[23] It developed from a group of young militant neo-Nazis in the Hamburg area, where it was initially based. On its fringes were a number of small and violent groupings that engaged in various criminal activities.[24] Kühnen's early actions had brought him several brushes with the law, but by 1978 he had attracted the serious attention of the state's prosecuting authorities; he and others were indicted in December 1978 on suspicion of forming a terrorist organisation and, after the so-called Bückeburg Terrorist Trial, he was sentenced in 1979 to a four-year prison term, being released in November 1982. Although in the beginning no more than a few dozen young activists, the ANS quickly pushed itself into the headlines, becoming involved in a major disturbance with the police in July 1978, when the latter broke up an ANS gathering on the theme of 'Justice for Hitler'. The ANS lost some of its impetus during the period that Kühnen spent in gaol, being described as having only a few members at the end of 1979.[25] However, the remaining stalwarts continued to be active in the early 1980s, engaging in public leafleting, graffiti-writing, flyposting, demonstrations and meetings.

After his release from gaol, Kühnen re-assembled the ANS – now calling itself the ANS/NA after formal amalgamation of the original group with similar ones from Frankfurt and Fulda – into the most influential branch of militant neo-Nazism. At the time of its proscription by the BMI in December 1983, it had some 270 members distributed into over thirty local branches. Also proscribed at the same time was a group called Operation Repatriation – Popular Movement against Foreign Dominance and Destruction of the Environment [*Aktion Ausländerrückführung – Volksbewegung gegen Überfremdung und Umweltzerstörung*, AAR], which – despite its protestations to the contrary – was adjudged merely a front organisation of the ANS/NA. In fact, the AAR had sought legitimacy by fighting in four constituencies in the Hesse Regional Parliament election on 25 September 1983, winning between 0.2 and 0.4 per cent of votes cast. Despite the proscription of the ANS/NA, as late as March 1988 four suspected continuing members were arrested in four different cities during a nation-wide search for militant neo-Nazi material that examined ninety-two dwellings in sixty-one cities and towns.[26]

As mentioned already, the immediate consequence of the ANS/NA proscription was the proliferation of militant neo-Nazi grouplets, a development assisted by the branch structure of the banned movement. However, that phase was short-lived. During 1984 and 1985, Kühnen encouraged his supporters to infiltrate the hitherto almost totally inconspicuous and insignificant FAP, which became in a sense a successor organisation to the ANS/NA. The FAP had originally been founded in Stuttgart, in 1979, by a one-time shopkeeper and teacher, Martin Pape (born in 1928). Although Kühnen was abroad or in custody from early

1984 until March 1988, he none the less orchestrated the take-over of the FAP by his supporters, much to the consternation of Pape. The latter's attempts to retain control were fruitless, although at the FAP's first national gathering in Stuttgart in June 1986, held when Pape could delay its calling no longer, he (Pape) was voted as a provisional figurehead leader, in part to diminish the attentions of the state upon the FAP's activities.[27]

The FAP was, until recently, self-avowedly a party appealing to youthful males and there is much evidence that this section of the population provided almost all its activists. It recruited particularly among German skinheads (a subculture that the Germans regard as an import from England). There are reported to be about 2,500 skinheads in the Federal Republic, about 10 per cent of whom are active on the extreme right.[28] Many current FAP members remain celebrants of extreme machismo. In this spirit, the party had sought active support among football fans. One such group of fans – the so-called *Borussenfront* associated with the team, Borussia Dortmund – became notorious for its criminal activities, especially its attacks upon Turks. In 1985 its leader, Siegfried Borchardt (born in 1954), was sentenced to a term of imprisonment after leading an attack on a Turkish cultural centre. He and his followers moved into the FAP in 1984 and, since his release, he has become head of the North Rhine-Westphalia branch.

In its reports for 1986 and 1987, the BfV identified a loose grouping calling itself in abbreviated mode 'The Movement' as a central base of much 'neo-Nazi' activity. This – said the BfV – was deliberately loosely structured and many of its members were former ANS/NA activists, as well as current members of the FAP. In September 1986, Kühnen and his deputy resigned from 'The Movement', having been forced to do so – so it seemed – because of growing internal opposition to their homosexuality. Although in prison, Kühnen subsequently sought to reclaim his position, issuing calls to his followers to regroup around his deputy. Thus, in its 1987 report, the BfV claimed that there were then two wings to 'The Movement', one led by Kühnen and the other by Jürgen Mosler, Kühnen's successor in the original movement after his resignation. The BfV's reports claimed that the FAP has been thoroughly infiltrated and directed by 'The Movement', with most FAP members being active in the latter.[29] The BfV's 1988 report says that 'The Movement' has been subject to some loss of impetus because of its continuing bitter division into two wings.[30]

In the early years of its public visibility, the FAP's neo-Nazism involved the celebration of race and nation in its most extreme expressions. It was judged by the BfV to have had about 500 members nationally in

1987, with groupings in North Rhine-Westphalia, Hamburg, Hesse, Lower Saxony, Bremen and Baden-Württemberg, as well as smaller branches in Bavaria and Schleswig-Holstein.[31] It has differed from some other militant neo-Nazi groups in actually offering itself at occasional elections, although doubtless for possible publicity rather than because of expectations of success. The ANS had made the odd claim to electoral participation, as at the Hamburg City Parliament election in 1978, failing in the event to be listed because of its inability to collect sufficient nominating signatures. The FAP has participated, without success, in the Regional Parliament election in North Rhine-Westphalia in 1985 and in one or two local elections in Lower Saxony in 1986. In a number of more recent elections of various sorts, culminating in the European Parliament election of June 1989, it has polled a consistent 0.1 per cent of votes cast. This meant, in the last case, 20,107 votes nation-wide.

The FAP's activities have, in any case, been largely non-electoral. Its stickers are often to be seen in public places and its members have been involved in numerous contacts with the state, usually arising from their commission of acts of violence, including arson. For example, in November 1988 two former FAP officials in Hanover were imprisoned for arson attacks in September 1986 on a Turkish translation office and a house inhabited by foreigners.[32] The FAP's skinhead activists have also been associated with racial attacks upon foreigners, especially Turks. Its anti-foreigner demands have been of the crudest sort – of the 'Germany for the Germans – foreigners out' variety – and have been particularly directed against Turks in the Federal Republic. To ensure that its message was understood, it even produced stickers in both German and Turkish. Its Statement of Principles and Goals produced in 1986 elevated its policy on foreigners to the second of eight separate sections and, confident that a large majority of the German public was for repatriation, it called for a referendum on the foreigner issue. The party's literature prepared for the November 1986 Hamburg City Parliament election was especially unequivocal on this theme. The FAP demands: (a) Repatriation of foreigners; (b) German jobs for German workers; (c) No franchise for foreigners; and (d) An end to the 'crazy enthusiasm for integration'.

The FAP has constantly been on the brink of illegality and there were numerous calls, especially from the left (e.g., from the North Rhine-Westphalia Interior Minister, Herbert Schnoor), for its proscription. The group of the Social Democratic Party of Germany [*Sozialdemokratische Partei Deutschlands*, SPD] in the Hesse Regional Parliament also called upon the region's coalition government – formed by the Christian Democratic Union [*Christlich-Demokratische Union*, CDU] and the

Liberal Democratic Party [*Freie Demokratische Partei*, FDP] – to support a move in the Federal Council (the Federal Republic's second parliamentary chamber) by the SPD of Lower Saxony and North Rhine-Westphalia to ban the FAP.[33] However, the BMI has always held back from proscription – partly, so it would appear, because of the likelihood that its members would merely move to a new organisation in the event of a ban, just as many former members of the ANS/NA gravitated to the FAP. Also, it says that in 1988 a majority of the country's monitoring authorities expressed opposition to an attempt at proscription without a high certainty of success before the Federal Constitutional Court, feeling that an unsuccessful attempt to proscribe would merely legitimate neo-Nazism, although the BMI does claim to be keeping the proscription-issue under review.[34] However, such a move may have been rendered more difficult by the leadership change in the FAP. On 5 November 1988, its leader became Friedhelm Busse (born in 1928), after those surrounding Jürgen Mosler chose to replace Pape with him; Busse had joined the party only in 1986 after a long career in legal and illegal extreme-right organisations, including the NPD and later leadership of the now banned VSBD/PdA.[35] For a while, Kühnen's group had claimed the FAP leadership for a nominee of their own but, in January 1989, they recognised Busse and his associates as being in charge of the FAP,[36] doubtless because they themselves were into alternative political initiatives. Since his assumption of the headship, Busse has apparently sought to re-orient the FAP – taking advantage of the currently more favourable electoral climate towards the extreme right by discouraging the excesses of his more youthful and enthusiastic supporters. He is recognised as a long-term Strasserite and, without totally rejecting the FAP's pro-Hitler roots, he has sought to move it in a direction more sympathetic to the Strasserite line.[37] His moderation of style, if carried through, will certainly be a change from the sort of postures adopted by the FAP a couple of years or so ago.

Many of its members then saw themselves as in direct confrontation with the organs of the state. The Hamburg branch prepared a seven-page pamphlet on *Conduct before the Police, the Courts and Other Authorities*, which advised 'fighters' about their rights and, paradoxically, read in parts like a manual of formal civil liberties. However, it concluded as follows:

> At a time when almost all Germans have lost their honour and when loyalty has become a foreign word, we must especially maintain these two virtues. Our honour demands that we be Germans and nationalist fighters and stand up for such virtues.

Our loyalty demands that we do everything in our power for the party and for our comrades.

The other major theme in the evolution of the 'traditional' wing is the activities of Kühnen. As was mentioned earlier, he is credited by some authorities with leadership of one branch of 'The Movement'. However, after his release from gaol in March 1988, he worked to establish his new and now proscribed party, the NS – an abbreviation that needs little decoding. This group was formally founded on 15 July 1988 and has been described by some commentators merely as an electoral initiative for the FAP,[38] although it seems more convincingly regarded as having always been a semi-independent initiative by Kühnen, despite considerable membership overlap between the two groupings.

By the day before it was banned, the NS had collected the necessary 180 signatures to stand in the local elections in Frankfurt on 12 March 1989,[39] as well as in the smaller town of Langen; it intended to call its entry 'Foreigners Out List/National Assembly' [*Liste Ausländer raus/Nationale Sammlung (NS)*]. When proscribed, it had about 170 members, some of them former ANS/NA activists and most based in the Hesse region. The task of proscription had been made easier in the case of the NS than for the FAP by some outspoken public rejections of democracy by the former's deputy leader and the purported resemblance – according to the BMI – between its programme and that of the NSDAP presented in February 1920.[40] Immediately after the proscription, Kühnen announced his founding of a new party, to be called Initiative for the Popular Will [*Initiative Volkswille*, IV],[41] although one must wonder how seriously this was to be taken since, barely a month later, he was announcing that the still legal FAP would contest forthcoming elections in North Rhine-Westphalia. Indeed, around 100 former NS members from Langen merely reconstituted themselves publicly into an FAP group.[42]

As already suggested, Kühnen himself – though still one of the foremost pro-Hitler activists of militant neo-Nazism – is apparently making some tactical accommodation with the emergence of Strasserism. The choice of the 1920 NSDAP programme as a model for that of the NS may be symptomatic of this. Although Hitler had been involved in the former's compilation, whereas the Strasser brothers had not, it has been judged significant for its reference to 'breaking the shackles of finance capital'. The Strassers' greater keenness than Hitler's in later years to take this seriously is often regarded as one reason for the gulf that developed between them.[43] Still, whatever Kühnen's own limited concessions to Strasserism, he retains all his original admiration for Hitler, whom he described in a recent interview as 'a hero, a half-divine human being who was filled with particular energies and had a special mission in this world'.[44]

THE STRASSERITE WING

Thus, even 'traditional' militant neo-Nazism has been tainted by the growing popularity of Strasserism within the West German extreme right. However, this orientation has long existed as an autonomous tendency. The VSBD/PdA, proscribed in January 1982 for seeking the reestablishment of National Socialism, had been an early exemplar of the Strasserite tradition. The title chosen for the self-avowed successor organisation, the Nationalist Front–League of Social Revolutionary Nationalists [*Nationalistische Front–Bund Sozialrevolutionärer Nationalisten*, NF-BSN] is itself revealing, as is that of a group from Bremen that was incorporated into this new formation, the National Revolutionary Workers' Front [*Nationalrevolutionäre Arbeiterfront*, NRAF].[45] The amalgamated grouping was formed in Munich in September 1983. It became the principal component of the NF that was organised as a political party in November 1985. Although it sought to establish itself country-wide, it is significant only in a few places, notably Berlin, Bielefeld and Bremen – the last based on members of the former NRAF. The Bielefeld group is the most active, whilst that in Berlin is reputedly dominated by skinheads. Whether consciously or not, it had adopted the elided 'N' and 'F' symbol often used by the British National Front.

Although relatively small – credited with a total of only eighty members[46] – it has succeeded during the past couple of years in making considerable public impact, partly through street confrontations with its political opponents outside its central office in Bielefeld. Judging by the quality of its printed material, it is well financed. Its members have a reputation for criminal violence, especially against Turks. For example, in January 1989 a 19-year-old member was arrested after an arson attack on a residence inhabited largely by Turks, during which a German and three Turks, including a child, were burnt; the self-avowed motive was 'hatred of foreigners'.[47] The NF has an international reputation on the extreme right, having been invited to a gathering organised, in August 1988, in Belgium by the Odal Ring, although it is unclear whether the invitation was actually accepted.[48]

The NF has produced a range of policy statements and propaganda. In some respects, its demands differ little from those of 'traditional' militant neo-Nazism. Its action programme calls, for example, for the compulsory and graduated expulsion of all foreigners (except political refugees) within ten years. However, its publications portray their Strasserite emphasis in their very liberal use of words such as 'capitalists', 'imperialists', 'materialism', and so on. Thus, the fifth point of its ten-point Programme of Principles is headed 'Anti-materialist Cultural Revolution' and the sixth one is titled 'Anti-capitalist Social Revolution'.

THE CULTURAL AND SUPPORT GROUPS

During the 1980s, the BfV has also reported on a number of other, usually small, groups in the militant neo-Nazi wing of the German extreme right. Some of these are largely efforts associated with one or two dominant individuals who have attracted a small coterie of supporters. Examples are: the Citizens' and Farmers' Initiative [*Bürger- und Bauerninitiative*, BBI] associated with Thies Christophersen (born in 1918), a man long active in neo-Nazi circles who, in 1986, fled to Denmark (where he has been allowed to remain) in order to avoid the German authorities; the German Citizens' Initiative [*Deutsche Bürgerinitiative*, DBI]; and the Working Community of National Organisations/Populist League [*Arbeitsgemeinschaft Nationaler Verbände/Völkischer Bund*, ANV/VB], which is led by an NPD activist and has organised well-attended gatherings of extreme-right and militant neo-Nazi devotees.

Undoubtedly the most significant, however, is the HNG, presided over from Bielefeld by Christa Goerth (born in 1936), which was founded in 1979. It was estimated by the BfV to have something over 200 members in 1988[49] and thus, as can be deduced from Table 5.1, is well above the average group size. It seeks to portray itself as an extreme-right cross between Amnesty International and the National Association for the Care and Resettlement of Offenders (if that is not being flippant) – looking after the interests of imprisoned right-wing extremists in the Federal Republic and, in a few cases, abroad:

> It has purely pastoral functions and does not directly engage in political struggle. We take care of German patriots, who are often persecuted and imprisoned because of their fight for national interests in the Federal Republic of Germany. To the extent that it is possible, we provide financial help but above all we give comradely support.[50]

The HNG publishes a monthly newsletter of twenty or so pages printed (except for the cover pages) by an offset method. It reports on the prisoners whom it is supporting, usually about twenty of them. Over the years, Kühnen has been a major recipient of its support. Other interpretations of its motives and actions are less charitable than its own version. The BfV quotes various passages from its newsletter that suggest sympathy not merely for the prisoner but also for the crime.[51]

Much of the additional significance of the HNG derives from its bi-annual gatherings, to which come activists in the various strands of militant neo-Nazism in the Federal Republic, and from the relative catholicity of its criteria in choosing prisoners for support. It has therefore been a unifying body for some of the otherwise fractious groupings within militant neo-Nazism, although an article in the HNG's December 1988 newsletter makes clear that the organisation's affairs do not always proceed without some bitter internal wrangles – about money, about visits to prisoners, about attending trials, and so on.[52] It has also been suggested, on occasion, that too much of the organisation's finance has gone to assist Michael Kühnen.

In June 1987, a small rival-organisation to the HNG had been founded by Ernst Tag (born in 1947) from Ludwigshafen, after his earlier exclusion from the HNG because of his attacks on Kühnen. It is called the International Committee for the Assistance of Those Persecuted for National Political Reasons and Their Dependants [*Internationales Hilfskomitee für nationale politische Verfolgte und deren Angehörige*, IHV]. However, Tag's supporters are few and his recent brushes with the law have in any case curtailed the activities of the IHV to the production of a monthly news-sheet.

THE SOCIAL AND DEMOGRAPHIC CHARACTERISTICS OF MILITANT NEO-NAZIS

To the self-posed question: 'how many citizens of the Federal Republic must be counted as neo-Nazis?', Ginzel replied: 'between 1400 and 3,000,000'![53] One might now want to put the upper figure at 6,400,000, according to the results of a survey conducted in March 1989 by EMNID for *Der Spiegel*, this being the grossed-up figure of the survey's finding about the number of adults giving Hitler a positive score on an eleven-point affect-scale ranging from +5 to −5; the figure becomes 11,900,000 if one also includes those offering zero scores.[54] As Ginzel says, and as was noted earlier, there is much confusion about definition and thus about the consequent number who qualify. This chapter has self-consciously adopted the categorisation used by the BfV, while not necessarily accepting the restrictive manner in which it applies the 'neo-Nazi' label. Thus, we focus very deliberately upon the 1400, or upon those individuals who have been included within some number close to this in the BfV's annual monitoring. In fact, the object of our closest interest is a subset of this group, in those who may be regarded as participating activists, since the BfV's figures on the total number of activists include some whose support is merely financial. The figure of 1400 is that of militant neo-Nazi activists (according to this chapter's definition) reported for 1979 and used by Ginzel; it is also almost exactly the twelve-year mean for 1977-88, as reported in Table 5.1.

However, no research has obtained direct and systematic individual-level data on even this reduced number of activists. Instead, in order to make certain tentative inferences about the social and demographic characteristics of militant neo-Nazis, one must resort to the rather sparse information assembled and reported – often intermittently – by the BfV about those in the extreme right who have had brushes with the law of varying degrees of seriousness. The three categories used are described more fully in Notes a, b and c of Table 5.2 but summary descriptions, that imply a graduated scale of increasing seriousness, are given for the respective columns of that table: (a) suspects of punishable offences with extreme right-wing features; (b) right-wing extremists convicted of relevant punishable offences; and (c) right-wing extremists involved in various acts of planned or actual violence, i.e., those whom the BfV regards as 'militant'.

On a preliminary criterion of a similarity of numbers, as shown on a *per annum* basis in Table 5.2, it is reasonable to argue that those in category (a) above, the suspects of punishable offences with extreme right-wing features, approach most closely, in their aggregate characteristics, the universe of militant neo-Nazis in the Federal Republic in whom our closest interest lies. Certainly, this seems an acceptable method of seeking to describe the likely participating membership of groups such as the FAP or NF, although it must be conceded that the cultural and support groups such as the HNG may well differ – probably having memberships that are rather older, more female and more bourgeois. Even with this qualification, our general claim of some aggregate equivalence must be made with caution; there are obvious methodological problems in the use of data on those in Category (a) for the purpose of inference about the intended universe of those belonging to the FAP, NF and similar organisations. Not all such militant neo-Nazis have attracted the

Table 5.2 Social and demographic characteristics of various categories of militant extreme-right activists in the Federal Republic of Germany, 1977–86 (with relevant age-standardised comparisons for all males aged fourteen to sixty-five given in brackets)

	(a) Suspects of punishable offences with extreme right-wing features, 1981–83, 1985[a]	(b) Right-wing extremists convicted of relevant punishable offences, 1977–86[b]	(c) Right-wing extremists involved in various acts of planned or actual violence, up to 1985[c]
Age			
14 to 20	48%	39%	14%
21 to 30	30%	32%	56%
31 to 40	9%	12%	14%
41 to 50	7%	9%	11%
51 or more	7%	8%	5%
	Median age: 21.2 years	Median age: 24.0 years	Median age: 26.9 years
Gender			
Female	4%	5%[d]	2%
Employment status			
Unemployed	3%[e] [10%]	8% [10%]	25% [10%]
Educational attainment			
With a university degree[f]	1%[g] [6%]	2% [8%]	1%[h] [11%]

Table 5.2 (cont.)

Occupation[i]	(a) Suspects of punishable offences with extreme right-wing features, 1981–83, 1985[a]	(b) Right-wing extremists convicted of relevant punishable offences, 1977–86[b]	(c) Right-wing extremists involved in various acts of planned or actual violence, up to 1985[c]
Unskilled manual workers	14% } 39% [31%]	19% } 40% [34%]	13% } 49% [41%]
Skilled manual workers and craftsmen	25%	21%	36%
Non-manual workers	9% [20%]	13% [23%]	10% [30%]
School pupils and students	21% } 35% [42%]	12% } 32% [35%]	9% } 18% [18%]
Those in training or apprenticeship	14%	20%	9%
Other	17% [7%]	16% [8%]	23% [11%]
Number of individuals:	(4318)	(1738)	(268)
Mean number per annum:	1079.5	272.8	—

Sources:

The data on the characteristics of these categories of extreme-right activist are taken from various BfV annual reports, as elaborated in notes below.

The relevant age-standardised data for all males aged from fourteen to sixty-five have been calculated from a cumulation of three national surveys of the population aged fifteen or more of the Federal Republic of Germany that were conducted around the relevant time period under the auspices of the European Community's EUROBAROMETER series; these are Survey No. 20 (conducted from 27 Sept. to 4 Nov. 1983), Survey No. 21 (conducted from 14 March to 13 April 1984), and Survey No. 22 (conducted from 2 Oct. to 2 Nov. 1984).

Adjustments were made in the lowest age-category to accommodate the fourteen-year-olds missing from the EUROBAROMETER surveys. How various problematic variables from the survey were operationalised for this purpose is given in a note below. The author is grateful to the Belgian Archive for the Social Sciences for permitting his use of these data.

a The description of this category used in the annual reports has varied slightly from year to year; the text in the 1985 Report was 'suspects of punishable offences with extreme right-wing features', while that in the 1981 Report was 'suspects of infractions of the law with extreme right-wing features'. This difference seems inconsequential. Data under this category have been collected since 1977 but were not assembled for 1984. The data presented here are from 1981, firstly because information on gender composition, employment status and educational attainment could not be obtained for 1980, secondly because the data for 1979 and before were published with a slightly different age-categorisation from that used from 1980, and thirdly because data on occupational composition were not published for 1977 and 1978.

b The description of this category used in the annual reports has varied slightly; the text in the 1985 Report, which gave cumulated data from 1977 to 1985, was 'those convicted of punishable offences with extreme right-wing features' while that in the 1986 Report, which also reported the 1986 data, was 'those convicted of relevant punishable offences'.

c These data are from the 1985 annual report and refer to those extreme right-wing activists 'who are known to the Constitutional Protection authorities to have participated in recent years in acts of violence, to have threatened or planned violence, or to have been found in possession of weapons, ammunition or explosives.'

d This figure covers the years from 1977 to 1985.

e This figure covers the years 1983 and 1985.

f 'With a university degree' was operationalised as having had formal education up to twenty-two years of age or more.

g This figure covers the years 1982, 1983 and 1985.

h This figure covers the years up to and including 1984.

i For standardisation purposes, the coding used by the EUROBAROMETER studies was collapsed as follows:

'Manual workers' and 'small businessmen, craftsmen and employers' for the BfV's 'unskilled manual workers' and 'skilled manual workers and craftsmen'. In the 1981 annual report, the data for the 'self-employed' were presented separately; thereafter, to judge by a criterion of internal consistency (although this is not explicitly noted), they seem to have been included with 'skilled manual workers and craftsmen'.

'Students and those doing military service' for the BfV's 'school pupils and students' and 'those in training or apprenticeship'. The latter BfV category is not used by the EUROBAROMETER occupational code and those in training or apprenticeship may well be placed into other categories than that of 'student' by EUROBAROMETER, presumably usually 'manual workers' or 'non-manual workers'. The implications of this ambiguity are addressed in the text of the chapter.

'Farmers and fishermen', 'professionals' and 'senior managers' for the BfV's 'Other'.

attention of the law, although a high percentage of them have. Also, a proportion (though usually a minority) of those in category (a) were identified with more conventional extreme-right groups, such as the NPD or its youth wing, rather than with militant neo-Nazism. Some individuals (especially the youngest) may have committed offences with extreme-right features, although they were not enrolled members of any militant neo-Nazi group. However, in view of the simple demographic focus of the proposed analysis, it is unlikely that these examples of mismatch will introduce very serious biases.

Further, it is not deducible from the presentations of the BfV to what extent category (b) above is a subset of (a), or rather of (a) at some earlier period. Category (b) does include some more serious crimes than (a) – for which the least serious offences are such activities as graffiti-writing and flyposting. Thus, it does seem reasonable to regard (b) as a subset of (a) at some earlier period. A degree of uncertainty also exists about how far (c) is a product of (a) and of (b) respectively, although again it seems permissible to assume time-lagged subset relationships. Thus, the shifts from (a) to (b) to (c) – or certainly from (a) to (c) and from (b) to (c) – represent the career path within the movement of the truly dedicated and violent militant neo-Nazi.

Let us now examine what Table 5.2 says about the social and demographic characteristics of the three categories. The first point to note from these data is the quite marked disproportions of age and gender compared with the national population. We have encountered examples of older individuals, such as Busse and Christophersen, and even of older women, such as Goerth, but militant neo-Nazis tend to be young and almost exclusively male. For both categories (a) and (b) in Table 5.2, the modal age-range is around the teenage years, fourteen to twenty. For the militant and violent neo-Nazi core represented by category (c), the modal age is between twenty-one and thirty. Correspondingly, the median age rises from twenty-one, to twenty-four, to twenty-seven years as one progresses from (a) to (c) – an indication that, as argued earlier, these categories represent the career path of the most committed activists. Interestingly, the median age even of category (a) is higher than that of those reported by Dudek as perpetrators of 'neo-Nazi crimes' up to 1960, whose median was less than twenty. However, the equivalent figures for 1960 and 1961, in the wake of the Cologne synagogue-daubing in late–1959, were 28.6 and 30.4 years;[55] clearly, a lot of rather older Nazi sympathisers were moved to action by the Cologne incident. The emphasis within the militant neo-Nazi groups like the FAP and NF on machismo and confrontation leads one to anticipate their almost exclusively male character, perhaps symptomatic of which is the internal debate about homosexuality.[56] Even so, articles about the role of women in the movement do appear in the publications of these groups, whose propaganda material also sometimes features pictures of 'Aryan-ish' women.

In discussing the data on the employment status, educational attainment and occupational background of militant neo-Nazis, comparisons of distinctiveness with what will be called a criterion population are offered. Given that militant neo-Nazis are almost exclusively male and have a skewed age distribution, it is demonstrably inappropriate to use the total German adult population for such comparative purposes. Instead, the criterion populations are males aged between fourteen and sixty-five with their relevant social data age-standardised for the categories (a) to (c), using their respective age distributions in Table 5.2. Take employment status as an example. If the male population during the period in question had had any of the three age distributions shown for categories (a) to (c) in Table 5.2, the percentage of unemployed would have been 10 per cent, as indicated in brackets. These, then, are age-standardised male unemployment rates and they contrast with an unstandardised rate of 8 per cent (since, although the very youngest are still in school and hence not eligible to be unemployed, unemployment does tend to be higher among younger groups in the economically active population). All age-standardised comparisons were calculated using data from three cumulated EUROBAROMETER surveys conducted in the Federal Republic in 1983 and 1984, as explained in the description of sources of Table 5.2.

These analyses offer some interesting conclusions. Those in (a) were noticeably less likely to be unemployed than their criterion population (i.e., even allowing for the fact that many were still in full-time education). Those in (b) were perhaps slightly less likely to be unemployed than their criterion population. It is only in category (c) – containing individuals who have consciously opted for a serious criminal career in militant neo-Nazi circles – where the level of unemployment is disproportionate. Concerning educational attainment, only a tiny fraction in each category has completed a university education, far less than in the respective criterion populations, where one is already allowing for the fact that the modal age-groups of (a) and (b) are both too young to have completed a university course.

Reliable inferences about the occupational origins of these three categories of militant neo-Nazi are made difficult by the sometimes apparently rather cavalier approach to occupational classification on the part of the

BfV. This is doubtless a result in many cases of minimal occupational descriptions, which may also have led to a heavy use of the residual 'other' category. Additionally, there is some uncertainty about the comparability of categories used by the BfV and in the EUROBAROMETER studies, the latter being one of the standard categorisations of occupation used by French market research; this uncertainty applies particularly to 'those in training or apprenticeship'. It may well be that the criterion percentage in brackets for 'school pupils and students' combined with 'those in training or apprenticeship' (e.g., the 42 per cent for category (a)) should be somewhat higher and the complementary percentages for the other occupational groups (i.e., the 31, 20 and 7 per cent) somewhat lower. The unemployed seem to have been classified occupationally on the basis of their former job, although the BfV does not state this explicitly.

Taking these data, in the first instance, at face value, it may be noted that in all three categories there is a slight disproportion from manual backgrounds. However, in no case does the relevant percentage difference between the values for observed and criterion populations exceed 8 points (e.g., 39–31 per cent for category (a)), although it must be admitted that the differences would be rather larger if the criterion percentages had been artificially raised because of the uncertainty discussed above about those in training or apprenticeship. Thus, a background in a manual occupation is common among militant neo-Nazis but – it may be tentatively concluded – it is not hugely disproportionate to expectations based on the criterion population. There is an under-representation of those from non-manual backgrounds, which is particularly noticeable for the militant hard core in category (c), where the percentage difference is 20 points; of course these differences would be rather less if the criterion percentages had been artificially raised because of ambiguity about the those in training or apprenticeship. Next, in two of the three categories there is an under-representation of school pupils and students, as well as those in training or apprenticeship, once the age composition of the categories has been controlled for; only in category (c) is there even an equivalent presence. Of course, these conclusions would be reinforced if, for reasons stated earlier, the various criterion percentages ought to be somewhat higher. Finally, the discrepancy between observed and criterion population percentages in the 'other' occupational category suggests the possibility of further bias, albeit unavoidable, in these comparisons, since the BfV researchers may have over-relied on this residual category.

THE SOCIAL PSYCHOLOGY OF MILITANT NEO-NAZISM

During the past ten or so years there has been a publishing explosion in the Federal Republic on the extreme right. Some of this literature has focused directly upon militant neo-Nazism, especially its youthful support.[57] The tone and content of these writings vary – from the descriptive, through the apocalyptic, to the analytical and theoretical. However, what is common to very many of them is their special focus upon organisational aspects of these movements' development, upon the activities of those involved and upon the movements' ideological characteristics. For these purposes, especially the last, there is heavy reliance on secondary material – propaganda publications such as news-letters, party programmes and leaflets, as well as reported statements of leaders. In part because of difficulties in securing research access and co-operation, there are remarkably few studies that examine individual militant neo-Nazis, and even fewer that do so from the perspective of offering systematic social-psychological explanations of their behaviour, although it is true that there have been several studies of more general tendencies to right-wing extremism among the young.

Two examples of research into militant neo-Nazism that did make personal contact with their subjects are those of Pomorin and Junge and of Rabe, although both are now more than ten years old.[58] However, these authors were investigative journalists. Pomorin and Junge especially used what has now become known as 'the Wallraff method' (after Gün-ther Wallraff) and their principal interest was exposé, both of the indi-viduals' activities and of the network of contacts among them, rather than any sophisticated examination of motive. Rabe was rather more concerned with motive, stressing the comradely aspects of militant neo-Nazism, although his collection of material seems unsystematic. Dudek, in his lit-erature review of the study of youthful right-wing extremism, identifies numerous different approaches but social-psychological studies are only his eighth category out of ten; these have focused upon the political socialisa-tion, the dispositional profiles and the personality structure of right-wing activists.[59] Yet, as he makes clear, these studies tend to have a theoretical focus, offering explanations based on processes of narcissistic socialisation, or on types of authoritarianism derived from the work of Adorno and Milgram. There has been a certain interest in 'career analysis' employing a social-psychological perspective, which involves examination of the backgrounds of acknowledged extremists for traumatic events in childhood or adolescence (being an orphan, divorce of parents, and so on).[60]

Perhaps the best example of this research – important because it conducted personal interviews with its subjects – is the work of Hennig.[61] This was carried out between 1979 and 1982, but it remains one of the few studies to have achieved systematic interview material with its subjects. It was conducted under commission from the BMI of the SPD-FDP government, particularly in the light of the growth of militant neo-Nazism from the mid–1970s – a development upon which comment has already been passed – and the fact that perhaps 60 to 70 per cent of those so active were young and almost exclusively male. Although this study is now nearly a decade old, the fact that the number of neo-Nazis has remained fairly stable during the 1980s (as Table 5.1 showed) suggests that its findings may not unrealistically be applied to the present situation. The only major change of emphasis in the present era is an ideological one; Hennig's research was not concerned with hostility to foreigners inside the Federal Republic but instead focused on the traditional interests of the post-war extreme right – anti-Communism, anti-Americanism, and so forth. Of course, hostility to foreigners would be a major theme of any similar contemporary study.

Hennig conducted thirty-two interviews with young right-wing extremists between sixteen and thirty; their median age was twenty. Not all were involved in the militant neo-Nazi scene, as this chapter has defined it. Sixteen were involved in, or sympathetic to, such groups (fourteen connected with 'neo-Nazi' groups and two 'national revolutionaries', as Hennig defined them), while the other sixteen were active in, or sympathetic to, the youth wing of the NPD. The research attempted to understand the mix of predisposing factors behind commitment to neo-Nazi activism, emphasising the effects of the combination of relative deprivation, political alienation and particular extreme crises in adolescence. Thus, right-wing extremist activism among the young was held to have a materialist basis, in the sense that it was a reaction among some individuals to frustrations associated with the end of a long period of economic prosperity and the beginning of economic recession in the mid–1970s. Finally, drawing on both his interview material and also on information on the backgrounds of forty-two young people convicted between 1978 and 1980 for offences with extreme right-wing features, Hennig offered a sequential model for a career of increasing commitment to the extreme right. This starts with parental problems and progresses through difficulties in school, with girls and at work until, by about the age of eighteen, the individual is committed to 'political soldiering', and has broken away from the conventional career pattern.

THE LIKELY FUTURE OF MILITANT NEO-NAZISM IN THE FEDERAL REPUBLIC

Militant neo-Nazism in the Federal Republic in the 1980s is a story of evolution but also of stability. There have been changes in the significance of particular organisations (especially in the light of proscriptions, schisms and infiltrations), some new personages have emerged, and there have been developments in styles and activities (such as the emergence of the skinhead culture in parts of the extreme right and the increasing role of football support), as well as in ideology (the current popularity of Strasserism). However, there are many enduring features: today's principal strands of militant neo-Nazism can be traced back, in organisational terms, to the 1970s, and many of those active in contemporary militant neo-Nazism began their careers in that decade.

When contemplating the future, one might be tempted to be apocalyptic, seeing the current wave of hostility to foreigners in the Federal Republic as exactly the sort of resentment upon which militant neo-Nazism might draw. However, it is paradoxical that, perhaps precisely because of this trend, militant neo-Nazism may not grow in proportionate strength, since these issues have been co-opted by the electorally oriented extreme right – The Republicans, the DVU (List D) and the NPD. To be sure, the militant groups will pose persistent threats to public order, liable to take advantage of appropriate opportunities – such as the death of Rudolf Hess in August 1987 or the hundredth anniversary of Hitler's birth in April 1989 – and to encourage criminal attacks on the homes and persons of asylum-seekers and some foreigners.[62] Even if proscribed, they will, of course, continue to exist in some form because of the all-male camaraderie that they offer to certain individuals.

Some commentators have argued that attempts by groups such as the FAP to sanitise their image in order to participate in the electoral process pose a particular danger,[63] but it seems unlikely that they will be able to outbid more 'respectable' extreme-right groups whose leaders do not have the stigma of having spent long periods in gaol for their past activities. The continuing interest of the state in these movements is a further brake on their growth, whereas the state's monitoring of the DVU and the NPD is likely to remain much more passive. The numbers reportedly active in militant neo-Nazism have remained remarkably stable during the 1980s, as we have seen, but of even greater relevance is that these numbers have not been associated, in any clear way, with seemingly relevant political events during the decade, such as the growth in the membership of the DVU. Perhaps the lesson from the surge of militant neo-Nazism in the 1970s is that only a major economic collapse in the Federal Republic would produce further dramatic increases in such activism. While this possibility is not to be discounted, it seems less likely than a scenario in which a small number of militant neo-Nazis pose a low-level terrorist threat, by their actions, against groups such as asylum-seekers and Turks. The electoral extreme right, such as The Republicans or the NPD, would seem to pose a far greater contemporary danger to political stability; only if circumstances force an alliance between these groups and those of militant neo-Nazism would the latter really emerge as a serious threat to the state.

LIST OF ABBREVIATIONS

AAR	*Aktion Ausländerrückführung – Volksbewegung gegen Überfremdung und Umweltzerstörung* [Operation Repatriation – Popular Movement against Foreign Dominance and Destruction of the Environment]
ANS	*Aktionsfront Nationaler Sozialisten* [Action Front of National Socialists]
ANS/NA	*Aktionsfront Nationaler Sozialisten/Nationale Aktivisten* [Action Front of National Socialists/National Activists]
ANV/VB	*Arbeitsgemeinschaft Nationaler Verbände/Völkischer Bund* [Working Community of National Organisations/ Populist League]
BBI	*Bürger- und Bauerninitiative* [Citizens' and Farmers' Initiative]
BfV	*Bundesamt für Verfassungsschutz* [Federal Office for the Protection of the Constitution]
BHM	*Bund Hamburger Mädel* [League of Hamburg Girls]
BMI	*Bundesministerium des Innern* [Federal Ministry of the Interior]
CDU	*Christlich-Demokratische Union* [Christian-Democratic Union]
DBI	*Deutsche Bürgerinitiative* [German Citizens' Initiative]
DFF	*Deutsche Frauenfront* [German Women's Front]
DVU	*Deutsche Volksunion* [German People's union]
DVU (List D)	*Deutsche Volksunion (Liste D)* [German People's Union (List D)]

FAP	*Freiheitliche Deutsche Arbeiterpartei* [Free German Workers' Party]
FDP	*Freie Demokratische Partei* [Liberal Democratic Party]
FN	*Front National* [National Front]
HNG	*Hilfsorganisation für nationale politische Gefangene und deren Angehörige* [Organisation for the Assistance of National Political Prisoners and Their Dependants]
IHV	*Internationales Hilfskomitee für nationale politische Verfolgte und deren Angehörige* [International Committee for the Assistance of Those Persecuted for National Political Reasons and Their Dependants]
IV	*Initiative Volkswille* [Initiative for the Popular Will]
JF	*Junge Front* [Young Front]
NF	*Nationalistische Front* [Nationalist Front]
NF-BSN	*Nationalistische Front — Bund Sozialrevolutionärer Nationalisten* [Nationalist Front — League of Social Revolutionary Nationalists]
NPD	*Nationaldemokratische Partei Deutschlands* [National Democratic Party of Germany]
NRAF	*Nationalrevolutionäre Arbeiterfront* [National Revolutionary Workers' Front]
NS	*Nationale Sammlung* [National Assembly]
NSDAP	*Nationalsozialistische Deutsche Arbeiterpartei* [National Socialist German Workers' Party]
REP	*Die Republikaner* [The Republicans]
SPD	*Sozialdemokratische Partei Deutschlands* [Social Democratic Party of Germany]
VB	*Vlaams Blok* [Flemish Bloc]
VSBD/PdA	*Volkssozialistische Bewegung Deutschlands/Partei der Arbeit* [Popular Socialist Movement of Germany/Labour Party]
WSG Hoffmann	*Wehrsportgruppe Hoffmann* [Hoffmann Defence and Sporting Group]

NOTES

1. Although 'REP' is now the standard abbreviation for this party in official listings, 'The Republicans' is the conventional description in text.
2. Dr Gerhard Frey (born in 1933) is a long-time activist on the extreme right

in the Federal Republic and has been an enthusiastic founder of numerous initiatives and organisations to expand his stable of activities; he is now the publisher of three extreme-right weekly newspapers. In 1971, he co-founded the DVU, which he has headed ever since; this was initially devoted merely to the propagation of extreme-right ideas. In March 1987, he formally founded the German People's Union (List D) [*Deutsche Volksunion (Liste D)*, DVU (List D)]. Although an organisation different from the DVU itself (in the sense of having a separately counted membership), the DVU (List D) operates in practice as the electoral wing of the DVU.

3. H. J. Schwagerl, *Verfassungsschutz in der Bundesrepublik Deutschland*, C. F. Müller Juristischer Verlag, Heidelberg, 1985, pp. 35–6.

4. An initial, rather casuistical, distinction was drawn by at least two officials between 'right-wing *radical*' (rechts*radikal*) and 'right-wing *extremist*' (rechts*extremistisch*); see *Süddeutsche Zeitung*, 6 Feb. 1989, p. 6 (emphases in original) and *Der Spiegel*, 13 Feb. 1989, p. 60. The decision on whether permanent, as opposed to provisional, monitoring of The Republicans was to be undertaken by the BfV was originally to have been taken in September 1989 but was then postponed until November. In early June 1989, the Bavarian Minister of the Interior announced that this region was monitoring The Republicans; see *Süddeutsche Zeitung*, 8 June 1989, pp. 1, 24, and 16, 17, 18 June 1989, p. 12. Later, a similar decision was taken by the regional authorities in SPD-controlled North Rhine-Westphalia; see *Süddeutsche Zeitung*, 4 Oct. 1989, p. 1.

5. BfV, *Verfassungsschutzbericht 1981*, Bundesminister des Innern, Bonn, 1982. These reports are hereafter cited by the year whose events they described (e.g., BfV, *Annual Report 1981*); the year of publication is invariably the subsequent one. The BfV's annual report for 1987 was the most recent available when the major work on this chapter was being done, but some material from the annual report for 1988, which was published in early July 1989, has been incorporated.

6. The WSG Hoffmann, formerly led by Karl-Heinz Hoffmann (a commercial artist, born in 1937), was proscribed in January 1980. Some of its members subsequently went to Lebanon to receive commando training from Al Fatah. In 1986, Hoffmann himself was acquitted of the murder in Erlangen, in 1980, of the former head of the Jewish cultural centre in Nuremberg and the latter's female consort, but he received a nine-and-a-half-year sentence for various crimes committed in Lebanon and the Federal Republic, including counterfeiting, false imprisonment, grievous bodily harm and intimidation. He was subsequently released on four years' parole in July 1989.

7. The Strasser brothers, Gregor (1892–1934) and Otto (1897–1974), represented the 'left', anti-capitalist wing of the NSDAP and were influential in assisting the party's growth in northern Germany during the 1920s. Gregor Strasser led a group of sixty or so NSDAP deputies whom Kurt von Schleicher, chancellor from 2 Dec. 1932, had hoped to attract away from the rest of the NSDAP behind a constitutional progressive social programme; see W. Carr,

A History of Germany, 1815–1945, Edward Arnold, London, 1969, p. 356, and K. D. Bracher, *The German Dictatorship: The Origins, Structure, and Effects of National Socialism*, translated by Jean Steinberg, Penguin University Books, Harmondsworth, 1973, pp. 253–4 (first published in German in 1969). Gregor Strasser gave way to Hitler's insistence that he refuse an offered position in von Schleicher's government; he thereupon resigned his party posts and left politics. He was murdered on Hitler's order on the occasion of the so-called Röhm Putsch of June 1934.

Dr Otto Strasser had been expelled from the NSDAP in July 1930 and tried unsuccessfully to organise a competing party. During the Nazi period, he lived in exile in Czechoslovakia, Switzerland and Canada but returned to the Federal Republic after the War.

8. BfV, *Annual Report 1981*, p. 29.
9. BfV, *Annual Report 1988*, p. 117.
10. Because the BfV's limited application of the 'neo-Nazi' label is contestable, the expression is hereafter given within quotation marks whenever reference to this particular usage is intended.
11. BfV, *Annual Report 1988*, p. 129.
12. *Süddeutsche Zeitung*, 6 Mar. 1989, p. 7.
13. BfV, *Annual Report 1988*, p. 130.
14. BfV, *Annual Report 1988*, p. 117.
15. BMI, 'Verfassungsfeindliche Bestrebungen – Ihre ideologischen Grundlagen, Entwicklungen und Tendenzen: Rechtsextremismus', Paper presented to a Seminar of the BMI on 'The Protection of the Constitution in the Democratic State' at Bad Neuenahr, 10 Jan. 1989, p. 1.
16. This use of the word 'militant' is, therefore, slightly less restrictive than that of the BfV, which described around 200 'neo-Nazi' individuals in 1988 as being 'militant', intending by this that subset of right-wing extremists who during recent years had themselves carried out, or participated in, acts of violence or who had been in illegal possession of weapons, ammunition or explosive; see BfV, *Annual Report 1988*, p. 117.
17. For an extensive discussion of those parts of the extreme right in the Federal Republic that have been electorally successful, including The Republicans, the DVU (List D) and the NPD, see C. T. Husbands, *Racist Political Movements in Western Europe*, Routledge, London, 1990, ch. 5.
18. BfV, *Annual Report 1982*, p. 127.
19. Michael Kühnen (born in 1955, and thus still only in his early thirties) has been widely known on the neo-Nazi scene in the Federal Republic since about 1977. He is a former lieutenant in the *Bundeswehr*. He has already done several prison terms for offences arising from his neo-Nazi activities, the most recent being of three years and four months from Jan. 1985 for disseminating propaganda demanding the lifting of the ban on the NSDAP and for using the emblems of unconstitutional organisations. In March 1984, he attempted to avoid the authorities by leaving the country, eventually being extradited from Paris in Oct. 1984.

20. BfV, *Annual Report 1984*, p. 141.
21. BfV, *Annual Report 1988*, p. 119.
22. BMI, 'Verfassungsfeindliche Bestrebungen', p. 10.
23. An exposé, containing much material on Kühnen's early activities that estab-lished his notoriety, is Antifa-Kommission, *Hamburg – Stadt mit Herz für Faschisten; Dokumentation: Zehn Jahre Begünstigung der NSDAP-Umtriebe*, Kommunistischer Bund, Hamburg, April 1978.
24. BfV, *Annual Report 1978*, p. 31.
25. BfV, *Annual Report 1979*, p. 28.
26. *Frankfurter Allgemeine Zeitung*, 3 Mar. 1988, p. 1.
27. *Der Spiegel*, 16 June 1986, pp. 75-9.
28. BMI, 'Verfassungsfeindliche Bestrebungen', p. 8.
29. BfV, *Annual Report 1987*, p. 101, and BMI, 'Verfassungsfeindliche Bestre-bungen', p. 11.
30. BfV, *Annual Report 1988*, p. 118.
31. BfV, *Annual Report 1987*, p. 101.
32. *Süddeutsche Zeitung*, 30 Nov. 1988, p. 6.
33. *Süddeutsche Zeitung*, 22/23 Oct. 1988, p. 5.
34. BMI, 'Verfassungsfeindliche Bestrebungen', p. 16.
35. J. Pomorin, 'Friedhelm Busse, "Reichsstatthalter" von München', in J. Pomorin and R. Junge, *Vorwärts, wir marschieren zurück: die Neonazis*, Part 2, Weltkreis-Verlag, Dortmund, 1979, pp. 156–78.
36. BfV, *Annual Report 1988*, p. 119.
37. B. Grill *et al.*, 'Alte Parolen, neue Parteien', *Die Zeit*, 17 Feb. 1989, p. 16.
38. *Frankfurter Allgemeine Zeitung*, 10 Feb. 1989, p. 2.
39. *Süddeutsche Zeitung*, 8 Feb. 1989, p. 5.
40. *Frankfurter Allgemeine Zeitung*, 10 Feb. 1989, p. 2.
41. *Süddeutsche Zeitung*, 11/12 Feb. 1989, p. 1.
42. *Süddeutsche Zeitung*, 13 Mar. 1989, p. 6.
43. For a discussion of the NSDAP's 1920 programme, see Bracher, *The German Dictatorship* cit., pp. 114–16.
44. 'Ich, Kühnen: Deutschlands gefürchtetster Neonazi erklärt sich', an interview with Michael Kühnen by Christa Ritter, *Tempo*, Feb. 1989, pp. 82–6.
45. BfV, *Annual Report 1983*, p. 128.
46. BfV, *Annual Report 1988*, p. 122.
47. *Süddeutsche Zeitung*, 18 Jan. 1989, p. 19.
48. *Searchlight*, Feb. 1989, p. 7.
49. BfV, *Annual Report 1988*, p. 122.
50. Personal letter to the author from Christa Goerth, 24 Jan. 1989.
51. BfV, *Annual Report 1986*, pp. 165–6.
52. *Nachrichten der HNG*, No. 103, Dec. 1988, pp. 8–9.
53. G. B. Ginzel, *Hitlers (Ur)enkel; Neonazis: ihre Ideologien and Aktionen*, Droste Verlag, Düsseldorf, 1981, p. 17.
54. *Der Spiegel*, 10 Apr. 1989, pp. 150–60.
55. P. Dudek, *Jugendliche Rechtsextremisten: Zwischen Hakenkreuz und Odalsrune*,

1945 bis heute, Bund-Verlag, Cologne, 1985, pp. 87–8; however, because of age-categories that are not mutually exclusive, there may be slight discrepancies in these calculations.

56. One does see some women activists among militant neo-Nazis but they are very much a minority. In the past there have been occasional groupings intended specifically for women (such as one that was associated with the ANS in the late 1970s, the League of Hamburg Girls [*Bund Hamburger Mädel*, BHM]), itself a significant title because the word, *Mädel*, is a South-German colloquialism with implications of both frivolity and subordination. One hears little of such organisations today, although there is a very small group called the German Women's Front [*Deutsche Frauenfront*, DFF] associated with Ursula Müller (born in 1934) and her husband in Mainz.

    Given the derogatory attitudes towards women held by some militant neo-Nazis, this paucity of women is scarcely surprising. Thus, Kühnen, when recently asked about women in his movement, replied: 'The Italian aristocrat, Julius Evola, says that only the crystal-clear, granite dynamism of masculinity makes possible an aspiring civilisation. Female influences are a distraction. ... Intellectually we don't need them [women]'. In the same interview he remarked that 'homosexuals are especially suited for our task of winning our struggle because they do not want ties to wife, children and family'. See his interview with Christa Ritter, *Tempo*, Feb. 1989, pp. 82–6.

57. Two summaries of this literature, the second focusing on right-wing extremism among the young are: U. Backes and E. Jesse, *Totalitarismus, Extremismus, Terrorismus: Ein Literaturführer und Wegweiser zur Extremismusforschung in der Bundesrepublik Deutschland*, 2nd ed., Leske und Budrich, Opladen, 1985, pp. 103–84, and P. Dudek and H.-G. Jaschke, *Jugend rechtsaussen: Analysen, Essays, Kritik*, Päd. Extra Buchverlag, Bensheim, 1982.

58. Pomorin and Junge, *Vorwärts, wir marschieren zurückcit*; K.-K. Rabe, ' "Wir sehen uns als eine grosse Gemeinschaft": Begegnungen mit jungen Mitgliedern rechtsextremer Organisationen', in P. Lersch (ed.), *Die verkannte Gefahr: Rechtsradikalismus in der Bundesrepublik*, Spiegel-Buch, Hamburg, 1981, pp. 128–42.

59. Dudek and Jaschke, *Jugend rechtsaussen* cit., pp. 19–20.

60. For example, H.-G. Jaschke, 'Gewalt von rechts vor und nach Hitler', *Aus Politik und Zeitgeschichte: Beilage zur Wochenzeitung 'Das Parlament'*, 12 June 1982, esp. pp. 15–17.

61. E. Hennig, 'Neonazistische Militanz und Rechtsextremismus unter Jugendlichen', *Aus Politik und Zeitgeschichte: Beilage zur Wochenzeitung 'Das Parlament'*, 12 June 1982, pp. 23–37, and BMI, *Neonazistische Militanz und Rechtsextremismus unter Jugendlichen*, Verlag W. Kohlhammer, Stuttgart, 1982.

62. Despite some official fears of widespread disorder, Hitler's hundredth birthday on 20 April 1989 was marked largely by some private celebrations in extreme-right circles, although there were considerable anxieties among parts of the country's foreign population, amid advance rumours of pogrom-style attacks. There is some irony in the fact that Kühnen himself was obliged to

spend the day in hospital recovering from an appendectomy! See *Der Spiegel*, 24 Apr. 1989, p. 31.

63. Grill *et al.*, 'Alte Parolen, neue Parteien' cit., p. 16.

CHAPTER SIX

The Holocaust Denial: a Study in Propaganda Technique

Roger Eatwell

The Holocaust of Jews during the Second World War is part of modern collective memory. Images of the emaciated living, of rag-doll heaps of the dead, of gas chambers and ferocious SS guards, are vivid not just for survivors. Popular media, such as film and television, provide constant reminders of the twentieth century's potential for bestiality. Yet, during the 1970s and 1980s there was a notable growth of articles, pamphlets and books seeking to deny that there was a systematic Nazi policy of genocide. Such views might be considered the historical or political equivalent of the 'scientific' belief that the moon is made of green cheese. However, four opening points about the growth of this Holocaust-denial literature illustrate the dangers of dismissing its potential impact, especially at a time when there are signs that anti-Semitism may be reviving, and criticisms of Israel growing.[1]

Firstly, such propaganda should not be seen solely within the context of the limited circulations achieved by most contemporary Fascist publications. Laws banning the publication of Nazi works have hampered German Fascists from focusing on these arguments. However, among notable Holocaust-denial works which have circulated is Thies Christophersen's pamphlet Die Auschwitz Lüge, first published in 1973 by Kritik-Verlag (Mohrkirch). By 1979 over 100,00 copies had allegedly been distributed.[2] That year also saw the appearance of Wilhelm Stäglich's 498-page Der Auschwitz-Mythos, published by Grabert Verlag (Tübingen). This was quickly suppressed but, apparently, only after all but seven of its 10,000-copy run had been sold; subsequently, it has been republished in English and French, while German language editions are advertised for smuggling back to Germany.[3]

This republication of works abroad illustrates a second important point:

the international aspect of the Holocaust denial and, especially, the link between some of the groups and individuals involved. These international links can be seen most clearly through the activities of the American Institute for Historical Review (IHR), founded in 1978. Many leading European, American and Arab 'Historical Revisionists', as they prefer to be known, have attended IHR conferences and contributed to its *The Journal of Historical Review*. Among the most active have been Arthur Butz and Robert Faurisson. The former is an Associate Professor of Electrical Engineering and Computer Sciences at Northwestern University, Illinois. He is best known for his 315-page book *The Hoax of the Twentieth Century*, first published in 1976 by the Historical Review Press (Brighton). The latter has been a Senior Lecturer in Literary Criticism at the University of Lyon-2. His prolific works in the 1980s include the 304-page book *Mémoire en défense contre ceux qui m'accusent de falsifier l'histoire*, published by La Vieille Taupe (Paris). This contained a preface written by the left-wing American linguistician Noam Chomsky, a document which caused considerable outcry and surprise.[4] These points illustrate a third factor which should be underlined at the outset: some Historical Revisionists are highly educated. Among earlier ones who were capable of sustaining a more sophisticated level of debate, it is important to note Maurice Bardèche, the brother-in-law of the literary Fascist Robert Brasillach. Bardèche wrote several books and articles which anticipated Historical Revisionist themes, and edited the neo-Fascist journal *Défense de l'Occident*.[5]

In her book *The Holocaust Denial* (Beyond the Pale Collective, Leeds, 1986), Gill Seidel draws attention to a fourth point: the clear Fascist and/ or racist motivation of this literature. It is interesting, here, to note Richard Harwood's widely-distributed pamphlet *Did Six Million Really Die?* (Historical Review Press, Ladbroke, 1974).[6] On page 2, Harwood reveals his motivation when he writes:

> what happens if a man dares to speak of the race problem, of its biological and political implications? He is branded as that most heinous of creatures, a 'racialist'. And what is racialism, of course, but the very hallmark of the Nazi! They (so everyone is told, anyway) murdered Six Million Jews because of racialism, so it must be a very evil thing indeed. When Enoch Powell drew attention to the dangers posed by coloured immigration into Britain in one of his early speeches, a certain prominent Socialist raised the spectre of Dachau and Auschwitz to silence his presumption.

It is interesting to note that this is removed in the 1987(?) revised edition, which admits that a small number of errors crept into the original version. However, the revised edition includes a more esoteric reference to Fascism in relation to the former French distributor of the pamphlet, François Duprat, who was assassinated in 1978. The new introduction notes that Duprat's party, the *Front National*, was subsequently taken over by 'opportunists', a clear reference to the less overtly Fascist tone which emerged as support grew during the 1980s. If further evidence is sought about motivation, it should be noted that Harwood subsequently turned out to be Richard Verrall, a leading member of the British National Front during the 1970s. The apparently anodyne Historical Review Press, which published the pamphlet, has close links with British Fascist and racist organisations.[7] It has been active in distributing a wide range of literature, including works by Butz, Christophersen, Faurisson and Stäglich, and it distributes IHR publications. The motivation of other publishers has not always been strictly Fascist. In America, anti-Semitism seems more to be the key. Some money has also come from Arab sources, clearly with the desire of de-legitimising Israel. In France, Faurisson's works have been published by a left-wing collective called La Vieille Taupe, which includes Jewish supporters. Here again, anti-Israel sentiments, which are common in sections of both the Communist and non-Communist left, seem to be central (this position tends to be pro-Palestinian, seeing Israel as capitalist and imperialist – even racist – in the light of its policies towards the Palestinians).

The linking publishing theme is therefore political manipulation rather than a desire to engage in academic debate. In its more sophisticated form, this even involves a form of Gramsci-ism, the belief that the radical needs to fight at the level of ideas in order to undermine dominant cultural-political values. While such views are normally found on he left, the French *Nouvelle Droite* offers a notable example of 'Gramsci-ism of the right' (moreover, the extent to which contemporary Fascist tracts circulate at the international level means that this *Nouvelle Droite* position has been influential elsewhere). A leading member of La Vieille Taupe has even claimed that Louis Pauwels, the director of the French conservative newspaper *Le Figaro* and a leading figure in the *Nouvelle Droite*, met Faurisson in private and expressed support for Historical Revisionism. Pressure from advertisers, and the threat of legal action prevented Pauwels openly siding with Faurisson, but he later financed a trip to America for a 'revisionist' member of La Vieille Taupe.[8] While such testimony must be treated with extreme caution, it underlines the possibility that Historical Revisionism is viewed as useful by more respectable members of the right (and left).

These diverse political motivations are a vital perspective, but unduly emphasising them can lead to the belief that all Historical Revisionists are frauds in the sense that they are consciously lying. Most undoubtedly are but Faurisson, in particular, appears to believe what he is arguing. Certainly, his earlier writings on French literature had a tendency to adopt the Messianic view that he had seen the true light, whereas countless others had been deceived, a markedly similar line to his one on the Holocaust. Emphasis on the Fascist and racist links also means that Holocaust-denial arguments tend to be ignored or parodied. Once the political associations of the individual have been established, substantive debate of the *issue* seems unnecessary. Such an approach leads to underestimating the potential appeal of some arguments. Evidence as to their potential can be seen by the fact that the author Colin Wilson wrote a review of Harwood's pamphlet which reveals that he was clearly impressed.[9] The Henri Roques affair in France offers further evidence of the potential appeal of such arguments, even to academics (it also attracted considerable popular-media attention).[10] In 1985, a student was awarded a doctorate at the University of Nantes for a Historical Revisionist critique of the Gerstein document (see below). The degree was subsequently revoked as a result of a series of irregularities involving the connivance of some academics.[11] It is impossible to tell whether the individuals concerned were convinced by the arguments or saw them, more, as politically useful. Certainly, some had connections with various Fascist and racist groups. Nevertheless, there seems to be a strong case for analysing the appeal of Holocaust-denial arguments more systematically.

APPROACHING THE HOLOCAUST DENIAL

An important question when approaching the Holocaust denial is whether it would be better to ignore the literature. It could be argued that discussing such claims could both give them legitimacy in the sense that they are seen as worthy of debate, and increase their familiarity among those who might otherwise have been unaware of their existence. This may have been the best policy when such works were rare, but their recent growth makes a more specific response vital, especially as ignoring them could be seen as confirming a conspiracy (a common Historical Revisionist allegation) of silence.

It has been argued that such a response should focus on legal suppression.[12] Censorship raises a series of wide-ranging issues about democratic politics. However, even at the pragmatic level, it is possible to question whether legal proceedings can be deemed unequivocally useful. The threat of legal action (mainly under race relations laws) has probably served to deter the wider publication of Historical Revisionist arguments. On the other hand, there were various prosecutions against Faurisson in the 1980s, followed by appeals and counter-appeals. In the end, both sides claimed victory. The anti-racist groups stressed that Faurisson had to pay damages and was given a suspended sentence. He argued that the court had ultimately concluded that his work on the gas chambers was 'scientific', and that the charge that he had been deliberately negligent was not proven.[13] This process almost certainly helped keep alive an issue which might otherwise have remained on the fringes. The prohibition of the public sale of the French journal *Annales d'histoire révisionniste* in 1987 may have harmed its sales (it was limited to subscription sales) but it is not clear that it will limit the impact of the ideas. Holocaust denial works have circulated fairly widely in Germany in spite of bans. Moreover, banning may even increase the appeal of such works by reinforcing the claim that there is a conspiracy to suppress them.

This still leaves the problem of *how* to study such literature. Many social scientists have sought to analyse Fascist propaganda within the framework of quantitative content analysis, which seeks to measure the recurrence of key terms.[14] There have been a series of major objections to this approach. One concerns a failure to perceive that such terms, for example 'freedom', can have radically different meanings.[15] There is also the problem of the selection of texts. This is a particularly significant issue in the context of the Holocaust denial because it is useful to distinguish between two types of text.

The first, and by far the largest group, is the sort which involves an overtly Fascist or racist content. This would include crude works such as the grossly-mistitled Committee for Truth in History's *The Six Million Reconsidered,* published in 1979 by the Historical Review Press. This is littered with references to Jewish power, Zionism's baneful consequences and other familiar themes. It is not necessary to move beyond the contents page to see the tone: 'Zion's Own ''Six Million'' Plans ... The Tsarist Pogrom Myth ... Jews and Organized Crime ... Jews and Communism ... Epilogue in Palestine'. It would also include Harwood's *Did Six Million Really Die?* (mentioned above), though the tone of this is far less crude. The second group includes texts like Faurisson's article 'The Mechanics of Gassing', published in *The Journal of Historical Review* (No. 1, 1980), or the

Italian Carlo Mattogno's article 'Le Mythe de l'extermination des juifs', which appeared in the *Annales d'histoire révisionniste* (No. 1, 1987). Such texts are normally more 'academic', in the sense that they include extensive footnotes, and refer to major secondary works, e.g. Mattogno's forty-two page article has an average of almost two footnotes per page, including many leading works on the Holocaust and related areas.

Several objections could be made to this division. Firstly, it is not clear how to classify some works. Butz's *The Hoax of the Twentieth Century* is lengthy and has extensive footnotes, which might indicate that it should be classed as a type-2 work. On the other hand, it has limited references to Jewish influence and Zionism which place it in type-1. Secondly, it could be argued that the type-2 works are normally published by people with clear Fascist, racist or anti-Zionist intentions. Why, therefore, separate them out from type-1 works, which often have the same publishers? A third objection concerns the fact that an absence of crude Fascism or racism in a particular test does not mean that the author has not expressed such views in other texts, especially in those not intended for widespread circulation. A common distinction in analysing contemporary Fascist propaganda concerns the differences between its public ('exoteric') and private ('esoteric') appeals. This distinction is undoubtedly relevant to many Historical Revisionists. David McCalden, for example, when wearing his public hat as Director the IHR, tried to present an academic facade (he left the IHR in 1982, mainly because of friction with its founder, Willis Carto). However, in a limited-circulation tract he referred to the sponsor of the 1988 Oxford conference on the Holocaust in the following terms: 'Typically, the wealthy [Robert] Maxwell has bought himself a Holocaust© Expert© in the form of Prof. Yehuda Bauer, who cannot make up his mind these days whether to sell his services to the *nouveau riche* Slovakian-Jewish barrow-boy Maxwell, or to the *nouveau riche* Iraqi-Jewish barrow-boy Vidal Sassoon'.[16] It is hardly necessary to be an expert in anti-Semitic stereotyping to recognise the old themes of the wandering, money-centred, scheming Jew.

However, distinguishing between two types of Holocaust denial text underlines a strategy delineated in a La Vieile Taupe samizdat circular of 1986 and seems to fit a more general Holocaust denial perspective on how to exert influence. The La Vieille Taupe tract advocated agit-prop developments for popular consumption, accompanied by a deepening of the historical and theoretical knowledge of the Holocaust for more educated audiences (this involves the classic Communist distinction between 'agitation' for the less educated and 'propaganda' for the educated, a terminology not mirrored in the West, where the term 'propaganda' tends to have more pejorative connotations). Such a division still leaves the problem of how to approach the texts. Quantitative content analysis could be used to analyse type-1 Historical Revisionism, though whether such an investigation would produce anything worth while is another matter. It seems far less suitable for the type-2 texts, which do not include the ideological framework of normal Fascist propaganda. Indeed, type-2 texts tend to read like academic history articles (the main exception is the currency of words such as 'myth', which more than hint at conspiracy theory). Thus, such an approach would not pick up the key *values* which are the focus of social science content studies of Fascist propaganda of the classic Hitler-speech type.

In the following description of Historical Revisionism, a form of qualitative content analysis is therefore used which seeks to create a general account of the major arguments. In constructing this model, it is important to note the following points. Firstly, such an approach risks sanitising the debate by making it seem more credible, and especially by underplaying the overt Fascist or racist aspects of type-1 arguments. This seems acceptable in the context of this chapter where such links are clearly stated, and where a major purpose is to seek to understand any potential appeal to educated audiences. Secondly, the order of presentation of an argument can influence its force. For example, psychologists have debated the question of whether arguments are most powerful when presented in climactic, or anti-climactic manners. The order of the following model tries to reflect what have been qualitatively judged to be the most frequently-used Holocaust-denial claims. It begins with what have become the most common assertions, and ends with less frequent arguments (though an increasing Historical Revisionist perception of the possibilities of the last argument given below, the 'scientific' one, is changing the balance). Thirdly, the model begins with a series of brief quotations which set out what the more cogent Historical Revisionists do *not* claim. They frequently state that their position is travestied by critics, and there is some truth in this. For example, the Publisher's Preface to Seidel's *The Holocaust Denial* misleadingly claims that 'Now it is being argued that Jewry emerged unharmed' from the war.[17] Another work claims that 'The Revisionist propaganda is a reiteration of the forgery ... *The Protocols of the Elders of Zion*'.[18] Holocaust-denial arguments may share conspiracy theory as the basis of their appeal, but they are not based on forgery in the sense of creating documents (though the Hitler diaries, 'discovered' in 1983, conformed very much to the Historical Revisionist view of the world).[19]

Historical Revisionists often argue that Jews ultimately benefited from the Holocaust because the 'myth' led to the establishment of Israel, reinforced group solidarity at a time of assimilation, and hindered a revival of anti-Semitism. However, they do *not* normally deny the following points (all the quotations are taken from the IHR's pamphlet *The Worldwide Growth and Impact of 'Holocaust' Revisionism*, published by the IHR in 1985 in Torrance, pp. 19–20):

> The existence of a vast network of concentration camps ... The fact that Jewish, and other, practitioners of illegal behind-the-lines partisan warfare were executed by German *Einsatzgruppen* ... And the fact that in these round-up operations *some innocent people* ... were indeed killed ... The fact that many Jews perished ... and that their casualties from all causes – including natural attrition, disease, malnutrition, bombings, military actions, pogroms conducted by indigenous Eastern European populations, *Einsatzgruppen* actions, nameless ad-hoc atrocities and general wartime havoc – numbered unquestionably in the hundreds of thousands ... The fact that some atrocities *did* occur ... None of this is denied. *What is denied is that there was a deliberate German policy of systematic extermination of Jews.*

Historical Revisionist arguments can usefully be grouped under five main headings, though there tends to be some overlap. They will not be dissected until the following section as the object, here, is to reconstruct as accurate an account as possible of the more 'academic' type of Holocaust-denial case. However, it is important to note that it is not possible completely to divorce content from technique.

1. Documentary, trial and confessional evidence

Stäglich notes that 'As a source material for historiography, documents of every kind are assigned pre-eminent rank'.[20] Much play is, therefore, made of the assertion that, in spite of the Allies capturing vast quantities of German documents, no specific order can be found in which Hitler clearly orders the killing of the Jews, or in which key aspects of the Holocaust are set out. As Harwood argues: 'It should be emphasised straight away that there is not a single document in existence which proves that the Germans intended to, or carried out, the deliberate murder of Jews.'[21] This claim holds that many of the so-called key documents which are alleged to have been part of the planning of the Holocaust are open to different interpretations. For example, at the famous Wannee conference in January 1942, which saw the gathering of leading Nazi figures involved in the 'Final Solution', no reference was made to the experimental gassings which had allegedly been carried out during the preceding year, nor to future gassings. For Historical Revisionists, this constitutes evidence that it was simply a discussion of Jewish population numbers which is seen as perfectly understandable in view of Nazi plans to resettle them in camps.

Butz, in his book *The Hoax of the Twentieth Century*, has tried to show that the language about the Holocaust to be found in documents is open to different interpretations – a line which has been followed by others. The term 'Final Solution' (*Endlösung*), it is argued, can be found in contexts where it clearly refers to emigration, or resettlement in Jewish ghettos. The phrase 'Special Treatment' (*Sonderbehandlung*), normally seen as designating those to be gassed, can also be found in reference to prominent figures, such as the French Socialist leader Léon Blum, who survived the war. In these cases, 'Special Treatment' referred to providing better accommodation or rations. This argument holds that there is a paradox between occasional highly provocative Nazi speeches about the fate of the Jews, for example Hitler's speech in the Reichstag on 30 January 1939, and the alleged euphemisms of the documents. For Historical Revisionists this poses no fundamental problem. Rhetoric was part of the Nazis' style, part of their social control. Conventional accounts of the Holocaust, it is held, need a rationale based on an Orwellian double-think: they have to hold that the Nazis in public could be viciously anti-Semitic, but in private dealt only in euphemisms.

Evidence from the post-war trials, especially Nuremberg, is particularly attacked.[22] In part, this involves an attack on the very legality of the victors trying the vanquished, for example charge number one (conspiracy to wage aggressive war) could be seen as applying to one of the judging nations, the Soviet Union, which had invaded both eastern Poland and Finland during 1939–40. More specifically, trial procedure is attacked on two counts. Firstly, much of what was admitted in evidence was not cross-checked. This is seen as hardly surprising in view not only of the presumption of guilt on the part of the accused, but also of the allegedly high percentage of Jews working for the various prosecutors. Secondly, it is argued that much testimony derived from torture, the threat of being handed over to the Russians, or the promise of leniency in return for a co-operative attitude. Thus Albert Speer, Hitler's architect, 'court' confidant, and Minister of Munitions during the war, was given the relatively light sentence of twenty years because he told the court what it wanted to hear: namely, that Hitler headed an evil empire (though he – Speer – knew nothing of the worst atrocities).

Faurisson, Roques and others have sought to prove, through internal textual criticism, that much of the court or interrogation information is worthless. Their use of the Gerstein document is a good example of this approach. Gerstein was an SS officer in charge of procuring Zyklon B crystals (which served both as a fumigator and as a source of lethal gas). He was interrogated in France at the end of the war, before committing suicide. Historical Revisionists look for internal contradictions in such testimony, or for patently ludicrous statements, for example the claim that hundreds of victims were packed into gas chambers of only a few square metres. They allege that such claims prove that the witness was simply saying what he believed his captors wanted him to say.

Finally, the controversial British historian David Irving wrote, in a letter which appeared in *The Spectator* on 25 November 1989, that the Auschwitz death books had been found in a Moscow archive. They revealed that 74,000 people had died in the camp, which he noted was 'of course, bad enough: nearly twice as many as died in the July 1943 RAF attack on Hamburg' (see below for further examples of this tendency to compare the Holocaust with Allied 'atrocities'). Irving added that his documentary research in the New York Yivo Institute revealed an order that deaths in Auschwitz should be carefully recorded; he thus argues that the documented 74,000 deaths can be treated as an accurate figure – a dramatic reduction on the accepted figure!

2. Jewish and other survivor testimony

Considerable attention is also paid to survivor testimony. It is frequently claimed that there are countless oral and written accounts about gas chambers existing in camps which are now accepted as not having been involved in the mass gassing campaign, for example Dachau or Ravensbrück.[23] 'I-too-was-there' evidence has also been used to counter claims of gas chambers. Christophersen's pamphlet *Die Auschwitz Lüge* often figures prominently because the author worked as an army agricultural researcher in Auschwitz for eleven months. Great play is made of the fact that the Allies had aerial reconnaissance shots of Auschwitz, which was a major centre of war production. None of these, it is alleged, reveals evidence to support conventional Holocaust-survivor accounts, for example there were no groups waiting for 'selections', or to enter gas chambers; there were no crematoria with constantly burning chimneys.

It is worth concentrating on a single article. It clearly impresses the Historical Revisionists as it has appeared in both the *Journal of Historical Review*, and in the *Annales d'histoire révisionniste* (though the latter has generally seemed short of substantial new material). Its author is Howard F. Stein, an Associate Professor of Psychiatry at the University of Oklahoma. The editorial of the IHR journal notes:

> Dr Stein is himself of Jewish origin, and believes that forty of his relatives died in Europe during World War Two. His focus is not so much on history as meanings. He feels that it is wrong to label the Holocaust a 'hoax' or 'lie' because the people who are propagating it actually believe in it themselves. It is this phenomenon of self-deception which he addresses in his very fine article.[24]

Or in Stein's own words:

> Whatever did happen in the Holocaust must be made to conform to the group-fantasy of what ought to have happened. For the Jews, the term 'Holocaust' does not simply denote a single catastrophic era in history, but is a grim metaphor for the meaning of Jewish history ... One is either anxiously awaiting persecution, experiencing persecution, recovering from it, or living in a period that is a temporary reprieve from it.[25]

Thus, Stein is arguing that the experiences of camp life were interpreted within a framework of a history of persecution. In camps where families were broken up, where the smells and sounds of industrial production were strong, even repellent, it was easy to imagine all forms of horror. This tendency was fuelled by the fact that some horrific acts did take place within the camps. Limited, non-systematic killings, were therefore incorporated into a collective picture of genocide because of the very nature of Jewish psychology when faced with incarceration in concentration camps.

3. Cui Bono?

A third form of argument is to pose the question: who benefits from the Holocaust 'myth'? Usually, the focus is upon the Jews and Israel.[26] Harwood claims that belief in the Holocaust was not only important in leading to the creation of Israel but, by the early 1970s, had led to £6 billion compensation being paid by West Germany. A 1988 article by Mark Weber claims that, at the end of 1987, the West Germany government gave a figure of eighty billion marks as the total sum paid in compensation.[27] More generally, belief in the Holocaust is seen as useful both in fostering Jewish solidarity and limiting the revival of anti-Semitism. Faurisson, in a samizdat circular, has attacked the film *Shoah* partly along these lines, claiming that Menachem Begin approved an allocation of $850,000 dollars towards the making of the film as it furthered Jewish national interests. The Holocaust is portrayed as a form of rite of passage; discovering the Holocaust, becoming immersed in the Holocaust, is part of the very process of becoming an adult Jew (it then continues as a way of bonding Jews together in a sense of shared past persecution and potential future threat).

The wartime Allies are also portrayed as beneficiaries of the Holocaust 'myth'. Belief in German atrocities helps deflect attention from alleged Allied war crimes, such as the fire-bombing of Dresden in the closing stages of the war, or the Soviet killing of Polish officers at Katyn. The Soviet Union, in particular, benefits because the Holocaust deflects attention from the gulags and the Stalinist terror. Indeed, the Soviet Union is often portrayed as a major factor in the creation of the Holocaust myth. It is argued that all the main alleged extermination camps are in what was to become Communist Europe. It was many years before Western observers were allowed into these camps, by which time they had been heavily rebuilt. Faurisson, for example, argues that what is now shown as the main gas chamber at Auschwitz appears on plans as a series of small rooms. Butz adds that the creation of Israel and subsequent US support for Israel has fostered the USSR's interests in the Middle East by preventing the Americans lining up fully behind anti-Communist Arab states.[28] The USSR, therefore, has a strong vested interest in keeping Holocaust memories alive.

4. Holocaust 'myths' and 'lies'

Another line of attack is to point to parallels with other myths and, especially, to attack the historiography of the Holocaust. It is often pointed out that the First World War saw a vast number of atrocity stories, including claims that the Germans boiled corpses into soap, or transfixed babies on bayonets. All the major stories later turned out to be fakes. Paradoxically, they featured prominently in First World War propaganda, whereas the Holocaust attracted little attention during the Second World War. Historical Revisionists argue that this points to the conclusion that much of the Holocaust is a post-war fabrication. It is often added that Allied intelligence services, and the Vatican, had considerable knowledge of what was happening in occupied Europe; thus, if there had been systematic genocide, these sources would have made more of it during the war.

It is noted that there are some fakes relating to the Holocaust which are even admitted by Jewish groups. Many photographs relating to the Holocaust are alleged to be faked, or presented in a misleading way.[29] Perhaps the most common charge of all, in terms of forgery, is the claim that Anne Frank's diary was clearly written after the War, a claim that has found some echo among journalists and others beyond the confines of Historical Revisionism.[30] The argument is based on the claim that parts are in ball-point pen, that the handwriting varies, and that the thoughts are beyond those of a young girl. In spite of the publication of a detailed defence of the validity of the work by a Dutch official organisation, Faurisson repeated the forgery claim in 1989.[31] However, the argument is not always featured. Butz, while clearly agreeing with the charge, argues that it is irrelevant to proof about the Holocaust as the diary refers to a period of hiding in Amsterdam. Anne Frank subsequently died in a typhoid epidemic in Bergen-Belsen.[32]

It is also frequently argued that the common images of rag-doll-emaciated dead are (when genuine) pictures of typhoid and other epidemic victims. These diseases took a heavy toll near the end of the war, when supplies of food and medicine broke down as Germany collapsed (Anne Frank died in March 1945). There were earlier major epidemics at Auschwitz and elsewhere. In these latter cases, large numbers of bodies had to be cremated quickly, or buried in pits. It is alleged that much of the Holocaust literature and, especially, imagery relate to these events. Such events, it is suggested, help explain the large number of crematoria in the camps; such crematoria were also needed simply because camps such as Auschwitz were large industrial-population centres.

Historians of the Holocaust are attacked for careless research, even deliberate distortion. Thus Faurisson, in a 1987 samizdat circular, claimed that the leading British historian Martin Gilbert had deliberately altered part of the Gerstein evidence for his book *The Holocaust*, enlarging the physical size of the gas chambers to make the evidence seem more plausible. He also claimed that Gilbert's books were full of manipulation and slipshod scholarship. For example, in *Auschwitz and the Allies* Gilbert writes that in 1942 'hundreds of thousands of Jews were being gassed every day at Belzec, Chelmno, Sobibor and Treblinka'.[33] As the hundreds of thousands is in words, not numerals, this cannot be a typographical error. The four million Jews, normally considered to have been gassed (rather than shot, etc.), therefore met their end in a month, according to Gilbert. Gilbert is a leading historian, so the fact that such an error can creep into his work is used by the Historical Revisionists to cast doubt on all historical accounts.

Historical Revisionists have put considerable efforts into trying to use population statistics to show that six million Jews cannot possibly have died. Much of this is derived from the works of French socialist Paul Rassinier, who was imprisoned in Buchenwald for resistance activities.[34] Harwood puts the argument concisely when he writes: '*The World Almanac* of 1938 gives the number of Jews in the world as 16,588,259. But after the war the *New York Times*, February 22nd 1948 placed the number of Jews in the world at a minimum of 15,600,000 and a maximum of 18,700,000'.[35] These figures are used to estimate Jewish losses, through epidemics, random killings etc., as in the hundreds of thousands.

5. 'Scientific' arguments

A final set of arguments can be grouped together under the heading 'scientific'. From his earliest writings, Faurisson tried to show the scientific impossibility of mass gassings, for example in his article 'The Mechanics of Gassing', he developed the remarkable claim that gassings, in the way alleged in Holocaust literature, were scientifically impossible. He used evidence from the gassing of single prisoners in US executions, and from the commercial use of Zyklon B. He noted that barracks which had been fumigated with Zyklon B were supposed to be left for twenty hours before special teams went to test them. In American executions, the problems of venting a single small room meant that the acidic vapours were turned into a salt, and then flushed out with water. Yet it is alleged that large gas chambers were quickly vented in camps which contained Germans as well as Jews. It is also claimed that teams, usually without masks, went into the chambers within minutes to remove bodies. A different scientific point was raised by the IHR's 1982 offer of $50,000 for evidence that a single Jew was gassed. It asked for forensic evidence – in particular, an autopsy showing that a single person had been gassed. The IHR claims that no one came forward.[36]

The controversial British right-wing historian David Irving has written: 'Unlike the writing history, chemistry is an exact science. Old fashioned historians have always conducted endless learned debates about meanings and interpretations ... Recently, however, the more daring modern historians have begun using the tools of forensic science'.[37]

Before 1988, Irving's public line accepted that Jews had been systematically killed, but he claimed this was not ordered by Hitler. His conversion to the Holocaust denial position came, allegedly, as the result of evidence compiled by an American expert in gas chamber construction, Fred Leuchter, who visited Auschwitz, Birkenau and Majdanek in early 1988. From his study of the design of the installations, Leuchter concluded that they could not have been used for mass gassings. Forensic samples taken in the gas chambers were analysed in the USA, revealing no significant traces of hydrocyanic gas, though comparison samples taken in delousing chambers for clothes revealed significant levels. This evidence was collated in a report that Irving published in 1989, a document which, he claimed, marked 'the end of the line' for the Auschwitz myth.[38] Irving clearly hoped that the report would exert an appeal even over academic audiences, for the cover states that free copies were being distributed to 'heads of the History, Chemistry, Physics and Engineering departments, the libraries and junior common rooms of every university in the United Kingdom' (though it is not clear how many, if any, were sent; certainly none appear to have arrived at Bath University).

PROPAGANDA TECHNIQUE ANALYSIS

Some books on propaganda list a small number of specific techniques which are seen as central to persuasion.[39] This approach has been rightly criticised on the grounds that there are literally thousands of verbal and non-verbal forms of persuasion.[40] Even in connection with Historical Revisionism, it is possible to delineate a substantial list of devices.

Some techniques are more common in type-1 arguments than in type-2. For example, type-1 texts tend to use a framework of keywords, repetition and stereotyping around the basic arguments. Thus, terms such as 'conspiracy', 'Zionist', 'International Capital/Capitalism' often figure prominently. *The Six Million Reconsidered* is a good example of this. Clearly, these terms, especially 'conspiracy', seek to play on anti-Semitic tendencies. They are not normally present in type-2 arguments, though it could be argued that the presence of words such as 'myth' reflects a more subtle awareness of propaganda technique. There is some evidence that educated audiences are more influenced by propaganda which allows them to make the last link for themselves. Thus, even if the often crude anti-Semitism of type-1 Historical Revisionism failed to alienate educated readers at the outset, it might lead to a lower level of retention of the basic message by too clearly stressing conclusions.[41]

This discussion raises the possibility that it might be best to analyse such texts in terms of hidden messages. One structure which has been common in much propaganda is the story of the martyr as hero. The hidden message in the Holocaust denial could read as follows: Hitler is dead, but he helped warn the world of the dangers of conniving Jews and of expansionary world Communism (stressing the anti-Communist side of Fascism is a common form of rehabilitation). This raises a fascinating area, but it moves away from directly countering the model of Historical Revisionism set up in the previous section. It is, therefore, necessary to revert to a more overt content-based analysis. Limitations on length in this chapter make it impossible to consider all overt techniques, or to counter every argument put earlier.[42] Nevertheless, four headings help to dismantle the basic technique.

1. Deception/lying

The whole of the Holocaust denial could be seen as deception, in the sense that it is hard to accept that most advocates believe the proposition that there was no systematic genocide. There is also clear lying within specific arguments. Two examples from Harwood's main pamphlet illustrate the point.[43] (a) He claims that by 1938 most Jews had left Germany, all with a 'sizeable proportion of their assets'. In fact, most Jews who were lucky enough to leave Germany lost the majority of their assets. (b) He claims that the International Committee of the Red Cross found no evidence, in its wartime visits to Germany and the occupied territories, of 'a deliberate policy to exterminate the Jews' (changed in the 1987(?) edition to 'no evidence whatsoever of "gas chambers"'). Harwood omitted to point out that the report he referred to specifically stated that there was a Nazi policy of extermination.

2. Selection/suppression

Much of type-2 Historical Revisionism avoids easily-traceable specific deception, as does the better type-1 literature. It relies more on selection, or rather suppression, as all history inevitably involves selection.

An example of suppression would be Harwood's quotation from Colin Cross's book *Adolf Hitler*. Harwood writes: 'Cross ... observes astutely that "The shuffling of millions of Jews around Europe and murdering them, in a time of desperate war emergency, was useless from any rational point of view'".[44] The clear implication is that Cross doubts the Holocaust, but reading his book shows, that, shortly afterwards, he uses this line of argument to demonstrate the fanatical anti-Semitism of the Nazis!

A more general example of suppression is a tendency to say little about the *Einsatzgruppen* period, or the euthanasia programme which helped set up the mechanics of gassing. There is also a focus on Auschwitz, which was an industrial complex of 100,000 people as well as a death camp. Little or nothing is said about other camps in Poland which had no such labour need and which operated for human destruction. Faurisson's 'scientific' discussion of gassing is particularly selective. It does not refer to the fact that Zyklon B was not the only form of gassing (carbon monoxide was also used in specially converted sealed lorry-backs, and in gas chambers). He fails to point out that the *Sonderkommando* who emptied the gas chambers were young Jews, for whom the Nazis would hardly impose rigorous safety standards. Gas chambers, with their bare walls, clearly would not retain dangerous pockets of gas as long as barracks, which he claims were left for a day before being entered after delousing. Moreover, the very fact that Zyklon B was regularly used on an extensive scale to fumigate barracks in camps shows that the venting problem in a large open space was not critical. These same points apply to Leuchter's arguments about the dangers of using gas in the camps. Other aspects of selection in the Leuchter report include his claim that Zyklon B would only be effective in warm temperatures, but that his visit revealed the chambers to be damp and cold. As the camps were unoccupied and as he visited Poland in February, the low temperature is hardly surprising; he omits to mention that central Europe in the summer is relatively hot. He also glosses over the fact that his samples were taken surreptitiously – hardly under controlled scientific conditions. Moreover, there are hypotheses which could explain why there should be higher concentrations of hydrocyanic acid in the walls of delousing chambers than in those of gas chambers: for example, the human body would absorb far more gas than clothes.

Overall, the focus of Historical Revisionism has increasingly centred on the evidence about the existence of gas chambers. Why Jews should have been in concentration camps is glossed over. Historical Revisionists sometimes point out that the British used camps during the Boer War, or that the Americans interned aliens during the Second World War. However, the Nazis' first concentration camps, such as Dachau (which was not specifically for Jews), were set up shortly after they came to power in

1933 – not during a war-emergency. Virulent anti-Semitic outpourings were a feature of the 'thought' of many Nazis, especially Hitler, well before the Second World War. It is true that there is a growing debate about the centrality of anti-Semitism to Nazism in general, but it is grossly disingenuous to portray the camps, with their concomitant degradation, torture and killings, as simply a response to the War.

3. Authority/status claims

In order to boost their arguments, academic credentials are stressed or invented. Thus: the Institute of Historical Review; its *Journal of Historical Review*; its annual conferences held in America; the Historical Review Press; the *Annales d'histoire révisionniste* – reminiscent, in its title, of the prestigious French history journal, *Annales*. The IHR managed to place an advertisement in the *London Review of Books*, and came close to placing a full-page one in *History Today*. The *Journal of Historical Review*, Winter 1980, listed seventeen members of its Editorial Advisory Board: nine were given as being current or retired academics. None were serious historians, but it is important to underline the fact that Historical Revisionism has attracted highly educated supporters.

In other cases, fraudulent academic or status credentials have been employed. The most notorious example is 'Richard Harwood', who not only used a pseudonym for *Did Six Million Really Die?*; he also found it necessary to state on the back cover that he was 'a writer and specialist in political and diplomatic aspects of the Second World War. At present he is with the University of London' (Harwood's name, and therefore this reference, is omitted from the 1987 (?) revised edition). Rassinier is frequently referred to as a 'Professor' or 'geographer'. In fact, he was an anti-Semitic writer and teacher. Harwood shows nothing if not nerve in referring to a book about Allied bombing and the post-war trials as being written by J. P. Veale, 'the distinguished English jurist' ('lawyer' in the revised edition).[45] Veale was in fact an obscure solicitor.

4. Evidence/proof

Ultimately, the key to the Holocaust-denial technique can be seen in the Historical Revisionists' concept of evidence and proof. Many of them stress that, at one point, they believed in the Holocaust but that their eyes had been opened when they looked more closely at the evidence.

Clearly, this raises the question of what is valid evidence and proof. Stäglich, a former magistrate, argues that:

> According to the time-honored principle of Roman law *in dubio pro reo*, he [the accused] must be acquitted when the facts of the case leave room for doubt, even though his innocence cannot be definitely established ... Thus the accused – the German people – are under no obligation to prove that 'gas chambers' did not exist. Rather it is up to our accusers to prove that they did.[46]

There are, unquestionably, some valid legal problems which can be raised about the Nuremberg trials and about other aspects of evidence relating to the Holocaust. However, it is important not to confuse legal and historical practice, for example hearsay, or evidence obtained under duress, may be invalid in a court of law but they are not necessarily ignored by historians. Moreover, it is important to stress that hearsay evidence or evidence obtained under duress constitute only a small part of Holocaust evidence. The knowledge that the Nazi state practised systematic genocide is based on normal historical methodology which uses as many sources as possible to reach a conclusion which is *beyond reasonable doubt*. It is not necessary that every piece of evidence be without a flaw, simply that the whole case be based on careful weighing of all the evidence. As such, it is possible to question whether the number of Jews who died was six million. Indeed, respectable writers have done so: Gerald Reitlinger gives a figure of just over four million.[47] Details of decision-making and of the process of genocide can also be questioned; again, there is a growing debate about these issues, especially whether the Holocaust was in some way inevitable. What cannot be doubted is that millions of Jews (and others) suffered appallingly, and that the Nazi state committed genocide.

The more sophisticated arguments stress the need for 'scientific' proof. There is a sleight of hand here in the sense that historical arguments cannot exhibit some features of 'paradigmatic' scientific arguments, for example repeatability. However, it is interesting to adapt the Popperian notion which holds that science can be demarcated from metaphysics because scientists are supposed to employ falsifiable conjectures. (The fact that this view of science can be criticised is irrelevant here.) The whole basis of Historical Revisionism relies on the fact that it will not accept falsification. Even when Historical Revisionism appears to conform to this Popperian notion, there is a trick. The IHR's offer of a $50,000 reward for forensic evidence seems to require just one autopsy. However, the Nazis clearly did not carry out autopsies on their own gas victims, whose bodies were subsequently cremated or burned. (Autopsies were carried out on those who died during the horrifying medical experiments inflicted on some camp inmates.) In some cases, corpses were even exhumed in order to burn them. This request for forensic evidence plays on popular images of large piles of rag-doll dead found at the time of the liberation of the camps. It is true that there were many dead in camps such as Dachau and Bergen-Belsen, but these were the victims of typhoid and maltreatment rather than of gassing. In the extremely unlikely event that an autopsy was found, the IHR would probably still manage to avoid considering this as proof. Such an autopsy could be challenged as a forgery. Even if this tactic failed, it could be argued that the person was not gassed in a mass gas chamber, but as a result of the random killings which Historical Revisionists accept did happen. Moreover, to be on the safe side, the IHR insisted that such evidence be examined by its own panel of 'experts'! Thus, even after a claimant, Mel Mermelstein, took the IHR to court over the $50,000 reward, and a judge had taken 'judicial notice' of the fact of gassings, the IHR still maintained that gassings had not been proven (the IHR claimed that the court awarded Mermelstein damages rather than the reward).[48]

More generally, the Holocaust denial relies on introducing an element of doubt into the argument, for example as some eyewitnesses may have remembered incorrectly, or even lied, it is held that all eyewitnesses cannot be believed. As there were myths of atrocities in the First World War, it is claimed that there are similar myths for the Second World War. However, as Descartes has shown, if we try to doubt everything, we find that there is nothing of which we can be certain except our own ability to doubt. Historical Revisionism relies on an unattainable conception of proof in which there is not the slightest doubt in any area.

THE APPEAL OF THE HOLOCAUST DENIAL

In view of the above discussion, the potential attraction of Historical Revisionism could be seen within two main psychological frameworks. Firstly, it appeals to those who are already Fascist or racist, or who have personality traits which lend themselves to such views. Secondly, it is especially appealing to those with a predisposition to view the world in terms of conspiracy theory. Such individuals are thus able to discount what psychologists call 'dissonance' (conflicting evidence): evidence as to the existence of the Holocaust, for instance, can be dismissed as the product of Jewish manipulation. Michael Billig has argued that 'psychological approaches to the study of conspiracy theory can basically be grouped around two themes: the study of cognitive and motivational factors'.[49] In the former case, there is a tendency to argue that the search for explanations is natural. Conspiracy theory appeals precisely because it offers a simple explanation of complex and diverse political events. In the latter case, the emphasis is more on the psychological compensations to be gained from a belief in conspiracy theory. Thus, there could be a sense of superiority which comes from believing that one knows a hidden truth; or repressed emotions could be projected onto the alleged conspirators. However, while these approaches are important, they seem better at explaining why the Holocaust denial might appeal to less rather than more educated audiences. They also ignore important non-psychological aspects of the potential appeal of such arguments.

The French sociologist Jacques Ellul has argued that education is not necessarily a defence against propaganda. Indeed, he believes that there are three reasons why educated audiences might be susceptible to propaganda: they receive large amounts of unverifiable, unsystematic information; they believe themselves capable of judging; and they tend to think that they ought to have an opinion on matters.[50] To this might be added the academic tendency to look for new arguments, to reject the 'conventional wisdom'.

Another way of considering the potential appeal involves looking at some epistemological problems in coming to terms with Historical Revisionist arguments. The difficulties can be seen most clearly by considering debates about the nature of scientific knowledge, a particularly appropriate analogy as some Historical Revisionists make great play of the scientific nature of their work. Harry Collins and Trevor Pinch have shown in their study of scientists' response to the paranormal that most reject such work outright because it does not fit existing theories. Proponents of paranormal views are usually seen as frauds.[51] There seems to be a parallel with much of the literature on Historical Revisionism, where critics have often clearly read little of what they criticise, and quickly resort to attacks on individual motivations. It could be countered that this is a grossly misleading parallel. Scientists dismiss the paranormal because it does not fit existing *theories*; the Holocaust denial is rejected because it contradicts well established *facts*. However, a final point about the sociology of science illustrates the problem of frameworks in discussing Historical Revisionism. It has become commonplace to argue that what we observe depends largely upon what we know, or rather believe we know. Much of the literature on the Holocaust has clearly been produced within a framework of what has become known as the 'Intentionalist' view of Nazi anti-Semitism. This holds that anti-Semitism was fundamental to Nazism, and the Holocaust the inevitable, or almost inevitable, consequence. Radical supporters of what has become known as the 'Functionalist' or 'Structuralist' school see anti-Semitism as little more than a rhetorical prop of Nazi agitation. The functionalist interpretation makes it more difficult to understand the Holocaust, especially when added to facts such as that some Jews were allowed to leave Germany as late as 1940.[52]

Academically, Historical Revisionism plays on the view that knowledge is ideologically structured, that the historian is not a totally impartial observer, however much he may try to follow the injunction to empathise. The editorial of the first *Annales d'histoire révisionniste*, published in 1987, specifically refers to the tradition of history, allegedly dating from Herodotus, which sees its main task as teaching lessons rather than discovering objective facts. As the early Judaeo-Christian historical tradition shared similar traits, Historical Revisionists seek to portray the history of the Holocaust as a latter-day version of the 'exemplar' rather than the Enlightenment philosophy of history. In other words, the goal is not the discovery of facts, even laws, in a neutral scientific spirit; the point is to teach morals, to defend the community's interest. The Holocaust is portrayed as a useful lesson to Jews to retain group solidarity; it is a means of combating anti-Semitism. It is important, in this context, to admit that there seem to be books on the Holocaust which have been written with the intention of stressing lessons rather than closely examining all facts (or with other non-historical motives in mind).[53] And in drawing such lessons, style, often based on emotive appeals, has sometimes transcended the demands of strict historical scholarship.

The same issue of *Annales d'histoire révisionniste* also plays on the revisionism which is inherent in all history. Lucy Dawidowicz has pointed out, that, in the case of Nazi Germany, major academic revisionism goes back to the early 1960s with the publication of A. J. P. Taylor's *The Origins of the Second World War*.[54] This viewed Hitler as a pragmatist in foreign policy, lacking a grand design. A notable contribution to late 1970s revisionism was David Irving's book *Hitler's War*.[55] This claimed that no documentary evidence could be found which showed that Hitler either ordered, or knew about the Holocaust. Himmler and the SS were portrayed as the guilty parties. Irving went on to offer a $1000 reward, through his short-lived magazine *Focal Point*, to anyone who could produce a genuine document showing that Hitler clearly had knowledge of the Holocaust. The debates in the 1980s between the 'Intentionalists' and 'Functionalists' are therefore only a part of a growing revisionism of Nazi history. The drift of this has been to challenge the totalitarian model of the 1950s with its emphasis on features such as the dominant leader purveying a clearly defined ideology.

Historical Revisionists in the late 1980s took particular comfort from aspects of the bitter *Historikerstreit* debate in West Germany.[56] This began with an attempt by the historian Ernst Nolte to 'relativise' the Holocaust, but soon spread to question central aspects of the 'conventional' wisdom on Nazi Germany. He claimed that the Holocaust was only one of many examples of terror and genocide in world history. Moreover, Nolte saw it as a reaction to fear born of the Russian revolution, and the ensuing terror and gulags. More specifically, he claimed that the World Zionist Organization had, in effect, declared war on Nazi Germany, and this gave grounds to treat Jews as prisoners of war! This argument is especially interesting for the questions it raises about the nature of history. For example, while Nolte does raise some important questions in comparative history, he seems motivated by a clear desire to rehabilitate aspects of Germany's past. At least, this seems the most charitable explanation of views such as his claim that there existed a Jewish declaration of war on Germany: how could diverse peoples, with no state, yet alone army, 'declare war'?

The French historian Pierre Vidal-Naquet has written in relation to Historical Revisionism that 'to deny history is not to revise it'.[57] This glosses over the fact that it is not always easy to provide a neat philosophical definition of what is history and what is propaganda. In some ways, the distinction is one of intention: the historian should seek to provide as objective an account as possible; the propagandist seeks to serve an ulterior political motive. The vast majority of Historical Revisionist writings have a clear political motive, usually anti-Semitic and/ or neo-Fascist. However, the distinction between history and propaganda cannot simply be one of intention. There are many works, which are usually seen as history, where there is a clear, overt, or at least implicit, political position; for example, are not most Western accounts of Fascism written from the perspective of the superiority of liberal democratic systems? And if intention is the sole key to propaganda, how should we view the writings of an Historical Revisionist who actually believed what he or she wrote?

Propaganda has, therefore, also to be understood in terms of the nature of the arguments. One such approach would be to claim that propaganda teaches us *what* to think, rather than *how* to think.[58] The distinction opens up fruitful avenues for further thought, but fails fully to resolve the problem in the sense that much history surely tells us what to think. A more helpful one-liner is the view that propaganda serves to *narrow* thought, whereas history serves to *broaden* it. The legitimate historiography of the Holocaust raises a vast number of questions. These include detailed questions about the procurement of transport for the Jews. It encompasses more general questions about the Nazi regime, for instance whether the system was truly totalitarian, or whether it was more chaotic and fragmented than has generally been assumed. Holocaust historiography even raises sweeping issues, such as the question of human nature, or the concept of progress. On the other hand, Historical Revisionism concentrates on a small number of issues and, on many of these, it is misleading, downright wrong, even dishonest. Historical Revisionism ignores vast amounts of evidence which contradict its position. As such, it is hardly likely to influence the central views of the professional historian or serious student of the Holocaust. Unfortunately, the history of propaganda indicates that the 'big lie' or the repetition of a small number of points, can, all too easily influence the views of the less well informed. It is, ultimately, for this reason that the central arguments and the propaganda technique of the Historical Revisionists are worthy of an essay in specific analysis and refutation.

NOTES

1. Measuring popular anti-Semitic attitudes is notoriously difficult. For brief surveys of such material, see the journal *Patterns of Prejudice,* 1966 – .
2. Various subsequent German editions. French edition, FANE, Paris, 1976. Reference to 100,000 copies distributed, in T. Christophersen, *Auschwitz*, Liberty Bell Publications, Reedy, W. Va., 1979. See also, Christophersen's journal *Kritik, die Stimme des Volkes*, e.g. No. 51, 1980.
3. English edition, *The Auschwitz Myth*, Institute for Historical Review,Torrance Ca., 1986. Quotations in the text are from this edition. French edition, La Vieille Taupe, Paris, 1986.
4. For a clarification of Chomsky's position, which was more a defence of free speech, see his interview in *Le Monde*, 24 Dec. 1980, p. 10.
5. See esp. M. Bardèche, *Nuremberg ou la terre promise*, Les Sept Couleurs, Paris, 1948; *Nuremberg II ou les faux-monnayeurs*, Les Sept Couleurs, Paris, 1950. German edition, K. H. Priester, Wiesbaden, 1957.
6. Various subsequent editions in several languages. Also published as *Six Million Lost and Found*, and republished with minor changes in 1987(?). These rely

heavily on the anonymous (D. L. Hoggan?) booklet *The Myth of the Six Million*, Noontide Press, Los Angeles, 1969.

7. The magazine *Searchlight* has regularly published evidence as to these links.

8. P. Guillaume, 'L'abominable vénalité de la presse', *Annales d'histoire révisionniste*, No. 7, spring–summer 1989, pp. 11–12.

9. C. Wilson, 'The Fuehrer in Perspective', *Books and Bookmen*, Nov. 1974, p. 31.

10. For example, see *Ouest France*, 1 and 2–3 Aug. 1986, p. 6.

11. See G. Wellers, 'A propos d'une thèse de doctorat "explosive" sur le "Rapport Gerstein"', *Le monde juif*, Jan.–March. 1986, pp. 1–18. See also H. Roques, 'De l'affaire Gerstein à l'affaire Roques', *Annales d'histoire révisionniste*, No. 3, autumn–winter 1987, pp. 103–25.

12. See S. J. Roth, 'Making the Denial of the Holocaust a Crime in Law', *IJA Research Reports*, March 1982, pp. 1–12.

13. For example, see J. Aitken (pseud. R. Faurisson), *Epilogue judiciaire de l'affaire Faurisson*, La Vieille Taupe, Paris, 1983.

14. For example, M. Billig, *Fascists,* Harcourt Brace Jovanovich, London, 1978.

15. Freedom can be understood within Lockean or Kantian perspectives, or in terms of 'negative' and 'positive' freedom. Fascism was an enemy of freedom in the Lockean sense (where it is seen as an external relation, e.g. between a man and the state). However, it could be argued that Fascism was not necessarily an enemy of freedom in the Kantian sense (where it could be conceived more in terms of self-realisation; thus a man could be in gaol, but free).

16. *David McCalden Newsletter*, No. 64, Jan.–Feb. 1987, p. 8.

17. G. Seidel, *The Holocaust Denial,* cit., p. viii.

18. Anne Frank Stichting, *The Extreme Right*, Anne Frank Stichting, Amsterdam, 1985, p. 18.

19. See 'Judgement on the Hitler Diaries', *Patterns of Prejudice*, Vol. 17, July 1983, pp. 26–9.

20. Stäglich, *The Auschwitz Myth* cit., p. 16.

21. Harwood, *Did Six Million* cit. p. 8.

22. For example, R. Harwood, *Nuremberg and other War Crimes Trials*, Historical Review Press, Ladbroke, 1978; Stäglich, *The Auschwitz Myth* cit.

23. For example, R. Faurisson, *Réponse à Pierre Vidal-Naquet*, La Vieille Taupe, Paris, 1982, pp. 26–8; S. Thion, *Vérité historique ou vérité politique?*, La Vieille Taupe, Paris, 1980, pp. 25 ff.

24. *The Journal of Historical Review*, No. 1, Winter 1980, p. 296.

25. H. F. Stein, 'The Holocaust, and the Myth of the Past as History', *The Journal of Historical Review*, No. 1, winter 1980, p. 310.

26. For example, C. E. Weber, *The 'Holocaust', 120 Questions and Answers*, Historical Review Press, Torrance, CA., 1983, pp. 8 ff.

27. Harwood, *Did Six Million*, cit., p. 2; M. Weber, '"Holocauste": réparations versées par l'Allemagne de l'Ouest', *Annales d'histoire révisionniste*, No. 6, Winter 1988/9, p. 51.

28. Butz, *The Hoax of the Twentieth Century* cit., esp p. 6.
29. For example, U. Walendy, 'The Fake Photograph Problem', *The Journal of Historical Review*, No. 1, Spring 1980, pp. 59–67.
30. E.g. *Sunday Times*, 30 Nov. 1980, p. 15.
31. R. Faurisson, 'Les écritures d'Anne Frank', *Annales d'histoire révisionniste*, No. 7, Spring-Summer 1989, pp. 45–50.
32. Butz, *The Hoax of the Twentieth Century*, cit., p. 37.
33. M. Gilbert, *Auschwitz and the Allies*, Michael Joseph, London 1981, p. 26.
34. The best example of Rassinier's work in English is the compilation *Debunking the Genocide Myth*, Noontide Press, Torrance, CA, 1978. Among the best examples of his work in French are: *Le mensonge d'Ulysse*, Editions Bressanes, Paris, 1950. Italian edition, La Rune, Milan, 1966. Reissued, La Vieille Taupe, Paris, *1979. Le drame des juifs européens*, Les Sept Couleurs, Paris, 1964. German edition, Pfeiffer, Hanover, 1964. Reissued, La Vieille Taupe, Paris, 1985.
35. Harwood, *Did Six Million* cit., pp. 6–7.
36. Institute for Historical Review, *The Worldwide Growth*, cit., pp. 1 ff.
37. D. Irving, 'Foreword' to *The Leuchter Report*, Focal Point, London, 1989, p. 6.
38. *The Leuchter Report*, cit., *passim*.
39. For example, J. A. C. Brown, *Techniques of Persuasion*, Penguin Books, Harmondsworth, 1963.
40. For example, G. N. Gordon, *Persuasion: the Theory and Practice of Manipulative Communication*, Communication Arts Books, New York, 1971.
41. For example, C. I. Hovland *et al.*, *Communication and Persuasion*, Yale University Press, New Haven, 1953.
42. This chapter, therefore, avoids detailed reference to historical sources on the Holocaust.
43. Harwood, *Did Six Million,* cit., pp. 3, 24–5.
44. Ibid., p. 20.
45. Ibid., p. 9. Veale used the pseudonym 'Jurist' when he published. *Advance to Barbarism*, Thompson and Smith, London, 1948. This, and its sequel, *Crimes Discreetly Veiled*, first published in 1958 by Cooper Book Company, London, were republished in 1979 by the IHR.
46. Stäglich, *Auschwitz Myth,* cit., p. 16.
47. G. Reitlinger, *The Final Solution*, Sphere Books, London, 1971.
48. Institute for Historical Review, cit., pp. 3–12.
49. M. Billig, 'The Extreme Right: Continuities in anti-Semitic Conspiracy Theory in post-war Europe', in R. Eatwell and N. O'Sullivan (eds), *The Nature of the Right,* Pinter, London, 1989, p. 159.
50. J. Ellul, *Propaganda*, Vintage Books, New York, 1973.
51. H. M. Collins and T. J. Pinch, 'The Construction of the Paranormal', in R. Wallis, (ed.), *On the Margins of Science*, University of Keele Press, Keele, 1978.
52. See J. P. Fox, 'The Final Solution: Intended or Contingent?', *Patterns of*

Prejudice, Vol. 18, July 1984, pp. 27–39.

53. For example, M. Gray, *For those I Have Loved*, Bodley Head, London, 1973.

54. L. S. Dawidowicz, 'Lies about the Holocaust', *Commentary*, Vol. 70, June 1980, p. 31.

55. D. Irving, *Hitler's War*, Hodder and Stoughton, London, 1977.

56. On these debates, see R. Evans, *In Hitler's Shadow: West Germany's Historians and the Attempt to Escape from the Nazi Past,* Tauris, London, 1989.

57. P. Vidal-Naquet, *Les assassins de la mémoire*, Maspéro – La Découverte, Paris, 1987, p. 150.

58. Brown, *Techniques of Persuasion* (cit.), p. 21.

The author would like to thank the editors of this book and James Darragh for comments on an earlier draft.

CHAPTER SEVEN

The Extreme Right in Spain: a Dying Species?

Sheelagh Ellwood

In 1985, the European Parliament set up a Committee of Enquiry into the rise of Fascism and racism in Europe. Two members of the Committee visited Spain to collect material for their research. They were surprised (and disturbed) to find that the related phenomena of racism and Fascism seemed to arouse little interest among Spaniards.[1] Both Spain's recent history and her future objectives seemed to be at variance with such indifference. Only ten years earlier, Spain had emerged from forty years under the autocratic, anti-democratic rule of general Franco, whose regime had once been the ally of Hitler and Mussolini and was known to have sheltered the erstwhile followers of these dictators. It was difficult, too, to understand how Spaniards could assume that the reappearance of Fascism in Europe had no implications for them at a time when their country aspired to be an integral part of Europe and, indeed, was then on the verge of becoming a member of the EEC. In the following pages, we shall look at some possible explanations for these apparent paradoxes. We shall also try to answer a question which springs inevitably from them: is there a solid basis for the optimistic assessment Spaniards implicitly make of their country, as being a Fascist-free zone? In order to broach these questions about today's Spain, we must first look briefly at the origins of the extreme right there, in the first third of the present century.

The roots of the rabid nationalism, ultra-authoritarian attitudes and disdain for parliamentary democracy as a political system which characterise the Spanish extreme right today go back to the collapse of the Spanish empire in the latter part of the nineteenth century. Later, in the 1920s and, especially, in the 1930s, the feelings of resentment and fear harboured by the middle classes against what they saw as, on the one hand, an inefficient political class and, on the other, the threat of an increasingly

147

organised and vocal working class, began to crystallise into political movements which claimed to defend conservative interests against both liberalism and Communism. At a time when Fascism was rapidly gaining ground elsewhere in Europe, similar movements made their debut in Spain. What was ultimately to be the longest-lasting of the Spanish fascist organisations, Spanish Phalanx (*Falange Española*, FE), was created in 1933, the year that Adolf Hitler became Chancellor in Germany. Unlike its German and Italian counterparts, however, FE remained a minority organisation. Its numbers were increased and its social base broadened slightly in early 1934, when it joined forces with another Fascist group, the Committees for National Syndicalist Attack [*Juntas de Ofensiva Nacional-Sindicalista*, JONS], but the new party, the Spanish Phalanx of Committees for National Syndicalist Attack [*Falange Española de las JONS*, FE de las JONS] was still unable to attract a nationwide, mass following.

When a military coup was staged in July 1936 to oust the legitimately elected government of the day, FE de las JONS joined the insurgents. For the duration of the Civil War to which that coup led, the party backed its political commitment to the anti-democratic cause with men, women, arms and propaganda. I have examined elsewhere the role of FE de las JONS during the Spanish Civil War.[2] For the purposes of the present discussion, the importance of the War lay in the fact that it enabled the party to pass from being a political nonentity to occupying a position of state power as a source of ideological legitimation and structural organisation for the military régime born in and from the war. On 19 April 1937, the leader of the insurgent armies and self-styled head of the Spanish State, general Francisco Franco, issued a decree which amalgamated all the rightist political organisations supporting the military enterprise. Franco himself assumed the leadership of the new party, which was called Spanish Traditionalist Phalanx of Committees for National Syndicalist Attack [*Falange Española Tradicionalista y de las Juntas de Ofensiva Nacional-Sindicalista*, FET y de las JONS].[3] This unwieldy title indicated that it was the extreme, rather than the moderate, brand of rightism which was to provide the organisational and ideological framework of the Franco régime.

Because the ideological bases and political structures of Francoism remained unchanged throughout the 39 years that the Franco régime lasted, this hybrid, quasi-single party survived, formally intact, to the end. In social, economic and cultural terms, however, Spain changed a great deal in the course of those years and when Franco died, on 20 November 1975, barely six months elapsed before a Law of Political Associations was introduced which set the stage for dismantling the single party and legalising a democratic, pluralist, political system. In fact, behind the official facade of FET y de las JONS, only the Traditionalist and Falangist sectors of the old party retained the ideological positions and physical existence they had had prior to April 1937. The other parties had disappeared as organised groups and their Catholic conservatism had been transformed by their ideological heirs into positions sufficiently progressive to cause their advocates to be referred to as the Franco régime's 'tolerated opposition'. By the time the Law of Political Associations was passed, in June 1976, Traditionalism was largely confined to the northern province of Navarre and to Seville, in the south, whither its followers had withdrawn to winter quarters in 1939, on realising that Franco's victory in the Civil War was not going to bring a monarchical restoration in the person of their Pretender.

As for the *Falange*, a tendency to internal fragmentation inherent in the per-Civil War party had re-emerged after Franco's death and, by 1976, there were four rightist groups each laying claim to the original title, *Falange Española de las JONS*. These were the Spanish National Front [*Frente Nacional Español*, FNE]. Authentic Spanish Phalanx [*Falange Española (auténtica)*, FE(a)], the National Syndicalist Co-ordinating Committee [*Junta Coordinadora Nacional Sindicalista, JCNS*] and a group without a name, made up of notoriously violent right-wingers whose leader was the chief of another extremist group, the Warriors of Christ the King (*Guerrilleros de Cristo Rey*). Each claimed to be the direct descendant of the party founded in 1933 and accused the others of having 'betrayed' the original doctrine by their collaboration with the Franco régime.

The question of which group might legitimately call itself *Falange Española de las JONS* was finally resolved in October 1976, by the assignation of the title to the FNE. In fact, it mattered very little what these groups called themselves, for their style and their discourse were the same as they had been forty years earlier and everyone recognised them as remnants of an anti-democratic past. They still wore the navy blue shirt and yoke-and-arrows symbol adopted by the *Falange* as its uniform in 1933; they still sang the Falangist anthem, 'Face to the Sun' (*Cara al sol*); and they still rejected traditional rightist anathema, such as Basque and Catalan nationalism or Marxism. Indeed, in 1977, during the campaign for the first democratic elections since 1936 – in which the Falangists participated despite their openly admitted contempt for parliamentary democracy – they based their appeal on the idea that their tenets were as valid in the 1970s as they had been in the 1930s, on the grounds that they had not been applied, simply usurped, by the Franco régime.

This ingenious argument found little response in the Spanish electorate.

Taken as a whole, the extreme right polled less than 1 per cent of the total number of votes cast on 15 June 1977.[4] Its nearest rival, the conservative Popular Alliance [*Alianza Popular*, AP] obtained 8.21 per cent of the vote, while the Spanish Socialist Workers Party [*Partido Socialista Obrero Español*, PSOE] accounted for 29.21 per cent and the winning centre-right coalition, Democratic Centrist Union [*Unión de Centro Democrático*, UCD], took 34.74 per cent.[5] Between them, FE(a), and two of the groups which had participated in the JCNS, Independent Spanish Phalanx [*Falange Española (independiente)*, FE(i)] and the José Antonio Doctrinal Circles [*Círculos Doctrinales José Antonio*], polled 40,359 votes.[6] The main extreme rightist group, the '18 July' National Alliance [*Alianza nacional '18 de julio'*], having adopted a line which defended, rather than reneged on, the Francoist heritage, received 64,558 votes, which represented 0.36 per cent of the total.[7] Not one of the extreme rightist candidates was elected to either of the two parliamentary chambers. These results made it abundantly clear that, whether or not it presented the defence of Franco's memory as part of its programme, the extreme right had no appeal for a majority of people who identified with the idea of a modern, democratic, Europeanist future, not with ideologies which they associated with a repressive and outmoded past.

The results of fresh general elections, held two years later, in March 1979, appear, at first sight to belie this statement, for while the Socialist, Communist and centrist parties each made only slight advances, the extreme right increased its poll from 0.6 to 2.2 per cent of the total vote. In the wake of the 1977 débâcle, the *Círculos Doctrinales* had joined forces with FE de las JONS as National Union [*Union Nacional*, UN], which polled 379,463 votes, or 2.1 per cent of the total.[8] Blas Piñar López, leader of the third group integrated in the National Union, New Force [*Fuerza Nueva*, FN], was elected for Madrid. In fact, these results did not reflect a real shift to the right so much as a 'settling down' of the electoral panorama after the 'novelty' of the 1977 poll. Many of the dozens of tiny groups which had put up candidates in 1977 did not run again in 1979 and regional parties played a role in 1979 which they had not played in 1977. Most significantly, the conservative vote went down in 1979 by 2 per cent on the 1977 figure. Very probably, the votes gained in 1979 by UN (274,546) came largely from the 500,000 lost by AP.[9]

That conservatism in general and extreme conservatism in particular had few supporters in post-Franco Spain was shown by two key – and not unrelated – events which occurred in the 1980s: an attempted *coup d'état*, in February 1981, and a socialist victory at the polls, in October 1982.

Form the point of view of the present discussion, it was not the coup itself, but its failure and, particularly, popular reaction to it that were important. It is very difficult to say whether there was any civilian involvement in what appeared to be an operation organised and executed solely by officers from the army and the para-military police force, the Civil Guard. No civilian connections emerged in the subsequent trial, beyond the minor role played by a former employee of the Francoist trade union system, notorious for his ultra-rightist political views, Juan García Carrés.[10] Without concrete evidence, it would be equally difficult to estimate how much socio-political support the coup would have had if it had been successful. However, the reaction of the majority of the armed forces, of the political parties and of the Spanish people suggested that such support would have been minimal. An enormous demonstration, held in the centre of Madrid (and in other cities all over Spain) on the night of 27 February, three days after the coup had been definitively aborted, showed that, in general, people actively wanted peace and democracy.

In the light of the very real sense of danger generated by those events, and of the strong emotional response they provoked, it is easy to understand that, when general elections were held in October 1982, there was a massive swing towards the Socialist Party as an emphatic gesture of dissatisfaction with the internal squabbles of the governing centrist coalition and of dissaffection from everything associated with a return to the past. The PSOE landslide did not reflect a conscious *ideological* choice on the part of the majority of the electorate, so much as a deeply felt desire for *change*, as newness – new faces, new ideas, new policies. And that was what the PSOE promised, with its electoral slogan 'Socialism is freedom. For change'.

The total discredit of the old order was clearly reflected not only in the results of the October 1982 election, but also in those of the June 1986 poll. In 1982, the largest of the extreme right-wing groups, the coalition UN, polled a mere 100,899 votes in the whole of Spain.[11] In the light of this result, its leading candidate, Blas Piñar, announced the dissolution of his own party, New Force, on 20 November 1982, the seventh anniversary of Franco's death. A few months later, in February 1983, the veteran right-winger and former Francoist Minister, Raimundo Fernández Cuesta, announced his resignation as president of FE de las JONS . In spite of the UN's poor showing in 1982, FE de las JONS presented candidates on its own ticket when the next elections were held, in June 1986. As in 1977, 1979 and 1982, the 1986 electoral platform of FE de las JONS was based on the alleged validity of the original, 1930s

Falangist concepts. Their result — 32,663 votes, or 0.16 per cent of the total — was consistent with the 40,000-vote ceiling registered by *Falange* purist options in previous years.[12]

At this point, it is possible to answer two of the questions raised at the beginning of the present chapter: why did Spaniards feel uninvolved with respect to the possible existence of neo-Fascism in the Spain of the 1980s and why were they so uninterested in the problem of its growth in Europe? The answer to the first part of that question was that no one was interested in the extreme right, because it scarcely existed; and it scarcely existed, because no one was interested. In a situation of free, political competition and at a time when both the popular mood and the historical moment were overwhelmingly in favour of democracy, reactionary, anti-democratic options attracted only minimal electoral support from a die-hard minority of urban, middle-class voters fearful of the 'chaos' Francoism had taught them democracy would bring and hostile to any change which might endanger social and economic privileges acquired during the Franco régime. On account of its organisational and electoral weakness, the extreme right was not perceived even as a *potential* threat to the new, democratic order.

With respect to Europe, where, by contrast, neo-Fascism clearly did exist, there were two main reasons for Spanish unconcern. First, forty years of Francoist isolationism had contributed to a lasting feeling that what went on beyond the Pyrenees had nothing to do with Spaniards. Secondly, and partly as a result of this, the fact that the autochthonous breed of Fascism appeared to be a thing of the past made people think that, whatever was happening elsewhere, it couldn't happen in Spain and, therefore, there was no need to take any notice of it.

We come, now, to the third of our initial questions: is it correct to assume that Fascism in Spain is a dying species? If we consider electoral results as 'solid' evidence and, in the case of post-Francoist Spain, there is no reason to doubt their reliability, then the immediate answer is, as we have seen, that there *is* some basis for that assumption. However, the fact that people did not *vote* for the extreme right's candidates does not of itself necessarily imply its disappearance as a socio-political force, not least because electoral statistics tell only part of the story. They do not, for example, tell us anything about the rightist groups which did not participate in electoral contests.

It is difficult to give an accurate and detailed account of the extra-parliamentary right in terms of the social composition, size, internal structure or economic resources of its components. In the first place, reliable, verifiable data are not available from published sources.[13] In the second, the fact that the extreme right is not averse to the use of physical violence against those to whom it takes a dislike leads one to be wary of carrying out one's own, first-hand research. Nevertheless, on the basis of the few sources which are accessible and of personal observation in Spain, and bearing the methodological difficulties in mind, it is possible to sketch an outline of what these groups are and how they operate.

The first thing to note is their tendency to extreme fragmentation: in 1984, it was estimated that as many as 400 groups existed throughout the country.[14] Occasionally, they appear to have a certain capacity for organising propaganda campaigns. Such is the case of the Spanish Committees [Juntas Españolas, JJ.EE.], centred in Madrid; or Spanish Statement [Afirmación Española, AE], said to be run by a Spanish publisher (Alberto Vasallo de Number) and to have some thirty high-ranking army officers among its members.[15] More typically, however, ultra-rightist groups in Spain are little more than tiny nuclei of adolescents. They have little material or organisational infrastructure and few activities other than spraying graffiti on walls, shouting abuse in front of cinemas showing films they disapprove of, and participating in decreasingly attended demonstrations on Francoism's commemorative dates. Their message is essentially backward-looking. For some, the central figure is Franco; for others it is the founder of *Falange*, José Antonio Primo de Rivera or one of the other pre-war Falangist leaders. For all, the external paraphernalia, the lexicon, the iconography and the ideological content are culled from the 1930s, regardless of the fact that the Falangist yoke and arrows painted on walls, the protests against 'reds' and 'masons', the blue shirts and roman saluting seem anachronistic in post-Francoist Spain. Indeed, the impression these groups give is that the Spanish extreme right is ahistorical.

In addition to these small groups, there are also a series of larger nuclei, for which the smaller ones can, of course, always serve as a recruiting ground.

The organisation which shared with FE the title of the Francoist party, the Traditionalist Communion [Comunión Tradicionalista, CT], cannot, strictly speaking, be considered fascist, on account of its monarchical principles, its profound Catholicism, and its non-revolutionary character. Nevertheless, its extreme conservatism, rabid anti-Marxist, anti-democratic postures and corporativist economic ideas make it eligible for inclusion on the extreme right of the political spectrum. Towards the end of the 1960s, and after a series of internal schisms, CT split into a progressive sector of a social-democratic nature, and an ultra-conservative sector. The latter has proven connections with Italian and Latin-American extreme rightist organisations and has, on occasions, used violence against the social-democratic sector. It participated in the 1977 elections as part of the '18 July' National Alliance, but has not taken an active part in contempoary politics since then.

Until its dissolution in 1982, the paragdigmatic ultra-right group was New Force, differentiated from FE de las JONS by the former's greater readiness to use physical violence as a political instrument, by its more overtly Catholic integrist nature, and by its tendency to invoke Franco, as well as Primo de Rivera, as its hero-figures. FE de las JONS stalwarts often accused New Force of making illegitimate use of the Falangist blue shirt, while New Force considered the Falangists, at best, as 'softies' and, at worst, as undercover leftists.

The leader of New Force, Blas Piñar, is the only person on the extreme right who could be classified as a charismatic leader. By profession a solicitor, Piñar has always cultivated the suave elegance of the aristocratic Primo de Rivera, usually besuited and with the slicked-down hair characteristic of the FE de las JONS founder, although, at close quarters, Piñar in fact bears a closer resemblance to the 1950s leader of Argentinian *justicialismo*, Juan Domingo Perón, than to Primo de Rivera. Like both of them, Piñar's capacity for impassioned haranguing totally commands the awe and the fervour of his devotees. One of the latter wrote of him in 1977:

> Gentlemen, we must take our hats off to Blas Piñar. Always consistent, faithful and loyal to the same ideas, immaculate in his political practice ... That's why he attracts masses of young people and fills the People with enthusiasm ... Blas Piñar has never sucked off the teat of the previous régime[16] ... He unmasks the sanctimonious Christian Democrats, lashes the reds with his tongue and stands up to all the Francoists who are traitors to Franco.[17]

Even so, Piñar is not given to making outrageously provocative public statements in the style of the French extremist, Jean-Marie Le Pen.

Yet Piñar has never been able to act as a rallying point for the whole of the extreme right. The reasons may well be historical, rather than ideological. In spite of his strong personal connections with the Castilian city of Toledo, where he was born in 1918, Piñar was not in the habit of attending the annual ceremony to mark the anniversary of the time when, during the Spanish Civil War, Francoist troops entered Republican-held Toledo and rescued the remains of a contingent of anti-Republicans who had been besieged in the city's fortress (the *Alcazar*) for two months.

Piñar's presence at the fiftieth anniversary commemoration, in September 1986, caused considerable irritation among the 'regulars' who, it need scarcely be said, could not be suspected of left-wing sympathies.[18] Surprisingly, too, given the importance attached by the extreme right to the Civil War, Piñar has never used his past to legitimate his position as a political leader. On the contrary, he prefers to elude references to the past. The reason is clear, though rarely stated: on the day of the anti-Republican rising, 18 July 1936, Piñar was in Madrid. However, he did not return to Toledo (where his father was shortly to be among the besieged defenders of the *Alcazar*), nor did he enlist as a rebel volunteer. Instead, young Blas took refuge, first, in the Finnish, then, later, in the Panamanian legations, remaining in the latter until the end of the war in 1939.[19] This was hardly a convincing start for an aspiring *caudillo*. Seriously handicapped in the eyes of his extreme rightist clientele by his lack of a good Civil War curriculum, Piñar distracts attention from the shortcomings of the content of his claim to political authority by carefully orchestrated attention to its form. His catastrophist arguments and the vehemence of their delivery are designed to secure the kind of irrational, unquestioning allegiance commanded by such oratorial marathon-runners as Hitler, Mussolini, Castro or Stalin.

New Force always maintained good relations with South American and European rightist groups. Chilean and Argentinian *ultras* were frequently to be seen at its meetings, and the Italian group *Ordine Nuovo*, was a regular attender at New Force's annual rally, on 20 November, the anniversary of Franco's death. It has been suggested, too, that, in spite of being disbanded in 1982, New Force continued to receive financial support from foreign sources.[20] Certainly, the group continued to maintain, as its meeting place, two adjacent flats in the centre of Madrid and to publish a fortnightly magazine, also entitled *Fuerza Nueva*.

On a much smaller and more 'discreet' scale than New Force is a group which, though not explicitly a political organisation, indoctrinates its members with extreme rightist ideas and organises them as para-military commandos against the day when their 'Security Corps shall be a great army ...' after the style of 'the guards of imperial Rome or the army of Napoleon'.[21] Registered as a cultural organisation, New Acropolis [*Nueva Acrópolis*] is known to be a Naziphile organisation whose central offices are in Brussels and which has branches in 34 countries. In Spain, it was reported in 1985 as being active in 27 of the country's 52 provinces and as having about 1,000 members, most of whom were below the age of 30.[22]

Much closer to European neo-Fascism in both style and ideology than any of the groups mentioned so far is the group Spanish Circle of Friends of Europe [*Círculo Español de Amigos de Europa*, CEDADE]. Originally founded in West Germany in 1965, by a group of German, Italian and Spanish fascists, CEDADE was established in Barcelona in 1966 as 'an entity of Europeanist character, which would act as the spokesman for the sentiments of Spanish youth'.[23] In 1973, a branch was opened in Madrid. Between them, these two cities account for about 1,000 of the 2,500 members CEDADE was reported to have in Spain in 1985.[24] With Spain as the centre of its operations, CEDADE has created subsidiaries in various Latin-American countries, in France and in Portugal.

CEDADE takes its ideological inspiration directly from German National Socialism, and is differentiated from other Spanish rightist groups by its less insistently Falangist character, its overt anti-semitism and its Europeanist stance, which sees European unity as a cultural and racial issue, rather than a political or an economic one. CEDADE has organised a number of summer camps and congresses in Spain, although its proposed Congress of European Youth, planned for 1974, was ultimately prohibited. In recent years, CEDADE has not been very visible in terms of public meetings, proselytising campaigns, press statements or other newsworthy activities. Nevertheless, the group maintains and office in the centre of Madrid and has a stand at the large book-fair held annually in Madrid, offering mostly Nazi literature and music cassettes. It also publishes a magazine – *CEDADE* – and is capable of organising *ad hoc* propaganda campaigns. When Spain formally resumed diplomatic relations with Israel in 1986, CEDADE pasted up anti-Jewish posters and when the news of Rudolf Hess's death was announced in August 1987, CEDADE instantly papered Madrid and Barcelona with propaganda in his favour. These four activities, together with the relatively high quality of the design, paper and printing of the group's propaganda indicate an economic capacity superior to that of all the other groups, with the exception of New Force.

A French magazine, *Article 31*, wrote of CEDADE in 1985: 'The public activities of CEDADE are almost certainly no more than the visible tip of the iceberg. Does CEDADE serve as a co-ordinating and documentation centre for European Nazi movements? What logistic support might it have provided for "black" terrorism?'[25]

Those questions might equally be asked of all extreme right-wing groups in Spain. The answers are fragmentary and the evidence often circumstantial. Nevertheless, in recent years there have been numerous reports in the Spanish press of links between individuals known to militate in, or to sympathise with, Spanish ultra-rightist groups and international terrorist networks. The Bologna station massacre of 1980, for example, and the Milan–Naples train explosion of 1984, are alleged by Italian legal authorities to have been prepared in Spain, with Spanish explosives, by members of the Italian rightist organisations *Ordine Nuovo*, *Avanguardia Nazionale* and *Movimento Sociale Italiano*, operating from Madrid, Barcelona and the south coast, and in collaboration with a Spanish group called International Revolutionary Action Groups [*Grupos Revolucionarios de Acción Internacional*, GRAI].[26] Similarly, right-wing extremists wanted for terrorist actions in Italy are known to live, or to have lived, in Spain and are often suspected of having taken part in other terrorist actions there. Carlo Cicuttini, resident in Spain from 1972 onwards and responsible for the organisation of *Ordine Nuovo* outside Italy, is alleged to be implicated in the massacre of five left-wing lawyers in Madrid in January 1977.[27] He and Giuseppe Calzona, resident in Spain since 1974 and implicated in the murder of an Italian Communist (Alfio Oddo) in Monza, are reputed to be confidants of the Spanish police and to have taken part in operations against the Basque separatist organisation, ETA, in collaboration with two Spanish counter-terrorist organisations, the Spanish Basque Battalion [*Batallón Vasco-Español*, BVE] and the Anti-terrorist Liberation Groups [*Grupos Anti-terroristas de Liberación*, GAL], in turn said to be linked to Spanish police intelligence services. Elio Massagrande, founder member of *Ordine Nuovo* was arrested in March 1977, on the discover of an illegal arms factory in the centre of Madrid. Others involved were *Avanguardia Nazionale* terrorist, Stefano delle Chiaie, and the leader of the Spanish *Guerrilleros de Cristo Rey*, Mariano Sanchez Covisa.[28]

A more outlandish and, in some ways, more unnerving manifestation of right-wing extremism was the revelation, in May 1986, of meetings between a Spanish Army officer, colonel Carlos de Meer, and the Libyan leader, colonel Gaddafi. De Meer was president of a clandestine group formed in the summer of 1985, called the Coordinating Committee of National Forces [*Junta Coordinadora de Fuerzas Nacionales*], composed of 19 autonomous rightist groups. De Meer evidently travelled to Tripoli in January 1986, to negotiate Libyan financing to the tune of some £4.5 million, for the creation of a new right-wing party.[29] What, at first sight, appears to be a case of strange bed-fellows makes more sense when we remember that De Meer's activities coincided with a period in which the situation in the western Mediterranean had become extremely tense on account of the deterioration in relations between the US and Libya. This, together with Gaddafi's declaration, on 11 April 1986, that all cities in southern Europe might be considered military targets, and the presence of several US military bases on Spanish soil, perhaps led the Coordinating

Committee of National Forces to believe that its members and the Libyans could become fellow-travellers for purposes of subverting the existing order on Europe's south-western flank. Certainly, indications exist of Arab assistance for extreme rightist groups in Europe. In this connection, the implications of Spain's geographical proximity to North Africa, and the potential utility of having willing collaborators in Spain, are self-evident.

Disturbing though such activities are to anyone with democratic sensitivities, they are, nevertheless, beyond the bounds of legality and judicial mechanisms exist to pursue and suppress them. Society is not entirely defenceless against them. Thus, the Madrid arms factory was dismantled, De Meer was arrested and expulsion orders were issued against some of the Italian *ultras*.[30] Neo-Fascism is far more dangerous when it operates within the bounds of legality, for then democracy can find itself threatened by its own belief in the right of all law-abiding citizens freely to express their opinions. It is difficult to say whether or not this was taken into consideration by the Spanish extreme right. The fact remains, however, that when, in the autumn of 1986, New Force reappeared, it did so with the express intention of playing the parliamentary system according to the system's own rules.

After disbanding as an aggressively anti-liberal, anti-democratic party in 1982, New Force went to ground by converting itself into a 'study centre', the Centre for Social, Political and Economic Studies [*Centro de Estudios Sociales, Políticos y Económicos*, CESPE], with little or no external projection. When it re-emerged, four years later, it had adopted a new, more respectable look, abandoning the rabidly anti-European stance which, until then, had always been one of the hallmarks of the extreme right in Spain. It had also adopted a new name – National Front [*Frente Nacional, FN*] – which gave it immediately recognisable connotations of similar groups in other European countries. Indeed, at the constitutional meeting of the new party, Blas Piñar was accompanied by the (then) secretary general of the Italian MSI, Giorgio Almirante, and by a delegate from the French *Front National*, Jean-Marc Brissaud.[31]

The idea of returning to the political arena arose in May 1986. In June of that year, as a result of another conservative defeat at the polls, the decision was taken to create the National Front.[32] An open-air rally in July provided an insight into what were to be the party's composition and aims. The event constituted an almost surreal meeting of old and new waters. To begin with, the date chosen – 18 July – was also that of the 50th anniversary of the rising which initiated the Spanish Civil War. Most of the old paraphernalia was still present, too: the blue shirts, the New

Force badges, Spanish flags with Franco's crest on them, stalls selling cassettes of right-wing favourites and bronze busts of Franco. Even so, the two young men in full Falangist regalia were in an anomalous minority, and when a group of spectators tried to sing the Falangist anthem, they were rapidly silenced by the rest of the audience. The most significant change, however, was that the speakers, although as impassioned as ever, no longer harped on the Francoist past so much as on an ultra-Catholic future.[33]

When, on 1 March 1987, the new party held its first congress as such, its president, Piñar, spoke of the need to construct 'the Europe of Christianity' as a means to entering 'an epoch of prosperity and development'. In ethical terms, he said, this meant the rejection of 'abortion, euthanasia, and the corruption of youth', and the promotion of 'the institution of marriage' and the family. Politically, it meant unity between the countries of southern Europe, to protect themselves from the 'destruction of [their] economy to the benefit of that of the countries of northern Europe', and the 'recuperation' of 'absent Europe' – the countries of the Communist bloc.[34]

In spite of giving the crisis of 'liberal conservatism' as one of the motives for creating *Frente Nacional*, Piñar was emphatic in his rejection of the notion that his party would 'pull the chestnuts out of the fire' for Spanish conservatism.[35] As if to underline this, he announced that the National Front would not participate in the next domestic elections – local and regional government elections, set for June 1987 – but would only put up candidates for the elections to the European Parliament, also to be held in June 1987.

Behind the apparent paradox of a National Front which deliberately eschewed participation in domestic politics, lay two hard realities, which Piñar undoubtedly included in his calculations. In the first place, as the party's own electoral track record showed and the crumbling state of AP confirmed, the right in Spain was on a serious down-swing. In an electoral system based on proportional representation, the National Front stood very little chance of success in domestic elections. The elections for Strasbourg, by contrast, would be fought on the basis of a single, nation-wide constituency. This maximised its chances of amassing sufficient votes to obtain at least one Euro-MP. The second factor was that election to the European Parliament would not only provide the moral, political and strategic advantages of having an important international platform from which to broadcast the National Front ideology, it would also mean reception of European parliamentary funds. In so far as it would be part of the extreme-rightist parliamentary group formed by French, Italian and

Greek members, the Spanish National Front would be eligible for a share of the monies available to all groups. An ironic situation indeed: the temple of European democracy financing groups committed to the destruction of democracy itself.

The closing event of the National Front's electoral campaign, on 8 June 1987, was attended by Jean-Marie Le Pen and Nino Tripodi, president of the *Movimento Sociale Italiano*. Their interest in Piñar's candidacy was not simply one of ideological solidarity. The precarious existence of the European Right parliamentary group would be shored up if Piñar were elected, since it would thereby increase its three-country representation (the minimal requirement to form a parliamentary group in Strasbourg) to four. In the event, the National Front obtained only 123,000 votes in the whole of Spain and, consequently, Piñar was not elected.[36]

Did this mean, then, that the threat of neo-Fascism had been definitively routed in Spain? Certainly, the conditions which had favoured the growth of Fascism in industrialised, Western-European countries in the past were not present in Spain in the 1980s. For example, there was no racial or religious element, readily utilisable as a scapegoat 'explanation' for massive unemployment. Parts of the Spanish economy were undeniably in crisis, following the recession which affected the whole of Spain's economy in the 1970s. These, however, were mostly in the primary sector, such as mining, shipbuilding, or steel-making. By contrast, the secondary and tertiary sectors were well on the way to recovery by the second half of the 1980s, and it was these which employed the middle classes to whom the extreme right has traditionally directed its appeal.

Politically, too, the erstwhile clientèle of the extreme right did not feel itself threatened by the left as it had done in the 1930s. On the contrary, the anarchist left was a very marginal force, and the Communist left, though experiencing a resurgence of popular support from 1986 onwards, still lagged far behind the PSOE in terms of parliamentary seats and access to power. For its part, the PSOE had abandoned its explicitly Marxist positions for reformist centrism, while the conservative right was also intent upon presenting itself as a centre-rightist option. An observation made by Stuart Woolf with regard to 'traditional' Fascism seems relevant in this respect: 'Where no Bolshevik threat existed, it was difficult for a Fascist movement to act as a rallying-point of reaction, for the space had already been occupied by the politically powerful and socially respectable forces of the right.'[37]

Against this background, the situation of the extreme right in the 1980s was similar to what it had been in the first half of the 1930s: it was destined to remain marginal as long as the classes with most economic and political influence retained confidence in the ability of the parliamentary system to protect their interests by maintaining the existing political status quo. Unlike the majority of its extreme-rightist brethren, the National Front understood the changes which had occurred from 1982 onwards, and updated its analysis of the contemporary political and economic situation accordingly. Speaking in 1986 of what he termed the 'Fabian socialism [now] in power' in Spain, Blas Piñar said:

> I don't think Communism is the great threat to Spain ... Today, there is no conflict between Fabian socialism and means-of-exchange capitalism (money). On the contrary, socialism is the great political instrument of money and money capitalism offers all its enormous strength ... Money supports the installation of Fabian socialism in the countries of the west.[38]

Recognising the futility of 1930s-style revolutionary appeals (e.g. to nationalise the banking system) at a time when the centres of economic, financial and military power were satisfied with the policies of the Socialist government, the extreme right in Spain no longer tried to compete with the 'politically powerful and socially respectable forces', so much as to ride on their coat-tails. In this light, it becomes comprehensible that the veteran Falangist and close friend of Piñar, José Antonio Girón, should publicly pass favourable judgement on the leaders of the PSOE,[39] while Blas Piñar preferred the consolidation of his international image to lambasting the government of the day at home.[40]

Towards the end of the 1980s, the stagnation of Le Pen's appeal in France, and the death of Almirante in Italy had a dampening effect on the hitherto buoyant spirits of the National Front, which was not offset by the triumph of the neo-Nazi Republican Party in the West Berlin regional elections of January 1989. The elections to the European Parliament held in June 1989 dealt a further blow to extreme right-wing hopes of revival in Spain. While the German *Republikaner* gained six seats in Strasbourg and the French *Front National* held on to its existing ten seats, their Spanish comrades not only failed, as in 1987, to secure any seats, but also lost ground in terms of the number of votes they received. The *Frente Nacional* polled 59,783 votes – 63,016 less than two years earlier, while *Falange Española de las JONS* collected a mere 23,500 votes, which was 500 fewer than in 1987. In the light of this trend, the *Frente Nacional* did not put up any candidates for the general elections held four months later, on 29 October. FE de las JONS candidates did stand, but polled less than 50,000 votes. Had *Frente National* run, *Falange's* share of the poll would have been even smaller.

Surprisingly, perhaps, given the continual decline in electoral support for the extreme right, these disastrous results did not lead to the disbanding of its political organisations. They did, however, have the effect of sharpening the tactical divisions between those groups which explicitly rejected democratic parliamentarianism, and those which were prepared to participate in the electoral system. In addition, the 1989 election acted as a catalyst for a change of style in the latter.

A certain revival of illegal extreme rightist organisations was already visible in the universities in 1988.[41] This was subsequently reported to have spread to secondary schools and sporting venues.[42] Its principal exponent is an organisation called the Autonomous Grass-roots Groups [*Bases Autónomas*], whose *modus operandi* is direct confrontation with legality. The objective of this strategy, which members refer to as 'Basist chaos', is to create an atmosphere of destabilisation, in which an accumulation of small-scale violence aims to erode public confidence in the capacity of the institutions of the democratic parliamentary system to maintain order and stability.

At the legal end of the extreme rightist spectrum, CEDADE, the National Front and the JJ.EE. came to realise that clinging to people and posture associated with the pre-democratic past consistently undermined their objective of exercising some influence over contemporary political events. In a process similar to that undertaken by the conservative right in 1988-89, these groups shunted their original leaders – respectively, Mota, Piñar and Gómez Rovira – into the wings and effective control was taken over by young, executive-type men whose main concerns were efficient internal management and electoral success, rather than ideological purity and the cult of a charismatic leader.[43]

Time will tell whether this change of style will enable the extreme right to attract a larger following than it has achieved hereto. Considered only in national terms, the extreme right in Spain does not currently possess the strength to overthrow democracy. Today, however, neo-Fascism must be viewed as an international phenomenon, whose significance lies in its capacity to undermine the principle of democratic coexistence, rather than in its practice in any given geographical area. Its tactics – from within and without – are those of interconnecting sapper commandos, which do not require a complex infrastructure or a mass following. As we have seen, there are many such groups in Spain, some of them fully attuned to the international networks in which money, arms and influence circulate. It may be that, within the frontiers of Spain, there is no immediate cause for alarm. Spain, however, as successive post-Francoist governments have not tired of reiterating, is in Europe; and in Europe, there can never be room for complacency.

LIST OF ABBREVIATIONS

AE	*Afirmación Española* [Spanish Statement]
AP	*Alianza Popular* [People's Alliance]
BVE	*Batallón Vasco-Español* [Spanish Basque Battalion]
CEDADE	*Círculo Español de Amigos de Europa* [Spanish Circle of Friends of Europe]
CESPE	*Centro de Estudios Sociales, Políticos y Económicos* [Centre for Social, Political and Economic Studies]
CT	*Comunión Tradicionalista* [Traditionalist Communion]
FE	*Falange Española* [Spanish Phalanx]
FE(a)	*Falange Española (auténtica)* [Authentic Spanish Phalanx]
FE de las JONS	*Falange Española de las Juntas de Ofensiva Nacional-Sindicalista* [Spanish Phalanx of Committees for National Syndicalist Attack]
FE(i)	*Falange Española (independiente)* [Independent Spanish Phalanx]
FET y de las JONS	*Falange Española Tradicionalista y de las Juntas de Ofensiva Nacional-Sindicalista* [Traditionalist Spanish Phalanx of Committees for National Syndicalist Attack]
FN	*Frente Nacional* [National Front]
FN	*Fuerza Nueva* [New force]
FNE	*Frente Nacional Español* [Spanish National Front]
GAL	*Grupos Anti-terroristas de Liberación* [Anti-terrorist Liberation Groups]
GRAI	*Grupos Revolucionarios de Acción Internacional* [International Revolutionary Action Groups]
JCNS	*Junta Coordinadora Nacional Sindicalista* [National Syndicalist Coordinating Committee]

JJ.EE.	*Juntas Españolas* [Spanish Committees]
JONS	*Juntas de Ofensiva Nacional-Sindicalista* [Committees for National Syndicalist Attack]
PAN	*Partido de Acción Nacional* [National Action Party]
PCE	*Partido Comunista de España* [Spanish Communist Party]
PP	*Partido Popular* [People's Party]
PSOE	*Partido Socialista Obrero Español* [Spanish Socialist Workers Party]
UCD	*Unión de Centro Democratico* [Democratic Centrist Union]
UGT	*Union General de Trabajadores* [General Workers' Union]
UN	*Unión Nacional* [National Union]

Notes

1. Personal Conversation in Madrid, April 1985, with Geoffrey Harris and Glyn Ford, members of the European Parliamentary Committee of Enquiry into the Rise of Fascism and Racism in Europe.
2. S. Ellwood, 'Falange Española, 1933-1939: fom Fascism to Francoism', in R. M. Blinkhorn (ed.) *Spain in Conflict*, Sage Publications, London, 1986, pp. 206-23
3. The word 'Traditionalist' came from the title of the second-largest para-military force in the Francoist camp, the Traditionalist Communion [*Comunión Tradicionalista*, CT]. Politically, it was a monarchical organisation dating from the nineteenth century, that supported the cause of a branch of the Bourbon royal family which contested the legitimacy of the reigning branch's claim to the Spanish throne.
4. J. J. Linz, 'Il sistema politico spagnolo', *Rivista italiana di scienza politica*, III, 1978, p. 372, Various Authors, *Historia de la transición*, Diario 16, Madrid, 1984, vol. II, p. 466.
5. *Historia* cit., p. 466.
6. *Informaciones*, Madrid, 18 June 1977.
7. *Historia* cit.; Linz, *Rivista Italiana* cit., p. 372, gives 0.21 per cent. The '18 July' National Alliance was a coalition of the following rightist groups: New Force [*Fuerza Nueva*, FN], FE de las JONS, CT, Confederation of Combatants [*Confederación de Combatientes*], and National Action Party [*Partido de Acción Nacional*, PAN].
8. *El País*, 3 March 1979, pp. 10-13, and 21 Nov. 1982, pp. 18. J. Rodríguez Aramberri, in F. Claudin (ed.), ¿ *Crisis en los partidos politicos?*,

Dedalo, Madrid, 1980, p. 130; *Historia,* cit., p. 580.

9. *Historia,* cit., p. 580.

10. In July 1980, García Carrés participated with lieutenant colonels Tejero and Más Oliver in a meeting at which the idea of a *coup d'état* was mooted. At a further meeting of Army officers, in January 1981, Garcia Carrés was asked, as a civilian, to leave. He was ultimately sentenced to two years for 'conspiracy to military rebellion'. Juan García Carrés died in 1986.

11. *El País,* 21 Nov. 1982.

12. Author's computation, from data in *El País,* 23 and 24 June 1986.

13. The mouthpiece of the extreme right, *El Alcazar,* resuscitated as a weekly paper in 1987, after almost a year in abeyance as a daily. It devoted itself almost exclusively to acid criticism of current social and political events. Rightist publishing houses, such as DYRSA or *Fuerza Nueva,* tend to publish historiographical material such as memoirs or accounts of the Spanish Civil War, or works on the theory of Fascism, but not accounts of the composition and activities of present-day groups.

14. *Tiempo,* 26 Nov. 1984, p. 34

15. *Tiempo,* 3 Nov. 1986, p. 32

16. In spite of the fact that Piñar had held a number of official posts during the Franco régime, such as National Councillor of the Movement, National Councillor for Education and Director of the Institute of Hispanic Culture.

17. A. Royuela, *Diccionario de la ultra derecha,* Dopesa, Barcelona, 1977, pp. 15-16.

18. Personal observation, Toledo, Sept. 1986.

19. Anon. 'Vida de Don Blas', *Cuadernos para el diálogo,* 26 March 1977, pp. 21-22

20. *Tiempo,* 26 Nov. 1984, p. 31

21. From the *Nueva Acrópolis* "Leader's Manual", quoted in *Tiempo,* 13 May 1985, p. 40

22. *Ibid.*

23. J. Mota, *Hacia un socialismo europeo,* Ediciones Bau, Barcelona, 1974, back cover.

24. 'La Cedade', *Article 31,* VII, 1985, p. 14

25. Ibid.

26. *Tiempo,* 13 May 1985, p. 10

27. Ibid. Members of New Force were subsequently tried as the active perpetrators of the Jan. 1977 "Atocha massacre"; see *Diario 16,* 15 March 1977, pp. 16-17

28. *Tiempo,* 13 May 1985, p. 12

29. *Tiempo,* 3 Nov. 1986, p. 32

30. *Diario 16,* 10 June 1987, p. 10

31. *El País,* 27 Oct. 1986, p. 18

32. Blas Piñar, in *Diario 16,* 3 March 1987, p. 12

33. Personal observation at the *Frente Nacional/Fuerza Nueva* rally in El Escorial (Madrid), on 18 July 1986.

34. *Diario 16,* and 2 March 1987, p. 7

35. Personal observation at the *Frente Nacional/Fuerza Nueva* rally in El Escorial, on 18 July 1986.

36. *Diario 16*, 11 June 1987. The party spokesman, Luis Villamea, immediately issued accusations of fraudulent dealings at the polls and threatened to take the matter up with the European Parliament, for, he said, 'in Madrid alone we have more than 40,000 voters'. In fact, the official figure was absolutely consistent with successive electoral results for the extreme right since 1977, with the exception of 1979, discussed above.

37. S. J. Woolf, Introduction to S. J. Woolf (ed.), *Fascism in Europe*, Methuen, London, 1981, p. 7.

38. Blas Piñar, personal interview, Madrid, 17 October, 1986.

39. In an interview published in *Interviú*, 29 July 1987, pp. 16-19 Girón said of President González that he is 'a man who is full of good intentions, who always tries to resolve problems by the most agreeable means. He seems fairly moderate.' Likewise, PSOE vice-secretary general, Alfonso Guerra, was considered by Girón to be 'an alert and agile man, who has to play the villain of the piece, which doesn't mean he *is* a villain'.

40. See, e.g., the report of Piñar's guest-of-honour appearance at the 'Red, White and Blue Festival', organised by the French *Front National* at Le Bourget in Aug. 1987, in *Fuerza Nueva*, No. 945, 12-26 Sept. 1987, pp. 12-15

41. *Cambio 16*, No. 898, 13 Feb. 1989, p. 42-45

42. *El País*, 11 Dec. 1989, p. 20

43. *El País*, 10 Dec. 1989, p. 15

CHAPTER EIGHT

The Radical Right in Contemporary Portugal*

António Costa Pinto

The neo-Fascist manifestations which have recurred periodically in European countries since 1945 have had no Portuguese equivalent as yet. For anyone supporting a restricted definition of Fascism and hence of neo-Fascism, it would hardly make sense to discuss this theme in Portugal. The concept of radical right is therefore to be preferred since it enables us to cover a wider spectrum closer to the reality investigated.[1] If we deal only with the emergence of neo-Fascism, we would be confined to the tiny groups and intellectual circles, set up in the early 1960s. These found no expression in the political spectrum either under the New State [*Estado Novo*, EN] created by Salazar in the 1930s, or under the democratic regime.

In investigating the Portuguese case, it is therefore important not to lose sight of the different realities covered by those two concepts. This is all the more necessary since the debate about the political nature of Salazar's regime is far from closed. In addition, some specific characteristics differentiated that regime from its European counterparts in the inter-war years. This fact had important consequences for the legacy left to the democratic regime after 1974.

The second point refers to chronology. On 25 April 1974, a military coup, which rapidly turned into a revolutionary process, ensured the transition towards, and later the consolidation of, a democratic regime, and the irreversible fall of the EN. Both Iberian dictatorships had survived the demise of European Fascism, and 1945 had not caused any significant break in the nature of either. Yet the downfall of the Axis caused some changes in the political system and a rapid downgrading of some institutions associated with Fascism. This was probably more true of Portugal than of Spain, and it was the starting point for the emergence of a minority located to the right of the EN, which, from then on, called itself an 'organic democracy'.

Until Salazar's political death in 1968, neo-Fascism and some nuclei of the radical right in Portugal defined themselves as a trend aimed at purifying the regime. The figure of the leader was always spared. With the advent of the dictator's successor, Marcello Caetano, who supported various reformist attempts in the last years of the authoritarian regime, some trends emerged which demarcated themselves from the new political power. They were the origin of the radical right groupings which were active in Portugal after the transition to a democratic regime. Hence their genesis from 1945, still under the EN, must be covered in a brief introduction.

THE LEGACY OF THE 'ESTADO NOVO'

A populist radical right has not been part of Portuguese political culture in the twentieth century. There were political movements similar to *Action Française* at the beginning of the century, but the elitism of their ideology was hard to combine with a populist strategy for political action. Though present in the ideological field, they never went beyond an elitist type of intervention.[2] The very short dictatorship of Sidonio Pais (1918) might have brought about such a constitution. However, the regime which imposed itself in the wake of a military dictatorship (1926) − Salazar's EN − always resisted that temptation.

There may be legitimate doubts about the relationships of causality between the ups and downs of radical right movements in contemporary Europe, and the historical Fascisms of the inter-war period. Yet it remains true that one of their legacies to post-war democratic regimes is an embryonic neo-Fascism. Even in countries where native Fascism only shared power thanks to enemy occupation, as in France, the more or less episodic emergence of this type of movement has remained a constant. Italy provides a clear example of this, while in Germany it was only an antagonistic electoral system which blocked its rapid reappearance after the Second World War. It was not so in Portugal.

Unlike other regimes of the 'Fascist period', Salazar's did not leave to posterity, after its fall, the symbols, organisation, ideology and human support capable of feeding a neo-Fascist party. One component of Francoism was a native Fascism which ultimately acknowledged him as head of the movement. In post-authoritarian Spain a neo-phalangism was possible, though it remained marginal. In Portugal it was impossible to introduce a neo-Fascist practice based on the abolished regime.

Though it shared some features and underwent the influence of Fascism, the EN differed from it in a number of basic aspects. Historically, it emerged from a military dictatorship, introduced in 1926 after a coup which abolished a liberal republic. It was not based on a Fascist-type party (which did not exist during the crisis and the downfall of liberalism).[3] The single party of the regime – the National Union [*União Nacional*, UN] – was created in 1930, from above and through a decisive intervention of the state apparatus. The corporative institutions, inspired by Italian Fascism, were tempered by the 'Social Catholicism' from which the dictator originated. In practice they were mere appendages of the state machinery, without life of their own or autonomy. Furthermore, the regime – unlike its Fascist counterparts – did not rely on the intense political mobilisation of the population.

It was at the height of the military dictatorship, when Salazar was emerging as a major candidate for the post of Prime Minister, that a Fascist party, the National Syndicalism [*Nacional Sindicalismo*, NS], headed by Rolão Preto, was set up. There was a leadership contest and the NS was repressed, indeed outlawed, in 1934. The following year, an attempted coup against Salazar resulted in the exile and persecution of its leaders.[4] The single party was also created to oppose this native Fascism. It was, in addition, intended to provide representation in a parliament which met infrequently, merely to ratify the decisions of the executive. It sank into lethargy until the end of the Second World War.[5]

The threat represented by the Second Spanish Republic and the start of the Civil War in that neighbouring country induced a shift towards Fascism in the regime. Salazar allowed the formation of the Portuguese Legion [*Legião Portuguesa*, LP], which sent volunteers to fight beside Franco, as well as a paramilitary organisation, Portuguese Youth [*Mocidade Portuguesa*, MP]. Both provided a Fascist political backing to the regime in the second half of the 1930s, but they remained under the strict domination of the state. MP was under the direct rule of the Ministry of Education and the LP was controlled by the army. There was no linkage with the party which was merely an institution of the regime, without any effective powers.[6]

Anticipating a new international situation after the defeat of Fascism, the regime prepared a cover-up operation in 1944. The single party was resurrected to ensure a 'certain victory' in the general and presidential elections, in which the opposition was allowed to participate. It took advantage of those brief interludes to denounce the dictatorial nature of the regime, until its fall in 1974.[7]

In the post-war period, the EN came to define itself as an 'organic democracy' and endeavoured, without too much difficulty, to conceal the outward signs of its association with Fascism. The paramilitary organisations, the MP in particular, acquired a more 'former-student' and 'sporting' character. The *Secretariado de Propaganda Nacional* (Secretariat for National Propaganda), entrusted with organising mass demonstrations throughout the 1930s, and led by António Ferro, an intellectual extrovert and admirer of Mussolini, changed name and leader. It acquired a more anodyne image as a promoter of 'tourism and information'. The LP, downgraded since 1939, when Franco won the Spanish Civil War, vanished from the streets and went into terminal decline.

In the unfavourable international climate of 1945, Salazar was able to secure the survival of his regime. This he owed to his neutrality during the war, to his military concessions to Britain and the United States, and to the rapid onset of the cold war, which gained him the recognition of the new international community (Portugal joined the UN and NATO, at the end of the decade[8]). However, changes at the level of institutions and of decision-making machinery proved very limited. There were no basic changes in 1945, as far as the authoritarian nature of the regime was concerned. It was only when Salazar was replaced by Marcello Caetano, in 1968, that a series of reforms took place, and that part of the political elite associated with the old dictator was removed.

Some of the characteristics which demarcated the EN from European Fascism may account for the fragility of the Portuguese radical right on the eve of the regime's fall.[9] The main one, no doubt, was the minimal autonomy of party institutions in relation to the state. One author rightly concluded that 'the truth about the way Portugal was governed from 1930 to 1974 was (that it was) an administrative state'.[10] Apart from administration, the little that existed disintegrated over time, if only for lack of functions, as the regime – once established – did not attempt any extensive or intensive political mobilisation. Political militancy was weak and participation in the single party or the paramilitary organisations remained limited since, from the inter-war period, but more explicitly after 1945, the regime promoted depoliticisation. Salazar never sponsored any ideological or mobilising organisation, even when confronted with a colonial war in the early 1960s.[11]

One of the subtlest ideologists of Portuguese neo-Fascism, writing in the short exile to which he was forced by the transition to democracy, wrote that Salazar was, in spite of everything, a sceptic about the potential of others. He was not a Fascist, but a reactionary and, as Drieu taught, they are polar opposites. He did not believe in popular energies, in the permanent revolution, in that collective sense of national mystique, perhaps manufactured by propaganda, but possibly the great moving-force of peoples. Salazar preferred the force of circumstance, of common sense, of routine.[12]

This statement anticipated how difficult it would be to find in the collapsed regime an ideological and political basis for neo-Fascist practice. However, until 1974, the figure of the Leader was never challenged.

The first properly neo-Fascist nucleus, demarcated from the native radical right entrenched in some institutions such as the old LP or the official press, was founded in 1959, around the review *Tempo Presente*.[13] It was a group of young intellectuals who, faced with the ideological and political decrepitude of the regime, and in the wake of presidential elections in which an opposition candidate (one General Humberto Delgado, with a governmental background and a military man to boot), achieved considerable popularity, sought to revive the 'Fascist' wing of the regime.

Though of marginal importance, politically, this group started the intellectual revival of the Portuguese radical right. The neo-Fascism to which they gave foundations and substance developed through the 1960s. The start of the colonial war gave them some governmental support. It also gave them a 'political struggle' with which they wanted to mobilise the energies needed to preserve the empire, threatened by African liberation movements. They started various university nuclei, such as the Young Portugal movement [*Movimento Jovem Portugal*, MJP], the Front of Nationalistic Students [*Frente de Estudantes Nacionalistas*, FEN], and the National Revolutionary Front [*Frente Nacional Revolucionária*, FNR].

Tempo Presente linked itself explicitly with Fascism, that 'unforgettable revelation of our youth'.[14] Contrary to the domestic and defensive radical right, this group embraced modern aesthetic values. It sought to deprive opposition intellectuals of their overwhelming monopoly in the intellectual field.[15]

The main political themes of the review revolved round a critique of the 'enemies within'. The main one, the real *bête noire* of the 1960s was the Catholic world, in which youth organizations and groups of intellectuals were beginning to break away from the dominant orthodoxy.[16] This movement, which was later legitimised by Vatican II, gave rise to a Catholic Opposition centre. A second theme focused on the 'technocrats', associated with the moderate economic boom of the 1960s. They were accused of lacking any ideological scruples and of defending European options incompatible with a multi-continental Empire. These accusations became sharper when the old dictator was replaced, and the sector associated with the Empire lost important positions within the state machinery.

The beginning of the colonial war in 1961, and its extension to several fronts in later years, provided the small neo-Fascist group with a leitmotif. It also ensured the support of various institutions, worried by the growth and the politicisation of the student movement, which was the main target of conscription. However, in this last struggle of the regime, Salazar − consistent with the total distrust he had always shown since the 1930s − did not rely on any large-scale mobilisation or 'refascistisation'. Once the control of the armed forces had been secured, by purging them of waverers, the war was hardly mentioned by the media, except for rare 'confrontations' with 'terrorists' from outside. This applied until the situation deteriorated dramatically in the early 1970s. For the neo-Fascists, 'it was a war without heroes or rather one in which heroes were hidden or concealed', without any encouragement of 'the cult of those who were fighting.'[17]

As for the political organisations proper, they were always very limited and exclusively linked with the student milieu, in which they had the secret support of the Ministry of Education, the political police and the old LP. Their appearance was nearly always merely part of a counter-propaganda strategy used by official bodies since 1945, when opposition organisations began to engage in semi-legal activities. Such was the case of the Patriotic Academic Front [*Frente Académica Patriética*, FAP] which was active in the late 1940s, but served merely as a mouthpiece for government propaganda.[18]

The previously mentioned Young Portugal Movement, founded in 1961, enjoyed more autonomy.[19] Its leaders wished to create a party which would conform to the organisational ideal type of the 1930s. They even managed to contact the old N S leaders to show their loyalty to the old principles of intransigent Fascism. In the meantime, some of them had moved a long way away and allied themselves to the 'democratic opposition', as was the case of Rolão Preto.[20] The MJP would be succeeded by the National Revolutionary Front [*Frente Nacional Revolucionária*, FNR] in 1966.[21]

Defining itself as a movement of young students and workers, the FNR did not hesitate to criticise the thirty dangerous years in which the regime itself promoted the 'apoliticisation of youth', with results which were all too obvious, as mobilisation for a colonial war coincided with the ageing of the ruling elite.[22]

In the ideological sphere, this group endeavoured to blend the European neo-Fascist themes of the 1960s with an updated version of National Syndicalist principles, defined as the Movement's official doctrine.[23] From the 1930s emerged the Fascist heroes, such as the Romanian Codreanu and the Spanish José António, from the 1960s Maurice Bardèche, Blas Piñar, and the whole international panoply of the most virulent, dogmatic and 'revolutionary' sector of European neo-Fascism. In France, as groups proliferated on the far-right, contacts with Pierre Sido's *Jeune Nation* movement were made.[24] In Italy this happened with the more radical faction of the *Movimento Sociale Italiano*, the splinter group *Ordine Nuovo*.[25]

Created as the university students' movement became more politicised, after the academic crisis of 1962, the MJP had a brief existence. Its main leaders were called up to serve in the colonial war. In 1964, the FEN which has already been mentioned, was created to fill the space thus vacated. The following year it became known by taking part, together with the LP, in the attack on the Portuguese Writers' Association.[26] A less clandestine existence was led by the FNR, which was based in the universities of Lisbon and Coimbra, where it organised meetings and action against the student movement.[27] More atuned to the ideological renewal of the French group *Europe-Action* of whom Zarco Moniz Ferreira was the correspondent in Portugal, the FNR appeared more future-oriented, and no longer considered NS as its official ideology.[28] This is not an exhaust-ive list of Portuguese neo-Fascist groups in existence until 1974. The model adopted, however, was that of the study-group, linked with universities, rather than the political party.[29]

Although it often shared the same editorial and thematic space with young neo-Fascism, the indigenous radical right was associated with a different generation and with ideological and cultural references much more closely related to traditional Portuguese anti-liberalism. Its programme expressed the resistance of a cultural and political universe which had been in decline since 1945. It was against the world of the United Nations, 'born with its back turned to God' as a strange alliance between 'American plutocratic utilitarianism and the militant atheism of communism'.[30] Its political expression did not extend beyond the publica-tion of reviews such as *Agora* and *Resistência*.[31]

In the editorial team of *Agora*, in its early phase, reappear old names of the 1930s, mainly the National Syndicalists who accepted Salazarism.[32] Its journalistic activity was limited to saying what diplomatic caution prevented the mainstream press from being open about. Catholic dogmatism, anti-cosmopolitanism and nationalist isolationism against a 'world in chaos': these central values of the Salazarist universe were asserted against the 'enemies within' and the pernicious influence of fashions from outside. The performer Cecilia Meireles, who 'sings what the people sing no longer', was contrasted positively with the Beatles[33] and the poet António Sardinha with Arthur Miller, the 'communist Jew', or Sartre, 'wrongdoer of literature and homosexual'.[34] On the eve of the dictator's removal, *Agora*, in a special issue on Fascism, published statements by representatives of various generations who had kept the ideological flame of the radical right burning during the long authoritarian regime. Nevertheless, all of them were politically marginal in relation to Salazarism.[35]

The removal of Salazar in 1968 and the coming to power of Marcello Caetano did not provide a favourable ground for the continued support or the benevolent neutrality of official bodies. Supported or covertly tolerated in the last years of Salazarism, the neo-Fascist nuclei foresaw the difficult problem of succession in a dictatorship bound up with the charismatic figure of its leader. Salazar, always respected, was secretly accused of lacking firmness, but any queries about his successor elicited a reply which announced problems: 'After him, nobody.'[36]

It was under the reformist experiment of Salazar's successor that both the radical right and the neo-Fascists openly distanced themselves from the authoritarian political power, sought alternative leaders, and even called for coup attempts.

As the single party was reorganised under *Marcelismo*, as the Liberalising sectors acquired an autonomous organisation, as censorship eased and as some opposition figures began to return home, the radical right dissociated itself from the leadership of the regime. It became known by public opinion, with its own spokesmen in the National Assembly and with the support of some Salazarist barons.

Nuclei such as Social Studies Circles VECTOR [*Círculos de Estudos Sociais VECTOR*] claimed the purity of the EN and set up a national network.[37] Symbolically, the first meeting of that organisation took place in 1969 at Fátima. Apart from the left, which then had more access to the media, its enemies were the reformists and the technocrats associated with Caetano. Some figures from that milieu became known in the struggle with the 'liberals' in the National Assembly.

While *Resistência* represented the hard nucleus of Salazarism, *Politica*, created in 1969, was the voice of neo-Fascism.[38] Neither the ideology nor the names changed much from what had existed in Salazar's last years.[39]

The only novelty was its organisation and its acknowledgement as a political trend, detached from power.[40]

In those years, a close association was forged between some opponents of Caetano's candidacy as a successor to Salazar, e.g. the former Minister of Foreign Affairs, Franco Nogueira, and these groups. Later, just before the downfall of the regime, this stance was adopted by members of the armed forces, e.g. by General Kaúlza de Arriage, who was capable of launching a *pronunciamento* against Caetano, in the context of the crisis unleashed by General Spínola.

THE RADICAL RIGHT AND THE TRANSITION TO DEMOCRACY

Some specific features of the transition to democracy, such as the lack of compromise with the old regime's elite and the 'anti-Fascist' radicalism of 1974–75, deeply affected the overall political realignment of the Portuguese right. For the radical right, this new situation was devastating, both politically and organisationally, but ideologically as well.

In the first two years, while political parties were set up and the new constitution was approved, the radical right was affected by a number of electoral prohibitions, political *saneamentos* (purges) and party bans. Hence, any quick reconversion of the elite of Salazarism or – at the outset – of the groups discussed here was impeded.[41]

It was under pressure from strong social and political movements led by the left and the extreme left, and in the shadow of illegality, that the two parties which stood for the centre-right and the right in the general election of 1975 were formed.[42] The adverse conjuncture in which they began life was made obvious both by the political programmes of the centrists and the social democrats, on the one hand, and by their own choice of leaders with no active political past under the old regime. Drawing up a balance sheet of those years, a Portuguese neo-Fascist got close to the truth when he stressed, years later, that these factors involved both parties in adopting 'programmes to the left of their leaders, who were to the left of militants and voters'.[43]

In the context of the transition to democracy in Southern Europe in the 1970s, the *saneamento* movement, which started immediately after the coup and developed throughout 1975, was a singularity of the Portuguese case.[44] Although it was ultimately rather limited, as was the whole process of 'defascistisation' after the Second World War, it still had significant consequences in that it prevented a rapid readjustment by most of the old regime's political personnel.

The first measures of the National Salvation Junta [*Junta de Salvação Nacional,* JSN], presided over by General Spínola, were directed towards a rapid and straightforward purge programme. The former president of the republic and the prime minister, together with some ministers, were exiled. The paramilitary and the police groups (the political police and the old anti-Communist militia, LP), who attempted resistance, were dissolved and a part of their elite entourage arrested. The single party, the official youth organisation and other institutions from the fascist era were also dissolved. The Armed Forces Movement (*Movimento das Forças* Armadas, MFA), which led the coup, proposed to retire 60 generals, the majority of whom had participated, some time before, in a public demonstration of solidarity with the old regime.[45]

The first legislation on *saneamento* included the demise of the civil service and the loss of political rights of all presidents of the republic, ministers, national leaders of the single party, and of the LP. At the local level, the clandestine and semi-legal opposition to the old regime – particularly the Portuguese Democratic Movement, [*Movimento Democrático Português*, MDP], a front organisation connected with the Communist Party [*Partido Comunista Português*, PCP] – occupied the majority of the town councils and expelled their previous leaders. The old corporative unions were occupied by the workers, the majority of whom were affiliated to the Communist Party. The pressure of left-wing political movements and the effect of 'liberation' prevented any action, which could have permitted the survival of the institutions and the national political elite of the dissolved regime, against the initial wish of Spínola.

The first policy declarations of the left-wing parties were, in general, fairly cautious as far as *saneamentos* were concerned. The Socialist Party asked in its first communiqué for 'the removal of all those directly involved in the previous government'. The Communists also made rather moderate declarations. Nevertheless, the first *saneamentos* occurred in various sectors, and the demands for purges were part of the first workers' strikes. In the Universities of Lisbon and Coimbra, lecturers and staff who had co-operated with the former regime were denied entrance by students' unions.

In response to these spontaneous movements, the provisional government issued the first regulations on civil servant *saneamentos* creating an inter-ministerial re-classification committee in order to bring to justice those who might reveal behaviour 'contrary to the established order after 25 April 1974'.[46] This committee functioned until 1976 and the legislation was reviewed several times, thus revealing the radicalisation of the political situation. At the beginning of 1975, the legal text itself referred to the previous regime as 'Fascist regime' and the behaviour of civil servants before the revolution became subject to *saneamento*.[47]

After Spínola's overthrow, the anti-capitalist thrust of events provoked a second wave of purges. Individual *saneamentos* were encouraged. The nationalisation of the most important firms and the expropriation of the great land-owners were called for. These two groups were considered the supporters of the previous regime by the two main agents of the second part of the process – the PCP and the ultra left-wing groups, which dominated the Portuguese revolution until the end of 1975. Purging and anti-capitalism were strictly connected in the second period.

In February 1975, the official reports on the purge process declared that 12,000 citizens were involved.[48] Between March and November 1975, this figure must have significantly increased, since, by 25 November 1975, when the purge movement was suspended, this number was approximately 20,000, if we consider all types of punishments: from the simple transfer to dismissal from work.

The proponents of the purge process were many and varied. If we exclude the first measures of the JSN immediately following the coup, it was however essentially the PCP and the small but influential extreme-left parties which led the movement.

The demands for purges were often led by workers' commissions independent of the unions, and organised according to place of work (the so-called *Comissões de Trabalhadores*) where the PCP had to share control with the extreme-left parties. Most of the 'wildcat purges' were implemented by these committees which occasionally escaped the control of the PCP bureaucracy.

In general, the purge movement did not keep to clear strategies and coherent patterns, being extremely diverse from sector to sector. The concept of 'collaborator' changed during the period of 'exception'. In 1974, the first purge movement was based on a strict concept of collaboration, but in 1975, with the burgeoning anti-capitalist wave, a number of traditional attitudes held by industrialists were considered as symbols of the old regime.

The purge deeply affected the top cadres of Salazarism, most of whom went into exile or retreated into political silence without giving much symbolic commitment to the reorganisation of the radical right at the time.

The young neo-Fascists, unaffected by the initial measures of purge and exile, since they had not exercised any eminent political functions under the former regime, were the first to initiate the creation of resistance parties, within the new legal order. These included the Progress Party [*Partido de Progresso*, PP], whose headquarters were ransacked and which was dissolved on 28 September, after the departure of General Spínola, as well as the Liberal Party [*Partido Liberal*, PL], and the Portuguese Nationalist Movement [*Movimento Nacionalista* Português, MNP].[49] Only the Christian Democrat Party [*Partido de Democracia Cristã*, PDC], survived this first offensive and achieved legal status, after having been prevented from contesting the first elections in April 1975. However, it is rather unclear whether the early PDC really did belong to the radical right. In fact this tiny party, which for many years was the only electoral contender representing the far right, went through very diverse phases and never united the main elements of that sector.[50]

After the party's dissolution, following the fall of Spínola, some nuclei began a clandestine struggle in 1975, as part of a major anti-Communist offensive.

At the beginning of 1975, the radicalisation and the shift to the left gave way to several organisations that played an important political role in the centre and north of the country, during the so-called 'hot summer' of 1975.

As already suggested, the situation changed in this period. The occupation of land in the south began; the great economic groups were nationalised; important company directors left the country; and even the Catholic Church lost control of its official broadcasting station. The latter was occupied by workers and journalists and turned into the mouthpiece of the revolutionary left.

Thus were created the conditions for the political fulfilment of one of the main themes of the ideological discourse of the radical right since the turn of the century: capital (Lisbon) versus province, Catholic north versus 'red' south.

The theorization of this dual political culture of Portugal was a constant element of Portuguese conservative and traditionalist thought: the hard-working Catholic north versus the Mozarabic south of the rural workers of the latifundia area and the urban world of Lisbon.

The anti-Communist political offensive of the summer of 1975 can only be compared to the anti-liberal social movements of the nineteenth century, even though hurried comparisons might lead to anachronism. However, we are clearly confronted with the first relatively successful mass mobilisation of the provinces since the middle of the nineteenth century. Local notables and Catholic churchmen played an important part in the movement, in the centre and north of the country.[51]

After his escape from the country, General Spínola created the Demo-cratic Movement for the Liberation of Portugal [*Movimento Democrático de Libertação Nacional*, MDLP] which was connected with the Portuguese Liberation Army [*Exército de Libertação Nacional*, ELP], and led part of the movement. These organisations were largely dominated by right-wing military men, associated with the provincial elites while the Church of Braga, the centre of the more conservative northern Catholic hierarchy of the country, provided connections with local notables. Financial support was forthcoming from northern industrialists and from some Western nations. The Spanish border and the police showed a collaborative neutrality. The hard core of the MDLP, created in Madrid in the mid–1970s, was formed by military men and the newly created ultra-right parties, which became illegal upon the fall of Spínola. However, some veterans of the colonial war led the operations. Alpoim Galvão, an army officer and veteran of the colonial war (he led the attack on Guinée-Conakry in 1970), recruited some military men and after dealing with Spínola, by that time in Brazil, created the movement.[52]

According to Galvão, the ELP was bringing together the more radical elements, who supported a return to the authoritarian regime, of which he did not approve. Nevertheless, there was co-operation between them. The ELP carried out several terrorist actions, bomb attacks and even political murders.

The ELP activities were of a classic political terrorism type. More important were the effective anti-Communist demonstrations, which usually led to the burning and pillaging of the PCP offices, and those of the MDP which still dominated part of the local administration.

The ELP, which has received little academic attention, relied on the decisive support of the Catholic hierarchy mainly in the north and particularly in the Braga diocese. A whole network of provincial parish priests did their utmost to link their anti-Communist activities from he pulpit with political demonstrations. It would be hard to describe the various clashes between the rural and provincial world, on the one hand, and the urban and working-class one, on the other, during the 'hot summer' of 1975, whether by referring to the social actors involved or from an organisational viewpoint. The truth remains that while in Lisbon a workers' demonstration besieged the Constituent Assembly, 50 kilo-metres north of the capital, on its rural outskirts, peasants beat up pickets and destroyed the headquarters of the PCP, after a demonstration of 'support for the lord bishop'.[53]

This whole dynamic process had an important impact in isolating the capital city, its industrial belt and the Alentejo region, shaken by strong radical movements. It was also in the north that organic links between the MDLP–ELP, the religious hierarchy and the local notables, closely associated with small business, made political action more effective.[54] It should be stressed that all this activity, including attacks on Communist headquarters in the centre-north of the country, took place with the support of local branches of the centre-right and Socialist parties.

In Lisbon it was the Socialist Party [*Partido Socialista*, PS], together with members of the armed forces belonging to the moderate left, who led the movement which came to a head on 25 November 1975. This date was crucial in containing the pre-revolutionary wave and in establishing a representative democracy. These sectors were the main recipients of large financial support from the West, mainly from the United States, which rapidly turned off the small tap available to Spínola and the MDLP.

The operational activities, terrorism included, of the MDLP and the FLP were mainly undertaken by soldiers or former soldiers. Some of them were arrested, but their connections with moderates during the 'hot summer' of 1975 and the promises made to many that everything would be forgotten, turned their trials into sensitive matters, dragging on for many years, and led to vendettas among the persons concerned.

The end of the revolutionary period and the gradual establishment of democracy from 1976 onwards led to the vanishing of illusions about an extreme-right restoration, and even about the minimum programme on which any such organisation could be based. The return of exiles to Portugal, the growing press activity of those who had been 'plundered' in 1974–75, and the search for anti-Communist 'military heroes', ended without leaving any trace. Decolonisation, made worse by the inability to mobilise the *retornados*, marked the end of an era in the political culture of the radical right.

The reintegration process of purged individuals went forward between 1976 and the early 1980s. Based upon new legislation, the most rapid measures were taken in the economic sector, where the 'wildcat purge' had been strongest. The governments implemented a set of incentive measures aimed at the return of emigrés or purged managers, in a climate of economic crisis and negotiations with the International Monetary Fund. The law declared that the purge of citizens for political or ideological reasons, occurring between 1974 and 1976, was legally non-existent.

Within the civil service, new legislation invited purged people to apply for rehabilitation. The purge committees were dismantled, and a rehabilitation commission was set up, which worked until the 1980s and rehabilitated individuals in the majority of the cases presented. However, in the light of present knowledge it seems that 'reintegration' did not mean a return to former positions. For example, in the case of the armed forces, the old elite remained in reserve or retired. Because of complicated administrative processes, it took longer to reintegrate the victims of legal purges.

In the same period an anti-leftist purge developed: militants from the extreme left and the PCP were dismissed from the media, state departments and public enterprises. This was particularly evident in the Ministries of Agriculture and Work, and in the nationalised banks where Communists had exerted a strong presence.

With the renegotiation of the pact between the democratic parties and the inheritors of the MFA, and the disappearance of military tutelage, some leading figures of the old regime returned to Portugal. The President, Tomás (who remained politically silent until his death), and some ministers returned from Brazil, and only Marcello Caetano refused permission to return, and died in Brazil in 1980.

However, these figures were not associated with a possible future revival of the native radical right, and the old ministerial elite of Salazar died in silence. Exceptions prove this rule: only one ex-minister made a political career in the new democracy: Adriano Moreira, former Minister of Overseas Territories, who was deputy and general secretary of the CDS for a short period. Two reformist ministers of Caetano's were brought back into the fold: the Secretary of State for Corporations, who introduced the liberalisation of the unions before the end of the regime, and also the architect of the education reform.

The new political climate of 'political reconciliation', which characterised the end of the 1970s, influenced some processes connected with the inheritance of the old regime, e.g., in the case of the members of the ex-political police.

Despite efforts by some military sectors to save the colonial branch of the political police, the entire body was, after brief resistance, totally dismantled. In 1974, in an atmosphere of persecution, those who had not fled spent the two years of the period of exception awaiting trial. Their trials were already organised in accordance with the new political ethos. Consequently, those who had not taken advantage of conditional freedom to emigrate were lightly punished by military courts, which were especially lenient towards those with good military records.

Among the few who had been gaoled in Portugal since 1974 was General Kaúlza de Arriaga. A veteran of the colonial war, whose name was much mentioned by the extreme right in the last years of the regime, he created in 1977 the Independent Movement for National Reconstruction [*Movimento Independente para a Reconstrução Nacional*, MIRN], later renamed Party of the Portuguese Right [*Partido de Direita Portuguesa*, PDP].[55] This party was the last attempt to unify various fringe groups associated with the old regime. With a moderate programme, demarcated from the authoritarianism of the past and seeking to defend the interest of white settlers from the former colonies, this party fought the general election of 1980, allied to the PDC. It did not win any seats, despite an electoral system based on proportional representation which enabled the extreme left to be represented in parliament, during the transition period, with less than 2 per cent of the vote.

The failure of the MIRN, which was dissolved soon after, symbolically marked the end of an era. To the ideological trauma caused by the loss of the colonies, which generated an abundant literature of recrimination, corresponded a very moderate sociological trauma for those affected – at least by comparison with similar processes.[56] Obviously the relatively peaceful integration of the *retornados* was not only caused by the 'gentle ways' of the Portuguese or by the sustained provision of financial support by the State. Sociological characteristics of the white community in Africa, such as relatively recent settlement (and thus family ties in the metropolitan country) or direct emigration to other countries, in particular South Africa, cushioned the shock.

The end of the 1970s, with the gradual withdrawal of the military from the political arena, the consolidation of parliamentary parties, and the settling down of their electorate, ended any chance of political reconversion for some populist military figures, tempted to capitalise on the success of their anti-leftist action in 1975.

THE RADICAL RIGHT IN THE 1980S

1989, the year of Euro-elections which marked a strengthening of the extreme right, particularly in West Germany, saw some meetings of Portuguese groups and international representatives of the same sector. However, no Portuguese organisation fought the elections.[57] It was also the year in which the centenary of Salazar's birth was commemorated by a number of public events, predominantly of a cultural nature.[58] It was in the field of culture that the most active groups concentrated their activities in the 1980s.

The core of Portuguese nationalism, the multi-continental 'Empire', on which the ideology of the extreme right had rested until the 1970s, was irreversibly destroyed. An abundant cultural activity revolved round its reshaping in the context of the European option and of the attendant threats to Portuguese national identity. Once again it was the (by now less) young neo-Fascist intellectuals of the 1960s who undertook this task. They were prompted by the belief that it 'would be more important, in the political sphere, to indoctrinate and influence the non-Marxist parties into moving to the right and to support strongly the leaders and groups who favoured this trend rather than to create autonomous rightist forces.'[59] Without repudiating their past heroes, they started a process of ideological revision and of breaking with simple anti-democratic reactionarism. An example was provided by Present Future [*Futuro Presente*, FP] where part of the neo-Fascist generation of the 1960s, in particular those who had not joined centre-right parties in the meantime, could be found.[60] This was far from dogmatic and militant neo-Fascism, and represented, instead, an attempt at doctrinal reformulation of the Portuguese right.[61]

This effort went on throughout the debate about the new geo-strategic location of Portugal, now smaller, and through the reassessment of 'nation' as a concept. The themes of the European and American new right were also introduced under a political system still dominated by socialist legacies from the revolutionary period.

Revealing a multiplicity of influences, the debate covered the contributions of North-American neo-liberals and 'anarcho-capitalists', of socio-biology, of Alain de Benoist's *Nouvelle Droite*, and of the classics of Portuguese traditionalism which were being revived. Classic themes of Lusitanian nationalist mythology, such as the Discoveries and the 'Atlantic calling' inherited from the colonial empire, the problem of the Iberian peninsula and the Spanish threat, and the decadence caused by nineteenth century liberalism, among others, were invoked to legitimate a new conservative nationalism or 'a Nationalism conceived as a political doctrine in which the Nation State is [...] the first value to preserve and to defend in the temporal order'.[62]

From the late 1970s, this cultural and ideological effort acquired various centres of growth. Among them were the private universities founded by lecturers purged from the state universities in 1974, a new privately owned press, and the youth organisations of right-wing parties, as well as some foundations associated with them.

A symptom of this rethinking of new ideological elements by the right and of the attempt to overcome dogmatism was the proliferation of cultural initiatives. These initiatives relied on the co-operation of young neo-Fascists, traditionalist monarchists, Catholic fundamentalists, right-wing dominated students' associations and other conservative sectors which developed through the 1980s, sometimes under the patronage of universally respected figures.[63] The latter ranged from Franco Nogueira, an old 'baron' of Salazarism and author of a monumental biography of the dictator, to Jorge Borges de Macedo, a distinguished historian and university professor. On the other hand, in a movement which was not unprecedented but was fairly unusual (the earliest precedent was during the First World War), various intellectuals associated with the left, which was undergoing a similar revisionist trend, shared in some of these initiatives and engaged in a dialogue in the media.

Since the transition to democracy, the radical right has been characterised by an absence of leaders with even minimal public impact, by the extreme weakness and fragility of party organisations, by the drifting away of its cadres and by an ideological crisis.

Virtually only the PDC has fought every election, and its results are so modest, even in conjunction with Kaúlza de Arriaga's MIRN-PDP in 1980, that no assumptions about electoral sociology can be drawn. Its scores have ranged between 0.3 and 1.1 per cent in general elections (see Table).

Table 8.1   PDC/MIRN and the Portuguese elections

Party	Year	N.º Votes	%
PDC	1976	28,226	0.5
PDC	1979	65,417	1.1
PDC/MIRN	1980	20,489	0.3
PDC	1983	36,365	0.6
PDC	1985	39,675	0.69

Prevented from standing in the first elections, deprived of any well-known personalities, despised by ideological neo-Fascism, the PDC found a refuge in propaganda on behalf of the former colonials.[64] As for the more ambitious but brief experiment of the MIRN, it occurred rather late and was damaged, indeed literally destroyed, by the electoral alliance of right-wing parties. In the 1980s, new and rather fragmented organisations emerged, but they were nearly always run by youngsters and were devoid of electoral impact.

On the other hand, neo-Fascism survived, residually, in the cultural field, through depleted youth organisations but without the symbolic presence of crowds in the streets, expressive propaganda, or electoral impact. Paradoxically, it was the gradual consolidation of the extreme right in the European Parliament in the second half of the 1980s, and the corresponding development of international structures which generated some unrest among the native radical right. Some of its leaders came to Portugal and made some noise in the media. Organisations such as the National Force–New Monarchy party, [*Força Nacional – Nova Monarquia, FN–NM*], created in 1989 through the merger of two youth organizations, are connected with this trend.[65]

CONCLUSION

The *Estado Novo* bequeathed a deep legacy to the young Portuguese democracy. It did not, however, bequeath to the country a neo-Fascist or radical right party, comparable to those in Germany, Italy or France. The origin of this absence, as has been shown, derives from the very nature of the political regime overthrown in 1974.

To disregard the chances of neo-Fascism as a legacy of the past does not amount to any forecast for the future. Movements of the far right have a potential in all industrial societies and Portugal is, obviously, no exception. Until the 1980s, some of the factors associated with the growth of such movements did not exist in Portugal. Their usual functions as conveyor belts for popular aspirations were lacking, as they had no social base or support. There had been the wholesale return of white settlers, caused by decolonisation. However, such factors as significant foreign immigration and its attendant popular xenophobia did not occur in Portuguese society.[66]

The most important shifts on the radical right occurred at the cultural level after a profound crisis bought on by the transition to democracy and by decolonisation. Nevertheless, the right and centre-right parties have, until now, absorbed whatever potential for autonomous growth in the political sphere the extreme right may have had.[67]

(Translated by Michalina Vaughan)

LIST OF ABBREVIATIONS

CDS   *Centro Democrático Social* [Social Democratic Centre]
ELP   *Exército de Libertação Nacional* [Portuguese Liberation Army]
EN   *Estado Novo* [New State]
FAP   *Frente Académica Patriotica* [Patriotic Academic Front]
FEN   *Frente de Estudantes Nacionalistas* [Nationalist Students Front]
FNR   *Frente Nacional Revolucionária* [National Revolutionary Front]

FN–NM *Força Nacional/Nova Monarquia* [National Force – New Monarchy]
FP *Futuro Presente* [Present Future]
JSN *Junta de Salvação Nacional* [National Salvation Junta]
LP *Legião Portuguesa* [Portuguese Legion]
MDLP *Movimento Democrático de Libertãçao de Portugal* [Democratic Movement for the Liberation of Portugal]
MDP *Movimento Democrático Português* [Portuguese Democratic Movement]
MFA *Movimento das Forças Armadas* [Armed Forces Movement]
MIRN *Movimento Independente para a Reconstrução Nacional* [Independent Movement for National Reconstruction]
MJP *Movimento Jovem Portugal* [Young Portugal Movement]
MNP *Movimento Nacionalista Português* [Portuguese Nationalist Movement]
MP *Mocidade Portuguesa* [Portuguese Youth]
NS *Nacional Sindicalismo* [National Syndicalism]
PCP *Partido Comunista Português* [Portuguese Communist Party]
PDC *Partido da Democracia Cristã* [Christian Democrat Party]
PDP *Partida de Direita Portuguêsa* [Party of the Portuguese Right]
PL *Partido Liberal* [Liberal Party]
PP *Partido do Progresso* [Progress Party]
PPD *Partido Popular Democrático* [Popular Democratic Party]
PPM *Partido Popular Monarquico* [Popular Royalist Party]
PS *Partido Socialista* [Socialist Party]
PSD *Partido Social Democráta* [Social Democratic Party]
UN *União Nacional* [National Union]

* The first version of this article was written when I was a Visiting Fellow in the Centre for European Studies, Department of Political Science, Stanford University, in 1988–89. I would like to thank its Director, Professor Philippe C. Schmitter, and to acknowledge the working conditions, as well as the stimulating intellectual climate I found there. I was also invited by Prof. Richard Herr to present and discuss this paper at the Iberian Study Seminar of the Institute of International Studies, University of California Berkeley, in May 1989.

1. For an introduction to the application of these concepts to post-war political movements, see K. V. Beyme, 'Right-Wing Extremism in Post-War Europe', *West European Politics*, XI, 2, 1988, pp. 1–18. In this article, I use the typology of right-wing movements developed by S. G. Payne, *Fascism: Comparison and Definition.*, University of Wisconsin Press, Madison, 1980, pp. 14–21, and R. Rémond *Les Droites en France*, Aubier, Paris, 1982 (4th edn.), pp. 15–45.

2. O *Integralismo Lusitano* was the main ideological challenge to the liberal order at the start of the century. Created under the influence of *Action Française*, this traditional, corporatist and anti-liberal royalist movement inspired anti-republican plots, but never became a political party. See M. Braga da Cruz, 'O Integralismo Lusitano nas origens do Salazarismo', *Análise Social*, XVIII, No. 70, 1982, pp. 137–182 and A. Costa Pinto, 'A Formação do Integralismo Lusitano: 1907–17', *Análise Social*, XVIII Nos. 72,73,74, 1982, pp. 1409–19.

3. On some of the failed attempts to set up Fascist parties after the First World War, see A. Costa Pinto, 'O Fascismo e a crise da Iª Republica: Os Nacionalistas Lusitanos, 1923–25', *Penélope*, 3, pp. 43–62.

4. On the radical right and Fascism at the time, see, A. Costa Pinto, 'The Radical Right and the Military Dictatorship in Portugal: the National May 28 League 1928–1933', *Luso-Brasilian Review*, Madison, XXIII, 1, 1986, pp. 1–15.

5. On the single party of the EN, see A. M. Caldeira, 'O Partido de Salazar: antecedentes, organização e funcões da União Nacional', *Analise Social*, XXII, 5, 1986, pp. 943–77; M. Braga da Cruz, *O Partido e o Estado do Salazarismo*, Presença, Lisbon, 1988, reviewed by the author in *Annales. Economie. Société. Civilizations*, XLIII, 1988, pp. 691–3.

6. On the origins of the MP, see A. Costa Pinto and N. Ribeiro, *A Acção Escolar Vanguarda, 1933–34*, História e Crítica, Lisbon, 1988.

7. On the opposition to Salazarism, see D. L. Raby, *Fascism and Resistance in Portugal: Communists, Liberals and Military Dissidents in the Opposition to Salazar, 1941–74*, Manchester University Press, Manchester, 1988.

8. See A. J. Telo, *Portugal na Segunda Guerra*, Perspectivas e Realidades, Lisbon, 1987.

9. On authoritarian regimes, see J. J. Linz, 'Totalitarian and Authoritarian Regimes', in F. Greenstein and N. Polsby (eds), *Handbook of Political Science*, Reading, Mass., 1975, vol. 3, pp. 175–411.

10. L. S. Graham, 'Portugal: The Bureaucracy of Empire', *LADS. Occasional Papers*, IX, 1973, p. 8.

11. For the interpretations of the EN, see M. de Lucena, 'Interpretações do Salazarismo: notas de leitura critica. I', *Análise Social*, LXXXIII, 1984, pp. 423–51 and A. Costa Pinto, 'O Salazarismo e o Fascismo Europeuos primeiros debates nas ciências sociais', *Salazar e o Salazarismo*, Publicações D. Quixote, Lisbon, 1989, pp. 155–88.

12. Nogueira Pinto, *Portugal os anos do fim. A revolução que veio de dentro*, Sociedade de publicações economia e financas, LDA, Lisbon, 1976, vol. I, p. 79.

13. This review was published from 1959 to 1961, and directed by Fernando Guedes. On this group, see E. Lourenço, 'Fascismo e cultura no antigo regime' *Análise Social*, XVIII, (72–73–74), pp. 1431–6.

14. A. José de Brito, *Tempo Presente*, No. 10, Feb. 1960, p. 12.

15. Its most prolific ideologist was A. José de Brito, still active in the 1980s.

Always a self-confessed neo-Fascist, he taught philosophy in a private university in Oporto, while publishing in the extreme-right press. His most interesting work, as far as Portuguese neo-Fascism in concerned, is *Destino do Nacionalismo Português*, Verbo, Lisbon, 1962.

16. See, for instance, the article by C. de Mello Beirão, *Tempo Presente*, No. 4, 1959, pp. 76–84.

17. J. Nogueira Pinto, *Portugal* cit., p. 122.

18. Its organ was the *FAP – Deus. Patria. Familia.*, which denounced opposition activities, and supported the politics of the government.

19. As did the National Syndicalist Portuguese Youth, [*Juventude Portuguesa Nacional Sindicalista*]. It published *Ataque*, which appeared on and off in 1961–62, as well as the ideological journal *Ofensiva*, which was clearly inspired by JONS, the matrix of Fascism in neighbouring Spain.

20. Z. Moniz Ferreira contacted the NS leader to seek his support. At the time, Rolão Preto, who had been actively involved with the candidacy of Humberto Delgado, belonged to the royalist opposition, which later presented 'independent' candidates and created the Popular Royalist Party [*Partido Popular Monarquico*, PPM] after the fall of the EN.

21. The national organ was *Frente*, which first appeared in October 1965.

22. *Ataque*, Nos. 6–8, Oct.–Dec. 1962, p. 1.

23. Z. Moniz Ferreira, 'Nacional Sindicalismo', *Ataque*, No. 13–14, May–June 1963, p. 4.

24. On the *Jeune Nation* movement see P. Milza, *Fascisme Français – Passé et Presént*, Flammarion, Paris, 1987, pp. 224–371.

25. See F. Ferraresi (ed.), *La destra radicale*, Feltrinelli, Milan, 1984, and by the same author, 'The Radical Right in Post-war Italy', *Politics and Society*, 16, 1 March 1988, pp. 71–119.

26. J. Morais and L. Violante, *Contribuicáo para uma cronologia dos factos económicos e sociais – Portugal 1926–1985*, Livros Horizonte, Lisbon, 1986, p. 185.

27. See the manifesto of the organisation in *Frente*, No. 5, April 1966, pp. 4–5.

28. *Europe-Action* was published between 1963, and anticipated some of the themes of the *Nouvelle Droite*. See Milza, *Fascisme*, cit., pp. 328–31.

29. See, e.g., the review *Itinerário*, first published in March–April 1965, more cultural than ideological, and *Movimento Vanguardista*, founded in 1969, which made repeated attacks on Caetano.

30. *Agora*, 8 Jan. 1966, p. 12.

31. *Agora*, No. 1, 18 Feb. 1961, *Resistência*, No. 1, 1968.

32. To begin with, its first director, Raul de Carvalho Branco and various contributors, such as Neves da Costa. In 1967, it became the mouthpiece of the neo-Fascist faction, as it attracted former leaders such as Valle Figueredo and Jaime Nogueira Pinto.

33. *Agora*, 20 Oct. 1965, p. 3.

34. *Agora*, 28 Aug. 1965, p. 3 and 26 Feb. 1966, p. 5.

35. See J. Nogueira Pinto, 'Fascismo 67', *Agora*, 4 Nov. 1967, p. 13.

36. J. Valle Figueiredo, in *Frente*, No. 6, July 1966, p. 1.

37. *Resistência* continued to be published after 1974 with remarkable regularity.
38. Edited by J. Nogueira Pinto; the first number appeared in Nov. 1969.
39. The most notable names being Lucas Pires and José Miguel Júdice, in Coimbra. The latter wrote a preface, from a neo-Fascist perspective, for the Portuguese edition of José António Primo de Rivera's writings. See J. M. A. Júdice, *José António Primo de Rivera*, Cidadela, Coimbra, 1972, pp. 11–51.
40. On the various factions, from the royalists to the neo-Fascists, see A. Valdemar ed., *Ser ou não ser pelo partido único*, Arcadia, Lisbon, 1973.
41. For an introduction to the *saneamentos* (literally 'cleanings out'), the political purges after the fall of the regime, see A. Costa Pinto, 'Revolution and Political Purge in Portugal's Transition to Democracy', in S. U. Larsen (ed.), *Modern Europe after Fascism, 1945–1980s*, Norwegian University Press, Bergen (forthcoming).
42. These were the Popular Democratic Party [*Partido Popular Democrático*, PPD] – later Social Democratic Party [*Partido Social Democrático*, PSD] – and the Social Democratic Centre [*Centro Democrático Social*, CDS]
43. J. Nogueira Pinto, 'A direita e o 25 de Abril' in M. Batista Coelho (ed.), *Portugal: O Sistema Político e Constitucional, 1974–87*, Instituto de Ciências Sociais, Lisbon, 1989, p. 203.
44. On this subject, see G. O'Donnell and P. C. Schmitter, *Transitions from Authoritarian Rule. Tentative conclusions about uncertain democracies*, The Johns Hopkins University Press, Baltimore and London, 1986.
45. On the coup and the Armed Forces Movement, see O. Saraiva de Carvalho, *Alvorada em Abril*, Bertrand, Lisbon, 1977, and D. de Almeida, *Origem e Evolução do Movimento dos Capitães*, Edições Sociais, Lisbon, 1977; see also P. C. Shmitter, 'Liberation by *Golpe*', *Armed Forces and Society II* (Nov. 1975), pp. 5–33; Douglas Porch, *The Portuguese Armed Forces and The Revolution*, Croom Helm, London, 1977; and, on the military in twentieth-century Portugal, M. Carrilho, *Forças Armadas e mudanças política em Portugal no século XX*, Imprensa Nacional, Lisbon, 1985.
46. See Decree-law No. 277/74 of 25 June 1974, *Diário do Governo*, 1st ser., No. 146, p. 744.
47. See Decree-law No. 123/75 of 11 March 1974, *Diário do Governo*, 1st ser., No.59, p. 375.
48. *O Século*, Lisbon, 27 Feb. 1975.
49. The P P's organ was *Bandarra*, edited by Miguel Freitas da Costa; only three issues were published.
50. See the book of one of its first leaders, an army officer who held governmental posts under the second provisional government and who followed Spínola in exile: S. Osório, *O equívoco do 25 de Abril*, Intervenção, Lisbon, 1975.
51. This contribution will not cover one aspect of extreme right activity, viz. the development of separatist movements in the Atlantic islands, particularly in the Azores.
52. On the ELP/MDLP, see A. Galvão, *De Conakry ao MDLP–Dossier secreto*,

Intervenção, Lisbon, 1976; A. Spínola, *Ao serviço de Portugal*, Atica/Bertrand, Lisbon, 1976, pp. 217–426; G. Wallraff, *A descoberta de uma conspiração – a acção Spínola*, Bertrand, Lisbon, 1976; P. de Abreu, *Do 25 de Abril ao 25 de Novembro – Memória de um tempo perdido*, Intervenção, Lisbon, 1983.

53. On this, see a case study by M. Espirito Santo, *Comunidade rural ao norte do Tejo (estudo de sociologia rural)*, Instituto de estudos para o desenvolvimento, Lisbon, 1980, pp. 199–214.

54. For a detailed description, see P. de Abreu, *Do 25 de Abril*, cit., pp. 144 ff.

55. On the formation of MIRN, see K. de Arriaga, *No Caminho das soluções do futuro*, Edições Abril, Lisbon, 1977.

56. See, e.g., the book by the former minister for Overseas Territories, S. Cunha, *O Ultramar a nacão e o 25 de Abril*, Atlantida, Lisbon, 1977, and A. Moreira, *A Nação Abandonada*, Intervenção, Lisbon, 1977. For some factual information on the decolonisation and the *retornados*, see Grupo de pesquisa sobre a descolonização portuguesa, *A descolonização portuguesa – aproximação a um estudo,* Instituto Amaro da Costa, 2 vols., Lisbon, 1979–82.

57. That is if we take no account of the PDC, which merely used the allocated TV time during the campaign.

58. Except for a very small visit (a hundred people or so) to the graveyard in his native village, Santa Comba Dão which is not to be compared with the annual pilgrimage to Franco's home at the time.

59. J. Nogueira Pinto, *A Direita* cit., p. 206.

60. No. 1, 1980, ed. by J. Nogueira Pinto.

61. See esp. J. Nogueira Pinto, 'Direita em Portugal – notas para uma autocrítica e projecto', *Futuro Presente*, Nos 9–10, 2nd ser., pp. 10–16.

62. J. Nogueira Pinto, 'A direita e as direitas – algumas questões prévias', *Futuro Presente*, No. 7, 2nd ser., p. 11.

63. It would be pointless to list them exhaustively. In the second half of the 1980s literally dozens of magazines, associations, etc. mushroomed. See, e.g., *Portugueses-revista de ideias*, first published in Dec. 1987, whose early issues reveal a variety of ideological influences. For the international affiliations of these groups, see C. O. Maoláin, *The Radical Right. A world directory*, Longman, 1988, pp. 229–33.

64. This is the only reference made in its party political broadcast for the European parliament of 1989.

65. Founded in June 1989, it adopted the name *Partido Força Nacional*, and declared that it had, on that date, 1,200 members.

66. At the end of 1989, Portuguese public opinion was surprised by the appearance of 'skinhead' groups leading violent anti-black activity in the two main cities of the country. In Lisbon, a young Trotskyist militant was killed, and in Oporto several attacks against black immigrants took place.

67. For a pessimistic outlook, see T. Gallagher 'From Hegemony to Opposition: the Ultra Right Before and After 1974' in L. Grahm and D. L. Wheeler (eds.), *In the Search of Modern Portugal. The Revolution and its Consequences*, Wisconsin University Press, Madison, 1983, p. 97.

CHAPTER NINE

Neo-Fascism in Modern Greece

Vassilis Kapetanyannis

INTRODUCTION

The political history of modern Greece is marked by a legacy of conflicts, instability, polarisation and fragile legitimacy. Political processes and political development have been confronted by powerful pressures from outside the parliamentary system. Until very recently, the military occupied a dominant position in the country's political and institutional setting, exercised undue influence over the political process, and showed little hesitation in interrupting and/or abolishing parliamentary institutions. It is no accident, therefore, that Greece has been seen as a 'praetorian society' having endemic political instability. Undoubtedly, however, the Greek political system has had a longer experience of liberal democratic rule than some other Mediterranean countries such as Spain or Portugal.

Western parliamentary institutions were imported into the country in the last century. However, early parliamentarianism, albeit of an oligarchic, restrictive type, had to operate within a social and economic context quite different from that of advanced West-European countries. The demise of Greek oligarchic parliamentarianism and the transition to broader forms of political participation and representation occurred at a time when industrial capitalism was very weak. In any case, its impact on the process of political development can in no way be compared with the effects of industrialisation on political institutions in Western Europe.[1]

The national schism of 1915, caused by the clash between the pro-Entente liberal Venizelos and the Germanophile King Constantine, acquired the dimensions of a serious confrontation between throne and parliament, and marked the beginning of a series of military coups and countercoups. The involvement of army officers in the party-political affairs of the country was such that it can amply justify the claim that the military clientele of each political party became the arbiter of political disputes.[2] The first Greek Republic, established in 1924, was short lived. King George II was restored to his throne in 1934. This was a turning point in Greece's modern political history. Two years later, on 4 August 1936, a quasi-Fascist military dictatorship was imposed by General Metaxas with the king's full support and patronage. It is important to put the Metaxas regime in its broader social and political context and to understand its nature, since all subsequent neo-Fascist ideologies and groups draw heavily from the official proclamations, practices and experiences of Metaxas's proto-Fascism.

Equally, the lack of any serious neo-Fascist and extreme-right organisations in Greece today and their failure to establish themselves, both during the military dictatorship (1967–74) and after its collapse, cannot be adequately explained without direct reference to political developments which occurred after the First World War. A brief account of the historical background is therefore necessary to make sense of the present situation.

THE INTER-WAR PERIOD

Inter-war Greece was still a predominantly agrarian society. In the main, the dominant class of peasant smallholders emerged from the distribution of the 'National Lands', the previously Turkish properties taken over by the Greek state.[3] Radical land reforms were effected, particularly after the Asia Minor Disaster of 1922 (the defeat by the Turks).

Not only did these reforms accommodate the demands of the huge refugee population, numbering approximately 1.2 million, who were driven out of Asia Minor, they also created a massive new stratum of smallholders largely dependent on state agencies for support and survival.[4] By 1930, Greece had irrevocably become a country whose smallholders constituted the main social class.[5]

On the political level, the two major bourgeois parties, the Liberals [*Filelefteroi*] of the charismatic Elefterios Venizelos (1864–1936) and the staunchly royalist People's Party [*Laiko Komma*, LK], commanded the loyalties of the peasantry, whereas the newly founded Communist Party of Greece [*Kommounistiko Komma Elladas*, KKE][6] was never able to make any significant inroads in the countryside. The peasants were kept firmly within the clientelistic networks of the two major parties which were fundamentally divided over the issue of the throne.[7] On the other hand, although the KKE's influence within the working class was very limited, industrial capitalism had made little advance in inter-war Greece.[8]

Moreover, Greek society was highly homogeneous from the linguistic, religious, cultural and national points of view. There was no foreign ethnic group in a dominant economic and/or cultural position to attract hatred from other social groups and be made a scapegoat for the country's social and political ills. The refugee problem did not provide a social basis for the growth of Fascist or extreme right-wing movements feeding on massive human misery or wounded nationalist feelings. Patriotism did not prove a vehicle for any Fascist movement. The fragile legitimacy of the political parties and political institutions played into the hands of the military, not of any would-be Fascist leader.

The period of the Republic (1924–35) was a turbulent one. However, despite the serious economic crisis of 1932, and a degree of labour militancy led by the Communists, a Fascist movement was, again, virtually absent. General Metaxas's party of Free Believers [*Elefterofronoi*, EL], for instance, had only two deputies elected in the 1932 general election, as against nine Communists, in a 250-seat parliament. A few right-wing organisations inspired, to some extent, by National Socialist ideas made their appearance during this period but were rather insignificant in terms of both size and political impact.[9] These organisations[10] failed, also, to spark off any massive movement in support of Fascist ideologies and/or goals. However, pressure from military and monarchist elements was mounting. A new National Socialist organisation, the Panhellenic National Front [*Panellinio Ethniko Metopo*, PEM] made its appearance and was responsible for some acts of terrorism against the Communists in Athens.

The abortive pro-Venizelos military coup of 1 March 1935 was followed by an anti-Venizelos backlash, and the hand of military and royalist elements was strengthened. A rigged plebiscite on the issue of the restoration of the monarchy held in November 1935 produced, predictably enough, a 95 per cent majority and King George II returned to the throne. New elections held on 26 January 1936 were, on the whole, conducted fairly under a system of proportional representation. However, the result was inconclusive. The Communist-dominated Popular Front held the balance of power in a hung Parliament, and, despite an agreement with the Liberals, the two major parties finally gave their vote of confidence to Metaxas when he was appointed Prime Minister in April 1936.

The Chamber was not to meet again for ten years. A nation-wide general strike, proclaimed for 5 August, served as a pretext for Metaxas to secure the king's assent to the suspension of a number of key articles of the Constitution on 4 August.[11] The nightmare of the '4th of August' dictatorship had begun with little resistance.[12] Metaxas, a marginal political figure, was now invested with unlimited powers which he exercised until his death in January 1941.

THE '4TH OF AUGUST' REGIME

Metaxas embarked on the reshaping of the Greek state and society. His basic objective was to establish a totalitarian state and to 'discipline' the Greek people by evolving the concept of the Third Hellenic Civilisation, a more than conscious imitation of Hitler's Third Reich. He aped many of the trappings of Fascism and Nazism. The regime tried to buy off the support of the workers and peasants by introducing labour and social legislation. Some of his chief ministers, like the Press and Propaganda Minister Nicoloudes, never concealed their admiration for Fascist regimes, although, officially, the Greek regime shied away from such explicit references.[13]

The regime's anti-plutocratic, anti-capitalist and anti-parliamentary rhetoric failed to create any enthusiastic, large-scale political mobilisation in support of the dictatorship. The style of government remained paternalistic and authoritarian,[14] but beneath the surface of nice talk lay the brutal reality of oppression, persecution, systematic torture, censorship and terror. Resistance to the regime was ruthlessly crushed by the 'efficient' Public Security Minister, Constantine Maniadakis, with his notorious Special Security Branch. Lacking a political following, and having acquired some degree of autonomy *vis-à-vis* the King, Metaxas sought to obtain a power base of his own by setting up the National Youth Organisation (*Ethniki Organossis Neolaias*, EON) and the Labour Battalions (*Tagmata Ergassias*, TE), membership of which (at around 600,000) was compulsory. In any case, with Metaxas's death this Fascist youth movement effectively collapsed.

During Metaxas's rule, a number of more-or-less serious military plots to overthrow him failed. The military were deeply divided, while a group of army generals was actively plotting with the Germans behind the scenes. The paradox was that, despite his ideological loyalties, Metaxas sided with the British and the allied camp against the Axis powers.

OCCUPATION, RESISTANCE AND CIVIL WAR
(1941–49)

On the morning of 28 October 1940, Metaxas was presented with an ultimatum by the Italians which he instantly rejected. At that time Greece was the only country to have sided, of her own volition, with the Allies, when Britain stood alone.[15] The Greeks drove the invading Italians back, deep into Albania, and when the war was reduced to deadlock, Hitler decided to intervene in order to secure his southern flank in his preparations to invade Russia.

General Tsolakoglou, the Commander of the Western Macedonian front and one of the prominent figures of the pro-German military faction, surrendered his troops (without government authorisation) and signed an armistice in April 1941. He was soon to be rewarded when the Germans installed him as the first Quisling Prime Minister of Greece. The king and the government headed by the banker Tsouderos had already fled, first to Crete and, after its fall to the Germans, to Egypt.

Resistance to the occupation forces (Germans, Italians and Bulgarians) took on formidable proportions. The most powerful groups were the Communist-led and controlled National Liberation Front [*Ethniko Apelefterotiko Metopo*, EAM], founded in September 1941, and its military arm, the National Popular Liberation Army [*Ethnikos Laikos Apelefterotikos Stratos*, ELAS]. Despite the terror and horrifying reprisals of the occupation forces against acts of resistance, the movement quickly embraced the great majority of the Greek population, although the Quisling governments organised a number of Fascist and extreme right-wing collaborationist groups which were assisting the Germans to defeat resistance in any possible way. The most notorious of these groups were the Security Battalions [*Tagmata Asfaleias*, TA].[16]

In the Middle East, new Greek military units were formed from the remnants of the Greek army, under the aegis of the British Command. These units were highly factionalised along political lines. Pro-EAM elements had fomented mutinies in the units stationed in Egypt, demanding the formation of a government of national unity in exile to be based on the Political Committee of National Liberation [*Politiki Epitropi Ethnikis Apelefterossis*, PEEA], the so-called 'Government of the Mountain', created by EAM in mid-March 1944. The mutinies were suppressed by the British, the units were purged of leftist elements and large numbers of those involved were interned.[17]

During this period, many clandestine organisations were formed by officers. Most of them were right-wing, pro-royalist and anti-Communist. The most prominent and active of these organisations in the post-civil war era, the Sacred Bond of Greek Officers [*Ieros Syndesmos Ellinon Axiomatikon*, IDEA], originated in the Middle East during 1943–44. There were many other groups of lesser importance.[18]

A national unity Government under George Papandreou, with the participation of EAM ministers in minor posts, was formed in the Middle East and landed in Greece in October 1944. Papandreou had the full support of Churchill who was obsessed by his desire to prevent the establishment of any Communist-controlled regime in Athens and to crush the backbone of EAM at any cost. He had previously secured a free hand in Greece under the Yalta agreement with Stalin. Early in December 1944, a bid for power by the Communists failed when the military tide turned with British intervention. In February 1945, a political settlement was reached. ELAS agreed to disarm.

However, the terms of the agreement were never to be implemented. The right-wing backlash and white terror followed. KKE and EAM followers, ELAS ex-resistance veterans and left-wingers were systematically persecuted and often tried and gaoled. Collaborators were not brought to justice and were on the loose. Violence by right-wing bands and gangs, such as that of the notorious X (Hi), particularly active in the Peloponnese, was widespread. This reign of terror paved the way for elections in March 1946. However, the left decided to abstain and thus excluded itself from Parliament – with disastrous consequences. The slide towards civil war gathered momentum with the return of the king after a plebiscite in September 1946, the fairness of which is still very much in doubt.

In the winter of 1946–47, a fully fledged civil war broke out. The 'Democratic Army', the KKE's military arm, was to be led to defeat in 1949 by a variety of factors. These included: the abandonment of guerrilla tactics, internal dissent, Tito's closing of the frontiers, a massive infusion of American military and economic aid, and the better leadership and efficiency of the national armed forces.

The Americans, with the declaration of the Truman Doctrine in 1947, had replaced the British as the patron-power of Greece, and their influence over Greek affairs in the coming years was to be enormous.[19]

The civil war left a bitter legacy of bloody political divisions. Right-wing groups and illegally operating gangs, under the auspices and control of state security services, were instrumental both in starting the civil war and in committing atrocities. These developments were to have lasting effects on the country's political system and political culture.

THE POST-CIVIL-WAR STATE AND MILITARY DICTATORSHIP (1948–74)

After its victory, the right imposed a quasi-parliamentary regime. This 'repressive parliamentarianism'[20] was controlled by the triarchy of throne, army and the political right. Within this power bloc, the army played the dominant role, an important aspect of which was its political, ideological and, to a lesser extent, financial dependence on the United States.[21]

Beyond its own vast security apparatus the Greek army was in a position to exercise direct or indirect control over the key 'civilian' intelligence and security services which, in fact, were heavily militarised. Files were kept on the majority of the population[22] (between 80 and 90 per cent), and, in addition, there was a nationwide system of identity cards. These services became the centre of plots, counter-plots, and military conspiracies. Moreover, the military were also in control of the Battalions of National Defence [*Tagmata Ethnikis Amynis*, TEA], which were officered, commanded and trained by the army. The threads connecting the Security Services with the 'parastate' organisations were also numerous. It seems that parastate organisations had started to appear and proliferate, under legal or illegal covers, around 1957–58. This was the time of rising popular discontent expressed clearly by the electoral triumph of the left in 1958 which, under the banner of the United Democratic Left [*Eniaia Demokratiki Aristera*, EDA], became the major opposition party in Parliament against all the odds.[23]

Obviously, what distinguished these parastate organisations from their European counterparts was that they were not mass organisations expressing or leading mass movements, but rubber-stamp associations, with few members in most cases, recruited mainly among the petty criminal and political underworld. They were used as an instrument for doing the 'dirty work' so that official state organs could, publicly, keep their hands clean. They were also used in other provocative actions and, more openly, in student politics.[24] Their obscure existence came into broad daylight with the assassination of the left-wing deputy Lambrakis,[25] in Thessaloniki, in May 1963.

Generally, the term *Security State* seems appropriate to define the post-civil war state; its main features were:

1. The dominant role of the army as a state institution;
2. The growth of security services and para-military, parastate organisations;

3. A dual legality inscribed in, and parallel to, the official constitutional order;
4. A restricted range of political rights and liberties;
5. Categorisation of citizens according to discriminatory political and ideological criteria;
6. The identification of external and internal enemies;
7. The politics of exclusion by legal, administrative and police methods (banning, exiling and imprisonment for political opponents);
8. An ideology of anti-Communist subversion and national security.

These principles defined the operational criteria of the repressive state apparatuses.

Especially after 1958, more funds were allocated for psychological warfare and, in 1959, two more security agencies were added to an already overprotected state. Prisons were still full of political detainees and places of internal exile for political opponents were to be found all over the country.[26] The public administration was purged and the institutionalized practices of requiring certificates of 'civil loyalty' and of strict security screening were widespread. This regimentation of society required an enormous army of functionaries, estimated at nearly 60,000.[27]

The rise of George Papandreou's movement of democratisation in the early 1960s, which became known as 'the unyielding struggle', was to erode the regime's own sources of legitimacy. The landslide victory of Papandreou's Centre Union Party [*Enosis Kentrou*, EK] in the February 1964 elections produced an overall majority in Parliament, broke the right-wing parties' monopoly of power, and carried the promise of a democratic, reformist government.

However, the government was short-lived. With the active involvement of King Constantine II, Papandreou's government was toppled in 1965, and the country slipped into a protracted and deep political crisis having as its epicentre the political control of the armed forces. The crisis was 'resolved' by military intervention in April 1967. This time, a group of middle-ranking officers, acting more or less autonomously, abolished parliamentary institutions and established a military dictatorship which lasted for seven years.[28] The traditional political system[29] crumbled under the pressures of rapid economic development and intense and protracted political mobilisation.

The seven-year military dictatorship[30] did not fundamentally alter the status and role of right-wing ideologies in Greek society. The military conspirators who gravitated round Colonel Papadopoulos, the leader of the 1967 *coup d'état*, were now elevated to key ministerial posts. Their political ideas were crude, naïve and extremely vague. Generally speaking, the regime's ideology was *sui generis*, but it leaves a residual sensation of much of it having been heard before. There is no doubt that, behind the changing rhetoric and verbiage of the regime's main ideological propagandists,[31] one can isolate persistent references to the ideological principles of Metaxas's regime, frequent religious overtones, a right-wing populist approach, and crude anti-Communism. Among the most recurrent themes, were: national security, alleged social decadence, and the need for the political re-education of the Greeks who had lost their way in the jungle of modernity and irresponsible parliamentarianism.[32]

Members of the military junta maintained close links with the tame '4th of August Party'[33] [*Komma tis 4 Avgoustou, K4A*], named after the date on which Metaxas established his dictatorship in 1936. The fortnightly left-wing paper *ANTI* carried numerous reports, between 1974 and 1977, documenting the various new parastate organisations created by the military regime, such as the National Movement of Young Scientists [*Ethniko Kinima Neon Epistimonon*, EKNE] and, more importantly, the relations between the Greek military regime, the K4A and 'New Order' [*Nea Taksi*, NT] with Italian far-right groups. It was reported, in this context, that Greece was a convenient hideout for Italian neo-Fascists like Elio Massagrande, deputy leader of *Ordine Nuovo*, or Clemente Graziani, leader of the organisation and of the International of neo-Nazism. It was also argued that the Italian fugitive neo-Fascists had made Greece their headquarters for organising a *coup d'état* in Rome on 2 June 1974.[34] The assassination of Christos Mantakas, a Greek studying in Italy, in February 1975, led the Italian authorities to discover many vital clues about the activities of Italian neo-Fascists.[35] It is reasonable to assume that the Greek Colonels were eager to export their 'model' to Italy, were conditions looked more favourable. Massagrande was arrested in Greece early in 1975, following a request by the Italian authorities, well after the fall of the military junta in July 1974. This indicates the extent to which Italian neo-Fascists had made Greece their operational base during the dictatorship.

However, the Greek colonels failed to legitimise their power[36] and create any mass support inspired by their 'ideals' and 'ideas'. The regime collapsed amid chaos and the national tragedy of Cyprus, invaded by Turkey in July 1974. Seven years of brutal and unpopular dictatorship had ended as abruptly as they had begun.

1974 AND AFTER

The transfer of power from military to civilian leadership under Constantine Karamanlis inaugurated an entirely new phase in modern Greek politics. Karamanlis's gradualist approach to the serious problems that confronted him was evident in the timing of the measures he adopted. He defused the near-war situation with Turkey, formed a government of national unity and proceeded carefully in restoring civil authority over a demoralised and disintegrated military. His strategy succeeded in full.[37] He was also able to consolidate the new parliamentary regime and establish the most liberal political system in the post-war period. The KKE was legalised and could now compete on an equal footing with other political forces, despite its split.[38]

The new open, competitive and democratic regime passed successfully the test of functionality and stability[39] with the smooth transition of power from the conservative New Democracy [*Nea Demokratia*, ND] to a radical-socialist party, the Panhellenic Socialist Movement (*Panellinio Socialistiko Kinema*, PASOK), in October 1981, when the latter's leader Andreas Papandreou won a landslide victory at the polls. The protagonists of the 1967 military coup were tried and sentenced to death, although the government rushed to commute their sentences to life imprisonment.

In December 1974 a plebiscite on the divisive issue of the monarchy was held. Support for a republic soared to 69 per cent of the total vote.[40]

Since 1974, social, economic and, above all, political conditions have not been conducive to the creation and/or proliferation of extreme right-wing groups. The collapse of the military regime, under the burden of its own incompetence and crimes, completely demoralised, confused and disorganised the far right. Although ND, under the leadership of Karamanlis, won the general elections of 1974 and 1977, the wave of radicalism sweeping the country appeared unstoppable. The charismatic Papandreou, who founded the PASOK in 1974, succeeded in leading the movement to power shortly after, by sweeping to victory in 1981 and by winning, convincingly, a second term in office in 1985 with an overall majority.

During the period following the downfall of the military regime, it was the far left that made its presence felt in the country's public life in the form of many, apparently small, underground groups which embarked on a series of terrorist activities and political assassinations. Their activities and image, modelled on the Italian Red Brigades, failed to move those in whose name their 'Robin Hood' game was played.

However, while the 'revolutionary' left took up arms to achieve its aims, the far right tried parliamentary tactics to make its voice heard. This does not mean that right-wing organisations have altogether disappeared from the Greek political map. Although, according to some sources,[41] nearly 150 groups, which were Fascist, royalist or associated with the military dictatorship, appeared during 1967–84, none survived for more than a few months. The '4th of August Party' is still around and faithful to its national socialism. Its influence, however, is insignificant.[42] Given the circumstances in which the military regime collapsed, it is not surprising that the extreme right of the political spectrum made a very poor showing at the first freely conducted general election of November 1974. The National Democratic Union [*Ethniki Demokratiki Enosis, EDE*] received no seats by scoring only 1.1 per cent of the total vote: 54,162 votes out of a total of 4,912,356. EDE was headed by Petros Garoufalias, who, as Minister of Defence in George Papandreou's government in 1965, had been at the very centre of the grave political crisis which led to the military intervention of 1967. Garoufalias then refused to resign his post when Papandreou asked him to do so.[43] With the backing of the king, Garoufalias played a key role in the political plots and manoeuvres of the day which forced Papandreou to resign and allowed the king to carve up his party by tempting many MPs and senior Cabinet members to defect from the ruling Centre Union party and form their own government with the support of the main opposition right-wing party, the National Radical Union [*Ethniki Rizospastiki Enosis*, ERE].[44] Garoufalias this time tried to appeal directly to the supporters of the military regime and called for the restoration of the monarchy. A more serious regrouping of the far right emerged in time for the 1977 elections. A new political formation, the National Camp [*Ethniki Parataxis*, EP], led by Stephanos Stephanopoulos, won 6.8 per cent of the total vote (349,851 votes out of 5,129,884), and secured five seats out of a total of 300. Stephanopoulos was Prime Minister in 1965–66 (after defecting[45] from Papandreou's party) and a Minister in several pre–1965 governments. The EP consisted of an assortment of right-wing revivalists of various shades, disenchanted with Karamanlis's policies, and of royalist diehards. It is true that, after 1974, Karamanlis sought to distance ND from the authoritarian right, in contrast with the policies he followed in his administrations of the 1950s and 1960s. In the course of the 1977 electoral campaign, Karamanlis came under heavy fire from the ultra-right which accused him of having split the camp of 'nationally minded' Greeks by, for example, legalising the KKE and making substantial concessions to the left. The EP preached strong anti-Communism, promised to grant an amnesty to the ring leaders of the 1967 military coup and to rehabilitate those in higher education who were sacked for collaborating with the military regime. It also believed in a more *laissez-faire* economy.[46]

Although Stephanopoulos, a long-standing political opponent and rival of Karamanlis, did not manage to deprive the latter of an overall majority in Parliament, he nevertheless now constituted a force to be reckoned with and a serious threat to ND's right flank. For the 'enlightened right' the EP, in fact, represented a national danger and was no more than an opportunistic coalition of royalist and pro-junta supporters who had turned their guns against Karamanlis in order to destroy the democratic and parliamentary system established after 1974. Although the new ultra-right formation emphasised that the monarchy was not an electoral issue, its deputy leader, Spyros Theotokis, a former ERE deputy, was a prominent royalist.[47] The Camp, though, was soon to develop centrifugal tendencies.[48] Three of its five deputies defected in 1980 to support Karamanlis in his bid to become President[49] of the Republic, and the 'Party' disintegrated. Theotokis himself was invited to co-operate with new Democracy and rejoined its ticket in the October 1981 elections. Subsequently Theotokis won a seat on ND's national list.[50]

George Rallis, who succeeded Karamanlis in the leadership of ND, and in the premiership of the government, made some pre-electoral concessions to the far-right in order to secure their withdrawal from the electoral contest, in the face of the growing threat of Papandreou's 'Marxist' PASOK. These moves, however, did not prevent the latter from winning a landslide, with a massive 48 per cent of the total vote. In the meantime, in 1979, the United Nationalist Movement [*Enomeno Ethniko Kinema*, ENEK] was formed. This organisation had Fascist, national-socialist and racist views, but made no particular impression upon the political scene. However, the standard for the disintegrated ultra-right was borne, in the 1981 election, by Spyros Markezinis, the puppet-Prime Minister of Greece's military dictatorship in 1973, when the regime tried to 'liberalise' itself for a short time. The new right-wing party, called Progressive Party [*Komma Proodeftikon*, KP], was launched on 7 December 1979. It secured 1.4 per cent of the total vote (77,465 votes out of a total of 5,670,941). However, the party won 1.95 per cent of the vote in the European elections which were conducted simultaneously and, thanks to the simple proportional representation system applied in these elections, it secured one of the 24 seats allocated to Greece in the European Parliament.

The difficulties of right-wing groups in consolidating a solid electoral base were exacerbated by the lack of any serious, stable leadership and organisation. It is not surprising, therefore, that another electoral formation, the National Political Union [*Ethniki Politiki Enosis*, EPEN], was hastily set up to contest the June 1984 European election.

The election developed into a bitter contest on all issues as Papandreou had taken up the challenge of the ND leader, Evangelow Averoff, who had succeeded Rallis in the leadership, in the wake of his party's devastating 1981 electoral defeat. Amid such a polarised campaign, EPEN managed to win 2.29 per cent of the vote (136,642 out of a total of 5,956,060) and elect one MEP, who joined the group of the European Right. EPEN made no secret of its ideological and political links with the protagonists of the 1967 military coup whose release from prison it had constantly demanded. It is characteristic that the former dictator, George Papadopoulos, had secretly recorded a message which was played at a meeting of EPEN's founding members. In December 1984, Jean-Marie Le Pen hosted an Athens meeting of the Group of the European Right, which provoked violent protest demonstrations mainly by left-wing groups, and led to eight policemen being injured and four protesters arrested.[51] During a press conference afterwards, the leader of the French National Front demanded the release of the imprisoned leaders of the military junta, calling them 'political prisoners'.

Despite EPEN's initial relative success in regrouping the far right and gaining some publicity, the problems besetting this part of the political spectrum, did not go away. ENEK scored only 0.03 per cent of the total vote in the 1984 European elections, while EPEN was unable to hold most of its votes gained in the 1984 European elections.

In the general election the following year, it scored a poor 0.6 per cent and won no seats at all in the *Vouli*, the national parliament. Despite this setback, EPEN continues its activities today and publishes a weekly political newspaper, the *Ellinikos Kosmos* (Greek World) with a strong anti-Communist line (circulation figures are not available). There are also a few other daily and weekly papers which disseminate extreme right-wing and totalitarian ideas with strong anti-Semitic overtones, but their circulation is insignificant.[52] The common denominator of all these publications, representing small far right-wing groups is their anti-Communism, anti-Semitism, and deep hostility towards democratic and parliamentary institutions.

In the general and European elections conducted simultaneously in Greece on 18 June 1989, the far right failed again to make any impression, in contrast to the considerable surge in the vote of *Die Republikaner* in West Germany and of the *Front National* in France in the European election. EPEN, for instance, scored only 1.16 per cent of the total vote and lost its single seat in the European Parliament, whereas ENEK's share of the vote was a poor 0.23 per cent. EPEN took only 0.32 per cent of the vote in the general election.

CONCLUSIONS

I have used a number of interchangeable expressions, such as far or extreme right-wing, neo-Fascist, etc., to describe forces on the right of the political spectrum, and have placed in a meaningful context a phenomenon which is by no means insignificant or marginal in modern Greek politics. I qualified this statement by referring to the fact that, in terms of organisation and political strength, these groups were marginal and quite often no more than mere appendages of the security branches of the state. Far more important, since the inter-war period, has been the role of extreme right-wing ideologies, embodied as operational ideologies in the Greek state and its coercive apparatuses. Typically, it is only since 1974 that New Democracy, as the new political formation of the right-wing conservative part of the political spectrum, has abandoned traditional, simplistic anti-Communism and excessive reliance on state coercion.

It is also characteristic of the post–1974 era in Greek politics that, once eradicated from State bodies or made redundant, extreme right-wing ideologies ceased to play a political organisational role by rallying all groups under their banner and giving them cohesion. Once discarded from the mainstream of Greek politics by no longer being at the core of conservative ideologies, right-wing extremism found its 'proper' dimensions. Having been stripped of this ideological mantle, it was confined to small groups. Despite their temporary electoral revival in 1977, they never constituted a real challenge either to the conservatives as a political party or to the government of the day.

From a *social* point of view, Greece is not so polarised as to create and reproduce marginalised sections of the population living under extremely harsh conditions and thus vulnerable to right-wing ideologies. So far, social conditions in the country have not created any dynamics of mass discontent which could be easily exploited by extreme right-wing groups.

The economic system, the pattern of capitalist development and property relations have not produced a large stratum of dispossessed people, nor a large agricultural and/or industrial proletariat which could be potentially mobilised by Fascist groups or constitute the social basis of such a movement.

From a political point of view, the left – the Communists in particular – is far better placed to attract and mobilise discontent for its political purposes. The traditional Greek Communist left has vast material resources, a strong trade union presence and powerful media and mass organisational networks. Even the 'revolutionary left', in the context of the great publicity it gained after 1974 for its terrorist attacks and socio-political diatribes, must have greater recruitment appeal and access to vulnerable social and/or age groups under present circumstances. On the other hand, there is no tradition of Poujadism in Greece. Old and new petty bourgeois economic and social strata usually register their protest by voting for the major political parties, and not by supporting extreme political movements and/or forming their social backbone. It must be stressed that Greek political parties are multi-class formations in many respects: in the social composition of their membership, in their electoral support and in their policy-making. When in opposition, they promise everything to everybody; when in government, they are characterised by strong bureaucratic, clientelistic practices and display exceptional skills in satisfying sectional, particularistic and corporatist demands as well as in co-opting social groups into the power bloc. These functions and practices of the political parties do not leave much room for the development of right-wing extremism. However, whereas under present conditions the Greek ultra-right groups do not have the capabilities of mass recruitment and political mobilisation, and, more generally, conditions are not such as to make this feasible, there is always the possibility of some growth at the expense of ND. The possibility of a number of disappointed supporters of this party turning to the extremes cannot be ruled out, although any mass desertion cannot reasonably be expected. From an *electoral* point of view, under conditions where the system is coming increasingly closer to simple proportional representation, it is not unreasonable to assume that a bigger slice of the total vote will go to the far right. At the same time, the opposite may well prove to be the case: with a realistic prospect of a conservative party winning an overall majority in a general election and forming a government, the electoral appeal of the far-right will probably vanish and its vote shrink. Voters will probably want to jump on the bandwagon, even at the last minute, so as to be on the winning side.

A third possibility, still from an electoral point of view, is a modest or stagnant performance at the polls, which (given a hypothetically bizarre political arithmetic and a hung Parliament) might allow the ultra-right to hold the balance of power and blackmail a conservative party short of an overall majority. However, this possibility is very remote.

Finally, it need hardly be stressed, here, that the totalitarianism and racism of all extremist movements of the right tend to overlap, and the Greek case is no exception to the rule. Although the challenge of neo-Fascism is far more serious in other European countries than it is in Greece, it would be unwise to underestimate a dangerous movement which is using democratic institutions in order to destroy them.

LIST OF ABBREVIATIONS

EAM   *Ethniko Apelefterotiko Metopo* [National Liberation Front]

EDA   *Eniaia Demokratiki Aristera* [United Democratic Left]

EDE   *Ethniki Demokratiki Enosis* [National Democratic Union]

EEE   *Ethnikistiki Enosis Ellados* [Nationalist Union of Greece]

EEK   *Elliniko Ethnikosocialistiko Komma* [Greek Nationalist Socialist Party]

EK   *Enosis Kentrou* [Centre Union]

EKM   *Ethnikosocialistiko Komma Makedonias Kai Thrakis* [National Socialist Party of Macedonia and Thrace]

EKNE   *Ethniko Kinima Neon Epistimonon* [National Movement of Young Scientists]

EL   *Elefterofronoi* [Free Believers]

ELAS   *Ethnikos Laikos Apelefterotikos Stratos* [National Popular Liberation Army]

EN   *Ethniki Nemesi* [National Nemesis]

ENA   *Enosis Neon Axiomatikon* [Union of Junior Officers]

ENEK   *Enomeno Ethniko Kinema* [United Nationalist Movement]

EON   *Ethniki Organossis Neolaias* [National Youth Organisation]

EP   *Ethniki Parataxis* [National Camp]

EPEN   *Ethniki Politiki Enosis* [National Political Union]

ERE   *Ethniki Rizospastiki Enosis* [National Radical Union]

EYP   *Ethniki Epiressia Pliroforion* [National Intelligence Service]

FS   *Foititiko Somatio* [All Student Union]

IDEA   *Ieros Syndesmos Ellinon Axiomatikon* [Sacred Bond of Greek Officers]

KKE   *Kommounistiko Komma Elladas* [Communist Party of Greece]

KP   *Komma Proodeftikon* [Progressive Party]

K4A   *Komma tis 4 Avgoustou* [4th of August Party]

KYP   *Kratiki Epiressia Pliroforion* [State Intelligence Service]

LK   *Laiko Komma* [People's Party]

ND   *Nea Demokratia* [New Democracy]

NT   *Nea Taksi* [New Order]
PAO   *Pnevmatiki Ananeotiki Ormi* [Intellectual Renovating Momentum]
PASOK   *Panellinio Socialistiko Kinema* [Panhellenic Socialist Movement]
PEEA   *Politiki Epitropi Ethnikis Apelefterossis* [Political Committee of National Liberation]
PEM   *Panellinio Ethniko Metopo* [Panhellenic National Front]
PK   *Patriotiko Kinema* [Patriotic Movement]
SAN   *Syndesmos Axiomatikon Neon* [Association of Young Officers]
SEKE   *Socialistiko Ergatiko Komma Ellados* [Socialist Workers' Party of Greece]
TA   *Tagmata Asfaleias* [Security Battalions]
TE   *Tagmata Ergassias* [Labour Battalions]
TEA   *Tagmata Ethnikis Amynis* [Battalions of National Defence]

NOTES

1. N. Mouzelis, *Politics in the Semi-Periphery. Early Parliamentarism and Late Industrialisation in the Balkans and Latin America*, Macmillan, London, 1986.
2. Th. Veremis, *The Greek Army in Politics, 1922–1935*, Ph.D. thesis, Trinity College, Oxford University, 1974.
3. K. Vergopoulos, *To agrotiko zetema sten Hellada* [The agrarian question in Greece], Exantas, Athens, 1975.
4. G. Mavrogordatos, *Stillborn Democracy: Social Coalitions and Party Strategies in Greece, 1922–1936*, University of California Press, Berkeley, 1975.
5. According to the 1928 Census, 88 per cent of the heads of agricultural businesses owned their land.
6. The Socialist Workers' Party of Greece [*Socialistiko Ergatiko Komma Ellados*, SEKE] was founded in 1918. In 1920, the party joined the Third International and, in 1924, changed its title to Communist Party of Greece.
7. N. Mouzelis, *Modern Greece. Facets of Underdevelopment*, Macmillan, London, 1978.
8. G. Coutsoumaris, *The Morphology of Greek Industry and A Study in Industrial Development*, Center for Economic Research, Athens, 1963.
9. Y. Andricopoulos, 'The Power Base of Greek Authoritarianism', in *Who were the fascists?* Universitets Forlaget, Bergen–Oslo, 1980, pp. 568–84.
10. Andricopoulos, ibid., mentions the following: the Nationalist Union of Greece [*Ethnikistiki Enosis Ellados*, EEE], which had its headquarters in Salonica, where an 80,000-strong Jewish community was based; the Greek Nationalist Socialist Party [*Elliniko Ethnikosocialistiko Komma,* EEK]; the anti-Semitic National Socialist Party of Macedonia and Thrace [*Ethnikosocialistiko Komma Makedonias Kai Thrakis*, EKM], and the tiny All Student Union [*Foititiko Somatio*, FS]. This list was drawn up by the British Embassy at the

request of the Foreign Office, and despatched on 4 May 1934.

11. Two days earlier the king had rejected an offer by the two major parties in parliament to form a coalition government.

12. S. Linardatos, *Pos Ftassame sten 4e Avgoustou* [How We Reached the 4th of August], Themelio, Athens, 1965.

13. S. Linardatos, *H 4h Avgoustou* [The Fourth of August], Themelio, Athens, 1966. See also, 'H 4h Avgoustoy', *To Vima*, special issue, 3 Aug. 1986, pp. 15-34.

14. R. Clogg, *A Short History of Modern Greece*, Cambridge University Press, Cambridge, 1979. See also 'The Fourth-of-August Regime', *Journal of the Hellenic Diaspora*, Nos. 1 and 2, 1986, pp. 53-112.

15. C. M. Woodhouse, *Modern Greece: a Short History*, Faber and Faber, London, 1986 (4th edn).

16. A. Gerolymatos, *The Security Battalions and the Civil War*. Paper presented at the Conference on the Greek Civil War, University of Copenhagen, 1984.

17. H. Fleischer, 'The Anomalies in the Middle East Forces, 1941–44', *Journal of the Hellenic Diaspora*, special issue on 'Greece, 1940–1950', Autumn 1970, pp. 5-36.

18. For example, the pro-Fascist *National Nemesis* [*Ethniki Nemesi*, EN], the extreme royalist Union of Junior Officers [*Enosis Neon Axiomatikon*, ENA], the right-wing Association of Young Officers [*Syndesmos Axiomatikon Neon*, SAN], or others known only by their acronym like the PAN and the EE.

19. L. Wittner, *American Intervention in Greece, 1943–1949*, Columbia University Press, New York, 1982.

20. N. Mouzelis, 'Capitalism and Dictatorship in Postwar Greece', in *New Left Review*, No. 96, 1976, pp. 57-80.

21. V. Kapetanyannis, *Socio-Political Conflicts and Military Intervention: The Case of Greece, 1950–1967*, Ph.D. Thesis, Birkbeck College, University of London, 1986.

22. During the parliamentary debate on a new bill about the State Intelligence Service [*Kratiki Epiressia Pliroforion*, KYP], renamed National Intelligence Service [*Ethniki Epiressia Pliroforion*, EYP] in January 1984, figures of between 12 and 30 million files were officially mentioned. According to some reports, they could well number 35 million. See *ANTI*, No. 252, 20 Jan. 1984, pp. 11-13.

23. J. Meynaud, *Les forces politiques en Grèce*, Etudes de Science Politique, Lausanne, 1965.

24. A. Lentakis, *Neo-facistikes organoseis neolaias* [Neo-fascist youth organisations], EDA, Athens, 1963.

25. The Lambrakis affair was dramatised in the film 'Z' by K. Gavras, named after the book by the Greek novelist Vassili Vassilikos.

26. N. Alevizatos, *Les institutions politiques de la Grece à travers les crises: 1922–1974*, Unpublished Ph.D. thesis, Universite' de Droit, d'Economie et de Sciences Sociales de Paris, Paris II, 1977.

27. K. Tsoukalas, The Greek Tragedy, Penguin, Harmondsworth, 1969.

28. J. Meynaud, *Rapport sur l'abolition de la démocratie en Grèce*, University of Montreal, 1967.

29. K. Legg, *Politics in Modern Greece*, Stanford University Press, Standford, 1969.

30. C. Woodhouse, *The Rise and Fall of the Greek Colonels*, Granada, St Albans, 1985.

31. In April 1970, the publication of *Politiki Agogi* [Political Education], written by Th. Papakonstantinou, sometime Minister of Education in the regime, was announced. The book was widely distributed and used as a school textbook. George Georgalas, the regime's chief spokesman, published in April 1971 his *Ideologia tis Epanastaseos* [Ideology of the Revolution], which was given wide distribution. Savas Konstantopoulos, editor of the pro-regime newspaper *Elefteros Kosmos* [Free World], was another 'theoretician' of the dictatorship. George Papadopoulos himself has published seven volumes of *To Pistevo mas* [Our Creed] to state his 'case'.

32. R. Clogg, *The Ideology of the Revolution of 21 April 1967*, in R. Clogg and L. Yannopoulos (eds), *Greece under Military Rule*, Secker and Warburg, London, 1972.

33. The '4th of August Party' was founded in 1960 by Costas Plevris, who has openly propagated National-Socialist ideas. The organisation was particularly active between 1960 and 1967 in Thessaloniki, during the students' mobilisations. The emblem of the organisation (the two axes) was identical to that of the Italian neo-Fascist organisation *Ordine Nuovo*. According to *ANTI*, No. 62, 8 Jan. 1977, splinter groups like that of P. Dakoglou, nicknamed 'Achaioi' [Achaeans], were fanatical supporters of Brigadier Dimitri Ioannides, Commander of the notorious Greek military police which had tortured many of the victims of the junta during the dictatorship. Ioannides was responsible for the coup which overthrew Papadopoulos in 1973, and was, behind the scenes, the strong man of the new military regime until its collapse in July 1974. After the fall of the military regime, Dakoglou's group was renamed Intellectual Renovating Momentum [*Pnevmatiki Ananeotiki Ormi*, PAO]. Another splinter group of '4K', led by A. Dedrinos, was also renamed Patriotic Movement [*Patriotiko Kinema*, PK]. See ANTI, No. 62, 8 Jan. 1977.

34. *ANTI*, No. 19, 17 May 1975.

35. *ANTI*, Ibid.

36. Th. Veremis, 'Greece: Veto and Impasse, 1967–74', in C. Clapham and G. Philip (eds.), *The Political Dilemmas of Military Regimes*, Croom Helm, London, 1985, pp. 27-45.

37. N. Diamandouros, 'Transition to, and Consolidation of Democratic Politics in Greece, 1974–83. A Tentative Assessment', *West European Politics*, VII,2, 1984, pp. 50-71.

38. V. Kapetanyannis, 'The Making of Greek Euro-Communism', *Political Quarterly*, L, 4, 1979, pp. 445-60. See also idem, 'The Communists', in K. Featherston and D. Katsoudas (eds), *Political Change in Greece: Before and After the Colonels*, Croom Helm, London, 1988, pp. 120-55.

39. Th. Couloumbis and R. Yannas, 'The Stability Quotient of Greece's

Post–1974 Democratic Institutions', *Journal of Modern Greek Studies*, Dec. 1983, pp. 359-72.

40. R. Clogg, *Parties and Elections in Greece*, C. Hurst and Co., London, 1988.

41. *Decapenthimeros Politis*, Nos. 67-68, Dec. 1984, pp. 34-41.

42. European *Committee of Enquiry into the Rise of Fascism and Racism in Europe*, *Report on the Findings of the Enquiry*, 1985.

43. A Papandreou, *Democracy at Gunpoint*, Penguin, Harmondsworth, 1973.

44. P. Paraskevopoulos, *Ta Dramatika Gegonota, 1961–67: Georgios Papandreou* [*George Papandreou: The Dramatic Events of 1961–67*], Fytrakis-Typos, Athens, 1988.

45. Six of the fifty MPs who had defected were now participating in his candidate lists. See *ANTI*, No. 86, 19 Nov. 1977, pp. 12-15.

46. See the conservative political review *Politica Themata*, 15–21 Oct. 1977, and 18–25 Nov. 1977.

47. Theotokis was elected deputy for Corfu with Karamanlis's New Democracy Party in 1974. However, he was soon to express his strong disagreement with the party's neutral stand in the constitutional plebiscite that followed on 8 Dec. 1974, and ended the monarchy by a two-to-one vote. He resigned his seat four days later.

48. See *ANTI*, No. 106, 26 Aug. 1978, pp. 2-11.

49. Karamanlis was elected president on 5 May 1980 in the third and final parliamentary ballot by receiving 183 votes, three more than the minimum required.

50. Theotokis died in Athens in 1988 at the age of 79. See his obituary in *The Times*, 9 Sep. 1988, p. 18.

51. See *The Times*, 5 Dec. 1984, p. 6. Le Pen visited Greece again in Sept. 1988. The government spokesman said then that he was a *persona non grata* for the Greek government.

52. *Stochos* [Target], for instance, is an eight-page broadsheet weekly paper full of anti-Slav, anti-Moscow, anti-Jewish propaganda, and is extremely racist and chauvinistic. *Elefteri Ora* [Free Hour] is a six-page daily paper with an eight-page Sunday edition. It hosts the views of Costas Plevris, the leader of the '4th of August Party' and of other right-wingers. It is strongly anti-Communist and anti-Jewish. Its circulation is very low, around 1,500 copies daily (Nov. 1988) in the Athens-Piraeus area.

CHAPTER TEN

The Extreme Right in France: 'Lepénisme' or the Politics of Fear

Michalina Vaughan

THE AVATARS OF THE EXTREME RIGHT

The dichotomisation of politics into right and left is an integral part of the Revolution's legacy to republican France. The full endorsement of the organising myths which underpin the regime is held to be the birth-right of the left. In contrast, the ideological credentials of the right remain perennially open to challenge. The recent bicentennial celebrations highlighted yet again the divide between those who accept not only the Republic, but the Revolution as a whole (*en bloc*, in Clémenceau's words), and those whose acceptance is more or less heavily qualified. It is a moot point whether differences in values upheld by different sections of the right are of degree or kind. To stress the existence of a continuum from *centre-droite* to *extrême droite* is to hint at shared meanings or even at guilt by association. For instance, the disgrace of the Vichy regime was visited on the political right at the Liberation, regardless of the fact that Pétain's supporters were of diverse backgrounds and that de Gaulle in his youth had been a follower of *Action Française*, the monarchist organisation of Charles Maurras, so called after the daily paper published from 1908 to 1944.[1] An alternative approach consists in focusing on the plurality of *droites* and on the deep-seated ideological differences which demarcate them, as René Rémond has done in his classic work *Les droites en France* (Aubier-Montaigne, Paris, 1982). In accordance with his terminology, the 'Orléanist' trend – closest to the centre – has always stood for parliamen-

211

tary democracy, whereas its 'Bonapartist' counterpart has been populist, anti-parliamentarian and, to a degree, anti-capitalist. The former identified with the institutional structures of the Republic, the latter showed a readiness to adopt revolutionary means (albeit for reactionary ends). Thus, both accepted some elements of the tradition which the left tends to claim as its own. Yet, a repudiation of the whole revolutionary past and of republican institutions was characteristic of the 'legitimist' minority, committed to the restoration of the monarchy and – at the beginning of the twentieth century – of Catholicism as a state religion. This extreme right became so politically disaffected as to opt out of any participation in republican institutions. Described as *émigrés de l'intérieur* (emigrants within their own country) – in an allusion to the emigration of aristocrats during the Revolution – the legitimists remained estranged from mainstream society, contemptuous of the ruling elite and, by corollary, inclined to adopt a conspiracy theory of politics.

The tradition which they established by negating the legitimacy of post-revolutionary French institutions was cross-fertilised by a number of trends which emerged under the Third Republic, from the 1880s onwards. The exacerbation of nationalism by the defeat of 1870 stimulated the unrest which General Boulanger attempted to exploit, and provided an environment conducive to the so-called Leagues of Barrès, Déroulède and Drumont. The latter exemplified the increasing connection between popular aspirations to revenge over France's enemies and the anti-Semitism which considered Jews as their agents. The Dreyfus case displayed how widespread these emotions were and added fuel to them. Furthermore, the exploitation of financial scandals involving republican politicians enabled the nationalist right not only to discredit the ruling elite, but also to denounce Jewish capitalist interests. This was a fertile breeding ground for a new blend of populism, based on a denunciation of both parliamentary democracy and bourgeois capitalism.[2] According to the analyses of Rémond, these stirrings fit in with the 'Bonapartist' right, of which Boulanger could be considered an exponent. However, he had to acknowledge that as nationalism moved to the right, it 'contaminated' even the royalists of *Action Française* with an element of the Jacobin legacy. In advocating rebellion against a Republic, denounced as both insufficiently patriotic and too corrupt, its supporters became *contestataires*, increasingly willing to be defined as extremists. To the historian Sternhell, they were the heirs of a pre-Fascist radicalism of the right, which had openly advocated the use of violent means to effect socio-political change.[3] In the 1930s, this legacy was truly acknowledged when, despite their membership of a Monarchist association, the younger activists of

Action Française described themselves as 'revolutionary conservatives'. To prove that they meant business, they entered into alliances with the Leagues, which drew on both nationalism and revolutionary syndicalism in an attempt to mobilise the crowds along lines reminiscent of Fascist movements in other Western-European countries. A new blend of political themes borrowed from the traditional right and of social themes from the left, the advocacy of violence, and even the terminology (for instance, Georges Valois's movement was called *Le Faisceau* i.e. The Fasces) hint at Fascist leanings. This was plebeian company for the upper class, intellectually sophisticated *Action Française*. It would be interesting to review in detail the debate between Rémond, who argues that the French rights (in the plural) retained their originality and that the Leagues merely made a lot of noise, but did little harm, and Sternhell, who detects a spread of Fascism from the mid–1920s.[4] The latter hypothesis distinguishes between the moderates (Rémond's *Orléaniste* right) and the populists, closer to the extreme left in their discourse and tactics. However, whether to use a label is really a semantic issue. Whether Fascist or merely *fascisante*, an extreme right existed as a mobilising force rather than a submerged trend. It made capital out of the economic recession in the 1920s, out of the fears which were rife among an ageing population, weakened by the losses of the First World War and out of the rumours about corruption and/or inefficiency in high places. The anti-parliamentarian demonstrations in Paris in February 1934 showed that their supporters could be stirred to action.

Since the French economy had not been affected as adversely, these outbursts could not be compared with the riots, born out of despair, which paved the way for Fascism in Germany. Moreover, national pride had been assuaged by victory – despite the price paid for it. Still, these events were significant to the extent that they inspired the extreme right with a new confidence in its ability to bring about a change of political regime. Characteristically, 6 February 1934, when a mob attacked the Chamber of Deputies, was described by the writer Robert Brasillach (later sentenced to death for collaborating with the enemy, and executed) as ushering in 'Year One of the National Revolution.'[5] It was, of course, no coincidence that the *Révolution Nationale* should have been proclaimed in 1940 by Pétain as the only means available for national regeneration. That defeat should have been received by some nationalists as a 'divine surprise' can only be understood because the rejection of modernity, construed as decadence, and of parliamentarianism, perceived as bankrupt, had permeated their thinking. Thus, the Vichy regime was born out of a collapse of national morale and of state institutions which had long been predicted by the extreme right. Some individuals – de Gaulle was a case in point – responded as patriots rather than as ideologists. Others attempted to apply the traditionalist blueprint, with the aid of some opportunists and of some believers in an 'understanding' between Pétain and de Gaulle.[6] For the first time since 1789, the chief objective of officialdom was to put the clock back; the modern industrial world was repudiated and secular society rejected. The authority principle was to be asserted in the state, at work and in the family. The return to the land, the reliance on religious values to buttress the family and transform education – all these were well-known themes of the extreme right from the old days of *émigrés de l'intérieur*. The attempt to 'return France to the French' by implementing discriminatory legislation against Jews, freemasons and *Français de fraîche date* (recently naturalised French) belonged to an agenda developed since the 1880s.[7] Although all these policies were repealed at the Liberation, they were to be heard of again, when their supporters reappeared on the political scene.

BURIED WITH VICHY, REBORN IN ALGIERS

To begin with, the collapse of the Vichy regime drove the extreme right underground. In fact, the right seemed to have vanished altogether. *Pétainistes* went into exile or were tried, and sanctions involved (at the least) the loss of civic rights. Collaborators faced heavier sentences and, in some cases, got rough justice. Somewhat unfairly, the whole right seemed to be tarred with the same brush because its republicanism was suspect, even if its patriotism was not. Political credibility could only be regained by adopting protective covering i.e. joining a liberal or Christian-Democrat party and participating in coalition governments, initially dominated by the left. Under the Fourth Republic, the moderates gained more and more votes, achieved majorities in Parliament and could finally acknowledge their true allegiance, though they were not able to solve the Algerian crisis.[8] Hence, they were defeated by the nationalism of the extreme right, which acted as a midwife to de Gaulle's Fifth Republic.

After lying low for about a decade, supporters of the extreme right began to have an impact on French politics in the mid–1950s. Their first reappearance in Parliament occurred when Poujadism attracted the votes of the petty-bourgeoisie, a traditional clientele of reactionary populists. The appeal of Poujade was to small-scale shopkeepers and tradesmen threatened by policies of economic rationalisation and by urban growth.

The main plank of his platform was tax reform to benefit the self-employed.[9] It proved highly effective and, in 1956, his movement gained 11.6 per cent of votes cast and 52 seats in the National Assembly. One of the new MPs was called Jean-Marie Le Pen. A couple of years later, Poujadism had burnt itself out and Le Pen had quarrelled with Poujade. Still, its brief popularity bore witness to the persistence of 'a virus which France cannot eliminate'[10] – an instinctive resistance of the 'small man' to socio-economic change and, hence, a vulnerability to demagogy.

The outbreak of yet another virus – nationalist extremism – was unleashed by the protracted process of decolonisation. Both in Indochina and in Algeria, aspirations to independence were ascribed to Marxist infiltration by army cadres responsible for control. Hence, a virulent anti-Communism spread among the officer corps and furthered their connections with Catholic fundamentalism. The lessons of *Action Française* were explicitly invoked to advocate the need for counter-revolutionary groups to 'save the fatherland' and to 'defend Christian Western civilisation'. From the creation of the Algerian National Liberation Front [Front de Libération Nationale, FLN] in 1954 to the demonstration of European settlers in Algiers on 13 May 1958, which brought de Gaulle back to power, the army activists became increasingly determined to take the law into their own hands. They advocated the *droit d'insurrection*,[11] the right to rebel, which was the legacy of those *contestataires* whose true ideological colours are the theme of the Rémond–Sternhell debate.

The cause of *Algérie Française* became the rallying cry of the extreme right under the Fifth Republic. Illegal organisations proliferated while de Gaulle ruled.[12] In fact, anti-Gaullism was their stock-in-trade. This bitter resentment was fuelled by memories of de Gaulle's refusal to grant a pardon to old Marshal Pétain (who died in gaol in 1951), but was mainly prompted by his 'betrayal of the army's trust' in having negotiated with the FLN. Thus, it had all the added resentment characteristic of family feuds. Army officers traumatised by the loss of Algeria, and *pieds noirs* (European settlers repatriated to a 'motherland' they hardly knew, and who were not always of French descent) became as determined to rewrite history as the legitimist *ultras* had been after the Revolution. The failure of the army coup in Algiers in 1961 drove underground the conspirators of the Secret Army Organisation [*Organisation de l'Armée Secrète*, OAS]. Some clandestine groups operated outside the law, e.g. the Revolutionary Army [*Armée Révolutionnaire*, AR], while, on the margins of legality, the *Occident* movement attempted to organise protest. Dissolved in 1968 after an anti-immigrant demonstration, it spawned New Order [*Ordre Nouveau*, ON] in 1969. A number of strong-arm groups operated in the 1970s, e.g.

Club Charles Martel, Groupe Delta, Honneur de la Police, the students' *Groupe Union-Défense* (disbanded in 1973 to be reborn and connected in the 1980, with the Party of the New Forces [*Parti des Forces Nouvelles*, PFN] of which more later). The best known is the neo-Nazi Federation of National and European Action [*Fédération d'Action Nationale et Européenne*, FANE], reborn as National and European Fasces [*Faisceaux Nationaux et Européens*, FNE] – a deliberate return to the terminology of the 1930s.[13] According to the European Parliament's Committee of Enquiry into the Rise of Fascism and Racism in Europe, 'the violent nature of these groups is real enough but their impact should not be overestimated'.[14] Although they have some international connections (e.g. ON with the Italian *Movimento Sociale Italiano* and the *Nationaldemokratische Partei Deutschlands*, and the FANE with like-minded German groups), they lack financial resources to such an extent that some of their criminal activities are 'fund-raising' burglaries. Others are attacks against individuals – mainly Algerians and Jews. In 1980, the peak of their 'form', commandos of the extreme right claimed over 60 such actions.

This is not to say that the extreme right refrained from legitimate political activities in the aftermath of the *Algérie Française* trauma. In the referendum of April 1962, intensive lobbying yielded 9.2 per cent of the vote. In the presidential election of 1965, the *Algérie Française* candidate, Tixier-Vignancourt, managed 5.2 per cent in the first round. He was sponsored by his own party, the Alliance for Freedoms and Progress [*Alliance pour les Libertés et le Progrès*, ALP] and by a network of support committees with a secretary general, the former Poujadist MP, Le Pen. Although the two men quarrelled and parted company, this was a kind of dress rehearsal for the co-ordination of anti-Gaullists, fundamentalists, self-confessed neo-Fascists and the so-called neo-pagans, later to be known as the New Right [*Nouvelle Droite*, ND]. The time was not yet ripe, but it was already apparent that a national organisation would be needed if the extreme right sought to be legitimated through the ballot box. Such an outcome was rendered difficult by the proliferation of small, often short-lived groups between which antagonism was sharp. Ideological heterogeneity was not the only obstacle to co-operation; the personality characteristics of individuals did not help, since they were often embittered or even unstable.

In the aftermath of 1968, which was widely perceived as a 'cultural revolution',[15] the intellectuals of the extreme right sought to make their ideas respectable through quasi-academic publications under the auspices of the Research and Study Group for European Civilisation *Groupement de Recherche et d'Etudes pour une Civilisation Européenne*, GRECE].[16] Though it took nearly ten years for this *Nouvelle Droite* to be discovered by the media, its elitist discourse, its claims to be scientific and its emphasis on European culturalism were influential throughout the seventies in rehabilitating a number of ideas previously held to be indefensible.[17] The New Right's strategy of intellectual rearmament was the polar opposite of commando activism, but continuity of personnel and, in substance (though not in form), of major tenets can be traced back to the OAS[18] and beyond. Despite clear differences, particularly in the appraisal of Christianity, between *Nouvelle Droite* and *Action Française*, both posited intellectual reform as a preliminary to societal change, and both fostered a climate of opinion in which right-wing extremism could thrive.

While the ND redefined metapolitics and the commandos pursued their 'cottage industry' of violence,[19] attempts to establish the extreme right on a party-political basis did not prosper. The electoral successes of the MSI in Italy prompted members of ON to join with some of their former partners of the Tixier-Vignancourt campaign in setting up a new party, the National Front [*Front National*, FN] in 1972. This federation of groupuscules split, in no time, into rival parties and it was only a court order which granted to the faction led by Le Pen the right to be called FN, while the other became the PFN, led by Patrick Gauchon. Both before and after this split, the scores of the extreme right candidates were disastrous (1.32 per cent in the elections of 1973, and a mere 0.74 per cent for Le Pen, as presidential candidate, in the first round of the 1974 election).[20] Not a promising start, to say the least. The instability of the Front and its initial lack of appeal could be ascribed to its heterogeneity. It has been called *un fourre-tout idéologique* (an ideological hold-all) in which Monarchists were cheek by jowl with revolutionary nationalists, neo-Poujadists cohabited with Catholic fundamentalists, the last Pétainists mixed with OAS veterans, disappointed Socialists joined renegades from the mainstream parties of the right and anti-parliamentarians of every ilk met with tireless protesters.[21] Initially, it was no more successful than its 'terrible twin', the PFN.

From another groupuscule apparently doomed to obscurity, the FN rose to achieve credibility within a decade. By the autumn of 1983, it was capable of attracting over 10 per cent of votes in local elections.[22] This unexpected result can only be understood by reference to Le Pen's own rise to notoriety as a communicator and to his charismatic appeal (at least to a sizeable percentage of the electorate – fluctuating from over 10 to under 20 per cent). The image he projects and the skills he displays are as significant as the often contradictory messages he conveys. He has been eminently successful as a performer in gaining attention for his party and his programme. Therefore, it makes sense to discuss his *persona* first, his political philosophy next, and finally to account for their appeal as expressed by voting behaviour.

THE LIFE AND TIMES OF JEAN-MARIE LE PEN

The founder member of the NF could be considered exemplary to the extent that his background fits all the stereotypes of the extreme right.[23] The son and grandson of sailors, he was born in Brittany (in 1928), in the heartland of Catholic traditionalism. He was a war-orphan (*pupille de la nation*). He was educated by the Jesuits. If he is to be believed, he joined the *maquis* at the age of 16 and, allegedly, that is where he acquired his life-long hatred of the Communists, whom he accuses of trying to monopolise the Resistance movement. As a Law student (registered in Paris – on and off – between 1947 and 1953), he was involved in anti-Marxist politics, and was even elected president of the student union (*Corpo de Droit*). In 1953, he volunteered to serve in Indochina with the Foreign Legion as a parachutist – though he actually worked on the forces newspaper when he got there. Back at the Law Faculty, he met Poujade, accompanied him to a rally of the Union for the Defence of Shopkeepers and Tradesmen [*Union de Défense des Commerçants et des Artisans*] held at Rennes, and extemporised an impassioned speech, on the strength of which he was asked to stand for Parliament. Elected in a working-class Paris constituency in January 1956, he rapidly gained a reputation for the effectiveness of his vitriolic oratory. In particular, attacks on Mendès-France – alluding to a 'patriotic and quasi-physical repulsion' – were widely reprinted,[24] though often deplored as anti-Semitic.

Just as he was gaining a political reputation, Le Pen showed himself to be a man of action rather than a mere talker. He took six months' leave from Parliament to rejoin his former regiment. He was sent to Suez first and then to Algeria (from September 1956 to May 1957). Back in Parliament, he embraced the cause of *Algérie Française* with characteristic enthusiasm. By late 1957, he had left the Poujadists and sat as an independent. Re-elected in November 1958, he joined the group of *Indépendants Paysans* (going back to his Breton roots . . .). In the elections of November 1962, his anti-Gaullism lost him his seat. So far, his extreme right credentials were impeccable. The only missing feature was that Le Pen had never belonged to OAS – a fact which did complicate relationships within the FN (Mark One) prior to the split of 1973.[25] Out of parliament, he remained politically active, especially in the Tixier-Vignancourt campaign. In order to overcome financial difficulties, he set up a company for the production of records bringing to life the history of the twentieth century, through speeches made by Lenin, Churchill and Stalin and by royalists and anarchists.[26] Out of some 140 such records, the public prosecutor picked on a medley of songs from the Third Reich and Le Pen received a suspended sentence of three months, as well as being heavily fined for infringing the legislation on war crimes (eulogised in the lyrics). This was not the first time he had been in trouble with the police: as a student, he was known to be a *baroudeur* (a 'hard man'), occasionally arrested for violence (e.g. in a Pigalle cabaret in 1948). Boys will be boys, of course, and it was always on record that when Le Pen lost one eye during a fight at an electoral meeting in 1957, it was to protect a Muslim friend (a supporter of *Algérie Française*). Somewhat less predictably, the police had to be called at Aix-les-Bains in 1951 to curb his aggressive behaviour in a church, where he had been refused communion while drunk. A trivial detail, maybe, but revealing of a wild streak for which military life offered plenty of scope.

Lieutenent Le Pen was accused of having tortured a young Algerian of 19, arrested by the parachutists on 8 March 1957 and released on the 31st. A police report was drawn up at the plaintiff's request on the day after his release, but there was to be no prosecution. Its contents were first published in *Vérité-Libération. Cahiers d'information sur la guerre d'Algérie* in June–July 1962.[27] The reaction of Le Pen when asked about this aspect of his past during the now famous interview of 13 February 1984 ('L'heure de vérité' – The hour of truth – on the TV network *Antenne Deux*) was not to deny any facts, but to stress that the unit to which he belonged had been entrusted with a mission 'by a Socialist government' and acquitted itself of the obligations 'imposed by the military and political hierarchies of the time.'[28] It is the well-worn reasoning about 'obeying orders'. To the extent that there is abundant evidence of systematic reliance on torture during the Algerian war, Le Pen is not only defending himself, but his generation. Therefore, he may actually gain some support, at least among older voters as well as among the most fervent nationalists, unprepared to countenance any blemish on the army's good name. In addition, the younger age group may simply lack any interest in a remote past and may consider any criticisms of Le Pen's early career as diversionary tactics intended to discredit him. Be that as it may, no harm appears to have been done to the FN by revelations about the less savoury episodes in its leader's career.

Yet by no means all of these episodes can be ascribed to war-time emergencies or to military discipline – which are certainly redeeming circumstances for authoritarian nationalists, i.e. for the natural catchment of the FN. Paradoxically, Le Pen's record is far from reassuring in two spheres which have traditionally been of particular concern to the extreme right. Firstly, religion and, secondly, the family. Both institutions, which loom so large in his rhetoric, provide constraints that are hardly compatible with his exuberance. NF rallies begin with a Latin mass, but its leader would not have a crucifix in his house (*Le Matin* of 7 May 1987), according to the revelations made by his estranged wife at the time of their divorce. Should this source of information seem unreliable, he is on record as saying that he would rather send his children on holiday to a Communist-run camp than to 'les curés', the priests.[29] A touch of anticlericalism is in the French tradition, but it is still somewhat unusual for a devout follower of St Joan of Arc[30] to set so little store by the sanctity of family life. Not only did Le Pen marry a divorcee,[31] but the marriage was dissolved nearly a quarter of a century and three daughters later, after a most acrimonious and unseemly divorce. In 1987 – the year he was being taken seriously as a candidate for the presidency of the Republic – his image was hardly enhanced by the comment that the mother of his daughters, if she needed money, could get employment as a charlady, or indeed by her retaliation (posing for *Playboy* in an apron and no other garments). Hardly the behaviour expected of a pillar of Catholic traditionalism.

While this proneness to becoming involved in scandal must be an embarrassment to the more conventional milieux in which Le Pen recruits voters, two factors help explain that it should not have damaged him as much as might have been expected. On the one hand, he appears to have a gift for generating uncritical admiration. Thus, his considerable personal fortune was acquired through a controversial legacy[32] from an early recruit to the FN. As in the case of many charismatic leaders, he is expected to be somewhat 'larger than life', and his followers may well feel that ordinary standards do not apply. On the other hand, and more importantly, Le Pen's sympathisers do not conform to the pattern of the old-fashioned extreme right, respectful of established hierarchies and scathing about any sexual peccadilloes. His electorate tends to be both younger and, more often, male than that of the two main parties of the right in France – hence less influenced by religious beliefs. In each election, the Front has spread to working-class neighbourhoods from its initial bourgeois strongholds,[33] thus recruiting from among 'de-christianised' sections of the population. More will be said about this dual catchment area in connection with fluctuations in the FN's scores. At this stage, the point is that the vagaries of Le Pen's private life would not deter those voters to whom only the aspects of his message which relate to their own concerns are relevant and to whom the Catholic rhetoric does not matter. Precisely because the message is contradictory, the 'duality' of the Front's potential constituency can be explained.

LEPÉNISME

The political philosophy of the FN is largely reducible to Le Pen's writings and speeches. He is widely held to be a talented demagogue with undoubted debating skills, a love of rhetoric and a keen understanding of TV technique. However, it ought to be remembered that within his own following, he is taken seriously as an original thinker. He is 'master of the truth, guardian and supreme judge of orthodoxy, unfailing guide to action, visionary, prophet'[34] – no less! Such enthusiasm is hardly shared by the occasional NF voter. At any rate, though, there is a widespread belief that Le Pen's discourse is at least consistent, and that he is prepared to face unpopularity, accusations about his past and media attacks in order to put his ideas forward.

Insofar as these ideas add up to a system, its cornerstone is nationalism. Le Pen claims to be part of a 'long chain',[35] dating back to *Action Française* and to its forerunners. Predictably, the approach is deterministic rather than voluntaristic. Belonging to the French people is achieved by linear descent. This birthright yields exclusive exercise of citizenship and priority in terms of access to scarce and valued resources such as social security benefits, housing and education. The principle of 'national preference' (*Les Français d'abord* – the French first)[36] is derived from the basic democratic principle of national sovereignty vested in the people and of which the state is a mere representative – and an undependable one at that. The common sense justification of this exclusivity is derived from the analogy between the nation and the family. Once more, the *Antenne Deux* interview of February 1984 spelt out the common-sense view of proximity as a key to trust (the so-called 'concentric circles' approach to which Le Pen always returns: 'I like my daughters better than my cousins [*cousines*], my cousins better than my neighbours [*voisines*]; my neighbours better than strangers [*inconnus*], and strangers better than foes [*ennemis*]'[37] – the nearest and dearest being female, while outsiders and foes are male. No great knowledge of sociobiology is required to draw the conclusion that the preservation of a 'breed' is aimed at.

Concepts of natural selection are drawn upon by Le Pen in order to show that society cannot be based upon a concern for the week. It must be gladiatorial or collapse:

> By granting privileges to the weak, by favouring them excessively in all respects, one weakens the social body as a whole. One does the very opposite of what dog and horse breeders do. I am not against relief for misfortune, e.g. for the handicapped, but nowadays we have almost got to the stage where handicap is promoted.[38]
>
> The analogy of 'dogs and horses' not only suggests that defective specimens [...] ought not to have been bred and that compassion for them should be kept within strict limits[...]. It also hints at the need to keep thoroughbreds uncontaminated by miscegenation.[39]

This pseudo-Darwinian approach — with the expected references to the survival of the fittest — is explained as a realistic acceptance of human nature. Its counterpart is an apocalyptic warning. To disregard nature is to accept defeat in the struggle for survival. The decadence which threatens the Western world as a whole, and French society in particular, derives from an egalitarianism contrary to the hierarchical principle enshrined in nature: 'The egalitarian movement which consists of levelling age groups, the sexes and peoples, is to be criticised in my view because it masks reality, which is based on inequalities. [...] The theme of equality strikes us as decadent.'[40] That age-groups, as well as the sexes, have natural roles is illustrated by the model of the family, in which the authority principle is fully vindicated. The legacy of the past is inseparable from these natural hierarchies and the future can only be made safe if they are buttressed or — if need be — restored. Conservatism (a defensive attitude) is linked with proposals for the protection of core values — the family, the rights of the people, national identity. These consist in preserving the health of the social organism by attacking the ills to which it is subjected. The organic analogy, which is so common in any discourse of the right, is fully developed in order to justify *Lepénisme* as a symptom of healthy nationalism: 'If to be reactionary is to react like an organism reacts when faced with disease, then yes, I am a reactionary. Not to be a reactionary, is to sentence oneself to death. It is to let the disease or the enemy take over.'[41]

The 'disease' is the weakening of the family and the drop in the birthrate which makes the inflow of immigrants and their large families increasingly threatening to an under-populated country, likened to a house no longer filled. Immigration is 'a foreign invasion by osmosis',[42] admittedly peaceful, but whose long-term effects will be the same as the incursions of alien hordes, prepared to fight when denied bread, wine and women. The use of emotive analogies and value-laden vocabulary is analysed by Honoré,[43] who shows how family imagery (father, brother, patrimony, legacy, mother, son, generation, blood, love) is used when discussing the national identity of the French people and how threats to it are given sexual connotations (intrusion, rape, miscegenation, cuckolding, homosexuality, prostitution).

The genetic and cultural threat to national integrity must be resisted by a number of policies, some destined to protect the French family, and the mother in particular, others to curb abortions, and yet others to restrict the rights of immigrants, whether to the acquisition of nationality by birth on French soil or to family allowances. Ultimately, the top priority will be to challenge immigration, the blame for which is ascribed to the suicidal policy of French governments over the years, and to enforce 'national preference'. This would entail discontinuing any assimilation of foreigners to nationals by laws and regulations, expelling any immigrants who behave in ways 'unworthy of French hospitality', and gradually repatriating others. This drastic programme is justified by the logic of inbuilt inequalities. The Third World is not capable of the achievement which made the West what it is; the Muslims, and the North Africans in particular, are neither willing nor able to assimilate, nor are Africans. They are simply not deserving, they do not work hard enough, they would drag any society down. The fear of downward-levelling through miscegenation is compounded by that of contamination by alien value systems and life-styles. Despite the stress on differences, held to be natural and therefore valuable, there is no doubt that some ethnic groups are ranked higher than others in the hierarchy of *assimilables* (capable – or worthy? – of being assimilated). Back to the concentric circles and the cousins preferable to the mere 'neighbours' – especially if they live 'next door' (across the Alps or the Pyrenees), rather than on the other side of the Mediterranean. Proximity is not only a spatial category, but a cultural one. This is where Christianity plays an important part as an intrinsic component of national identity. The Islamic immigrant is doubly alien, in cultural as well as ethnic terms, whereas the Spaniard or Portuguese shares with the French a religious dimension which can make assimilation easier. Once more, the concentric circles come into play, so that 'strangers' would be preferable to 'foes' (e.g. former dependents like Algerians).

To claim a share in the Christian legacy of the past is a prerogative of the right: 'The right seems to me to be philosophically linked with the natural order, with the Christian message, even though there are atheists on the right, and agnostics as well'.[44] While it is surely doubtful that 'the Christian message' conforms to 'nature', since its objective is to curb natural impulses, there is also a contradiction between the tribute paid to Catholic traditionalism and the strong materialist undertones of Le Pen's discourse. His commitment to 'popular capitalism' links freedom of choice to the possession of private property. The harshness of competition under capitalism – pilloried by the Poujade movement in its time – is accepted as a means of rewarding merit and effort. It is a prerogative of the family to pass a patrimony on from generation to generation, thus protecting individuals from the vagaries of the labour market.[45] Hence, without property there is neither freedom nor security. The creation of wealth is the task of individuals, caring for their families and struggling for survival. The state should not interfere with this process, but should merely ensure that its citizens and their property are protected from any aggression. Its basic duties are 'to defend the Nation and its people, to maintain order, to dispense justice'.[46] It is this fundamental concern for order, for the assertion of authority and the control of delinquency, which reconciles the religious and the economic dimensions. When Le Pen asserts 'I think that Monseigneur Lefebvre does a little of what I attempt to do in politics',[47] he highlights which aspect of Catholicism is closest to his own view. It is the punitive rather than the compassionate. The state must be more repressive because society must be 'cleaned up'. The pernicious elements to be sanctioned range from the unions (the socialist threat to economic freedom), to homosexuals and drug addicts (the physical threat of AIDS) and – last but not least – to immigrants (the alien threat to national identity). Although, in each instance, the arguments are presented by reference to the organic analogy (i.e. the dichotomisation of health and disease in society), religious justifications are also available (by reference to 'station in life', to procreation as a duty, and to the preservation of a Christian community from unbelievers). Whichever line is chosen, one feature remains unchanged: the endorsement of order, of state authority, of the law, of paternalism. In sharp contradistinction to the advocacy of economic liberalism (with an occasional dig at international trusts – no doubt a residue of Poujadism), there is a fierce rejection of libertarian values in both ethical and political matters.

For all its inconsistencies, the message is powerful, precisely to the extent that it is simplistic. It appears to invoke elementary common sense and to put forward obvious solutions (*y a qu'à* – nothing is needed but to . . .) to boldly-defined problems. 'Everything comes from immigration.

Everything goes back to immigration':[48] unemployment, 'invasion' of council housing by the minorities, overcrowding in schools, currency drain, rising crime-rate, even the spread of AIDS, all social ills can be traced back to the same root-cause, and therefore a simple remedy can be prescribed for all of them. The method is not exactly a new one. Le Bon's classic study of crowd psychology foresaw its success: 'Pure and simple assertion, unconnected with any reasoning and any proof, is a sure means of making an idea enter into the mind of crows'.[49] The simpler the idea, the more readily acceptable it proves. The *Maghrébins* (North Africans) have merely taken over from the Jews as the alleged cause of all social ills. It could be said of Le Pen, as Barrès exclaimed about Boulanger, that it is the person rather than the programme in which people put their trust.

LE PEN'S CONSTITUENCIES

The increased receptiveness of public opinion to Le Pen's discourse is correlated with a shift to the right, initiated by the backlash following 1968 and by de Gaulle's withdrawal from politics, since, without him, Gaullism was less and less a *rassemblement* (a rally). While power was uneasily shared in the 1970s by the nationalist/populists (not called *Chiraquiens* yet) and the 'Orléanists' (from Pompidou to Giscard), anti-egalitarian themes became more and more common. As the recession began to bite, public policies restricted immigration, at the time when the ND was propagating pseudo-scientific arguments in support of exclusion.[50] A growing sense of personal insecurity, linked with the presence of immigrants, and a demand for 'law and order' measures, appeared to peak towards the middle of the decade.[51] The extreme right was bound to capitalise on this upsurge of negative emotions and Le Pen could claim that he was daring to speak out on behalf of the common Frenchman, reduced to silence by the hypocrisy of the main parties (*la bande des quatre*, the gang of four – Gaullists, Giscardians, Socialists and Communists, all tarred with the same brush). Resistance to social change – which had accounted for the success of Poujade – served Le Pen equally well, but it no longer took the form of rejecting capitalism. It consisted in the *refus de l'altérité*, rejection of the 'other', the immigrant who is highly visible (by virtue of racial characteristics) and resistant to assimilation (by virtue of his cultural background, and of his religion in particular). He is 'the enemy within' (a familiar character in the demonology of the extreme right), denounced as a potential offender, as a drain on state resources and as a competitor (both on a tight labour market and on an inadequate housing market). All ethnic minorities, but Algerians in particular, are described as an uncontrollable demographic threat (through the high birth-rate and through miscegenation), and as a territorial threat (through the formation of ghettos).

The common denominator to which *Lepénisme* appeals is fear: 'Today the man who is of the right is he who instinctively feels threatened by others, by immigrants, by women, by children and, in general, by everything that is alien to him'.[52] The pervasiveness of this theme was exemplified by the setting up, under the auspices of the Gaullist party, of *Légitime Défense* as an association in 1978, of *Sécurité et Liberté* in 1979, and by the bulldozing, in 1979, of a refuge for immigrants at Vitry (by order of the Communist-dominated local authority). In such a climate of opinion, the extreme right necessarily exploited the widespread sense of insecurity[53] – hence Le Pen's definition of 'security as the first freedom' was particularly enticing. Even though this sense of insecurity receded gradually after the mid–1970s, the justification of immigrant labour as contributing to national prosperity could no longer be used.[54] This meant that the ethnic minorities could be construed as expendable. Furthermore, a socialist majority could be more readily blamed for disregarding the national interest on ideological grounds – and the 'orthodox' right which used such arguments in opposition found itself pushed further into an anti-immigrant stance by the competition (*surenchère*) of the NF.

The turning point in the electoral scores of the FN occurred in 1983, i.e. after the decrease in the sense of insecurity. A number of other considerations must be taken into account to explain this upswing (which, in any case, is more marked for the FN than for Le Pen personally, thereby confirming his early charismatic effect).[55] Firstly, the introduction of proportional representation helped the minor parties, FN included, in the Euro-elections of 1984 and the general election of 1986. Secondly, local elections (at Dreux, Aulnay and in the Morbihan department in 1983) and Euro-elections are not as 'committal' as presidential or parliamentary ones. They provide an opportunity for expressing resentment at, and giving a warning to, the main political parties. Furthermore, they have a cumulative effect, in attracting the attention of the media and in convincing people that a vote for the FN would not be wasted in future. This appeared a good deal more credible in 1983, after a 16 per cent score in the local elections at Dreux, than in 1978 when the corresponding results was 2 per cent. Thirdly, the spread of conservative values affected the whole of the right in the 1980s, thereby prompting some Gaullist and even, occasionally, some Giscardian voters to support the FN.[56] This 'slide to the right' was favoured by the dissemination of new political themes (security/immigration) over which the traditional parties wavered. Consequently, the clear, if simplistic, position of Le Pen was increasingly contrasted with the inability of the political elite to confront the everyday problems of life in France. The less politicians are trusted and the less they are believed to be speaking the truth,[57] the more willingness there is to vote for 'the odd man out'. As the *état de grâce* – the period of indulgence towards the new Socialist administration – ended, and as new austerity policies were implemented, the hour of the FN appeared to have come. In the parliamentary elections of 1986, Le Pen was returned as MP for Paris – back in Parliament after 20 years (his 'traversée du désert' or period in the wilderness – an expression used by analogy with de Gaulle's exile in Colombey-les-Deux-Eglises under the Fourth Republic).

A number of data confirmed the new-found strength of the FN. From a (self-confessed) membership of 20,000 in spring 1984, it reached 50,000 a year later. Its score of 10.87 per cent in the Euro-elections of 1984 showed areas of considerable influence (e.g. 21.39 per cent in the Nice area, an average of over 19 per cent in the whole South-East, 14.53 per cent in the Paris area, 13.2 per cent in Corsica). These coincided with regions where the *pieds noirs* settlers are numerous and also where the presence of immigrants is keenly resented.[58] The South-East in particular – with its Italianate political tradition of clientelism and with well-established ties between local politicians and organised crime, e.g. in Marseilles and Nice, has always been the neo-Fascist heartland. The same areas of concentration characterised the NF results in the local elections of 1985, where its candidates gained 8.8 per cent of votes cast. As it had put up no candidates in approximately a quarter of *cantons*, this apparent decline in relation to the Euro-elections was actually a consolidation, even a slight increase, in urban constituencies. In the general election of 1986, with its vote down to 9.8 per cent, the FN showed the same regional pattern (peaking in the South-East, with 22 per cent of the vote in the Marseilles area, and around Paris), but with a changing electorate. Its voters were becoming younger, less middle class and less likely to have voted previously for a party of the right; they were more pessimistic than the average about the role of their country in the world, about unemployment and about the future of the economy.[59] In addition, they were disenchanted with all political parties: predictably, nearly three-quarters of them voiced their dissatisfaction with the Socialists, but over half felt that way about the Gaullist-Giscardian coalition of the right. They tended to view the whole political class as corrupt: an opinion expressed by 71 per cent of them (as against 42 per cent of the French in general). Thus, the catchment area of the FN remained geographically circumscribed, but shifted downwards in the social scale and towards younger males.

That the intake of the FN should be young and predominantly male[60] is striking, since this distinguishes it sharply from the parties of the right, as does its relatively high intake of clerical and manual workers – even compared with the Socialist Party. This youthfulness of its activists means that they have no direct experience of the Vichy era or even of decolonisation. Some have transited through the *Occident* movement, but nearly half – in a sample dating back to 1978 – had no political past at all, a proportion which has certainly increased in the meantime. As a result, the 'complexes' of the past are shrugged off with greater ease than by older age groups. There is no hesitation in asserting extreme views, both in the valuation of authority and in that of the in-group ('the tribe' to be protected from outsiders).[61] The avowed motivation for supporting the FN is the dislike and fear of immigrants, linked with a concern for security. The two main themes of Le Pen's discourse are clearly echoed by his supporters, but in the reverse order – his emphasis being always on law and order, while his disparagement is not limited to ethnic groups, but extends to other 'undesirables', such as AIDS sufferers and homosexuals. These attempts to capitalise on 'moral panics' are better adapted to the nostalgia for the past prevalent among fundamentalists and other traditional supporters of the extreme right. They find less of an echo among the new constituency in which religious practice is low and views about sexual morality (about abortion in particular) are more emancipated than among supporters of the two main right-wing parties. A common antagonism, in both categories, towards established parties and towards politicians in general, is in tune with Le Pen's attacks against the 'gang of four'. The votes for him and his party are always protest votes, with a component of nostalgia dominant until 1986 and an element of anomie in the new, suburban lower-class strongholds, often formerly dominated by the Communist Party. By its very nature, this support is fluctuating and highly dependent on an emotional response to the leader.

Media exposure was therefore crucial to the creation of Le Pen's credibility as a candidate for the presidency of the Republic, and not only to the diffusion of his views. Attempts to tone down his message, in order to reassure a wider audience, occasionally gave way to a more spontaneous reaction. The first slip-up, the reference to the Holocaust as 'a point of detail' during an interview in September 1987, was damaging in so far as it revived fears about the extremism of the FN, even among some of its more 'respectable' supporters and sponsors.[62] A year later, the play on words: *Durafour crématoire* (from the name of the Civil Service minister

Durafour and *four crématoire* or gas oven) was found distasteful even by FN leaders, so that the single MP the party boasted at the time, Yann Piat, was expelled for her criticism of Le Pen's 'barrack-room joke'. Yet neither his verbal infelicities, nor his matrimonial troubles did the presidential candidate any real harm. In the first round, in April 1988, he gained 14.4 per cent of votes, thus establishing a record for the extreme right and, apparently, managing to hold his different constituencies – neo-Poujadist, white-collar and suburban working class. He even widened his geographical base somewhat, especially in eastern France (where nationalism always had a strong hold), but with inroads in the South-West and in his own Brittany. The extent to which this was a protest vote was shown in the second round of the election, when over a fifth shifted their allegiance to Mitterrand, rather than supporting the candidate of the right, Chirac. The extent to which it was 'personalised', attracted by one man's charisma, was demonstrated in the general election of June 1987, when the Front went down from 32 MPs to one. The policy of electoral agreements with right-wing parties had occasionally served them, but had not delivered votes for FN candidates. Once more, it appeared to have been marginalised and the image of Le Pen to have deteriorated (according to *Le Monde*, 69 per cent of the French considered him 'a dangerous man' and 61 per cent a racist).[63]

Yet again, the Euro-elections showed that the FN had become a feature of the French political landscape. With 11.73 per cent of the vote, it gained ten seats in Strasbourg, achieved the third highest score of all parties (behind the orthodox right and the Socialists) and influenced, to a considerable extent, the political discourse of Giscard's right. The opportunity to be in the news again – when one of the new FN Euro-MPs was in the chair as Father of the House and caused an exodus in protest – was no doubt the first of many. Le Pen's ability to generate scandal is only exceeded by his zest of it and by his survival skills.

AN INCONCLUSIVE CONCLUSION

The chequered career of Le Pen is certainly not at an end yet, and its future course is as unpredictable as his behaviour has been so far. The growth of the NF, from an insignificant groupuscule to a party capable of rallying between 10 and 20 per cent of French voters, is inseparable from the flamboyance of his personality and from the simplistic generalisations of his message. But the former can be a drawback when he really 'lets rip', while the latter has remained largely unchanged over the years. If it has contributed to lowering the tone of political debate in France, it has been unoriginal in content, echoing the vituperations of the extreme right at the turn of the century. Its impact is enhanced by unemployment, by the fears surrounding the Single European Market, by the low esteem in which the public holds established political parties, and, above all, by the rejection of minorities. By enabling failure and insecurity to be blamed on outsiders, Le Pen legitimates irrational, deeply entrenched beliefs which have been the stock-in-trade of the extreme right for generations. He is the conscious carrier of a disease for which there is no known cure as yet.

LIST OF ABBREVIATIONS

ALP   *Alliance pour les Libertés et le Progrès* [Alliance for Freedoms and Progress]

AR   *Armée Révolutionnaire* [Revolutionary Army]

FANE   *Fédération d'Action Nationale et Européenne* [Federation of National and European Action]

FLN   *Front de Libération Nationale* [National Liberation Front]

FN   *Front National* [National Front]

FNE   *Faisceaux Nationaux et Européens* [National and European Fasces]

GRECE   *Groupement de Recherche et d'Etudes pour une Civilisation Européenne* [Research and Study Group for European Civilisation]

ND   *Nouvelle Droite* [New Right]

OAS   *Organisation de l'Armée Secrète* [Secret Army Organisation]

ON   *Ordre Nouveau* [New Order]

PFN   *Parti des Forces Nouvelles* [Party of the New Forces]

NOTES

1. On the political philosophy of *Action Française*, see J. P. Apparu ed., *La droite aujourd'hui*, Armand Michel, Paris, 1979, pp. 117 ff.

2. C. Nicolet, *L'idée républicaine en France (1789–1924)*, Gallimard, Paris, 1982, p. 16, analyses the evolution of the nationalist right towards radicalism, nationalism and populism from the 1880s onwards. See also, Z. Sternhell, *La droite révolutionnaire (1855–1914)*, Seuil, Paris, 1978, who described this tradition as pre-Fascist.

3. Z. Sternhell, *Ni droite, ni gauche. L'idéologie fasciste en France*, Seuil, Paris, 1983, in particular pp. 58 ff.
4. For full information on this debate, see earlier version of Rémond's accounts of the right, i.e. R. Rémond, *La droite en France de 1815 à nos jours*, Aubier, Paris, 1954, and *La droite en France de la Restauration à la Cinquième République*, Aubier, Paris, 1963, as well as *Les droites*, cit. (which is a rejoinder to Sternhell, *La droite*, cit.).
5. R. Brasillach, *Les captifs*, Plon, Paris, p. 115.
6. The close relationship between the two, before the war, gave added verisimilitude to this assumption. Pétain was the godfather of De Gaulle's son, and it was to him that De Gaulle's book was dedicated.
7. R. Paxton, *Vichy France*, Barrie & Jenkins, London, 1972.
8. B. Criddle, 'France: legitimacy attained', in E. Kolinsky (ed.), *Opposition in Western Europe*, Croom Helm, London, 1987, pp. 108 ff, emphasises the importance of the Algerian crisis for relations between right and extreme right.
9. S. Hofman, *Le mouvement Poujade*, Colin, Paris, 1956.
10. A. Siegfried, *Tableau politique de la France de l'Ouest sous la Troisième République*, A. Colin, Paris, 1913, p. 495, quoted by Perrineau in N. Mayer and P. Perrineau, *Le Front National à découvert*, Presses de la Fondation Nationale des Sciences Politiques, 1989, p. 37.
11. Two authors of attempts on De Gaulle's life, Bougrenet de la Tocnaye and Bastien-Thiry, claimed this right. See Rémond, *Les droites*, cit., pp. 369 ff.
12. F. Duprat, *Les mouvements d'extrême droite en France depuis 1944*, Albatros, Paris, 1972, pp. 56 ff.
13. See J. M. Theolleyre, *Les Neo-Nazis*, Messidor, Paris, 1982, and J. Algazy, *La tentation néo-fasciste en France*, Fayard, Paris, 1984.
14. European Community, *Report on the Findings of the Enquiry*, Luxemburg, 1985.
15. Rémond, *Les droites*, cit., p. 269.
16. P. A. Taguieff, 'La stratégie culturelle de la Nouvelle Droite en France (1968–1983)' in R. Badinter *et al.*, *Vous avez dit Fascismes?*, Arthaud-Montalba, Paris, 1984, pp. 20 ff.
17. M. Vaughan, 'Nouvelle Droite: Cultural Power and Political Influence', in D. S. Bell (ed.), *Contemporary French Political Parties*, Croom Helm, London, 1982, p. 52 ff.
18. M. Vaughan, 'The Wrong Right in France', in Kolinsky (ed.), *Opposition*, cit., p. 276.
19. European Community, *Report*, cit., p. 39.
20. A. Rollat, *Les hommes de l'extrême droite: Le Pen, Marie, Ortiz et les autres*, Calmann-Lévy, Paris, p. 57.
21. Idem, p. 7.
22. The two main sources – sharply contrasting in intent and approach – are the hagiographic J. Marcilly, *Le Pen sans bandeau*, Grancher, Paris, 1984, and the highly critical E. Plénel and A. Rollat (eds.), *L'effet Le Pen*, Le Monde – La Découverte, Paris, 1984.

23. J. Y. Camus, 'Origine et formation du Front National', in N. Mayer and P. Perrineau, *Le Front National*, cit., pp. 20 ff.

24. See Marcilly, *Le Pen*, cit., p. 199.

25. Ibid., p. 28.

26. Ibid., p. 28.

27. Details in *Le Monde*, 14 Feb. 1984 (article by E. Plénel), p. 10.

28. 43 per cent of respondents in a SOFRES survey, conducted in 1985, believed that if he had actually been a torturer in Algeria, this would not disqualify Le Pen as a politician. See SOFRES, *Opinion Publique*, Gallimard, Paris, 1985.

29. J. Ferniot, *Pierrot et Alice*, Grasset, Paris, p. 28.

30. In the *Antenne 2* interview, Le Pen said that he 'voted for Joan of Arc' in the second round of the presidential election (of 1974). He wants the saint's day (8 May) to be a national holiday. See J. Marcilly, *Le Pen*, cit., pp. 147 ff and p. 157.

31. Pierrette Lalanne was the former wife of a theatrical impresario (and friend of Le Pen, for whom she left her husband). Their marriage took place soon after he ceased to be an MP and she helped him launch his recording company.

32. In 1976, Mr and Mrs Le Pen inherited some thirty million francs from Hubert Saint-Julien Lambert, whose family were the biggest cement producers in France. Lambert – a nationalist writer on military matters – died aged 42, leaving his whole estate to the Le Pens. The Lambert family initially challenged this will, but the matter was settled out of court. See Plénet and Rollat, *L'effet Le Pen*, cit., pp. 229 ff.

33. See N. Meyer, in Meyer and Perrineau, *Le Front National*, cit., pp. 256 ff.

34. P. A. Taguieff, 'La métaphysique de Jean-Marie Le Pen' in N. Mayer and P. Perrineau, *Le Front National*, cit., pp. 173–4.

35. European Parliament, *Report*, cit., p. 38.

36. J.-M. Le Pen, *Les Français d'abord*, Carrère/Lafon, Paris, 1984.

37. M. Vaughan, in Kolinsky (ed.), *Opposition*, cit., p. 283.

38. Le Pen, in Apparu ed., *La droite*, cit., p. 175.

39. M. Vaughan, in Kolinsky (ed.), *Opposition*, cit., p. 282.

40. Le Pen, *Les Français*, cit., p. 183.

41. Ibid., p. 176.

42. Marcilly, *Le Pen,* cit., p. 190.

43. J. P. Honoré, 'La hiérarchie des sentiments', in *Mots*, No. 12, 1986, pp. 129–57. In June 1989, at a special meeting of Euro-MPs of the extreme right from five countries, Le Pen reasserted that he had no objection to the presence of Portuguese immigrants in France, provided that 'national preference' applied to employment. See *Expresso* (Lisbon), 16 June 1989, p. B3.

44. Le Pen, *Les Français*, cit., p. 71.

45. Ibid., p. 140.

46. Ibid., p. 115.

47. J. Marcilly, *Le Pen*, cit., p. 106.

48. *Le Monde*, 12 June 1987, p. 6.

49. G. Le Bon, *Psychologie des foules*, 1895, quoted in G. Paicheler, *Psychologie des influences sociales* Delachaux & Niestlé, Paris, 1985, p. 55.

50. G. Albet and M. Sajous, *Contrepoint, ou l'art d'être Républicain*, Third International Lexicology Conference at St Cloud, 1984.

51. See data in Meyer and Perrineau, *Le Front National*, cit., pp. 70–1, about the peak of insecurity in 1975 (at 70 per cent of sample) and the drop to 59 per cent in 1984.

52. J.-M. Domenach, 'Des Transferts', in J.-P. Apparu (ed.), *La droite*, cit., p. 66.

53. R. Dulong and J. Léon, 'L'insécurité est-elle de droite?', in G. Abet and M. Sajous, *Contrepoint*, cit., emphasise the exploitation of cases of self-defence or of militia-creation by the extreme right, and stress its ambivalence towards the police.

54. G. P. Freeman, *Immigrant labour and racial conflict in immigrant societies*, Princeton University Press, Princeton, 1979, pp. 280 ff.

55. In 1973, the average FN score was about 2 per cent, but Le Pen's own, in Paris's 15th *arrondissement*, was 5.2 per cent. Even in the parliamentary elections of 1981, when the FN barely reached 1 per cent, he achieved 4.4 per cent in the 17th *arrondissement*.

56. C. Yamal, 'Le RPR et l'UDF face au FN: concurrence et connivence', *Revue politique et parlementaire*, 1984, LXXXVI, No. 913, pp. 6 ff.

57. J. Charlot, 'La transformation de l'image des partis politiques français', *Revue française de science politique*, 1986, XXXVI, 1, pp. 5 ff.

58. 57 per cent of foreigners in France live in the three main areas of FN concentration, i.e. Île-de-France, Rhône-Alpes and Provence-Côte d'Azur (*Le Monde*, Jan. 14 1984, p. 000).

59. H. Sofres, *L'é'tat de l'opinion*, Seuil, Paris, 1988, p. 131 ff (The age-group under 35 was up to 43 per cent of the Front's electorate in 1987, according to a SOFRES poll; the lower-middle and working class was up to 61 per cent, and the percentage of those who were sympathetic to the two main parties of the right was down to 12 per cent – as against 31, 37 and 39 per cent respectively in 1984).

60. C. Ysmal, 'Sociologie des élites du FN', in Mayer and Perrineau, *Le Front National*, cit., pp. 107 ff.

61. J. Stoetzel, *Les valeurs du temps présent: une enquête européenne*, PUF, Paris, 1983, shows a greater sense of isolation and more dislike of interaction with people who do not share their views, as well as more worries about the future among supporters of the extreme right in all European countries.

62. *Le Monde*, 1 Jan. 1987, p. 6. One of the main providers of funds for Le Pen, *Causa*, an organisation of the Moon sect, gave warnings to Le Pen, through its representative Pierre Ceyrac, that anti-Semitic statements would have to be avoided.

63. *Le Monde*, 6 Jan. 1989, p. 8.

CHAPTER ELEVEN
The New Right in France

Douglas Johnson

One day in February 1893, Xavier Rollin, who was a mason working in Paris, asked for a day off. He had, he said, to visit a relative who was ill somewhere in the suburbs. He was given his day off. But he did not turn up for work the next day, nor on subsequent days. After a week's absence, as one can readily imagine, his wife and his work-mates were extremely worried, and about this time, on a Sunday, a number of these same work-mates spent part of their leisure time visiting the morgue on the Île Saint-Louis. Whether this was a normal way of spending a Sunday afternoon or whether it was a special expedition arising from their anxiety concerning the missing Rollin, is not certain. But perhaps it does not matter. Among the corpses that had been fished out of the Seine or had been found on the public highway, and which were displayed to the public so that they could be identified, they recognised their friend. He had the same face, the same moustache, even in death, they thought, the same somewhat mocking expression which had characterised him in life. Deeply moved, they asked to see the clothes which the dead man had been wearing. They were shown the blue overalls that a worker normally wore; these, though, were covered with white plaster. There could be no doubt: it must be their friend.

When Madame Rollin came to see the corpse, she had no doubt either and she tearfully identified her dead husband. Everything seemed sad, but simple. There was only one further formality to be gone through. The measurement of the corpse, and a comparison of these measurements with the official anthropometric records which the police kept. Presumably Rollin had a criminal record; and presumably the corpse also possessed a criminal record. At all events, the authorities asserted that in spite of the positive identification made by all those who knew Rollin best, the corpse could not be his. The shape of the corpse's ear did not tally with the records of Rollin's ear. And sure enough, a Rollin, who was alive but probably not well, emerged shortly from the prison where he had been held on a charge of drunkenness.

This is, one would have thought, a story which is amusing in its tragi-comedy rather than edifying in its suggestions. Many explanations could be given as to how the misunderstanding arose. The author of the an-thropometrical system, Bertillon, has had a popular rather than a scientific reputation (in the *Hound of the Baskervilles* he is presented as a more impressive scientific investigator than Sherlock Holmes). The whole story may, in any case, be inaccurately represented. How extraordinary, then, that it should be presented as a key passage by Henri de Lesquen in his book *La Politique du Vivant,* published on behalf of the *Club de l'Horloge,* an independent group of higher French civil servants and technocrats. The biological implications are made explicit. The individual exists in all his physical originality. Socially he may be confused with someone else. Even within the intimacy of his family, confusion can exist. But scientifically he is different from any other person. One man is different from another. Julian Huxley is called in as a witness. Individual human beings are sepa-rated from each other by degrees which are as considerable as those which separate one part of the animal kingdom from another. There is, thus, a fundamental variation; there are, therefore, distances; there can arise hostilities and mutual incomprehension. But all these are based upon scientific reality. The social and political consequences are clear. To en-deavour to treat human beings as if they were all alike is to start from a false premise. To suggest that men are born equal, or to aspire to some sort of equality, is to fly in the face of a socio-biological knowledge which was already illustrated in the days of Bertillon, but which has been more than confirmed by a great deal of subsequent investigation.[1]

This new point was not confined to the *Club de l'Horloge,* which tended to be an intellectual pressure group close to the sources of polit-ical power in France, especially Gaullist power and aspirations. It was founded in 1974 by a number of graduates of the *Ecole Nationale d'Administration* and of the *Polytechnique,* and took its name from the fact that its original meetings took place in a room at the *Ecole Nationale d'Administration* which contained a particularly ornate clock. It claimed to be independent of other intellectual groups and it distinguished itself from them in so far as its members both sought and achieved active positions in politics.[2] Nevertheless it had many similarities with the *Groupement de Recherche et d'Etudes pour une Civilisation Européenne* (known as GRECE) and with the various organisations and publications which became known as 'la Nouvelle Droite' [ND].[3] GRECE was founded in January 1968 by a small group of young men. Many of them had earlier been associated with a university students organisation, the *Fédération des Etudiants Nation-alistes* formed in opposition to the *Union National des Etudiants Français,* which, allegedly, had supported the cause of the rebellion in Algeria from 1960 onwards, and with a number of not very successful peridicals such as *Les Cahiers universitaires, Défense de l'Occident, Europe Action* and *Valeurs ac-tuelles,* which had all been accused of being Fascist and racist. More sig-nificant, perhaps, is the fact that through these activities, the founders of GRECE had established a link with earlier right-wing thinkers and lead-ers, such as Doriot, Drieu la Rochelle, Brasillach and the Breton region-alists who had received Nazi support during the occupation. The years after 1965 saw the collapse of many of these right-wing endeavours, as, in the presidential election of 1965 and the general election of 1967, right-wing candidates had clearly failed. With the Algerian question settled once and for all and with *l'après Gaullisme* conspicuously on the agenda, a new start was necessary, and this was the reason for the creation of GRECE.

From 1968 onwards, GRECE shared the experience of many *clubs* which had, in a France dominated by Gaullism, become an accepted means of political discussion and expression. There were dissensions and rivalries amongst its members; individuals came and went; seminars and colloquia were held with varying degrees of success. But, gradually, prog-ress was made. The review *Nouvelle Ecole,* which had circulated privately among members of the group, became public from 1969 onwards; the same happened to the review *Eléments,* from 1973; between 1975 and 1976, bulletins were circulated in military, medical and educational circles; in 1976 a publishing house, Copernic, was founded; and in 1978, with the launching of the Saturday supplement of the newspaper *Le Figaro,* called *Le Figaro Magazine,* some members of GRECE became known to a wide public. From June to September 1979, the *Nouvelle Droite* became the term by which this group of writers was known (contrary to their wishes) and they became the subject of considerable interest, with news-papers publishing an unprecedented number of articles and interviews concerning them.[4]

The first problem concerning the ND is to understand why it created such a sensation during the summer of 1979. Articles about these thinkers had been published earlier and had aroused little interest.[5] It appeared that a moment had come when there was a particular need to discover something new. There were the *nouveaux philosophes* (Bernard-Henri Lévy, Jean-Marie Benoit, Jean-Paul Dollé and, in spite of his denials, André Glucksmann), the *nouveaux historiens* (Georges Duby, Pierre Chaunu, Emmanuel Le Roy Ladurie, Jacques Le Goff), the *nouveaux économistes* (with Jean-Jacques Rosa), the *nouveaux sociologues* (with

Evelyne Sullerot); there was, of course, the *nouvelle cuisine* and there was talk of *un nouveau romantisme*. It was suggested that all this stemmed from the discrediting of the old creeds. No-one believed in Marxism or in the Soviet Union any more. The churches had little appeal. Since 1968, revolution seemed impossible. De Gaulle had no successor as the leader of the nation. Liberalism and capitalism were both uninspiring and unsuccessful. Since intellectuals detest a vacuum, something had to take the place of what was missing.

At the same time, the nature of the ND's presentation of ideas was attractive. Alain de Benoist was continually surveying the literature of the past, and his book, *Vu de droite,* which received a prize from the *Académie Française* in 1978, was a collection of reviews. When the public had the impression that they were being bombarded by publications and that they were saddled with an intolerable burden of past thinkers, it was very satisfying to have someone who was prepared to act as a guide. In this, Alain de Benoist resembled Bernard-Henri Lévy, except, it was said, that he appeared to have actually read the books which he was talking about.[6]

The French public is attracted towards superlatives. René Mayer was known as the richest and most intelligent man in the National Assembly. General Salan was the most decorated soldier in France. Raymond Barre was the finest economist in the country. And soon it was whispered that Alain de Benoist had the best private library in Paris. He was said to be capable of explaining, in simple terms, the most complicated ideas and to bring to life a whole series of half-heard names, from Kant to Wittgenstein, from Hegel to Karl Popper. He was a reassuring figure when compared to the young intellectuals who had seemed so threateningly aggressive in 1968, or to the structuralists and their associates who were so incomprehensible at all times. Furthermore, such an 'encyclopédie vivante' was to be encountered in a glossy magazine (also containing articles about tourism and restaurants) which, in 1979, was distributed free.

There were two other features which aided the success of the ND. One was that they were not afraid of being associated with the word 'right'. Since the Liberation, no-one wished to be classified as belonging to the right politically. No-one, or hardly anyone, had claimed to be in that tradition or had willingly accepted being placed on the right-hand side of the hemicycle of the Assembly. Words like 'centre' or even 'centre-gauche' had been preferred. This sensitivity demonstrated that the normal aims of social democracy were shared by everyone within a framework of general consensus. By this, was meant the search for general prosperity, the demand for greater equality and the achievement of social and economic security. The fact that a group had appeared which did not accept these priorities, and which accepted a label which said so, was striking and unusual.[7] The other feature was that the ND was attacked as being dangerous. The very fact that they had received their greatest publicity through the newspaper *Le Figaro,* whose owner had, at best, an ambiguous attitude during the war, at worst an unpatriotic one, was sufficient to suggest that one was witnessing a revival of French Fascism. It was alleged that racist articles had appeared in early numbers of *Nouvelle Ecole,* and that while such manifestations had, then, been confined to a few isolated and unimportant groups, the fact that they could now achieve a mass circulation was a direct threat to democracy in France. There was, thus, a general denunciation of the ND. Even when writers were careful to say that they were observing not a French version of Hitlerism but a revival of the old, traditional and irrelevant right, it was emphasised that such a resurrection was disagreeable and unwelcome.[8] But the more the ND was attacked in these terms, the more it defended itself, the more it appeared in the public gaze and the greater the importance it assumed.

Naturally, other reasons were given to explain the success, or the scandal, of the ND. It was said to be an invention of the left. Embarrassed by the revelations of the Soviet gulag and by the supposed discrediting of Marxism, disappointed by the failure to bring about a union of the Socialists, Communists and Radicals and to win the elections of 1978, the left was quick to seize upon the opportunity of creating a scare. What *France-Soir* called 'la basse police intellectuelle' of the left brandished the old monster of fascism in order to give life to what was a strategy in a shambles and a cause which many thought of as lost.[9] The Giscardiens, then in power, were also believed to have an interest in magnifying the importance of the ND. They constantly sought to enlarge their support in the centre and they were only too pleased to suggest that they were liberals who had nothing in common with the right as exemplified by the ND and which they too viewed with hostility and apprehension. The man most directly responsible for bringing the ND into the public eye, the editor of *Figaro Magazine,* Louis Pauwels, explained in an interview what he considered to be the farcical nature of such exaggerations. He claimed that the ND hardly existed; that those who sought to make it appear as a sinister force had commercial motives, since they wished to attack the economic success then being enjoyed by his magazine. He denied that he was a member of GRECE or of the *Club de l'Horloge* and he scorned the idea that his publication had accepted the ideas of the ND. However, such declarations did not put an end to the controversy (possibly because Pauwels had not been as explicit as he might have been:

he did not mention his long-standing association with *Nouvelle Ecole* or the similarities between some of his own publications and those of the ND).[10]

One is obliged to conclude that there was a general fascination with the ND, both on the right and on the left.[11] It is conceivable that people were disarmed by the claim that GRECE was a laboratory of ideas and a centre for reflection, and that its leaders had no intention of leading an active political party. This may have coincided with the development of a certain public indifference to organised political parties. Alain de Benoist rejected any connection with a traditional right that was nationalist, militarist, religious, populist and, on occasions, racist and monarchist, and which sought to put crowds in the streets (as on 6 February 1934 in Paris) or deputies in the Assembly. He was amused, although in the long run irritated, by those foreign journalists who asked him how many parliamentary votes he controlled.[12] The only active political organisation which openly claimed any affinity with the ND was the *Parti des Forces Nouvelles,* the French branch of Euro-Right. It claimed that it had called for the formation of a ND as early as 1974, and that it had organised a forum with GRECE and with interested individuals (including Louis Pauwels) in that year. However, the leaders of the PFN, such as Pascal Gauchon and Alain Robert, had turned to Jean-Louis Tixier-Vignancourt as their leader and, with him, were then engaged in a rivalry with Jean-Marie Le Pen and the *Front National* for leadership of the extreme right. Its intellectuals, such as Yves Van Ghele, had been obliged to leave GRECE once they had become activists, militating in favour of the PFN. Its position, therefore, was confined to the statement that it and the ND were 'de la même génération' and 'de la même famille intellectuelle'.[13]

The discussion of whether the ND was a reincarnation of the old traditional right or not, or whether it was a camouflaged and coded post-war version of pre-war Fascism, has continued to be debated ever since the heady days of the summer of 1979. Some observers note that in a confidential memorandum it was determined to be prudent with regard to its vocabulary, but that, in spite of such precautions, one finds in its publications the essential mix of race-politics and race-science, and that its language is that of classical Fascism.[14] Raymond Aron, while being particularly anxious to be fair to Alain de Benoist and to avoid any suggestion that he was a National-Socialist or a Fascist, nevertheless concluded that his manner of thinking and reasoning was often similar to that of the National-Socialists and the Fascists.[15] René Rémond, the historian of the right in France, has observed a resemblance between the role of Charles Maurras in the *Action Française* and that of Alain de Benoist in the ND, a role which extends to their method of work, as well as to their vision of an active cultural group in conflict with a political establishment.[16]

Naturally, observers as sophisticated as Aron and Rémond were always well aware of the circumstances that cause the ND to be distinguished from any of its ancestors, whether French or not. Yet, it is true that Alain de Benoist has dominated his movement, as did Maurras. It is significant that both of them were more concerned with the cultural rather than with the political, and that both of them saw their work as something which had to be accomplished within a long framework of time. They both made a fundamental distinction between the day-to-day running of a society and the accepted political climate of that society. In 1979, Alain de Benoist was able to point out that the left had never been in power since the Liberation, but that the accepted political culture, whether it was expressed by intellectuals or by *instituteurs,* was dominated by the ideology and the assumptions of some sort of Marxism. In a manner which had been made familiar by Gramsci and by Althusser (two thinkers whom he claimed to admire), his object was to change the values and the assumptions of French society and to influence the prevailing ideological apparatus without having to gain any political victory, and without having to promote any institutional change. By constantly challenging old axioms, by bringing forward thinkers relegated to oblivion and by promoting ideas which were strongly in contradiction with certain values and principles that had been taken for granted, the ND sought to stake a claim and to be accepted. In this way, it is true that it can be compared to such figures as Barrès or Maurras or to certain fascist thinkers, all of whom challenged prevailing liberalism. But, it need hardly be said, this in no way makes it comparable to the *squadristi* or to the Brown Shirts.

The challenge from the ND came essentially over three themes. Firstly, there was the rejection of equality. They argued that everyone must understand that men were not born free and equal. The study of primitive and ancient societies confirmed this. No community could take as its basis a purely arithmetical and theoretical equality, and no community should endeavour to construct such an equality. Secondly, there was the need for elites. Without a hierarchy, a society would have no sense of responsibility. A hierarchy classifies people according to their abilities and according to their tasks. Without this there can be no harmony. Thirdly the understanding of society depends upon science, that is to say sociobiology, rather than upon moral concepts. Human nature has an instinctive basis, however much this may be modified by social learning, and it is the genetic variety in the species which is vital for survival and for the success of the evolutionary process. In other words, what determines the nature of a society of a society are the ethnic rather than the economic factors.[17]

It is not surprising that these simple ideas should have had a certain success. People had become cynical about the possibilities of achieving social equality. New elites were constantly being created and it seemed sensible to accept them. Contact with the Third World suggested that there were fundamental differences between groups, and it did not seem unreasonable to suppose that biology might some day be recognised as being as important in political life as economics.

There was nothing surprising, either, in the fact that the ND was hostile both to the Soviet Union and to the United States (it was this latter hostility which aroused the most disapproval from Raymond Aron). No intellectual movement in France in 1979 would have stated otherwise. What was more unusual was its opposition both to Christianity and to Marxism. The basis of this attitude has been explained by Alain de Benoist as being an attack on a senseless form of history. Christianity, or Judaeo-Christianity as he has always preferred to call it, supposes that there was once a moment of ante-history, the Garden of Eden, which was destroyed by the original sin of Adam and Eve. There will also be a period of post-history when the Redeemer returns. Marxism, equally, supposes that there was once a time of primitive communism when men lived happily together. One day, though, mankind committed the fault of dividing up property and labour, and there developed a system of classes which set the exploiters against the exploited. But this will also come to an end when those most exploited succeed in dominating all society. Then, exploitation will cease, harmony will reign and the state will wither away. For Christians as for Marxists, mankind is dominated by a past, a present and a future. Mankind has therefore lost its freedom and the possibility of self-creation. It is not simply the church, the chapel, the ghetto and the gulag which have to be rejected, as if they were bad examples of good ideologies. Christianity is the Bolshevism of ancient times, monotheism is totalitarianism, all attempts at imposing equality are equally stultifying and barren. The philosophy of the ND is that of a new anthropology. Man is a defiant being, a creature of unlimited possibilities.

It is not surprising that these aspects of the ND were not appreciated by the readers of *Figaro Magazine* or were mentioned by those who sought to frighten liberals with the bogy of immediate Fascism. The insistence upon the values of paganism may have had a passing appeal for societies which found some attraction in the mysteries of Eastern religions, but this was hardly likely to be lasting. What was most challenging, and therefore least acceptable, was the ND's questioning of accepted ideas about progress. History, they claimed, was not a linear process; history was chaos. The world and the future will be what mankind wishes to make of them. None of the rules and laws which have been accepted as universal need be accepted at all. Everything is open to question. There is no reason why men should accept the cult of weakness and humility that was inaugurated by Christianity; no reason why the cult of egalitarianism should be derived from the supposition that men wish to satisfy their material needs in the same economic manner; no reason to accept the rule of some superman with outstanding intelligence or strength. But if history is chaos, history none the less exists. Just as animals have their sense of order, of defence, of territory, of gradation, so men live in groups which develop their instincts, differences, intuitions, beliefs and varied forms of rootedness. History may be chaos, but that is all the more reason to believe, with Nietzsche, that the future belongs to the man with the longest memory. History may be chaos, but that is all the more reason to believe in what exists rather than in what ought to exist. Universal and abstract concepts are names which have no corresponding realities.[18]

It could be argued that such a method thinking is devastating in its destructiveness, and that if it ever, for a short time, achieved a certain popularity, however limited, it was because no-one obeyed Alain de Benoist's advice that the texts of the ND should be carefully read and studied. But it must be admitted that there are other reasons why the vogue of the ND was short-lived. It was a phenomenon of the media, and as such was bound to be temporary, by definition. It was, as was pointed out at the time, a characteristic of Parisian intellectual life to take up a current of thought, to give it importance and then to drop it. There is a tendency in all cultural and political pressure groups, especially in France, for individuals to fall out and for organisations to divide and to sub-divide, and this has happened to the ND. Financial support, however discreet, is not necessarily permanent.

The political climate has also changed. The victory of the left in 1981 was in itself significant, but the progressive abandonment by French Socialists of many of their egalitarian ideas removed an issue from the debate that had existed in 1979. The preoccupation with modernisation, which became a fetish for the Socialists under Prime Minister Laurent Fabius, pushed the hostility of the ND towards the modernisation of life by machine into the background.[19] The emergence of the *Front National* as a political party which wins votes means that allegations of racialism and anti-Semitism are concentrated upon Le Pen and his supporters, and there are no commentators who wish to analyse Alain de Benoist's remarks about the Jewish diaspora made in a pamphlet which few people have read. Above all, perhaps, attention is focused upon the future organisation of Europe. But this is the decadent, technological, crypto-Christian Europe that the ND has always attacked. We are a long way away from the Indo-European civilisation from which Europeans have according to Alain de Benoist, sprung, especially from the cultures, the mists and the forests of northern Europe.

If in the late 1970s *La Monde* was filled with articles discussing the ideas of the ND, in the 1980s it was filled with articles discussing the silence of the intellectuals. Alain de Benoist is a victim of the belief that, within a vast consensus of agreement about the importance of material benefits, there is no longer any role for intellectuals. But he believes that his time will come. He still thinks that the great issue of the present and the future is the struggle between paganism and monotheism. He believes that it is the duty of the radical right, rather than the radical left, to combat accepted ideas, assumptions and values, and so to challenge the camp-followers of conformity.[20]

NOTES

1. H. De Lesquen, *La Politique du Vivant,* Club de l'Horloge, Paris, 1979.

2. It is noticeable that certain prominent members of the *Club de l'Horloge* have recently joined Le Pen's *Front National,* e.g. Jean-Yves le Gallou, who was formerly the secretary-general of the *Club,* a member of the *Parti républicain* and assistant to the mayor of Antony, in the southern suburbs of Paris. He explained his position in the *Front National's* weekly paper, *National-Hebdo,* 12 Sept. 1985. Yvan Blot, who was President of the *Club* until 1985 and who was closely associated with Jacques Chirac as mayor of Paris, was elected to the European Parliament as a member of the *Front National* in June 1989. See his interview in *Le Monde,* 2 June 1989, in which he explains his progressive disappointment with Chirac's party, and *Le Nouvel Observateur,* 7–13 Sept. 1989, p. 28, which describes him as the *maître-à-penser* of Le Pen.

3. The most authoritative work on GRECE is A. -M. Duranton-Crabol, *Visages de la Nouvelle Droite. Le GRECE et son histoire,* Presses de la Fondation Nationale des Sciences Politiques, Paris, 1988. This publication is a version of a thesis which was submitted to the University of Paris–Nanterre in 1987, the full text of which, with a copious bibliography, is deposited in the library of that university. On the subject of the relations between the *Club de l'Horloge* and the ND, see three articles in *Le Matin,* Paris, 25, 26, 27 July 1979.

4. Alain de Benoist vigorously denied, in an interview with the author, 23 Jan.

1980, any association with 'la droite traditionnelle', and therefore thought the term 'Nouvelle Droite' inappropriate. He did, however, state, on another occasion, that in the early 1960s he had been a militant in extreme right-wing circles (see Duranton-Crabol, *Visages,* cit., p. 20). Pierre Vial, the sec-retary-general of GRECE, claimed that his group was concerned rather with the elaboration of 'une nouvelle culture de droite' but which, however, felt itself to be nearer to 'une nouvelle gauche' than to the traditional right (*Le Monde,* 24 August 1979, p. 2).

5. J. Brunn, *La Nouvelle Droite. Le Dossier du Procès,* Nouvelles Editions Oswald, Paris, 1979, is an anthology of these articles. A bibliography of the ND and of kindred movements in Italy is in *Mots,* No. 12, 1986, pp. 204–24.

6. T. Sheehan, 'Paris: Moses and Polytheism', *New York Review of Books,* 24 Jan. 1980, p. 13.

7. A. Fontaine, *Le Monde,* 11 July 1979, p. 1.

8. A. Kriegel, *Le Figaro,* 10 July 1979, p. 2. Several writers in the daily edition of this newspaper, including the editor, Jean d'Ormesson, expressed their disagreement with ideas published in the supplement.

9. *France-Soir,* 10 July 1979.

10. Louis Pauwels, interviewed by Georges Suffert, *Le Point,* 13 Aug. 1979, pp. 28–9. See also L. Pauwels, *Comment devient-on ce que l'on est,* Stock, Paris, 1978, and his preface to the collective work published under the name of Maiastra, *Renaissance de l'Occident,* Plon, Paris, 1979.

11. J.-F. Kahn, *Le Nouvel Observateur,* 13 Aug. 1979, p. 13, makes this point.

12. Author's interview with Alain de Benoist, 24 Jan. 1980.

13. *Le Monde,* 30 July 1979, p. 6. The ideology of the *Parti des Forces Nouvelles* is stated in its pamphlet, *Propositions pour une nation nouvelle,* Paris, 1978 (2nd edn).

14. M. Billig, *L'Internationale raciste. De la psychologie à la science des races,* Maspéro, Paris, 1981, pp. 123–49. G. Seidel, 'Le fascisme dans les textes de la Nouvelle Droite', *Mots,* No. 3, 1981, pp. 47–62.

15. R. Aron, *Mémoires,* Julliard, Paris, 1983, p. 701. He was very anxious that the ND should not be accused of causing the terrorist attack on the syna-gogue in the rue Copernic in Paris, and he took every opportunity of saying this.

16. R. Rémond, *Les Droites en France,* Aubier, Paris, 1982, pp. 283–5.

17. For the many sources of Alain de Benoist's ideas, see A.-M. Duranton-Crabol, *Visages,* cit.

18. P.-A. Taguieff, 'Alain de Benoist philosophe', *Les Temps Modernes,* Feb. 1984. vol. XIX-XXX, pp. 1439–78, and April 1985, pp. 1780–1842, criticises the nature of the philosophy of the ND and places it in its context in Europe, as well as discussing its attitude towards the controversy over the Holocaust in France.

19. G. Faye, *Les nouveaux enjeux idéologiques,* Editions du Labyrinthe, Paris, 1985.

20. Author's interview with Alain de Benoist, 26 Oct. 1987. On this occasion he said that, contrary to press reports, *Nouvelle Ecole* had 10,000 subscribers and that *Elements* regularly sold between 15,000 and 20,000 copies.

CHAPTER TWELVE
The Far Right in Contemporary Britain

Gerry Gable

In the winter of 1987 the National Front (NF) celebrated its twentieth birthday. In this paper I would like to chart the changes in the National Front and the broader far right movement in Britain since their modern origins twenty years ago and to show how, with international help, a small and very dedicated group known as the Strasserites has ascended to power. These take their name from the Strasser brothers who were the backbone of the Brownshirt movement in Germany even before the Nazis took power. When Hitler purged the Brownshirts in 1934, one brother was murdered and the other fled into exile, only returning to Europe after the Second World War.[1]

THE NATIONAL FRONT'S BEGINNINGS

The National Front was born out of an amalgamation of far-right groups during the winter of 1966–67. Its initial membership came in the main from three large groups: the British National Party (BNP) with 1500 members, the League of Empire Loyalists (LEL), 2000 strong, and the Racial Preservation Society (RPS), with around 500 followers. Other smaller groups also became part of the new organisation, and a few months later the avowedly Nazi Greater Britain Movement (GBM), led by John Tyndall, came into the NF.

In its first year the NF's membership totalled around 4000. It had a number of publications which the groups had brought in with them, such as *Spearhead*, owned and edited by Tyndall, and *Candour*, the personal broadsheet of A. K. Chesterton, the NF's first leader. Other publications such as *National Front News, Nationalism Today, Bulldog* and maybe a dozen others have come and gone over the years. Many local branches produced their own brand of propaganda, often openly Nazi in content and style, illegal, and almost always vicious in approach to Jews and blacks. Black crime and Jewish control were two of the regular themes. The leadership included almost every noteworthy post-war Fascist organiser and activist with the exceptions of Oswald Mosley and members of the hierarchy of his party, Union Movement (UM), and Colin Jordan who had founded, and was at that time still leading, the National Socialist Movement (NSM) in between frequent terms of imprisonment.

THE NF'S GROWTH TO 1974

Over the next seven years the NF flourished, while some of the old guard dropped away. These included Chesterton, who had been Oswald Mosley's pre-war political secretary and had founded the LEL in the 1950s, John Bean, also a former activist in the LX and organiser of the neo-Nazi National Labour Party (NLP) from 1958 to 1960, during which time he helped set up the BNP, and Andrew Fountaine, a former navy commander and Conservative parliamentary candidate who had been forced out of the party in the 1950s for his blatantly anti-Jewish sentiments. His estate in Norfolk was used for Nordic radical international gatherings in the late 1950s, at the time when he was involved in establishing the BNP. New blood was injected into the organisation by the intake of disgruntled Conservatives opposed to the leadership of Edward Heath, who was seen as soft on immigration and law and order, the two key planks of the NF's policy. These included former parliamentary candidates like Roy Bramwell and local Monday Club organisers like Gillian Goold as well as local councillors such as John Kingsley Read in Blackburn.

By the first of the two 1974 general elections the NF's membership had peaked at 17,500 and their percentage of votes in both national and local elections was steadily increasing well beyond the odd-ball and fringe vote of the earlier post-war, far-right groups. The success of the NF had even prompted Mosley to try several times to return to the hustings, with disastrous results. This led to him finally bowing out from the political scene and to most of his inner circle leaving UM to form the League of St George (LSG) in the mid-1970s. Although the new members came from the Conservative Party, most of the NF's votes were coming from traditional Labour voters in the inner cities.

THE STRASSERITE COUP AGAINST TYNDALL

The Front now appeared to be under the absolute authority of the leading NSM activist John Tyndall, a street politician of little charm and small intelligence, but with a well-organised Praetorian guard of old GBM members around him in the key NF posts. But just when he seemed to have gained total control, the leadership was swept out of his grasp by a group of young Strasserites and ex-Conservatives who replaced him with John Kingsley Read.

It appears that a number of internal rows over Tyndall's style of leadership – in the main his refusal to share power or adopt a more Strasserite policy – had led to a split at the top of the party. It is thought that the main reason he was ousted was that he reneged on his oath of allegiance to the Nazi secret society, Column 88, into which he had been inducted at the age of nineteen. This covert organisation, named after the pre-war Nazi student fifth column in Vienna before Hitler marched into the city in 1938, has existed in this country since the war years. Its aim is to ensure the internal security of the movement, punish those who break their oaths of allegiance and conduct paramilitary training for those deemed suitable. It has also run a very professional infiltration of democratic organisations over the post-war period. It is linked to similar groups abroad.

In 1967, at the time of his rise to power in the NF, Tyndall had written to the US Nazi party leader, Dr William Pierce, to explain that he had not abandoned his faith in the swastika and Hitler, but that the British public were not prepared to accept open Nazism yet; so the NF must hide behind the Union Jack and phoney patriotic jargon until the time was ripe to go public with a mass Nazi movement. Rhodesia and the defence of the white minority, illegal regime of Ian Smith was a prominent theme of their public activities, and the old sun-wheel symbol, common to most post-war neo-Nazi groups in Britain, was dropped in favour of the Union Flag. On Remembrance Sunday parades, which at that time were attended by some thousands of members or supporters, bemedalled ex-servicemen were pushed to the fore.

Column 88 clearly saw Tyndall's opposition to developing an openly Nazi programme of ideas for the last quarter of the twentieth century as out of step with its own radical position, which was influenced by the more internationalist approach being preached by François Genoud and Guy Armundraz of the New European Order. They were busy making accommodations along political rather than racial lines, and the idea of a strong united Europe was well up on the agenda. Certainly these men had no compunction about making deals with Arab nationalists, for instance, and with Irish and other revolutionary groups, if it enhanced their own progress. Tyndall, on the other hand, was without a doubt a little islander who believed that he would only find foreign support in the white Commonwealth or the deep south of the USA. The French and Spanish were almost as alien as blacks and Jews to his way of seeing the world.

Shortly before his death in 1984, John Kingsley Read admitted that, when he was chairman of the NF, the young Strasserites were obtaining funds from Column 88 sources abroad as well as from right-wing Arab sources, in order to run the NF and to produce large amounts of propaganda.[2] In charge of this operation was a young graduate called Richard Lawson. Read also witnessed the illicit arms deals involving Steven Brady, a young Ulsterman, and Leslie Eric 'Lutz' Vaughan, the intelligence officer of Column 88. These arms were destined for loyalists in Ulster.

The creation of the LSG which aimed to explore, behind closed doors, the old Nazi ideas and the new approach, had frightened Tyndall and his younger but cleverer organiser, Martin Webster. Webster had followed the same path as Tyndall from the NSM to the GBM and into the NF. In 1976, the NF declared the League a proscribed organisation. NF members were prohibited by Martin Webster from making trips to the annual nationalist rally at Dixmuide in Belgium, where the old guard and the new Nazis could meet and plan operations that were, in many cases, illegal.

The other rising star of this period in the mid–1970s was David McCalden, another young Ulsterman, who directed his energies towards the student movement and animal-rights groups. He later went to live in California where, with the godfather of the American anti-Semitic right, Willis Carto, he founded the Institute for Historical Revisionism, an anti-Jewish operation which encouraged the re-writing of history, in particular suggesting that the Holocaust had not taken place. The Institute's other themes all emanated from the basic idea of 'Jewish evil' put forward in the Protocols of the Learned Elders of Zion, the infamous anti-Jewish tract that first emerged as a propaganda weapon in Tsarist times in Russia. McCalden arranged the Institute's early funding from Arab sources.

THATCHER'S ELECTION AND THE CHANGE IN THE POLITICAL SCENE

After Tyndall regained the NF leadership, the Strasserites left to form the

National Party (NP). But both groups were fast approaching the political wilderness as far more important changes were taking place in the mainstream of British political life. With the election of Margaret Thatcher as leader of the Conservative Party in 1975 on a ticket of more restricted immigration, and a strong policy on law and order and on Ulster, there was very little reason for the Conservative dissidents who had joined the NF not to return to the Conservative fold. Thatcher's television interview of January 1978 in which she said she understood how English people felt about being 'swamped' by those of alien cultures was the final wink and nudge to return home. Roy Painter was free to re-enter the Conservative party without any promises on his part or any pre-conditions being set.[3] Painter was a typical example of a Conservative defector to the NF. A former working-class Conservative parliamentary candidate in Tottenham (North London) in 1974, he became an NF election candidate in the same constituency, and a party activist.

Tyndall was left with a rump organisation. The suggestion that he was being punished for his disloyalty to Column 88 was being echoed in every far-right quarter. Column 88 had shown how powerful it was behind the scenes. The 1979 general election, which swept Thatcher to power, ended the NF's dreams of ever achieving any sort of political recognition via the ballot box.

Further splits left around 5000 members in the NF, which came under the control of Andrew Brons, another former associate of Jordan and Webster. Tyndall then set up the New National Front (NNF) and later resurrected the BNP. Both these groups have been openly Nazi in style, in particular in the role of Tyndall as sole, unelected leader. Hitler and his racial and political programmes are openly praised in the party's journals. Despite the fact that Tyndall has since 1982 managed to run two publications, *Spearhead* and *The British Nationalist*, with occasional editions of a youth paper called *The Young Nationalist*, he has only been able to maintain a membership of around 800, of whom only very few have been activists.

Colin Jordan gave up the leadership of the British Movement (BM), which the NSM was now called, because of legal problems following the strengthening of the race relations laws by several Acts of Parliament between the late 1960s and the mid-1980s. He took to living in the country in Yorkshire and to producing occasional duplicated copies of *Gothic Ripples*, an anti-Semitic broadsheet named after the publication of his mentor, the late Arnold Leese, leader of the pre-war Imperial Fascist League (IFL). This was a small but violently anti-democratic, pro-Hitler organisation whose main theme was an almost hysterical anti-Semitism.

Mosley's organisation, UM, has gone, and apart from a few ultra-fringe groups such as WISE (Welsh, Irish, Scots, English) and Choice, it is only the NF that comes to the mind of the public whenever British racism or Fascism is mentioned. A key NF member once said that ownership of the name NF was like owning the name of Heinz if you were a baked beans manufacturer – it is the name everyone knows.

THE RE-SHAPING OF THE FAR RIGHT

By 1983 the British far right lined up as follows: the BNP, the NF, the LSG, the National Socialist Action Group (NSAG), the National Action Party (NAP), a range of sections of the Monday Club (a fringe group close to the Conservative Party), and the Federation of Conservative Students. The latter organisation was so far right that it had to be shut down by the Conservative Party leadership in 1988.

It was clear at this point that the British right was ripe for reshaping and modernisation. An injection of funds, a new organisation, new policies and, above all, an overall strategy were needed to take it into the next decade. First of all the old guard, or those among it who would not step into line, would have to be removed and replaced, and the best place to start was with the largest group, the NF.

In 1983 Martin Webster felt secure in his full-time job at NF headquarters. He was virtually running the organisation himself, organising its troops who were now down to around 4000, editing its publications and paying lip-service to the leadership of Andrew Brons who lived in Harrogate, sufficiently far from the party headquarters in Croydon (South London) to cause Webster no problems. A new breed of activists had appeared on the scene in the previous few years: Ian Anderson, educated at Oxford; Nick Griffin, a Cambridge graduate; Derek Holland from East Anglia, also a graduate; and a working-class, street-fighting, anti-hero figure; Joe Pearce, from a working-class estate in Dagenham (East London). Pearce was the only leading member of the new leadership who could claim working-class origins that were genuine, and this gave him street credibility with the young skinhead followers who are in the main lumpen working-class.

Webster's close friend Michael Salt was the NF's office manager, and between them they had a very good idea of what was going on at every level of the organisation. Webster was close on forty and the oldest member of the inner circle.

A NF organiser for Central London, Michael Walker, had turned his home in Pimlico into a lodging house and meeting place for all sorts of Nazis from Italy, France, Germany and the USA. He was the translator of the works of the French new-right leader, Alain De Benoist, and was now extending his connections into Tory far-right groups such as Tory Action and David Irving's circle of political contacts, the Focus Study Group and the Clarendon Club. He was also forging lines of communication with ecological groups such as Green Peace and alternative energy organisations. His ability to communicate in several languages gave him the chance to approach European nationalist groups such as Basques, Bretons and Flemings. However, more than anything else, he was establishing links with groups that stood for a Europe of nations, but a united one that would stand against both US and Soviet influence.

Martin Webster had been seen by friends and enemies alike as the cleverest political in-fighter on the far right, hardly ever missing a trick. He had been worried by the growing contacts that Griffin, Holland and even Brons had forged with a group of exiled Italian Fascists from the *Nuclei Armati Rivoluzionari*. This organisation takes a Third Position stance [i.e. it distances itself from both capitalism and communism], and has became synonymous with violence, bombings, shootings and robberies for party funds. The two key Italians in London at that time were Luciano Petrone and Roberto Fiore. Petrone was on the run for the murder of two Italian police officers and a £12 million bank vault raid in Spain. He was living in Chelsea with a British woman whose child's nanny was the girl-friend of the second Italian, Roberto Fiore. When Fiore's child was born, his girl-friend took the child and went to live with the Hancock family in Brighton, who are involved in all Fascist publishing both in the UK and across Western Europe and Scandinavia. They are members of the LSG and Column 88, and have played a key role in the international Nazi movement over the last 20 years. Fiore was convicted in Italy, in his absence, on charges of organising an armed group and sentenced to a nine-year term of imprisonment. He was to be the main contact with the NF's young Strasserites.

Webster had always maintained a double standard as far as law-breaking was concerned. He would allow his members to step over the line on minor matters but would inform the police about anybody with a gun or explosives. This he did out of self-preservation rather than any real regard for the law. As party boss he knew that if ever conspiracy charges were levelled against the NF, he would certainly be in the dock; he therefore did his utmost to create a clean image.

This time, however, Webster's spy network failed him and in a Saturday afternoon coup he was ousted along with Michael Salt, and cut off from the headquarters and membership lists. Within hours, other old guard members got their marching orders. In the months that followed, a series of court hearings failed to resolve the NF's internal disputes but in the end the new guard, who included Anderson, Griffin, Holland, Wingfield, Pearce, and even Brons, were in a position to oust Webster at the NF's Annual General Meeting, using the rule book.

Webster waited a while and then tried in vain to set up his own small political group, Our Nation (ON). It made the headlines because one of its architects, a former NSM and NF member called Denis Pirie, was working in a sensitive post in Whitehall. For a time, Colin Jordan's former wife, the synagogue arsonist Françoise Dior, assisted Webster with funding. Tyndall sat on the sidelines crowing at the downfall of his former friend and later political adversary. Today, ON still meets on rare occasions for a meal and after-dinner speech, but Webster has gone into semi-retirement, running his own small commercial type-setting business in North London.

In what was described as a period of political Pol Potism, the advocates of the new regime were prepared to get rid of almost the entire membership, in the same way as Pol Pot had destroyed the entire Khmer middle class to advance his ideas. Most members over 30 years of age were excluded from the NF, any argument was met with instant expulsion and the Italians went as far as suggesting, at the height of Webster's fight back, that he should be assassinated if he continued to be a thorn in their side.[4] The British Fascists seem not to have had the same enthusiasm for this form of political difference-settling. Through the Italians, Pearce and Holland gained introductions to Libyans and pro-Iranian Iraqis in Britain and France. Arrangements were well under way for regular funding when Pearce and Anderson were arrested and charged for producing *Bulldog*. Pearce had already served one term of imprisonment on the same charge. For a short while this poured cold water on the international link-up, but some funding for an insert for *Nationalism Today* entitled 'Victory for Palestine' had already passed into the party's funds. The Griffin faction had been drip-fed by Fiore and his associates with hundreds of pounds each month during the takeover of the NF. Strong suggestions continue that some funds from the Spanish bank-vault raid found their way to the NF to help promote destabilisation at international football matches.

PRODUCING 'POLITICAL SOLDIERS'

The new group was given printing equipment by the Hancocks and bought modern typesetting machines and some computers. They then began to move out of London to a series of secret locations around the country in preparation for a new form of organisation.

Fiore and others won a court case against their expulsion back to Italy, but Petrone's murder of the two Italian police officers resulted in his being sent home. Fiore moved in with Michael Walker, and about ten others of his group have continued to remain in Britain and work with the NF and Walker.

The reading list for NF members changed dramatically overnight and the ideas of the Strasser brothers have come to the fore as have those of Julius Evola the spiritual founding father of the NAR in Italy and of the Third Position. Now it is a case of 'give us the new recruit and we will produce the "political soldier" '. The ideas of Evola, a friend of Goebbels and Himmler, were so extreme that Mussolini had him arrested before the war.[5]

The NF leadership intentionally allowed the membership to run down to just under 1000 in early 1984, but by the end of that year it was back up to around 3000. They have now instituted a system of recruitment with various levels of membership and oaths of allegiance that give them absolute control over the members. Today you cannot join the NF – the NF chooses you if they think you are suitable material either as a street fighter (and future terrorist?) or as an organiser and propagandist. You can be a 'Friend of the Movement', a trainee cadre or a cadre, and after that you take further steps up the ladder of command.

Almost at once, the new regime brought in a man named Garry Gallo from Washington DC. He stayed in Britain for a year using, among his five other aliases, the name Rossi. In 1984 the NF told the authorities that his job was to help them set up the commercial side of the organisation, that is to sell T-shirts, badges, key-rings, records, tapes and books. In reality he was here to teach them how to run a clandestine organisation. He was assisted by ex-police officer Jim Capes, who knew how to deal with police interrogation and how to conceal material from police raids. Behind the scenes Richard Lawson was instructing the NF on the replacement of old policies with new ones that were ecology orientated. Michael Walker's growing network inside environmental groups was also of considerable help. Young members were sent out to join CND protests against US bases, following the example of the new right in Germany, but at the same time the NF argued in favour of the British nuclear deterrent.

Ulster became one of their prime areas for recruitment and action. Since the NF became involved there, attacks by loyalists against the Royal Ulster Constabulary have increased. One of the Front's key organisers, Andrew McLorry, a schoolmaster, has been sent to prison for bombing RUC homes using some of his pupils to deliver the bombs.

But NF criminal activity has not been confined to Ulster and the football terraces. A member of the *Bulldog* production team, Paul Hanmore, was sent to prison for life for the murder of an Asian cashier during an armed robbery in 1985. Several other members, including Joe Pearce and Martin Wingfield, have been sent to prison for offences under the Race Relations Acts, and many more, such as Ian Stuart Donaldson, leader of the rock band 'Skrewdriver', and his associate, Des Clarke, have been put away for serious assaults.

In the north of England where the NF have targeted areas of ex-tremely high youth unemployment, like Consett, where 84 per cent of school leavers are without a job, the violence has been similar. There the local NF organiser, Kevin Turner, got four years for cutting out a man's eye in a pub fight, which by all accounts was not over a political matter. Attacks on the police – something Webster was always careful to keep to a minimum – have resulted in at least two senior activists in London being sent to prison in 1988.

In 1983 the NF took on the services of Graham Gillmore, one of their members who had just returned from service in southern Africa. There he had served in specialist cross-border killer commandos of the South-African army, and had previously fought for the Smith regime in Rhodesia. He started to train a select group of members in modern guerrilla warfare, but moved out of the limelight after public attention was drawn to an NF weekend camp where he showed participants how to strip down hand-guns in the company of the military commander of Column 88, Major Ian Souter Clarence. He moved to Peterborough, but was exposed in 1987 while recruiting mercenaries with the help of a former NF parliamentary candidate, Tony Hilton.

Reports from local trade union clubs, youth clubs, animal rights groups and even anarchist organisations all indicate that the NF members with whom they are now in contact are better educated politically, have a fair degree of organisational ability, and try to find areas of agreement or accommodation instead of highlighting differences. The NF's role in vio-lent animal rights activities and the 'stop the city' demonstrations in

London called by direct action anarchist groups are only two examples of their involvement in events that help to destabilise society. The NF also appeared during the Wapping printers' strike and, more recently, in 1987, tried to intervene in the Kerton's trade-union dispute in Sheffield. Their involvement in the National Council for Civil Liberties in 1985 almost led to its collapse.

A CAREFUL PLAN

The question to be asked, then, is does the NF merely reflect a society that has seen a growth in street violence and mass unemployment in recent years, or is it working to a carefully-put-together plan? What follows may show the latter to be the case.

In 1986, after the final cleansing from the NF of all vestiges of the Webster years, a second coup took place, which left the 5000 members split, with around 2000 in the Griffin camp and 3000 with Brons. Both groups have money coming in from sales, membership and supporters' fees and donations, and receive clandestine support from secretive supporters. Both are producing publications and are conducting their activities along the lines they promise their followers. Both, in their own way, are equally successful and continue to grow. The Brons camp, which includes Joe Pearce, Martin Wingfield, Ian Anderson and Tom Acton, is growing faster because of its less stringent entry qualifications and more street-orientated activities. The Griffin camp, which contains Pat Harrington, Derek Holland and Graham Williamson, is going for quality rather than quantity in membership, and clearly sees itself as training the future leadership for any mass organisation in this country.

A study *Searchlight* conducted in 1984, based upon detailed inside information, showed that, even in non-election years and with only 3000 members, the NF was capable of raising at least £168,000 per year. In an election campaign, this increased dramatically. The joint income of both groups is likely to be over £250,000 a year. They are employing more and more full-time workers, producing better quality printed propaganda material as well as tapes, records, badges and items of clothing. To provide an additional source of income the groups have been given, since 1987, large quantities of books by the Libyan regime for re-sale to the NF's cadres for training courses. Sales of their newspapers go on not just in this country, but all over the West, including the USA.

Separate from all the other fascist groups is Ian Stuart Donaldson's Blood and Honour. This is a magazine, rather than a party, with 1400 subscribers in a number of countries, including Eastern Europe and the USA. This pool of youngsters attracted to fascist ideas forms a fertile recruiting ground for the more-established fascist parties.

British fascist organisers are now at work in Ulster, Sweden and Norway and exchanges with US groups having a similar political stance are being stepped up. The number of training camps in Spain and Ulster for the less legitimate of their activities have also been increased. Such activities in Britain are now becoming more difficult to sustain except where they are run under the guise of survivalist courses in the style of the far right in the USA. In a number of Hungerford–type shoot-outs in several parts of the USA between 1980 and 1988, the people concerned have turned out to be members of secret Nazi groups who had attended such camps.

The conversion of the outbuildings at the country home of Nick Griffin's father was completed in 1986 to provide the NF's first training facilities. Most of the initial training courses for cadres have taken place there. Young members who have attended training courses are often sent to take control of existing NF branches, frequently displacing older members. NF branches have been instructed that branch minute-books should be kept for no more than four months, after which they must be burned, and that membership lists must not be kept at the homes or places of employment of membership secretaries. This is another indication that the NF increasingly sees its future as an illegal organisation.

On the eve of his last term of imprisonment, Joe Pearce told a *Time Out* reporter that after the electoral disaster of 1979 the NF stumbled along from crisis to crisis with no clear objective. But he went on to say: 'In the last few years... the movement has analysed what power is and how to get it'.[6]

THE IDEOLOGY OF NATIONAL REVOLUTION

So, if there exists a master plan, who designed it and upon what is it based? We have already seen that the ideas of the Strassers and Julius Evola, plus something more than G. K. Chesterton's and Hilaire Belloc's 'distributionism', i.e. the idea of a decentralised economy and state,[7] are the main quasi-ideological drive of the party.

One has had to go back to John Tyndall's letter to William Pierce of the American Nazi Party explaining how the NF could not be openly Nazi because it would be stuck in the mire of the Second World War and the death camps. Since that letter was written in 1967, the historical revisionists have certainly been more active in trying to re-write that period of history in a more acceptable fashion.[8] But in Germany and elsewhere the movement has now moved on to what it terms 'beyond Hitler'. In fact it has moved back almost to before Hitler, with an ideology popular among German right-wing extremists in the early 1920s: that of national revolution, national Bolshevism, a return to the land and to the days of the Teutonic knights, trade guilds and a society regimented along lines that would leave the knights or the 'political soldiers' in control. To bring about what they see as a new 'golden epoch', they must tear down the existing system by subversion and destabilisation. They know it is not a battle that can be won face on in an open manner, but will need years of hard work to a common end. They justify their change of tactics by pointing to the successive failures of post-war groups on the far right.

It has been superficially suggested by political commentators in West Germany that these new young zealots are not the strict descendants of the old Nazis because of their disavowal of Hitler; there is, however, evidence that funding passes down from the old Nazis to the new breed through third parties. The demonstrations at the time of Rudolf Hess's death in August 1987 brought together Nazis of all age groups from parties that, on paper, are far apart, such as the *Nationaldemokratische Partei Deutschlands*, and the most extreme national revolutionary cells who, as part of their struggle, have bombed US bases in West Germany. Actions of such groups bring pressure on the democratic system of their country and so enhance the neo-Nazis' chances of success through being seen as revolutionary underdogs taking on the state. The new right's support for both sides in Ulster and for black extremists like Louis Farrakhan and his masters in Iran and Libya, is all part and parcel of the same programme.

To find the recent public roots of this programme we must go back to 1979 to the publication in the USA of *The Turner Diaries*, a book written by a man calling himself Andrew Macdonald, who is in fact none other than William Pierce. The book is set in the not-too-distant future in the United States, a country described as under the control of the Zionist Occupation Government. Its hero, Earl Turner, forms an under-cover Nazi resistance group which, after some years, wins control of the world for the 'white race'. In the early days of the book's story, a group called 'The Order' does many of the things the NF are doing now in this country: infiltration, and community campaigning in parallel with military training and activity. To undermine society it encourages odd-ball extremist groups and ethnic minorities to become involved in violence. It forges dollars and credit cards to destabilise the currency and economy and selectively bombs and kills, starting with those who would expose it and its programme.

The Turner Diaries has become the *Mein Kampf* of the 1980s, and is far more readable and exciting for the average cadre intake of the NF than the latter. The book also advises, as do leading members of existing paramilitary groups, that the overall structure of a country's far right should be re-arranged to give it the greatest chance of survival and success.

Within three years of the book appearing, a group calling itself The Order had come into existence in the USA and Canada. It brought together the hardest elements of the existing far right, such as the US Nazi Party, paramilitary sections of the Ku Klux Klan and the Aryan Nations network. In 1983 they were forging dollar bills, carrying out payroll robberies to the tune of millions of dollars, and killing those who stood in their way, such as a young Jewish broadcaster called Alan Berg who was exposing them on his radio show on the West Coast of America. Berg was murdered with a sub-machine gun. His killers are now behind bars along with the killers of tax investigators and a couple of state-troopers and FBI agents who were all looking into the Order's activities. Other cells of the organisation are still active on the West Coast and in the economically depressed Mid-Western states of Kansas and Oklahoma. In one siege, where a man barricaded himself inside a school building and shot it out with the police, it was later revealed that the man had undergone survivalist training and was a member of The Order.

JORDAN'S PLAN – AND THE REALITY

In 1986 Colin Jordan emerged from the shadows of years of self-imposed exile and put pen to paper in issue 45 of *National Review*, the journal of the LSG, which is internationally respected on the far right. Jordan proposed a twin-strategy of infiltration and terrorism as a way forward for the Nazis in Britain, a policy very familiar to readers of *The Turner Diaries*. He saw a complementary role for the main British right groups. Tyndall's BNP would rub shoulders with ultra-Tories and the NF would be organised in such a way as to have both a public face and the makings of a group that could go underground. It would have to contain people who would be prepared to live as political activists for years and also be prepared to make the sacrifice of spending long years in prison.

But, based upon his own long experience of successive failures of the right in Britain, his view was that it was the only way ahead.

The BNP took in a number of former officers of the Federation of Conservative Students in 1986, and claims still to have members concealed inside Conservative organisations. The split in the Front, which could well be cosmetic, allows one group to pursue a public policy and the other to go deeper and deeper underground. Clues to the real structure of the NF can be found, because at this stage it is not sufficiently advanced to be able to do a complete job of separation. For example, both groups have their own box numbers for communications, but *Searchlight* found that the key holders were picking up mail for both groups. In the organisation of their printing arrangements Tom Acton, although in the Brons camp, is now a partner of Hancock at his print-shop in Uckfield, Sussex, where senior members of the Griffin camp are regular visitors. In the north of England, what had been an unofficial working relationship between the Brons faction and the BNP has now become a public accord. And as they go more public, Griffin and his overseas connections dig in deeper.[9]

Derek Holland, who became the chairman of the NF after Nick Griffin was assigned to other duties for the party, has been instrumental in developing their most recent campaign in support of Louis Farrakhan His policy of apartheid for blacks in the USA and his praise of Iran and Libya, are in line with their own position. To help them launch this campaign, Mat Unger, alias Mat Malone, Gary Gallo's number two in the National Democratic Front (NDF) in the USA, was flown into Britain. Since the late 1970s, Holland has held out the most sympathetic hand to the Iranians and Libyans. He also co-edited a publication called *Rising*, which was the voice of the Italian exiles when they first arrived in Britain.

When a conference was held in Tripoli in April 1987 to commemorate the first anniversary of the American bombing, among all kinds of fringe groups present were members of the Canadian Nazi Party, which is also a Third Position group closely allied with Gary Gallo's new party and with some links to the British NF.

Links between senior British Nazis and West German and Italian terrorists also reveal a Middle East connection. In 1985, two West German terrorists were arrested at the home of Major Ian Souter Clarence, the military commander of Column 88. The two were wanted for the bombing of more than 20 US bases in West Germany. A third man, Odfried Hepp, escaped capture and was eventually arrested in the Paris apartment of Georges Abdullah, the hit-man of the Palestinian Abu Nidal group. When the liner 'Achille Lauro' was hijacked and an elderly Jewish passenger murdered, one of the demands put forward was for the release of their comrade, Hepp.

When, in 1987, *Searchlight* interviewed the 28-year-old German terrorist Gerhard Topfer, who had been a member of far-right groups since the age of fourteen, it found that he had travelled the same path as other Third Position members in Western Europe, having been passed from group to group including Arab and Irish ones.[10] Events in the last two years point even more strongly to the terrorist political stance of the National Front and its allies.

There have been growing connections between the NF and black Islamic militants in this country. Meetings between them have taken place in London, Manchester and Leeds. In Leeds and Manchester an upsurge of anti-Semitic activity, including fire-bomb attacks on two synagogues, has occurred. After the Leeds attack of 1987, the West Yorkshire police issued a photofit of one of the bombers, who is said to be of Middle-Eastern appearance. The NF's publications and book lists are promoting heavily the works of Gaddafi and Khomeini to political soldiers and cadres of the new-style movement. When some thousands of pro-Palestinian and pro-Islamic protesters gathered in London to demonstrate over current events in Gaza and on the West Bank on 23 January 1988, over twenty NF activists turned up to participate, but left after complaints from other demonstrators. At least two senior members of the NF, Patrick Harrington and Graeme Williamson, joined Muslim extremists on the 1988 Quds (Jerusalem) day march.

The development of NF terror links in Ulster and across the border in the Irish Republic is rapidly taking on a much more sinister turn. The two Loyalist politicians John McMichael and George Seawright, who were assassinated in 1987 had close links with the NF. David Seawright, the younger brother of George, is a fully paid-up member of the NF. McMichael's political plan for the future of Ulster was getting remarkably close to the NF's idea of an independent state with slightly adjusted borders and some co-operation with ultra-nationalists in the Republic. There, a new Nazi group, the Social Action Initiative, came out with a similar set of ideas to those of McMichael and the NF, and the new group's leader, Derrick Turner, also known as Sean O'Neill, a former soldier with the United Nations' UNIFIL force in the Lebanon and now a serving rating in the Irish navy, went north to meet John Field, the NF's full-time officer in Ulster in summer 1988. The meeting in fact took place in the Ulster Defence Association (UDA) headquarters. Apart from recruiting from the membership of other Nazi-style organisations in the Republic, and a formal link with the British NF and an admitted link with the UDA, Turner is thought to have been recruiting heavily among former members of the provisional IRA who had been expelled for 'indiscipline', a euphemism for extortion and unauthorised murders. One of these recruits, a long-term unemployed, married man with a family, but with no visible means of support, is thought to have been sent on training courses to West Germany for two weeks in September 1988 and to the United States earlier in the year. It is now known that it was Derrick Turner's former organisation, the Irish National Socialist Party, that safe-housed Gerhard Topfer in 1984 in south Dublin. So it should come as no surprise, knowing of Topfer's Middle-Eastern connections, that Turner's new group is advising its members to have contacts with Libya via the People's Bureau offices in West Germany. Three NF leaders, Patrick Harrington, Nick Griffin and Derek Holland, visited Libya as guests of that country's Foreign Office in September 1988. They were exposed in a Channel 4 television programme, *Disciples of Chaos*, transmitted on 5 October 1988, in which Harrington, speaking officially for the NF, praised Libya, refused to condemn the IRA as terrorists and stead-fastly defended the convicted Italian terrorist Roberto Fiore and the NF's association with him. In the same period, their publication *National Front News* roundly praised the Sons of Glyndwr, the group claiming responsibility for a bombing campaign in Wales and England during 1988 and 1989. There is still a strong rumour that the NF has a seat on the UDA military council and that Special Branch surveillance of the Front has been replaced by that of MI5 because of these strong paramilitary links.[11]

LIST OF ABBREVIATIONS

BM	British Movement
BNP	British National Party
GBM	Greater Britain Movement
IFL	Imperial Fascist League
LEL	League of Empire Loyalists
LSG	League of St George
NAP	National Action Party
NDF	National Democratic Front
NF	National Front
NLP	National Labour Party

NNF   New National Front
NP   National Party
NSAG National Socialist Action Group
NSM   National Socialist Movement
ON   Our Nation
RPS   Racial Preservation Society
UDA   Ulster Defence Association
UM   Union Movement

NOTES

1. On the Strasser brothers, see Christopher Husbands's chapter 'Militant Neo-Nazism in the Federal Republic of Germany in the 1980s', in this volume, note 7.
2. Personal conversations with the author.
3. Personal conversations with the author.
4. *Searchlight*, No. 112, Oct. 1984, p. 4
5. On Julius Evola, see R. Griffin, 'Revolts Against the Modern World', *Literature and History*, XI, spring 1985, pp. 101–123; R. H. Drake,'Julius Evola and the Ideological Origins of the Radical Right in Contemporary Italy', in P. H. Merkl (ed.) *Political Violence and Terror. Motifs and Motivations*, University of California Press, Los Angeles, 1986, pp. 161–89.
6. *Time Out*, No. 805 Jan. 23–29 1986, p. 15
7. 'Distributionism' was propounded earlier this century by anti-Semitic writers like G. K. Chesterton and Hilaire Belloc and, in its modern form, is practised in some ways in Libya. The main exponents of distributionism for the British right in the 1980s were Joe Pearce and Tom Acton who, in two articles entitled 'Radical Populism' and 'Radical Realities' in the February 1987 issue of the Flag Group magazine, *Vanguard* (No. 6, pp. 8 and 9), put forward a better thought-out case for decentralisation than their opponents in the political soldiers' wing of the NF ever did.
8. See Roger Eatwell's chapter 'The Holocaust Denial' in this volume.
9. In 1989 *Searchlight* revised its view as to whom Colin Jordan saw as the real 'political soldiers'. Today it is convinced that they are the reconstructed British Movement with its inner-core cell group, the British National Socialist Movement.
10. *Searchlight*, No. 143, May 1987, p. 3.
11. Since this chapter was written, major upheavals have taken place on the far right, with the disclosure of links between MI6 and Roberto Fiore and the subsequent collapse of the organisation in terms of members. By late 1989, the membership was down to fifty people.

Primary Sources

Ar Aghaidh (*Forward*) (published by the Social Action Initiative, Cork.)

D. Holland, *The Political Soldier*, National Front, London, 1985.

A. Macdonald, *The Turner Diaries*, The National Alliance, Washington, DC, 1978.

National Front News (published by the National Front, London), Nos. 105–15.

National Review (published by the League of St George, London), Nos. 45 and 46.

Nationalism Today (published by the National Front, London), issues covering 1984 to 1987.

The Nationalist (published by the National Democratic Front, Maryland, USA).

Rising (published by Derek Holland, Paul Matthews and NAR exiles in London), 1982–83.

Scorpion (published by Michael Walker, London), 1983–87.

Yesterday and Tomorrow. Roots of the National Revolution, The Rising Press, London, 1984.

Secondary Sources

Searchlight, issues covering 1984 to 1989, with particular reference to Nos 103, 104, 127, 129, 133, 147, 148, 163, 165, 173-81.

Various Authors, *From Ballots to Bombs. The Inside Story of the National Front's Political Soldiers*, Searchlight, London, 1989.

CHAPTER THIRTEEN
Women and the National Front

Martin Durham

In the little over twenty years since its formation, the British National Front (NF) has gone through a dizzying series of mutations. Passing through a short-lived period of electoral advance in the mid–1970s, it has shed a large number of members in a succession of bitter rows and, finally, in the mid–1980s, split into two rival groups, both of which claim the name National Front.[1]

In recent years, the NF's political strategy has significantly shifted, most notably in its downplaying of elections. Behind such shifts lies a process of ideological rethinking which has led both NFs to claim fealty to a radical nationalist tradition whose most important figures are the dissident Nazis Gregor and Otto Strasser, and the British social critics Hilaire Belloc and G. K. Chesterton.[2] For the more radical of the two groups, the *National Front News* faction, the notion of a 'Third Way' between capitalism and Communism has gone so far as to lead to an enthusiasm for such seemingly unlikely allies as the Libyan and Iranian governments. The other NF, grouped around the paper *The Flag*, has been unwilling to allow its radical stance to threaten the coherence of a race-centred view of world politics. Instead, it has presented itself as closer to the old NF, a stance which both allows it to attempt to win back former members and to manoeuvre to win over at least some of the elements of the distinctly less radical British National Party, another remnant of the old NF led by its former Chairman, John Tyndall.

Since its inception, there have been important changes in the NF's ideology, strategy and policy proposals. Although more difficult to establish, there have also been shifts in its patterns of recruitment, and in the social background, age and geographic concentration of its members and supporters. In all of these areas, there is need for more research, building on the studies of the NF produced in the 1970s and early 1980s. Any examination of the Front's development since the late 1960s needs to have a strong sense of its capacity to change organisationally and ideologically. But important areas of continuity remain, and any study would need to focus on a number of persistent themes – above all race, anti-Semitism, and a partly concealed and, more recently, partly modified National Socialist ideology.[3] Yet, in exploring what the NF means by racial nationalism, how this has been modified over time and who it appeals to, there is a constant danger that we will neglect a vital element both in how it ideologically constructs the world and how it draws support. This element is gender.

Existing studies of the NF have tended to omit gender issues and, in particular, the question of the role of women. Yet, as numerous writers have reminded us, German National Socialism was deeply concerned with such issues, particularly around motherhood and population, and we might well expect those British groups who draw on this tradition to share these concerns.[4] In addition, changes in the family and in sexual values, the rise of feminism and other developments in post-war Britain are exactly the kinds of shifts that one would expect to generate anxieties – anxieties that the extreme right would share and attempt to amplify, independently of whether it owed its ideological formation to Nazism or to some other form of authoritarian nationalism. In the late 1970s a number of writers raised crucial questions about the relationship between the NF and women and, in part, this chapter attempts to take this work forward.[5]

In the discussion that follows, material from the different phases of the NF's development will be examined in order to explore the continuities and discontinuities in its views on women. In such a study, it is important to bear in mind two crucial and interrelated aspects of the NF's ideology – the centrality of race and its explanation of the forces behind national decline. Thus, according to Richard Verrall, the editor, in the late 1970s, of its magazine, *Spearhead,* there is a 'conspiracy' which seeks to create a World State controlled by international finance. This conspiracy is allied with Communism to destroy nation states 'and the racial homogeneity which gives them cohesiveness'.[6] Part of this attack on race and nation, according to John Tyndall writing in the same period, is 'the threat of mass immigration of alien races and their potential to breed and inter-breed among our own people'.[7] The more radical elements who subsequently captured the NF were likewise concerned with racial purity. Thus, in his 1984 pamphlet, *Fight for Freedom!,* Joe Pearce, who had risen to prominence through his work in the Young National Front, declared that 'racial preservation' was the key question. 'The true Nationalist', he wrote, 'would oppose miscegenation even if all the races were intellectually equal'.[8] As we will see, a conspiracy theory figures in the NF's treatment of issues of gender just as it does in race. More importantly, fear of racial 'inter-breeding' and of the white race being overwhelmed is the organising principle behind much of its concern with gender.

It is in its discussion of race and population, then, that the Front's view of women can be most clearly seen. While the NF raised the subject on a number of occasions, it was most centrally discussed in two articles, the first by John Tyndall in late 1968, the second by Richard Verrall at the beginning of 1977.

Birth controllers, Tyndall argued, believed that all families were to be treated in the same way, yet only some families were of 'absolutely sound stock'. In normal circumstances they would find prosperity and be able to 'have plenty of children to inherit their desirable qualities', while the 'least desirable' would be restricted in the number of offspring who might survive. But the Pill was prescribed for anybody, and as a result the most intelligent made the most use of it, while the 'most ignorant and backward' multiplied. Nor did overpopulation justify such an approach. Contraception was not curbing the population explosion and, indeed, some countries were actively pursuing an increase in their birth-rate. The question, therefore, was not whether Britain was overpopulated in relation to its resources, but whether it was overpopulated in relation to other powers. Confronted by 'teeming coloured populations everywhere posing their own special threat to the bastions of white culture and stability', Britain needed an improvement of its birth-rate, both in quantity and quality. To this end, he concluded, 'all ephemeral social considerations should be subordinated'.[9]

If anything, Richard Verrall's article of almost a decade later[10] made even clearer the centrality of population to a racial nationalist politics. There was, he argued, no more fundamental question than that of racial survival, and when we looked at the modern world we saw 'a small boat in which the beleaguered White races are slowly sinking as the rising tide of the coloured world population threatens to swamp it'. Decades of Western liberalism had obscured this and worsened the situation by the indiscriminate encouragement of birth control among the very group that was threatened by low fertility. That contraception was promoted among whites, he argued, suggested that the West was 'either in the grip of some peculiar liberal death wish, or at the mercy of forces which are deliberately promoting the progressive reduction of White peoples throughout the world as a dominant racial factor'. Both the numbers and 'the racial quality of the White world' were declining, Verrall claimed, and at some point, 'the White man' would have to take 'unprecedented measures to secure for himself his rightful place on the planet'. In order to do so, a Nationalist population policy was vital. Other countries, including Germany and Italy in the 1930s, had pursued a policy of increasing population but, today, population was either neglected or its reduction even encouraged. Instead, what was needed was 'an education programme which will eliminate the moral and political sensitivity which has surrounded population policy, and has inhibited governments from taking the necessary action'. In such circumstances, government should *'positively encourage, by every means possible, the raising of large families'* (italics in the text). This would entail reducing the cost of parenthood, introducing child welfare schemes, repealing the 1967 Abortion Act and ending the 'national and governmental mania' for promoting contraception. 'What is required here', he argued, 'is simply a complete reorientation of government policy where state encouragement to build a family is the priority, instead of state discouragement to build one, as at present.' Through financial incentives such as low-interest mortgages for young couples, increased efforts to lower infant mortality and encouraging woman's role as mother, 'the building of large families' could be brought about.

It was in the light of arguments such as these that the NF discussed 'The family and population' in its 1979 election manifesto.[11] Britain needs a higher birth-rate, it argued, and large families should be made economically feasible. But it was also vital to oppose the levelling-down effects of punitive taxation, egalitarian education and 'racial mixing'. 'Alone among parties', it proclaimed, the NF sought to 'reverse those trends which make for a decline in our population qualitatively as well as quantitatively'.

As we have already noted, Verrall had included among his proposals the repeal of the 1967 Abortion Act. Because, he wrote, government should encourage by every possible means a return to large families, 'It goes without saying that the present permissive abortion laws should be scrapped'. Indeed, he added, it could well be that abortion should be completely illegal. His opposition to abortion was expressed exclusively in terms of its effect on the birth-rate: in Communist Rumania, he noted, fertility had fallen with lax abortion laws and risen when abortion policy had been reversed.[12] When we examine NF policy on abortion, however, we find a more complicated picture: if the threat to racial fertility is often put forward as the basis for opposing abortion, on other occasions this is completely obscured by the NF's adoption of the more familiar argument that abortion, as such, is morally wrong.

If we look at an article on abortion in the late 1970s, we find it attacked as the product of liberal permissiveness, compared to 'Herod's massacre of the innocents' and described as debasing and de-feminising to women – all arguments current within the anti-abortion movement. 'For nationalists', the writer went on, there were 'even more cogent arguments' – that most abortions in Britain were of whites and that in the face of the 'high coloured birthrate' this represented a racial death wish. Britain, he argued, has already lost more of its young to 'the abortionist's knife' than it had in the two World Wars. Abortion did not merely represent selfishness and fear of the future: 'Above all, it is a calculated weapon in the hands of the nation-wreckers, the Final Solution to the problem of European pre-eminence.'[13]

Argued in this way, NF opposition to abortion was fundamentally different from that of such groups as Life or the Society for the Protection of Unborn Children. At its most blatant, one NF writer could even declare that 'one hears that black women frequently avail themselves of abortion facilities, and that since 1968 there has been a fall in the number of mixed-race births, but does a bad means ever justify a desirable end?'[14] However, if its attitude to abortion was often argued on a racialist basis, on other occasions it was defended in exactly the same way as it is by non-racialist anti-abortionists. Thus, in the early 1970s, the NF paper, *Britain First,* praised Catholic doctors for refusing to take part in abortions and for taking the view that 'sanctity applies to unborn babies', while in 1980 *Spearhead,* commenting on David Steel's continued support for the 1967 Act, insisted that human life came into existence at the moment of conception and that there was no difference between killing a human being before birth and after.[15]

Opposition to abortion was important enough for the Front to be part of its policy in successive general elections. The election address produced for the 1974 general election included the demand 'Repeal Abortion Act', and at the subsequent NF Annual General Meeting, delegates voted to oppose abortion on demand, but qualified their position by permitting abortions on 'special medical grounds'.[16] Four years later, once again at an AGM, Verrall was the proposer of a successful motion to repeal the Abortion Act and only permit abortion on 'genuine medical grounds'.[17] It was this position that appeared in the NF's manifesto for the 1979 election. Similarly, the 1983 manifesto envisaged only allowing abortion on grounds of serious danger to the woman, serious malformation of the foetus or rape.[18] But this position was not reached easily for, as *Spearhead* revealed, some members of the Front were opposed to an anti-abortion stance.

According to the magazine's account of the 1974 AGM, there had been 'very passionate exchanges' during the debate on abortion before the successful amendment was passed.[19] In the following issue, one of its leading figures, Martin Webster, made use of his regular column to reveal that the resolution which the AGM eventually agreed had contained criticism of the NF leadership's decision to include 'unqualified opposition to abortion' in the October 1974 election address. Most members at the meeting, Webster commented, had recognised that a political party should not 'adopt official policies on questions pertaining to private morality'.[20] This quickly elicited a critical response from another leading activist, Malcolm Skeggs, who, while agreeing that the NF should not try to turn itself into 'a sort of adjunct of the Festival of Light', insisted that abortion was not a matter of private morality but was the taking of a human life.[21] Later in the year, a prominent woman member, Joan Sandland, also appeared in the letters column, this time arguing that the NF should work for the kind of social conditions that would lessen the demand for abortion rather than driving 'women back to the back street butcher'.[22] NF leaders, evidently, were not agreed on the subject.

'Lively debate' likewise occurred at the 1978 AGM, the supporters of the motion explicitly arguing that abortion was not a matter of personal morality. Following the split in the mid-1980s, the *National Front News* faction retained a strongly anti-abortion stance, arguing, in late 1987, in 'Abortion: The Nationalist View' that abortion was 'intrinsically evil' and had been brought about by a decadent society which encouraged an attitude of materialistic self-interest. While Life and SPUC campaigned against abortion, it went on, they were unlikely to win against a powerful pro-abortion lobby. Abortion could only be ended by a revolution based on natural laws and values, and the only movement which fully recognised this was the NF.[23] Despite the subsequent appearance of critical letters in the paper, this has very much remained the organisation's position.[24]

The *Flag* group, however, appears more hesitant on the issue. In two separate news reports in one issue of its paper, abortion was described as 'murder'. Yet a subsequent report in its magazine of the defeat of the anti-abortion Alton bill (1988), while criticising Parliament for failing to debate the issue seriously, merely suggested that whether one supported the bill or not, it should not have been talked out. The clue to this divergence was to be found in the same issue of the magazine, with the appearance of an anti-abortion article under the heading 'Debate'. 'The subject of abortion has traditionally been a very controversial one within Nationalist circles', the editor noted, and readers' comments would be welcome. Letters duly appeared, both for and against abortion.[25] Less concerned than the *National Front News* group with ideological homogeneity, the *Flag* faction appears to be continuing the internal debate of the 1970s.

If the dominant tendencies in the NF have been bitterly hostile to abortion, how does it view birth control? As we have seen, much of the NF's discussion of the subject has focused on condemning the promotion of birth control among whites. As with abortion, however, such views have attracted criticism from within its ranks. In 1969, *Spearhead* published a letter claiming to speak 'for a great majority of members' in rejecting Tyndall's views. Birth control, it argued, was vital for women unable to afford to bring up another child. Tyndall, who replied in the same issue, returned to the subject the following year when he complained that student members, seemingly infected by leftist views, had taken to sending letters to the magazine criticising so-called 'reactionary attitudes' towards such issues as contraception.[26] But while often hostile to birth control, the Front did not suggest, as it had done with abortion, that contraception should be banned. In his 1968 article, Tyndall had been careful to claim that 'We have no right to dictate to husbands and wives that they should have large families' and that a future Nationalist government would leave 'the choice of family size to every husband and wife'.[27] Likewise, the October 1974 election manifesto combined calling for 'a vigorous birth-rate' with the assurance that 'we see it as no part of the function of the State to issue gratuitous advice to families as to how many children they should have. This is a matter for parents alone to decide.'[28] The 1974 AGM, Martin Webster had claimed, had been opposed to making issues of private morality matters for party policy, and the NF's opposition to abortion was explicitly argued on the grounds that abortion was not purely personal. The same could have been argued about contraception, considering the importance of the birth-rate to the Front, but would have been deeply contentious. To argue against abortion, the NF could talk in terms of the unborn child; to seek to ban birth control would have been to champion a state intrusion into private lives far more Draconian than members or electorate could accept. Its opposition to birth control, then, remained comparatively in the background of Front propaganda, and, however unconvincingly, it assured supporters that a nationalist government would not enforce a population policy.

As we have seen, for the NF of the 1960s and the 1970s, population policy was crucial, not only to raise the white birth-rate but to improve the 'quality' of the race. With the departure of Tyndall and Verrall in the early 1980s, however, this concern has tended to recede. A 1987 issue of *National Front News* praised the French government for using financial incentives to increase the birth-rate, while Steve Brady, a leading figure in the Front, wrote a discussion-article in one of its magazines earlier in the 1980s, in which he proposed shaping 'our evolutionary destiny' by 'a gradual, scientific and humane programme of eugenics'. More recently, an article in *Nationalism Today* has declared that a future Nationalist Society would use 'tax incentives' in order to encourage 'large, healthy families'.[29] But such references are rare. The modern NF continues to espouse a racialist politics, but appears to have little interest in either increasing the white birth-rate or in eugenics. Why should this be so?

Here we are necessarily forced to be speculative. In recent years the *National Front News* faction's radicalism had led it to proclaim affinity with radical Islam and, even more disconcertingly, with black separatists.[30] Despite this development, however, it is stretching the imagination too far to think that it is no longer concerned with racial numbers (and this is even more the case with the more traditional *Flag* grouping). With the NF still incontrovertibly racist, three other possible reasons suggest themselves. Firstly, Tyndall and Verrall's arguments about the declining quality of the white race gave all the appearance of characterising the white middle class as genetically superior. The NF of the 1980s, however, sees itself as representing white workers and argues radical economic and social policies which sit uncomfortably with any suggestion that poverty is nature's reward for failures. Secondly, both Fronts have taken up ecology as a central part of their world-view, and this is likely to have an effect on population policy. Brady, for instance, in a recent article on 'the rising tide of colour' makes no reference to raising the white birth-rate (let alone to eugenics) and even suggests that Britain could, in the future, find a population level 'more in harmony with the capacity of the environment and ecology to support'.[31] Finally, both factions look to G. K. Chesterton, Hilaire Belloc and Distributism for their ideological roots. This tradition is expressly Catholic in its opposition not only to capitalism and to Communism but to eugenics. Some of the leading figures in the modern NF are ultra-traditionalist Catholics, and one such figure, Paul Matthews, wrote from a Catholic perspective in condemning Brady's earlier article on eugenics. 'The imagination reels', he declared, 'to see how any programme for abortion, euthanasia, the slaughter of the sick and lame of society can be humane; and the practical questions are scarcely less than the moral: who is to have the power of life and death? Who are the unfit?'[32] The NF remains firmly racist but looks to working-class cadres, sees itself as championing exploited whites against capitalism and is strongly influenced by forms of Catholic social theory. It is not particularly surprising, then, that it is considerably less exercised by eugenics than it was in the heyday of such figures as John Tyndall and Richard Verrall. Indeed, on ecological grounds, even the urgency of raising the birth-rate might seem outdated, as long as the races are separated and white racial purity preserved.

This centrality of race has other implications for the NF's views on gender. 'Race-mixing destroys our People', declares a recent issue of *National Front News*, articulating a theme central to racial nationalist ideology.[33] In a world-view in which race is all, white women are crucial as child-bearers for the race. But they are also seen by individual men as their companion and possession, and it is impossible to understand the NF without drawing attention to a key element of its propaganda – that black men are seeking access to 'our women'. Frequently, in the 1970s, *National Front News* carried reports of cases of rape and other sexual offences allegedly carried out by black men, while in late 1983, for instance, in its youth paper, *Bulldog*, the cover story proclaimed 'Black pimps force White girls into prostitution'.[34] It is likely that such articles speak to sympathetic readers in different ways – in women evoking fear, in men anger and a racial and sexual 'protectiveness'. In the early 1980s, the front-page of *National Front News* could carry a picture of a man, woman and child with the caption 'White Man! You Have a Duty to Protect Your Race, Homeland and Family!' An earlier issue of *Bulldog* spelt out the message more clearly still – 'Next time you see a "humane, compassionate" Black just think of the safety of your White womenfolk ... think of your mother, your sister, your girlfriend'.[35] That this is not merely 'protectiveness', but is tied up with sexual rivalry is rarely spelt out – instead it is best seen by noting the fondness of *Spearhead*, in the 1970s, for cover photographs of a white woman and a black man, with the encoded message such representations carry for the male nationalist reader of 'they' having what is rightfully 'ours'.[36]

The NF's appeal to women works in a different way. 'White Women are Muggers' Main Target', the second issue of *National Front News* claimed in 1976, and two years later one woman electoral candidate, Helena Steven, issued on 'open letter' on immigration and violence. 'If you are a White woman', she wrote, 'then the biggest problem facing you is ... Black violence'.[37] But neither in reality nor in the imagination can violence against women and sexual attack be kept clearly separate, and it is likely that for both genders among NF supporters, the fused image of the Black mugger and rapist is a potent element of their hostility to immigration, and that this, in turn, blurs into the consensual sexual relationships between races that racial nationalists abhor.

The NF seeks to appeal to women, but how does it view their place in society? As we have seen, the population policy envisaged by Verrall in 1977 had emphasised woman's role as mother. What was central, he argued, was 'a society that respected and cherished the feminine role as principally one of the wife, mother and home maker'. This, he insisted, was not a male chauvinist view but a rejection of the 'rebellion against nature' that was displayed in 'the contemporary derision of maternity and domesticity'.[38] The following year, he returned to this theme in a discussion of socio-biology. An examination of 'male dominance and female passivity', of 'male aggression and female domesticity' in the animal world, he suggested, demonstrated their biological basis and discredited feminist claims of sex roles being socially conditioned.[39]

For Tyndall too the restoration of traditional sex roles was crucial. Most Front members, he declared in 1970, wanted 'a society in which the differentiation between the sexes is clearly marked' and 'the values of real manhood and real womanhood' prioritised.[40] Such views were reiterated later in the 1970s, when the Front received much attention in the media. 'I would like to see real manhood and real womanhood once again valued', he told *The Times* in 1977. In his view, he told another journalist, 'women are of supreme value in the home. As a supportive factor'.[41] The party's 1979 manifesto, while avoiding Tyndall's more blatant views, denounced values and behaviour which weakened the distinction between masculinity and femininity.[42]

As with race, the NF is fond of resorting to 'scientific evidence' in such matters, and we have already noted Verrall's use of socio-biology. In 1978, *Spearhead* published an abridged version of an article on 'The Feminine Condition' by Alain de Benoist, a leading figure in the French New Right. The article argued that the sexes were fundamentally different, with men inclined towards aggression and the urge to conquer, while women had such attributes as submission, tenderness and passivity. Quoting from the anti-feminist writer Arianna Stassinopoulos, the psychoanalyst Carl Jung and others, de Benoist argued that the sexes were complementary in their roles. Jung, he noted, had declared that by taking up 'masculine callings', being active in politics and engaging in study, woman had departed from 'her feminine nature'.[43]

Spearhead's hostility to changes in gender relations was rarely far from the surface in the 1970s. Thus, in the same issue as the de Benoist article, appeared an article on 'the Erosion of the Family', in which juvenile delinquency was attributed 'to a large degree' to 'the growing number of mothers going out to work'.[44] This hostility could even appear as a casual comment at the end of an article celebrating the authoritarian regime in Portugal. It was true, the author noted, that 'it's a man's country, here, and women have taken a somewhat secondary place' but they were not unhappy, despite what 'certain World Rulers' might claim. After all, 'Governments knew perfectly well what happened in countries where women have been given full power; where so much time and money have been wasted'.[45]

More recently, there have been some signs of dissent from such views. In a 1984 article in *Nationalism Today*, leading activist John Field argued that 'many Nationalists' were wrong to see the struggle for women's rights as a 'device with which to divide the White race'. Nationalist men, he claimed, should 'protect and aid ... their racial sisters', but too often they reacted with apathy or even hostility. In ancient times, 'Whites treated their women with respect', but more recently, a women's movement had emerged to fight for economic and social justice in 'reaction against the outrages of the industrial revolution'. The present form of this movement, he claimed, had fallen under Jewish control but this could be reversed, and already Jewish feminists were complaining of anti–Semitism in the women's movement. Nationalists, he argued, were wrong if they believed that women's place was in the home. In the future society, women would not be forced by economic necessity to 'abandon home and family to get a job' and motherhood would be 'the noblest profession to which any White woman can aspire'. But they would still be free to pursue careers and would be rewarded justly. Furthermore, women now were living in a society in which they had to go out to work and faced such problems as sexual harassment, discrimination and unequal pay. Nationalists, he concluded, should support their struggle.[46] Another activist, Frank Burden, in a letter shortly afterwards, congratulated Field on his argument. Feminists, he claimed, misrepresented 'our womenfolk' and it was up to racial nationalists to take up women's 'very real and genuine problems'.[47]

Field's article, although very different from the dominant view of the 1970s, hovered uneasily between the mirage of winning feminists to the NF and calling on white men to 'respect their women'. Subsequent material, however, suggests that his view does not mark a new departure for the movement. *National Front News* in 1988 expressed the hope that 'true women's groups' would emerge committed 'to the beauty of femininity and the sacred role of motherhood'.[48] *Nationalism Today*, for its part, published a two–part article on Front policy towards the family.[49] The future of the nation, it argued, was threatened by the decline of 'good family life'. The Industrial Revolution had destroyed the economic independence of the family and capitalists had driven mothers out to work, away from their natural role as child-rearer, home-builder and 'support of the breadwinner'. The women's liberation movement had arisen to promote hostility between the sexes. Nationalists had to resist these developments by re-asserting the centrality of 'the organic family' as the basis of the nationalist movement and the future nationalist society. In the future society, a mass-propaganda campaign, particularly in the churches and in the media, would be backed up by pro-family legislation. In an order in which abortion was illegal, family businesses encouraged and commitment favoured over isolation and selfishness, women would find fulfilment. They would be equal, the article insisted, and would be perfectly free to combine 'a profession and Motherhood' if they so chose, but it would be the latter that would be their vocation and the basis of '*all material and spiritual life*' (italics in the text).

If in one NF there appear to be tensions between traditionalist and partly modernist elements, the same process seems to be occurring in the other. This was strikingly revealed shortly after the split, when a *Flag* faction pamphlet, *100 Questions and Answers About the National Front*, rejected the suggestion that the NF wanted women confined to the home. The NF fully supported, it declared, 'the changes in society over the last twenty years or so which have allowed women a full and equal role in society'. However, it added, 'some women' did not want a 'full time career and we would make sure that economic and social factors do not force women into careers which they do not want'.[50] To express support for the changes in women's role in recent years was a quite remarkable statement by any organisation claiming the name 'National Front'. Other evidence, however, suggests that 'the old Adam' is still alive and well in the *Flag* group. Writing in late 1987, Joe Pearce took the opportunity of a review of a book by the radical feminist Andrea Dworkin to portray feminism as nonsensical and to offer in its place Chesterton's traditionalist views concerning natural sex differences and the importance of woman's role as mother. The following month, NF activist Tina Denny replied strongly with a defence of the women's rights movement of the late nineteenth and early twentieth century. Nationalists, Denny claimed, did not devalue the early labour movement, despite its subsequent development. They should take the same view of the women's rights movement, rejecting present-day feminism but supporting the historic fight for women's citizenship.[51] Denny approached the issue at a tangent, drawing no conclusions for women in the late twentieth century. Yet, more mutedly than Field, she was clearly raising criticism of the orthodox nationalist line. In both factions, however, albeit more hesitantly than in the Tyndall–Verrall period, that orthodoxy remains strong.

When we consider the NF throughout its history, one of its most noticeable characteristics is its overwhelming masculinity. It is not merely that its membership is preponderantly male, a characteristic which it shares with other political parties, or even that all its leading figures have been men. As particularly evidenced in its support among football fans, much of the NF's appeal rests on the existence of a virulent machismo. Yet, if less visible, women have been active in the NF since its inception. Women are certainly a minority of its members and it is likely that their involvement in the most public (and potentially confrontational) activities of the movement – marches and street-sales – is lower still. None the less, photographs and reports in both NF and anti-NF publications show that women are often involved in such activities.[52] It is far more difficult to document women's participation in internal activities, but some evidence exists concerning their participation in branch meetings and AGMs.[53] Not unsurprisingly for a male-led movement, women are often to be found responsible for its social activities or for the provision of refreshments at its events.[54] But while it is likely that most of the women in the NF play relatively limited roles in its activities, this is not true for some.

If we look, for instance, at the NF leadership, its essential character was vividly displayed in the late 1970s in a *Spearhead* photograph of an all-male National Directorate.[55] Yet, at other times, women have appeared on the Directorate, holding, at peak, 4 out of the 18 seats at the end of 1980.[56] Women have also stood as general election candidates: 1 out of 10 candidates in 1970, 6 out of a total of 107 in the two 1974 contests, 36 out of 303 in 1979, 6 out of 60 in 1983.[57] In local elections, comparable figures have not been compiled, but in these too there have been women candidates. In the 1977 Greater London Council elections, for instance, 21 of the 91 candidates were women.[58] Women have played a part in local organisation, often as branch secretary, treasurer or election agent.[59] But they have also been branch organisers[60] while in the Young National Front, too, some women have achieved leading roles, whether as the one woman on a five-strong National Secretariat or as local organiser.[61]

Women activists in the 1970s were, as was true of the movement as a whole, often older than those who came to the fore subsequently, and those who appeared by name in *Spearhead* (frequently as election candidates) were often presented in terms of their role in the family. Thus Sheila Wright, a general election candidate in 1970, was described as a 'Wolverhampton housewife with two sons aged eight and four', while a 'Mum's Army' of 'six housewives, most of them National Front members', were praised for their pelting of the Labour Home Secretary, Roy Jenkins, with flour 'bombs' in protest against government policy on race.[62]

In the late 1970s, however, the NF decided to launch the Young National Front (YNF). As the YNF came to absorb more of its energies, the dominant image of women in the party shifted in both age and tone. Its publications began to carry photographs of young women members modelling NF T-shirts with such captions as 'One good reason for join-ing the YNF!' or 'Out in Front!'.[63] Shortly after *Bulldog* was launched, material on football and rock music began to be accompanied by a recent photograph of a 'Bird', sometimes named, sometimes an unidentified supporter at some Front event.[64] Some were described as NF activists and a very early issue carried an appeal by a woman member for 'More Girls' to join the NF, although the emphasis was on social events with 'lots of guys to chat you up in the bar afterwards'.[65] Much of the time, however, women in *Bulldog* were objects rather than subjects. As an early issue promised potential members, YNF discos gave a good opportunity to 'drink with fellow white racialists. And, more important, our female members are all the right colour'.[66]

Women in the Front of the 1970s had chosen to belong to a party led by John Tyndall, with his notion that their 'intuitive abilities' made them invaluable to the party but incapable of leadership. 'You might say', he had declared, 'that it is a reflection upon the abilities of the men in the Conservative Party that their present leader is a woman'.[67] For the first half of the 1980s, they had belonged to a party which looked at them as potential 'pin-ups'. In addition, there was still their future role as mother of the race. Indeed, for those who have been members for some time, they may already have made the transition. Tina Dalton, photographed in a YNF T-shirt for a NF publication earlier in the 1980s, has subsequently appeared in the pages of the *Flag* as Tina Denny, 'a housewife and mother'. But women members are not solely defined by these roles. As the paper emphasised, she is the NF's Administration Officer, and more recently, now Tina Wingfield, she has been its candidate at a parliamentary by-election.[68] Another activist, Caralyn Giles, has been frequently photographed for its publications (its photo-album, *We Are The National Front*, has a montage of three pictures with the caption 'lovely blond white girl'). But she has also been a council election candidate, a YNF local organiser and a NF branch secretary.[69]

Claims have been made several times in recent years of an increase in female involvement in the NF. *Bulldog* reported in 1978 a 'large increase' in girls joining the Front, while in the first issue of *Nationalism Today* it was claimed that, as the YNF had 'moved into 1979, it was noticed that more and more girls were becoming active on NF demonstrations'. This was to be welcomed, the article continued, as until then the vast majority of YNF activists had been male. More recently, the *Flag* faction has claimed that although there were 'more men than women in the movement . . . over the last few years this imbalance has been slowly decreasing and we hope that this will continue to be the case'.[70] There are obviously discrepancies in exactly when any change is supposed to have occurred, and what numbers are involved remains unclear. But if the proportion of women to men is changing in the NF, its resilient patriarchal traditions remain strong. One activist, Jackie Griffin, writing in *Nationalism Today*, has urged women to play a greater role in the movement. Too often, she writes, NF women are 'found behind the scenes, making cups of tea, addressing envelopes and folding circulars'. But while she holds that Front women have as much right as its men to be 'ideologists' and 'fighters', the main thrust of her argument is to take the most familial aspects of women's struggles as the way forward. Women's support for their families in the miners' strike and mothers' fear of nuclear war are offered as examples for 'a movement which is finding a way to link political matters with home building instincts'.[71] If there is space in the NF of the 1980s for arguing for greater equality between the sexes, the parameters of the argument remain set by traditional notions of woman's role.

In examining the National Front's views of women, at first sight little appears surprising. Most of its pronouncements on population, on abortion, on inter-racial relationships and on women's place in society are exactly as we might anticipate. The same, too, applies to the leading role of men in the party and the emphasis on women members as mothers or sex objects. The victory of the radicals in the early 1980s and the development of anti-capitalist (and ecological) economic and social policies has brought in its wake a move away from the 'selective breeding' emphases of Tyndall and Verrall, and even claims of a more favourable attitude towards women's equality. But the particular nature of the radicalism expounded in *National Front News* and, to a lesser degree, by the *Flag* group simultaneously pushes the NF towards a traditionalist view of women. The ruralist, medievalist, anti-capitalism of Chesterton and Belloc was hostile to the feminism of the early twentieth century, and when Joe Pearce quotes Chesterton on women or *Nationalism Today* attacks the Industrial Revolution for taking women out of the home, then we hear the voice of a male-defined politics thoroughly antagonistic to feminism.

Yet to assume that the modern NF is as simply anti-feminist as it was in the 1970s is to misread the situation. Just as it has sought to channel opposition to Cruise missiles and American bases (or support for the miners' strike) in a specifically racial nationalist direction, so too some NF activists have shown interest in attempting to fashion a racialist 'feminism'. I have already referred to Jackie Griffin's article on women in the Front and to John Field's comments on the inadequacies of nationalist views towards women and the tensions in the women's movement over Israel and Zionism. But even before the radicals' capture of the NF, *Spearhead* published an article in which a French 'feminist' nationalist argued that women should oppose large-scale immigration because non-European communities held 'reactionary' views towards women and represented a threat to the position white women held in western society.[72] No more than in Field's speculations did this article indicate that the NF had any serious hopes of finding sympathy among feminists. What it does indicate, however, is that racial nationalists need not necessarily define themselves as anti-feminist any more than they are always anti-strike or pro-nuclear.

In addition, the NF itself has recruited women (and men) with diverse attitudes towards patriarchal precedence in general and such issues as abortion in particular. In the earlier period, as we have seen, there were disagreements in the NF over abortion and contraception, and arguments around abortion have continued to the present day. The particular radicalism of the *National Front News* group, influenced by forms of Catholic social theory, has accentuated a traditionalist view of abortion and the family but this has not been a uniform process, and it is evident that, in both of the modern NFs, different views on abortion and on women's role within the movement exist and come into conflict.

Finally, even at its most Tyndallesque, the NF has always given some women in its ranks the possibility of taking on local and, on occasion, national responsibilities both within the organisation and in election contests. For a NF woman to be portrayed in its press as a housewife or mother is not incompatible with a role in the public sphere, and even women who are portrayed in NF publications in a sexualised way can still be regarded as political activists too. The NF of the 1970s was suffused with patriarchal values and so too is the back-to-the-land, back-to-the-family NF of the 1980s. But both diverge from the stereotypical picture—generated by Nazis and anti-Nazis alike – of Fascism as the paramilitary wing of patriarchy. The NF has been, and remains, an expression not only of racism, but often of an embattled masculinity. But post-war shifts in gender relations and sexual values have permeated all sections of British society, and not even such a resistant organism as the NF has been immune.

NOTES

1. Arguments in the 1970s were particularly concerned with the leadership of former National Socialist Movement member John Tyndall. Tyndall and his supporters left in 1980. A younger group came to prominence after his departure. Influenced by Italian radical Fascists, they espoused a ruralist society of family businesses and white workers' co-operatives, but came to blows over the direction of policy, and a new split took place in 1986. For the earlier period, see M. Walker, *The National Front*, Fontana, London, 1977; M. Billig, *Fascists. A Social Psychological View of the National Front*, Harcourt Brace Jovanovich, New York, 1978; M. Billig and A. Bell, 'Fascist Parties in Post-war Britain', *Race Relations Abstracts*, V, 1980, pp. 7–18; N. Fielding, *The National Front*, Routledge, London, 1981; S. Taylor, *The National Front in English Politics*, Macmillan, London, 1982; C. Husbands, *Racial Exclusionism and the City*, Allen & Unwin, 1983. On more recent developments, see R. Thurlow, *Fascism in Britain*, Blackwell, London, 1987, Ch. 12, and, for an account which rejects the authenticity of the 1986 split, see *From Ballots to Bombs*, Searchlight, London, 1989.

2. Gregor Strasser, a prominent figure in the Nazi Party, was liquidated after it came to power. His brother Otto had broken with the party earlier. They opposed what they regarded as Hitler's compromises with reactionary forces and betrayal of 'German socialism'. Chesterton and Belloc were advocates of Distributism, a doctrine which held that the widespread distribution of property was the only alternative to private or state monopoly. For these and other influences on the modern NF, see *Yesterday and Tomorrow. Roots of the National-Revolution*, Rising Press, London, n.d. (c.1983); D. Baker, 'A. K. Chesterton, the Strasser brothers and the Politics of the National Front' in *Patterns of Prejudice*, XIX, 3 1985, pp. 23–33.

3. For a decoding of NF publications of the 1970s, revealing a subterranean Nazi world-view, see Billig, *Fascists*, cit.

4. See e.g., T. Mason, 'Women in Nazi Germany', *History Workshop*, I, 1976, pp. 74–113, II, pp. 5–32; C. Koonz, *Mothers in the Fatherland. Women, the Family and Nazi Politics*, Cape, London, 1987.

5. See, in particular, V. Ware, *Women and the National Front*, Searchlight London, n.d. (c. 1978); Women and Fascism Study Group, *Breeders for Race and Nation*, n.d. (c. 1979).

6. *Spearhead* No. 103, March 1977, p. 11.

7. *Spearhead*, No. 88, Oct. 1975, p. 10.

8. J. Pearce, *Fight For Freedom!* Nationalist Books, London, 1984, pp. 9–10.

9. *Spearhead*, No. 21, Nov.–Dec. 1968, pp. 4–6.

10. *Spearhead*, No. 101, Jan. 1977, pp. 6–7, 10.

11. *It's our Country – Let's Win it Back!*, National Front, London, n.d. (1979), p. 57.

12. *Spearhead*, No. 101, Jan. 1977, pp. 7, 10.

13. *Spearhead*, No. 120, Aug. 1978, p. 5.

14. *Spearhead*, No. 79, Sept.–Oct. 1974, p. 14.

15. *Britain First*, No. 15, 25 March–7 April 1972, p. 3; *Spearhead*, No. 135, Jan. 1980, p. 3.

16. NF Oct. 1974 election address; *Spearhead*, No. 81, Feb. 1975, p. 18.

17. *Spearhead*, No. 126, Feb. 1979; pp. 18, 20.

18. *It's our Country*, cit., p. 56; *Let Britain Live!*, National Front, London, 1983, p. 21.

19. *Spearhead*, No. 81, Feb. 1975, p. 18.

20. *Spearhead*, No. 82, March 1975, p. 17.

21. *Spearhead*, No. 84, May 1975, p. 16.

22. *Spearhead*, No. 88, Oct. 1975, p. 16. Both Sandland and Skeggs were members of the NF's national leadership. *Spearhead*, No. 80, Jan. 75, p. 19. Sandland broke away from the Front soon after and was prominent in its short-lived rival, the National Party. Walker, *The National Front*, cit., p. 193.

23. *Spearhead*, No. 126, Feb. 1979, p. 18; *National Front News*, No. 97, Nov. 1987, p. 4.

24. *National Front News*, No. 102, Feb. 1988, p. 6. See *National Front News*, No. 104, April 1988, p. 6; No. 105, June 1988, p. 6; No. 106, n.d. (1988), p. 6; No. 108, n.d. (1988), p. 6.

25. *Flag*, No. 16, Feb. 1988, pp. 2, 5; *Vanguard*, No. 20, July 1988, pp. 4, 8–9; No. 22, Sept. 1988, p. 18; No. 23, Oct. 1988, p. 18.

26. *Spearhead*, No. 22, Jan.–Feb. 1969, p. 14; No. 31, March 1970, p. 19.

27. *Spearhead*, No. 21, Nov.–Dec. 1968, p. 6.

28. *For a New Britain*, National Front, London 1974, p. 12.

29. *National Front News*, No. 93, Aug. 1987, p. 1; *New Nation*, No. 6 winter 1984, p. 7; *Nationalism Today*, No. 44, n.d. (1989), p. 16.

30. For NF support for Khomeini as a fellow-fighter against capitalism and Communism, see, e.g., *Nationalism Today*, No. 45, n.d. (1989), pp. 8–9; for support for black separatism, see, e.g., *National Front News*, No. 102, Feb. 1988, pp. 1–2; No. 109, n.d. (1988), p. 1.

31. *Vanguard*, No. 19, June 1988, pp. 6–7.

32. *New Nation*, No. 7, Summer 1985, p. 16.

33. *National Front News*, No. 93, Aug. 1987, p. 1. See also, e.g., *National Front News*, No. 43, Nov. 1982, p. 3.

34. Ware, *Women*, cit., pp. 12–15; *Bulldog*, No. 35, Sept. 1983, p. 1.

35. *National Front News*, No. 35, Aug. 1981, p. 1; *Bulldog*, No. 11, Jan.–Feb. 1979, p. 3.

36. *Spearhead*, No. 65, June 1973, p. 1; No. 111, Nov. 1977, p. 1; No. 127, March 1979, p. 1.

37. *National Front News*, No. 2, May 1976, p. 1; Ware, *Women*, cit., p. 14. See also *National Front News*, No. 17, March 1979, p. 1. An undated leaflet (c. 1973), issued earlier in the decade by the Croydon branch, bore the heading 'WARNING! Attacks on White Women Are On The Increase In The South London Area'.

38. *Spearhead*, No. 101, Jan. 1977, p. 10.

39. *Spearhead*, No. 127, March 1979, p. 10,

40. *Spearhead*, No. 29, Jan. 1970, p. 7.

41. *The Times*, 30 Aug. 1977; *Sunday Telegraph Magazine*, 2 Oct. 1977, p. 15.

42. *It's our Country*, cit., p. 13.

43. *Spearhead*, No. 113, Jan. 1978, pp. 8–10.

44. *Spearhead*, No. 113, Jan. 1978, p. 20.

45. *Spearhead*, No. 75, May 1974, p. 11.

46. *Nationalism Today*, No. 25, Nov. 1984, p. 8.

47. *Nationalism Today*, No. 28, April 1985, p. 20.

48. *National Front News*, No. 105, June 1988, p. 2.

49. *Nationalism Today*, No. 43, n.d. (1988), pp. 14–16; No. 44, n.d. (1989), pp. 14–16.

50. I. Anderson, *100 Questions and Answers About the National Front*, Freedom Books, London, n.d. (c. 1987), p. 28.

51. *Vanguard*, No. 12, Sept. 1987, p. 11; No. 13, Oct. 1987, pp. 12–13.

52. See, in particular, the NF's 1981 photo-booklet, *We Are The National Front*.

53. For AGMs, see, e.g., *Spearhead*, No. 126, Feb. 1979, p. 20; *National Front News*, No. 62, Jan. 1985, p. 5. For branch meetings, see, e.g., Fielding, *The National Front*, cit., pp. 33–4, 50–52, 54.

54. See, e.g., *National Front News*, No. 70, Sept. 1985, p. 8; *Flag*, No. 1, Aug. 1986, p. 5.

55. *Spearhead*, No. 103, March 1977, p. 17.

56. *National Front News*, No. 28, Nov.–Dec. 1980, p. 4.

57. *Spearhead*, No. 34, June 1970, p. 15. F.W.S. Craig, *British Parliamentary Election Results 1974–1983*, Parliamentary Research Services London, 1984; *National Front News*, No. 48, July 1983, p. 4.

58. *Spearhead*, No. 105, May 1977, pp. 18–19; see also, e.g., No. 94, May 1976, pp. 18–19.

59. See, e.g., *National Front News*, No. 63, Feb. 1985, p. 6; *Spearhead*, No. 43, June 1971, p. 11; No. 113, Jan. 1978, p. 18. *Britain First*, No. 33, Oct. 1975, p. 4; *Flag*, No. 22, Aug. 1988, p. 6.

60. *Spearhead*, No. 27, Nov. 1969, p. 12; No. 86, Aug. 1975, p. 20; No. 113, Jan. 1978, p. 18; *Nationalism Today*, No. 36, Feb. 1986, p. 20.

61. See, e.g., *National Front News*, No. 67, June 1985, p. 1; *Nationalism Today*, No. 1, March 1980, p. 19.

62. *Spearhead*, No. 34, June 1970, p. 15; No. 88, Oct. 1975, p. 18. A somewhat younger woman candidate was described as a 'Charming housewife' in *Spearhead* No. 74, April 1974, p. 19.

63. *Spearhead*, No. 115, March 1978, p. 19; *Anglian News*, No. 12, July 1979, p. 1. *Anglian News* was a local NF publication.

64. See, e.g., *Bulldog*, No. 14, n.d., p. 3; No. 17, n.d., p. 3; No. 30, Nov. 1982, p. 3.

65. For the appeal for more members, see *Bulldog*, No. 4, Dec. 1977, p. 4. For 'birds' as activists see, e.g., *Bulldog*, No. 15, n.d., p. 3; No. 17, n.d., p. 3;

No. 28, June 1982, p. 3.

66. *Bulldog*, No. 9, Aug. 1978, p. 4.

67. *Sunday Telegraph Magazine*, 2 Oct. 1977, p. 15.

68. *Marching On With The National Front*, Nationalist Welfare Association, London n.d. (c. 1985), p. 11; *Flag*, No. 21, July 1988, p. 5; No. 24, Oct. 1988, p. 8.

69. *We Are The National Front*, cit., p. 46; *Bulldog*, No. 11, Jan.–Feb. 1979, p. 4; *Flag*, No. 8, May 1987, p. 7; No. 22, Aug. 1988, p. 6.

70. *Bulldog*, No. 9, Aug. 1978, p. 1; *Nationalism Today*, No. 1, March 1980, p. 18; *100 Questions*, cit., p. 29.

71. *Nationalism Today*, No. 33, Sept. 1985, p. 15.

72. *Spearhead*, No. 129, July 1979, pp. 14–15.

Select Bibliography

GENERAL

European Community	*Committee of Inquiry into the Rise of Fascism and Racism in Europe. Report on the Findings of the Inquiry,* Luxemburg, 1985.
J. H. Herz (ed.)	*From Dictatorship to Democracy,* Greenwood Press, Westport, CT, 1982.
C. T. Husbands	'Contemporary Right–Wing Extremism in Western – European Democracies', *European Journal of Political Research,* IX, 1981, pp. 75–99.
C. O'Maolain	*The Radical Right. A World Directory,* Longman, London, 1987.
Various Authors	*Right–Wing Extremism in Western Europe,* special issue of *West European Politics,* XI, 2, 1988.

ITALY

G. Cianflone and D. Scafoglio	*Fascismo sui muri,* Guida, Naples, 1976.
P. Corsini and L. Novati (eds.)	*L'eversione nera. Cronache di un decennio (1974–1984),* Franco Angeli, Milan, 1985.
R. H. Drake	'Julius Evola and the Ideological origins of the Radical Right in Contemporary Italy', in P. H. Merke (ed.), *Political Violence and Terror, Motifs and Motivations,* University of California Press, Los Angeles, 1986, pp. 161–89.
F. Ferraresi	'The Radical Right in Postwar Italy', *Politics and Society,* XVI, 1988, pp. 71–119.
R. Griffin	'Revolts Against the Modern World', *Literature and History,* XI, Spring 1985, pp. 101–123.
P. Ignazi	*Il polo escluso. Profilo del Movimento Sociale Italiano,* Il Mulino, Bologna, 1989.

Various Authors	*Fascismo oggi. Nuova destra e cultura reazionaria negli anni ottanta,* special issue of the *Notiziario dell'Istituto Storico della Resistenza in Cuneo e Provincia,* No. 23, June 1983.
L. B. Weinberg	*After Mussolini: Italian Neo–Fascism and the Nature of Fascism,* University Press of America, Washington, D. C., 1979.
M. Zucchinali	*A destra in Italia oggi,* Sugarco, Milan, 1986.

GERMANY

Bundesamt für Verfassungsschutz	*Verfassungsschutzbericht,* Bundesminister des Innern, Bonn, annually.
P. Dudek	*Jugendliche Rechtsextremisten: Zwischen Hakenkreuz und Odalsrune, 1945 bis heute,* Bund–Verlag, Cologne, 1985.
P. Dudek and H. – G. Jaschke	*Jugend Rechtsaussen: Analysen, Essays, Kritik, Pad. Extra Buchverlag,* Bensheim 1982.
P. Dudek and H. – G. Jaschke	*Entstehung und Entwicklung des Rechtsextremismus in der Bundesrepublik: zur Tradition einer besonderen politischen Kultur,* 2 vols., Westdeutscher Verlag, Opladen, 1984.
W. Heitmeyer	*Rechtsextremistische Orientierungen bei Jugendlichen: Empirische Ergebnisse und Erklärungsmuster einer Untersuchung zur politischen Sozialisation,* Juventa Verlag, Weinheim, 1988.
C. T. Husbands	*Racist Political Movements in Western Europe,* Routledge, London, ch. V (forthcoming).
R. Stöss	'The Problem of Right–Wing Extremism in West Germany' in K. von Beyme (ed.), *Right–wing Extremism in Western Europe,* Frank Cass, London, 1988, pp. 34–46

SPAIN

C. Díaz and A. Zucco	'La ultraderecha en Argentina', supplement to *El Periodista,* Buenos Aires, 28 Nov. 1986.
S. Ellwood	'Falange y franquismo', in J. Fontana (ed.), *España bajo el franquismo,* Editorial Crítica, Barcelona, 1986, pp. 39-59.
S. Ellwood	'Not so much a programme, more a way of life: oral history and Spanish Fascism', *Oral History,* XVI, 2, 1988, pp. 57-66.
S. Ellwood	*Spanish Fascism in the Franco Era,* Macmillan, London, 1987.

P. Preston	'General Franco's Rearguard', *New Society*, 29 Nov. 1973, pp. 519–21.
P. Preston	'Populism and Parasitism: the Falange and the Spanish Establishement, 1939–75', in M. Blinkhorn (ed.), *Fascists and Conservatives*, Unwin Hyman, London, 1990, pp. 138–56.
P. Preston	'Spain', in S. J. Woolf (ed.), *Fascism in Europe*, Methuen, London, 1981, pp. 329–51.
P. Preston	*The Politics of Revenge*, Unwin Hyman, London (forthcoming).
J. Rodríguez Puértolas	*Literatura fascista española*, Ediciones Akal, Madrid, 1986, 2 voll.

PORTUGAL

M. Braga da Cruz	*O Partido e o Estado no Salazarismo,* Presença, Lisbon, 1988.
T. Gallagher	'From Hegemony to Opposition: The Ultra Right Before and After 1974', in L. S. Graham and D. L. Wheeler (eds.), *In Search of Modern Portugal. The Revolution and its Consequences*, The University of Wisconsin Press, Madison, 1983, pp. 81-103.
M. de Lucena	*A Evolução do Sistema Corporativo Português*, vol. I – *O Salazarismo*, vol. II – *O Marcelismo*, Perspectivas e Realidades, Lisbon, 1976.
A. Costa Pinto	'A direita Radical em Portugal. Uma introdução', *Risco*, No. 12, Lisbon, Oct. 1989, pp. 67–85.
A. Costa Pinto,	'Revolution and Political Purge in Portugal's Transition to Democracy', in S. U. Larsen *et al*, *Modern Europe after Fascism, 1945–1980s*, Norwegian University Press, Bergen (in press).
J. Nogueira Pinto,	'A Direita e o 25 de Abril: ideologia, estratégia e evolução política', in M. B. Coelho (ed.), *Portugal. O sistema político e constitucional, 1974–87*, Instituto de Ciências Sociais, Lisbon, 1989, pp. 193-212.

GREECE

| R. Clogg and L. Yannapoulos (eds.) | *Greece Under Military Rule*, Secker and Warburg, London, 1972. |
| D. Close | 'Conservatism, Authoritarianism and Fascism |

in Greece, 1915-45', in M. Blinkhorn (ed.), *Fascists and Conservatives*, Unwin Hyman, London, 1990, pp. 200-217.

R. Clogg — *Parties and Elections in Greece*, C. Hurst and Co., London, 1988.

A. Lentakis — *Neo-facistikes organoseis neolaias* (Neofascist Youth Organisations), Athens, 1963.

S. Linardatos — *Pos ftasame sten 4e Augoustou* [How we reached the 4th of August], Themelio, Athens, 1965.

S. Linardatos — *H 4e Augoustou* (The Fourth of August), Themelio, Athens, 1966.

C. Woodhouse — *The Rise and Fall of the Greek Colonels*, Granada, St Albans, 1985.

FRANCE

J. P. Apparu — *La droite aujourd'hui*, A. Michel, Paris, 1979.

A. M. Duranton-Crabol — *Visages de Ia Nouvelle Droite. Le GRECE et son histoire*, Presses de la Fondation Nationale des Sciences Politiques, Paris, 1988.

G. Fay, — *Les nouveaux enjeux idéologiques*, Editions du Labyrinthe, Paris, 1985.

J. Marcilly, — *Le Peu sans bandeau*, Grancher, Paris, 1984.

N. Mayer and P. Perrineau — *Le Front National à Découvert*, Presses de la Fondation Nationale des Sciences Politiques, Paris, 1989.

P. Milza — *Fascisme français. Passé et présent*, Flammarion, Paris, 1987.

E. Plenel and A. Rollat — *L'effet Le Pen*, Le Monde – La Découverte, Paris, 1984.

A. Rollat — *Les hommes de I'extrême droite*, Calmann–Levy, Paris, 1985.

R. Rémond — *Les droites en France*, Aubier, Paris, 1982.

GREAT BRITAIN

From Ballots to Bombs, Searchlight, London, 1989.

M. Billig — *Fascists. A Social Psychological View of the National Front*, Harcourt Brace Jovanovich, New York, 1978.

N. Fielding — *The National Front*, Routledge, London, 1981.

C. Husbands — *Racial Exclusionism and the City*, Allen and Unwin, Winchester, MA, 1983.

T. Kusher and — *Traditions of Intolerance. Historical Perspectives on Fascism*

K. Lunn (eds.)	*and Race Discourse in Britain*, Manchester University Press, Manchester, 1989.
S. Taylor	*The National Front and English Politics*, Macmillan, London, 1982.
R. Thurlow	*Fascism in Britain*, Blackwell, London, 1987, ch. 12.
M. Walter	*The National Front*, Fontana, London, 1977.

Index

abortion and National Front (UK), 267-70, 279
Achaeans (Greece), 209
Action Française, 211, 212, 213, 239
Action Front of National Socialists *see Aktionsfront*
Acton, Tom, 255, 259
Adenauer, Konrad, 70, 71
Adolf Hitler (Cross), 135-6
Afirmación Española (AE), 153
Africa, 15
age of militant extreme-right activists, 103, 107, 108
Agora, 173-4
Aktion Ausländerrückführung (AAR) (W. Germany), 94
Aktionsfront Nationaler Sozialisten (ANS) (W. Germany), 93, 94, 96
Aktionsfront Nationaler Sozialisten/Nationale Aktivisten (ANS/NA) (W. Germany), 81, 91, 92, 94, 97
'Alberto Pollio' Institute for Historical and Military Studies, 34
Algeria, 14
Algerian National Liberation Front (FLN), 215
Algérie Française, 215, 216
Alianza nacional '18 de julio' (Spain), 150, 154
Alianza Popular (AP) (Spain), 150, 159
Alliance pour les Libertés et le Progrès (ALP) (France), 216
Almirante, Giorgio, 26, 29, 34, 35, 36, 38, 39, 43-4, 49, 158, 161
American Institute for Historical Research, 121
Anderson, Ian, 250, 252, 255
Annales d'histoire révisionniste, 124, 125, 130, 137, 141 anti-Semitism, 6-7, 141, 260
Anti-terrorist Liberation Groups (GAL) (Spain), 157
Arab Socialist Renaissance Party, 14
Arbeitsgemeinschaft Nationaler Verbände/Völkischer Bund (ANV/VB)

(W.Germany), 100
Armed Forces Movement (MFA) (Portugal), 176, 181
Armed Revolutionary Nuclei (NAR) (Italy), 37, 53
Armée Révolutionnaire (AR) (France), 215
Armundraz, Guy, 247
Aron, Raymond, 239
Asia, 13-14, 16
Auschwitz, 134, 136
Auschwitz and the Allies (Gilbert), 132-3
Auschwitz Lüge, Die (Christophersen), 120, 129
Auschwitz-Mythos, Der (Stäglich), 120
Austria, 8
Authentic Spanish Phalanx (FE(a)), 149, 150
Autonomous Grass-roots Groups (Spain), 162
Avanguardia Nazionale (Italy), 34, 36, 157
Averoff, Evangelow, 203
Azione Cattolica (Italy), 21

Ba'ath Party (Iraq/Syria), 14
Ba'athist regime, 16
Baden-Württemberg, 79-80, 81, 96
Balfour, Michael, 69
Balzarani, Barbara, 53
Bardèche, Maurice, 121
Bari, 24, 28
Basque country, 12
Battalions of National Defence (TEA) (Greece), 197
Bavaria, 79, 80, 81, 96
Bean, John, 246
Begin, Menachem, 131
Belgium, 8, 99
Belloc, Hilaire, 256, 264, 271, 278
Benoist, Alain de, 183, 237, 239, 240, 241, 242, 243, 244, 251, 273
Berg, Alan, 258
Berlin, 79, 99
Berlinguer, Enrico, 44

Bewegung, Die (The Movement), 80–1, 95, 98
Bielefeld, 99, 100
Billig, Michael, 140
birth control policy and National Front (UK), 266–7, 270
Blum, Léon, 128
Bobbio, Norberto, 64
Borchardt, Siegfried, 95
Borges de Macedo, Jorge, 184
Borghese, Valerio, 36
Borussenfront, 95
Boulanger, General, 212
Brady, Steve, 248, 271
Bramwell, Roy, 246
Brasillach, Robert, 121, 213
Brehl, Thomas, 81
Bremen, 81, 89, 96, 99
Britain *see* United Kingdom
British Movement (BM), 249
British National Party (BNP), 245, 250, 258, 259, 264
Brons, Andrew, 249, 250, 255, 259
Bulgaria, 15
Bulldog, 252, 272, 277
Bund der Heimatvertriebenen und Entrechteten (BHE) (W. Germany), 69–70
Bund Hamburger Madel (BHM), 118
Bundesamt für Verfassungsschutz (BfV), 72, 74, 78, 86–9, 90, 91, 92, 95, 100, 101, 102, 104, 107, 109
Bundesministerium des Innem (BMI), 91, 92, 97, 98
Burden, Frank, 274
Bürger-und Baueminitiative (W. Germany) (BBI), 100
Burma, 14
Busse, Friedhelm, 97
Butz, Arthur, 121, 125, 128, 131, 132

Caetano, Marcello, 181
Cambodia, 16
Campaign for Nuclear Disarmament, 253–4
Candour, 245
Capes, Jim, 253
Carto, Willis, 125, 248
Catania, 35
Catholic Centre Party (Germany) *see* Zentrum
Catholicism, political, 21–2, 30, 179
Ceausescu, Nicolae, 15
Centre Union Party (EK) (Greece), 198, 201
Chesterton, G.K., 245, 246, 256, 264, 271, 278

China, 14, 16
Chomsky, Noam, 121
Christian Democrat Party (Italy) *see* Democrazia Cristiana
Christian Democrat Party (PDC) (Portugal), 178, 184
Christian Democratic Union (CDU) (W. Germany), 73, 78, 80, 83, 96
Christian–Social Union (CSU) (W. Germany), 73, 78, 80, 83
Christlich-Demokratische Union Deutschlands (CDU), 73, 78, 80, 83, 96
Christlich-Soziale Union (CSU), (W. Germany) 78, 80, 83
Christophersen, Thies, 100, 120, 129
Citizens' and Farmers' Initiative (BBI) (W. Germany), 100
Clarence, Ian Souter, 254, 259
Club de l'Horloge, 235
Collins, Harry, 140
Column 88, 247, 88 254, 248
Comissoẽs de Trabalhadores (Portugal), 177
Comitati Civici (Italy), 30
Comitato di Liberazione Nazionale (CLN) (Italy), 27
Committee for National Liberation (CLN) (Italy), 27
Committee for Truth in History, 124
Communism, 4–5, 6, 9
Communist Party
   Greece (KKE), 192, 193, 196, 200, 201
   Italy, 24, 28, 32, 35
   Portugal (PCP), 176, 177, 179, 742
Confederazione Italiana Sindacati Nazionali Lavoratori (CISNAL), 29, 46
Constantine II, King of Greece, 198
Corsica, 12
Covelli, Alfredo, 19
Craxi, Bettino, 38
Croatia, 8
Cross, Colin, 135–6
Cuore di mamma (Samperi), 53
Czechoslovakia, 8

Dakoglou, P., 209
Dawidowicz, Lucy, 141
Défense de l'Occident, 121
de Gaulle, General, 73, 214
Delle Chiaie, Stefano, 34, 36
De Lorenzo, General, 33, 35
De Marsanich, Augusto, 29
Democratic Movement for the Liberation of Portugal (MDLP), 179, 180

Democratic Party of Monarchist Unity
(PDUM) (Italy), 19
Democrazia Cristiana (DC) (Italy), 21, 24, 28,
29, 30, 31, 34-5, 36, 38
Democrazia Nazionale (DN)(Italy), 36
demographic characteristics of militant neo-
Nazis, 101-9
Denny, Tina, 275, 277
Deutsche Aufbaupartei (DAP), 70
Deutsche Bauern- und Landvolkpartei (DB-Lp),
70
Deutsche Bürgerinitiative (DBI), 100
Deutsche Frauenfront (DFF), 118
Deutsche Konservative (DK), 70
Deutsche National Volkspartei (DNVP), 70
Deutsche Rechtspartei (DReP), 70, 71
Deutsche Reichspartei (DRP), 12, 71-2
Deutsche Stimme, 78
Deutsche Volksunion (DVU), 77, 80, 86, 89,
112, 115
Did Six Million Really Die? (Harwood), 121,
124, 137
Dior, Françoise, 252
Donaldson, Ian Stuart, 254, 255
Dorls, Fritz, 71
Dresden, 131
Druzes, 15
Dudek, P., 107, 110
Duprat, François, 122

Eco, Umberto, 49
educational background of extreme-right
activists, 103, 108
'18 July' National Alliance (Spain), 150, 154
Elefterofronoi (EL) (Greece), 193
Ellinikos Kosmos, 203
Ellul, Jacques, 140
Emilia-Romagna, 24
employment status of extremeright activists,
103, 108
Eniaia Demokratiki Aristera (EDA) (Greece),
197
Enomeno Ethniko Kinema (ENEK) (Greece),
202, 203, 204
Enosis Kentrou (Centre Union) (EK)
(Greece), 198, 201
Ente Nazionale di Assistenza (ENAS) (Italy),
29
Erhard, Ludwig, 70, 73
Estado Novo (EN) Portugal, 167, 168-75, 185
ETA, 157
Ethiopia, 15
ethnic minorities, 4, 12, 14
ethnic transfers, 10-11

Ethniki Demokratiki Enosis (EDE) (Greece),
201
Ethniki Organossis Neolaias (EON) (Greece),
194
Ethniki Parataxis (EP) (Greece), 201, 202
Ethniki Politiki Enosis (EPEN) (Greece), 203,
204
Ethniki Rizospastiki Enosis (ERE) (Greece),
201
Ethniko Apelefterotiko Metopo (EAM)
(Greece), 195, 196
Ethniko Kinima Neon Epistimonon (EKNE)
(Greece), 199
Ethnikos Laikos Apelefterotikos Stratos (ELAS)
(Greece), 195, 196
Europe-Action (France), 173
European Community, 79
European Parliament elections, 80, 86, 96,
147, 159-60, 161, 202-4, 226, 227, 229
European Right group, 86, 160, 203
Evola, Julius, 253
Exército de Libertação Nacional (ELP)
(Portugal), 179, 180
expellees, 69-70

Fabius, Laurent, 242
Faisceaux Nationaux et Européens (FNE)
(France), 216
Falange Española (FE), 8, 9, 148
Falange Española (*auténtica*) (FE(a)), 149,
150
Falange Española (*independiente*) (FE(i)), 150
Falange Española de las JONS (FE de las
JONS), 148, 149, 150, 151-2, 154, 161,
162
Falange Española Tradicionalista (*FET y de las
JONS*), 148, 149
Farrakhan, Louis, 257, 259
Fasci di Azione Rivoluzionaria (FAR) (Italy),
23, 27
Fascism, 4-5, 6, 7-8, 9
Faurisson, Robert, 121, 122, 123, 124, 129,
131, 132, 133, 136
Federation of Conservative Students (UK),
250, 259
Fédération d'Action Nationale et Européenne
(FANE) (France), 216
Fédération des Etudiants Nationalistes (France),
236
Federation of National and European Action
(FANE) (France), 216
Fellowship of Independent Germany
(GUD), 71
Ferreira, Zarco Moniz, 173

Ferró, Antonio, 170
Field, John, 260, 274
Figaro, Le, 122, 238
Filelefteroí (Greece), 192
Fini, Gianfranco, 38, 39
Finland, 8
Fiore, Roberto, 251, 252, 253, 261
Flag, The, 264, 269-70, 271, 275, 278
Flemish Bloc (VB), 86
Foggia, 28
Força Nacional - Nova Monarquia (FN-NM)
   (Portugal), 185
Foreigners Out List/National Assembly (NS)
   (W. Germany), 98
Fountaine, Andrew, 246
'4th of August Party' (K4A) (Greece), 199,
   201
France, 3, 8, 156, 211-44
Franco, General, 9, 20, 148, 154
Frank, Anne, 132
Frankfurt, 94
Frazier, Col. R.L., 67-8
Freda, Franco, 36
Free Believers (EL) (Greece), 193
Free Democratic Party (FDP)
   (W. Germany), 73-4, 78, 80
Free German Workers' Party (FAP), 80, 81,
   92, 94-8, 112
Freie Demokratische Partei (FDP)
   (W. Germany), 73-4, 78, 80, 97
Freiheitliche Deutsche Arbeiterpartei (FAP), 80,
   81, 92, 94-8, 112
Frente Académica Patriotica (FAP) (Portugal),
   172
Frente de Estudantes Nacionalistas (FEN)
   (Portugal), 171, 173
Frente Nacional (FN) (Spain), 158-60, 161,
   162
Frente Nacional Español (FNE), 149
Frente Nacional Revolucionária (FNR)
   (Portugal), 171, 172-3
Frey, Gerhard, 77, 80, 86, 88, 89, 114-15
Front de Libération National (FLN) (Algeria),
   14, 215
Front National (FN) (France), 77, 86, 122,
   161, 203, 217, 226-9, 239, 242
Front of Nationalistic Students (FEN)
   (Portugal), 171, 173
Fronte della Gioventù (Italy), 45, 46, 47, 51,
   53, 55, 56
Fronte Nazionale (FN) (Italy), 36
Fronte Universitario di Azione Nazionale
   (FUAN) (Italy), 29, 32
Fuerza Nueva (FN) (Spain), 38, 150, 151,
   154

Fulda, 94
Fumagalli, Carlo, 36
Futuro Presente (FP) (Portugal), 183

Gaddafi, Colonel, 157
Gallo, Gary, 253, 259
Galvão, Alpoim, 179
Garoufalias, Petros, 201
Gauchon, P., 217, 239
Gemeinschaft unabähngiger Deutscher (GUD),
   71
Genoud, François, 247
Gentile, Giovanni, 6
German Citizens' Initiative, (DBI), 100
German Conservatives (DK), 70
German Construction Party (DAP), 70
German Farmers' and Peasants' Party
   (DB-Lp), 70
German National People's Party (DNVP),
   70
German People's Union (DVU), 77, 80, 86,
   89, 112, 115
German Reich party (DRP), 71-2
German Rights Party (DReP), 70, 71
German Women's Front, 118
Germany, 6-7, 8, 9
   East, 11
   West, 11-12, 66-119
Gerstein document, 123, 129, 132
Gewerkschaft der Polizei, 79
Giannini, Guglielmo, 23-4
Gilbert, Martin, 132-3
Giles, Caralyn, 277
Gillmore, Graham, 254
Ginzel, G.B., 101, 102
Girón, José Antonio, 161
Goerth, Christa, 100
Goold, Gillian, 246
Gorbachev, Mikhail, 77
Gothic Ripples, 249
Graziani, Clemente, 199
Greece, 10, 191-210
Greek World, 203
Green Party (W. Germany), 78, 80, 83
Griffin, Jackie, 278
Griffin, Nick, 250, 252, 255, 256, 259, 261
Gronchi, Giovanni, 30
Group of the European Right, 86, 160, 203
Groupe Union-Défense (France), 216
*Groupement de Rechercheet d'Etudes pour la
   Civilisation Européenne* (GRECE), 216,
   235-6, 239
Grupos Anti-terroristas de Liberación (GAL)
   (Spain), 157
Grupos Revolucionarios de Acción Internacional

(GRAI) (Spain), 157
Guerrilleros de Cristo Rey (Spain), 149
Guomindang Party (China), 14

Hamburg, 81, 96
Hancock family, 251, 253, 259
Hanmore, Paul, 254
Harrington, P., 255, 260, 261
Harwood, Richard, 121, 124, 130, 133, 135, 137
Heidel, Volker, 81
Heimwehr, 8
Hennig, E., 111
Hepp, Odfried, 259-60
Hess, Otto, 71
Hess, Rudolf, 156, 257
Hesse, 81, 94, 96, 98
Hilfsorganisation für nationale politische Gefangene und deren Angehörige (HNG), (W. Germany), 93, 100-1
Hilton, Tony, 254
Historical Review Press, 122, 137
Historical Revisionism, 121-43
Hitler, Adolf, 8, 9, 67, 78, 83, 88, 98-9, 118
Hitler's War (Irving), 141
Hoax of the Twentieth Century, (Butz), 121, 125, 128
Hoffmann, Karl-Heinz, 115
Hoffmann Defence and Sporting Group (WSG Hoffmann) (W. Germany), 87, 90, 115
Hofmann-Gottig, Joachim, 80
Holland, Derek, 250, 252, 255, 259, 261
Holocaust, The (Gilbert), 132
holocaust denial, 120-46
Holocaust Denial, The (Seidel), 121, 126
Honore, J.P., 223
Hungary, 8

Ieros Syndesmos Ellinon Axiomatikon (IDEA) (Greece), 196
Immagine coordinator per un impero, Etiopia 1935-36 (Mignemi), 54
Imperial Fascist League (IFL) (UK), 249
Independent Movement for National Reconstruction (MIRN) (Portugal), 181, 182, 184
Independent Spanish Phalanx, [FE(i)], 150
Initiative for the Popular Will (IV) (W. Germany), 98
Initiative Volkswille (IV) (W. Germany), 98
Institute of Historical Review (IHR), 127, 133, 137, 138, 139, 248
Intellectual Renovating Momentum (PAO) (Greece), 209

International Committee for the Assistance of Those Persecuted for National Political Reasons (IHV) (W. Germany), 101
International Committee of the Red Cross, 135
International Military Fund, 180
International Revolutionary Action Groups (GRAI) (Spain), 157
Internatiönales Hilfskomitee für nationale politische Verfolgte und deren Angehörige (IHV) (W. Germany), 101
Ioannides, Dimitri, 209
Iran, 16
Iraq, 14, 16
Irish National Socialist Party, 261
Iron Guard (Romania), 8
Irving, David, 129, 133-4, 141, 251
Israel, 130, 131
Italian Confederation of National Workers' Unions (CISNAL), 29, 46
Italian Liberal Party (PLI), 24, 38
Italian Popular Party (PPI), 30
Italian Social Republic (RSI), 20, 26, 43
Italy, 7, 8-9, 12, 19-65

Japan, 14
Jeune Nation (France), 173
Jews, 6, 126-7, 131, 133
Jordan, Colin, 246, 249, 258
José Antonio Doctrinal Circles (Spain), 150
Journal of Historical Review, 124, 130, 137
Junge, R., 110
Junge Front (JF) (W. Germany), 91
Junta Coordinadora de Fuerzas Nacionales (Spain), 157-8
Junta Coordinadora Nacional Sindicalista (JCNS) (Spain), 149, 150
Junta de Salvacão Nacional (JSN) (Portugal), 176
Juntas de Ofensiva Nacional-Sindicalista (JONS) (Spain),148
Juntas Españolas (JJ.EE), 153, 162

Karamanlis, Constantine, 200, 201, 202
Katyn, 131
Kaúlza de Arriaga, General, 175, 181, 184
Kemal Atatürk, 14
Kemalists, 14
Kenya African National Union, 15
Khmers Rouges, 16
Kiel, 70
Komma Proodeftikon (KP) (Greece), 202
Komma tis 4 Avgoustou (K4A) (Greece), 199, 201

Kommounistiko Komma Elladas (KKE)
(Greece), 192, 193, 196, 200, 201
Kühnen, Michael, 81, 91, 92-3, 94, 94-5,
97, 98, 101, 116, 118, 119
Kunstmann, Hans Heinrich, 71
Kurds, 14, 16

Labour Battalions (Greece), 194
Laiko Komma (LK) (Greece), 192
Lapua movement (Finland), 8
Latin America, 13, 156
Lauro, Achille, 19
Lawson, Richard, 248, 253
League of Empire Loyalists (LEL) (UK),
245, 246
League of Expellees from the Homeland and
those without Rights (BHE)
(W. Germany), 69-70
League of Hamburg Girls (BHM), 118
League of St George (LSG) (UK), 246, 250
Leagues of Barrés, Déroulede and Drumont,
212, 214
Lebanon, 14-15
Lecce, 28
Leese, Arnold, 249
Legião Portuguesa (LP), 169, 170, 172, 173,
176
Légitime Défense (France), 226
Le Pen, Jean-Marie, 77, 86, 154, 160, 161,
203, 215-30 passim, 239, 242
Lepénisme, 221-5, 226
Lesquen, Henri de, 235
Leuchter, Fred, 134
Liberal Democratic Party (FDP)
(W. Germany), 97
Liberal Party (Greece), 192
Liberal Party (LP) (Portugal), 178
Libya, 14, 157-8, 261
Ligas, Natalia, 53
Linz, Juan, 21
Lisbon, 180
Liste Auslander raus/Nationale Sammlung (NS)
(W. Germany), 98
Lower Saxony, 81, 96, 97

McCalden, David, 125, 248
Macdonald, Andrew, 257
McLorry, Andrew, 254
McMichael, John, 260
Mambro, Framcesca, 53
Maniadakis, Constantine, 194
Mantakas, Christos, 199
Mao Zedong, 16
Markezinis, Spyros, 202
Maronite-Christians, 15

Massagrande, Elio, 157, 199
Matthews, Paul, 271
Mattogno, Carlo, 125
Maurras, Charles, 211, 239, 240
Maxwell, Robert, 125
Mechanics of Gassing, The (Faurisson), 124,
133
Meinberg, Wilhelm, 71
Meireles, Cecilia, 174
Mengistu's Workers Party of Ethiopia, 15
Mermelstein, Mel, 139
Metaxas, General, 192, 193, 194, 195, 199
Michelini, Arturo, 29, 32
Mignemi, Adolfo, 54
migrants in West Germany, 75-6, 79
Milan, 35
militant neo-Nazism, 90-119
Minority Rights Group (UK), 16
Mocidade Portuguesa (MP), 169, 170
Monarchist parties (Italy), 19, 24, 35
Monday Club, 250
Moreira, Adriano, 181
Mosler, Jürgen, 81, 95, 97
Mosley, Oswald, 246
Movement, The (W. Germany), 80-1, 95,
98
Movimento das Forças Armadas (MFA)
(Portugal), 176, 181
Movimento del '77, 37
Movimento Democrático de Libertação Nacional
(MDLP) (Portugal), 179, 180
Movimento Democrático Português (MDP), 176
Movimento di Azione Rivoluzionaria (MAR)
(Italy), 36
Movimento Independente para a Reconstrução
Nacional (MIRN) (Portugal), 181, 182,
184
Movimento Jovem Portugal (MJP), 171, 172,
173
Movimento Nacionalista Português (MNP), 178
Movimento Sociale Italiano (MSI), 19-42, 43,
157, 173 poster propaganda, 44-65
Müller, Ursula, 118
Munich, 99
Mussolini, Benito, 20, 21
Mythe de l'extermination des juifs (Mattogno),
125

Nacional Sindicalismo (NS) (Portugal), 169
Naples, 24, 28
National Assembly (NS) (W. Germany), 92,
98
National Camp (EP) (Greece), 201, 202
National Council for Civil Liberties (UK),
255

National Democracy group (Italy), 36
National Democratic Party of Germany
  (NPD), 12, 71-5, 77- 8, 80, 86, 88, 89,
  93, 97, 112
National Democratic Union (Greece), 201
National and European Fasces (FNE)
  (France), 216
National Fascist Party (PNF) (Italy), 22, 29
National Force – New Monarchy Party
  (FN-NM) (Portugal), 185
National Front (France) *see* Front National
National Front (Italy), 36
National Front (Spain) *see* Frente Nacional
National Front (UK), 245-83
National Front News, 264, 269, 270-1, 271,
  272, 274, 278, 279
National Labour Party (NLB) (UK), 246
National Liberation Front (EAM) (Greece),
  195, 196
National Monarchist Party (Italy) (PNM),
  19
National Movement of Young Scientists
  (EKNE), (Greece), 199
National Party (NP) (UK), 249
National Political Union (EPEN) (Greece),
  203, 204
National Popular Liberation Army (ELAS)
  (Greece), 195, 196
National Radical Union (ERE) (Greece),
  201
National Review, 258
National Revolutionary Front (FNR)
  (Portugal), 171, 172-3
National Revolutionary Workers' Front
  (NRAF) (W. Germany), 99
National Salvation Junta (JSN) (Portugal),
  176
National Socialism, 4, 7, 9, 14, 69, 265
National Socialist Action Group (NSAG)
  (UK), 250
National Socialist German Workers' Party
  (NSDAP), 66, 68, 70, 88, 98, 115
National Socialist Movement (NSM) (UK),
  246, 249
National Syndicalism (NS) (Portugal), 169
National Syndicalist Coordinating
  Committee (JCNS) (Spain), 149, 150
National Union (Portugal), 169
National Union (UN) (Spain), 150, 151
National Vanguard *see* Avanguardia
  Nazionale
National Welfare Association (ENAS) (Italy),
  29
National Youth Organisation (EON)
  (Greece), 194

Nationaldemokratische Partei Deutschlands
  (NPD), 12, 71-5, 77-8, 80, 86, 88, 89,
  93, 97, 112
Nationale Sammlung (NS) (W. Germany), 92,
  98
Nationalism Today, 274-5, 277-8, 278
Nationalist Front (NF) (W. Germany), 93
Nationalist Front-League of Social
  Revolutionary
Nationalists (NF-BSN) (W. Germany), 99-
  100
Nationalistische Front (NF) (W. Germany), 93
*Nationalistische Front-Bund Sozialrevolutionärer
  Nationalisten* (NF-BSN) (W. Germany),
  99-100
Nationalrevolutionäre Arbeiterfront (NRAF)
  (W. Germany), 99
Nationalsozialistische Deutsche Arbeiterpartei
  (NSDAP), 66, 68, 70, 88, 98, 115
Nazi Greater Britain Movement (GBM), 245
Nazis, 7-8, 66-7, 68-9, 70, 257 *see also* neo-
  Nazism
Nea Demokratia (ND) (Greece), 200, 201,
  202, 204
Nea Taksi (NT) (Greece), 199
neo-Nazism, 86-119
New Acropolis (Spain), 155
New Democracy (ND) (Greece), 200, 201,
  202, 204
New European Order, 247
New Force (FN) (Spain), 150, 151, 154,
  155, 158
New National Front (NNF) (UK), 249
New Order (ON) (France), 215
New Order (Greece) (NT), 199
New Order (Italy) *see* Ordine Nuovo
New Right (France) *see* Nouvelle Droite
New Right movement (Italy), 37
Nogueira, Franco, 175, 184
Nolte, Ernst, 142
North Rhine-Westphalia, 80, 81, 95, 96, 97,
  98
Nouvelle Droite (ND) (France), 37, 122, 183,
  216, 217, 235-44
Nouvelle Ecole, 238
Nuclei Armati Rivoluzionari (NAR) (Italy), 37,
  53, 251
Nueva Acrópolis (Spain), 155
Nuova Destra (ND) (Italy), 37
Nuremberg trials, 128

Occident movement (France), 215
Occorsio, Vittorio, 37
occupational origin of militant neo-Nazis,
  104, 108-9

Odal Ring, 99
Oddo, Alfio, 157
O'Neill, Sean, 260
Operation Repatriation (AAR)
    (W. Germany), 94
Order, The (USA/Canada), 258
Ordine Nuovo (ON) (Italy), 31, 34, 35, 155,
    157, 173
Ordre Nouveau (ON) (France), 215
Organisation for the Assistance of National
    Political Prisoners (HNG)
    (W. Germany), 93, 100-1
Organisation de l'Armée Secrète (OAS)
    (France), 215
Origins of the Second World War, (Taylor), 141
Ossowski, S., 5
Our Nation (ON) (UK), 252

Painter, Roy, 249
Pais, Sidonio, 168
Palermo, 35
Panellinio Ethniko Metopo (PEM) (Greece),
    193
Panellinio Socialistiko Kinema (PASOK)
    (Greece), 200, 202
Panhellenic National Front (PEM) (Greece),
    193
Panhellenic Socialist Movement (PASOK)
    (Greece), 200, 202
Pannella, Mario, 38
Papadopoulos, George, 203
Papandreou, Andreas, 200, 201, 202, 203
Papandreou, George, 196, 198
Pape, Martin, 94, 95, 97
Parti des Forces Nouvelles (PFN) (France), 38,
    216, 217, 239
Parti Socialiste Destourien (Tunisia), 14
Partido de Democracia Crista (PDC) (Portugal),
    178, 184
Partido de Direita Portuguesa (PDP), 182, 184
Partido de Progresso (PP) (Portugal), 178
Partido Liberal (PL) (Portugal),178
Partido Revolucionario Institucional (Mexico),
    13
Partido Socialista Obrero Español (PSOE), 150,
    151, 160
Partido Socialista (PS)(Portugal), 180
Partito Democratico di Unità Monarchica
    (PDUM) (Italy), 19
Partito Liberale Italiano (PLI), 24, 38
Partito Nazionale Fascista (PNF) (Italy), 22, 29
Partito Nazionale Monarchico (PNM) (Italy),
    19
Partito Popolare Italiano (PPI), 30

Partito Popolare Monarchico (PPM) (Italy), 19
Partito Radicale (PR) (Italy), 38
partitocrazia, 24, 27, 38, 47
Party of the New Forces (PFN) (France),
    216, 217, 239
Party of the Portuguese Right (PDP), 182,
    184
Patriotic Academic Front (FAP) (Portugal),
    172
Patriotic Front (Austria), 8
Pauwels, Louis, 122, 238-9
Pearce, Joe, 250, 252, 254, 255, 256, 265-6,
    275, 278
Pella, Giuseppe, 30
People's Alliance (AP) (Spain), 159
People's Party (LK) (Greece), 192
Peronistas, 13
Pétain, Marshal, 213, 214, 215
Petrone, Luciano, 251, 253
Piat, Yann, 229
Pierce, William, 247, 257
Piñar, Blas, 150, 151, 154-5, 158, 159, 160,
    161, 162
Pinch, Trevor, 140
Pirie, Denis, 252
Plevris, Costas, 209
Pnevmatiki Ananeotiki Ormi (PAO) (Greece),
    209
Poland, 69
Politica, 174-5
Political Committee of National Liberation
    (PEEA) (Greece), 195
political refugees, 76
Politiki Epitropi Ethnikis Apelefterossis (PEEA)
    (Greece), 195
Pomorin, J., 110
Popular Alliance (AP) (Spain), 150
Popular Monarchist Party (PPM) (Italy), 19
Popular Socialist Movement of Germany/
    Labour Party (VSBD/PdA), 90-1, 92, 97,
    99
population policy and the National Front
    (UK), 266-72
Portugal, 10, 20, 156, 167-90
Portuguese Democratic Movement (MDP),
    176
Portuguese Legion (LP), 169, 170, 172, 173,
    176
Portuguese Liberation Army (ELP), 179, 180
Portuguese Nationalist Movement (MNP),
    178
Portuguese Writers' Association, 173
Portuguese Youth (MP), 169, 170
    poster propaganda, 44-65
Poujadism, 214-15

Present Future (FP) (Portugal), 183
Preto, Rolão, 169
Primo de Rivero, José Antonio, 153, 154
Progress Party (PP) (Portugal), 178
Progressive Party (KP) (Greece), 202
propaganda posters, 44-65
propaganda technique and the Holocaust
    denial, 120-46
purges (*saneamentos*), 175-7

Racial Preservation Society (RPS), 245
Radical Party (PR) (Italy), 38
Rallis, George, 202
Rassinier, Paul, 133, 137
Rauti, Pino, 31, 38, 39
Read, John Kingsley, 246, 247, 248
Rebecchini, Aldo, 28
Red Brigades, 53
refugees, 11, 12, 69-70, 75
Reggio Calabria, 35
Reitlinger, Gerald, 138
Remer, Otto Ernst, 71
Rémond, Réne, 211, 212, 213, 239
Repubblica Sociale Italiana (RSI), 20, 43, 154
Republikaner, Die (REP), 11-12, 78-80, 83,
    86, 112, 161, 203
Research and Study Group for European
    Civilisation (GRECE) (France), 216,
    235-6, 239
Resistência, 173, 174
Revolutionary Action Fasces (FAR) (Italy),
    23
Revolutionary Action Movement (MAR)
    (Italy), 36
Revolutionary Army (AR) (France), 215
Rexists, 8
Robert, Alain, 239
Rollin, Xavier, 234-5
Romania, 8, 15
Rome, 24, 35
Roques, Henri, 123, 129
Rosa dei Venti (Italy), 36
Rousseau, Jean-Jacques, 2-3
Royal Ulster Constabulary (RUC), 254

Saar region, 69, 80
Sacred Bond of Greek Officers (IDEA), 196
Salazar, Antonio de Oliveira, 20, 167, 168,
    169, 170, 171, 172, 174
Salerno, 28
Salt, Michael, 250, 252
Samperi, Salvatore, 53
Sandland, Joan, 269
saneamentos, 175-7

Sardinha, António, 174
Scelba Law, 29
Schleicher, Kurt von, 115
Schleswig-Holstein, 70, 80, 81, 96
Schnoor, Herbert, 96
Schönhuber, Franz, 79, 80, 86
Schutz, Waldemar, 72
Scythe Cross, 8
Searchlight, 255, 259, 260
Seawright family, 260
Secret Army Organisation (OAS) (France),
    215
Secretariado de Propaganda Nacional (Portugal),
    170
Sécurité et Liberté (France), 226
Security Battalions (Greece), 195
Seidel, Gill, 121, 126
Shi'ites, 15, 16
Sicily, 28-9, 35
Sido, Pierre, 173
Silesia, 66
Six Million Reconsidered, The (Committee for
    Truth in History), 124, 134
Skeggs, Malcolm, 269
skinheads, 95, 96, 99, 112, 190
Slovak People's Party, 8
Social Action Iniative (Ireland), 260
social characteristics of militant neo-Nazis,
    101-9
Social Democratic Party of Germany (SPD),
    66, 67, 73, 78, 80, 83, 96, 97
social psychology of militant neo-Nazism,
    110-11
Social Studies Circles VECTOR (Portugal),
    174
socialism, 6
Socialist Party (PSI) (Italy), 24, 28, 35
Socialist Party (Portugal), 176, 180
Socialist Party of the Reich (SRP), 71
Socialist People's Libyan Arab Jamahirya, 14
Sons of Glyndwr, 261
South Africa, 15
Soviet Union, 5-6, 13, 69, 76-7, 131
Sozialdemokratische Partei Deutschlands (SPD),
    66, 73, 78, 80, 83, 96, 97
Sozialistische Reichspartei (SRP), 71
Spain, 8, 10, 147-66, 256
Spanish-Basque Battalion (BVE), 157
Spanish Circle of Friends of Europe
    (CEDADE), 156, 162
Spanish Civil War, 148, 155
Spanish Committees (JJ.EE), 153, 162
Spanish National Front (FNE), 149
Spanish Phalanx (FE), 148

Spanish Phalanx of Committees for National Syndicalist Attack (FE de las JONS), 148, 149, 150, 151-2, 154, 161, 162
Spanish Socialist Workers Party (PSOE), 150, 151, 160
Spanish Statement (AE), 153
Spanish Traditionalist Phalanx of Committees for National Syndicalist Attack (FET y de las Jons), 148, 149
Spearhead, 245, 249, 265, 268, 269, 270, 272, 273-4, 279
Speer, Albert, 128-9
Spiazzi, Amos, 36
Spiegel, Der, 79, 101
Spinola, General, 176, 179
Stäglich, Wilhelm, 120, 127, 138
State Shinto, 14
Stein, Howard F., 130
Stephanopoulos, Stephanos, 201, 202
Sternhell, Z., 212, 213
Steven, Helena, 272
Strasser brothers, 88, 98, 115, 116, 264, 280
Strasserism, 92, 98, 99-100
Strauss, Franz Josef, 79, 80, 82-3
Sturzo, Don, 30
Sunnites, 15
Syria, 14

Tag, Ernst, 101
Tagmata Asfaleias (TA) (Greece), 195
Tagmata Ergassias (TE) (Greece), 194
Tagmata Ethnikis Amynis (TEA) (Greece), 197
Tambroni, Fernando, 31
Taylor, A.J.P., 141
Tempo Presente, 171
terrorism, 13, 33, 87 as subject of posters, 52-3
Terza Posizione (TP) (Italy), 37
Thadden, Adolf von, 72
Thatcher, Margaret, 249
Theotokis, Spyros, 202
Thielen, Fritz, 72
Third Position (TP) (Italy), 37
Tixier-Vignancourt, Jean-Louis, 216, 239
Topfer, Gerhard, 260, 261
Traditionalist Communion (CT) (Spain), 153
Trieste, 31
Tripodi, Nino, 160
Tsolakoglou, General, 195
Tunisia, 14
Turkey, 14
Turks, 95, 96, 99
Turner, Derrick, 260-1

Turner, Kevin, 254
Turner Diaries, The (Macdonald), 257-8
Tyndall, John, 245, 247-8, 249, 252, 256-7, 264, 265, 266, 270, 273, 277
Ulster, 12, 254, 256, 257, 260
ultras, 13
unemployment, 75-6, 103, 108, 254
Uniāo Nacional (UN) (Portugal), 169
Unión de Centro Democrático (UCD) (Spain), 150
Union Movement (UM) (UK), 246, 250
Unión Nacional (UN) (Spain), 150, 151
Union National des Etudiants Français, 236
United Democratic Left (EDA) (Greece), 197
United Kingdom, 8, 245-83
United Nationalist Movement (ENEK) (Greece), 202, 203, 204
University Front for National Action (FUAN) (Italy), 29, 32
Uomo Qualunque party (UQ) (Italy), 23-4, 26, 35
Ustasha (Croatia), 8

Van Ghele, Yves, 239
Vasallo de Number, Alberto, 153
Vaughan, Leslie Eric, 248
Veale, J.P., 137
Venizelos, Elefterios, 191, 192, 193
Verrall, Richard, 122, 265, 266-7, 268, 273
Vidal-Naquet, Pierre, 142
Vieille Taupe, La, 122, 125
Vlaams Blok (VB), 86
Vlaamsch National Verbond (Belgium), 8
Volkssozialistische Bewegung Deutschlands/Partei der Arbeit (VSBD/PdA), 90-1, 92, 97, 99

Walker, Michael, 251, 253
Wansee conference, 127-8
Warriors of Christ the King (Spain), 149
Weber, Mark, 131
Webster, Martin, 248, 250, 251-2, 269, 270
Wehrsportgruppe Hoffmann (WSG Hoffmann) (W. Germany), 87, 90, 115
White Noise Club, 255-6
Williamson, G., 255, 260
Willner, Heinz, 72
Wilson, Colin, 123
Wind Rose organisation (Italy), 36
Wingfield, Martin, 254, 255
women, 103, 108, 118, 264-83

Woolf, Stuart, 160
Working Community of National
    Organisations/Populist League (ANV/
    VB) (W. Germany), 100
World Zionist Organization, 142
Worldwide Growth and Impact of
    'Holocaust' Revisionism, The (IHR),
    127
Wright, Sheila, 276

Young Front (JF) (W. Germany), 91
Young National Front (YNF) (UK), 277
Young Portugal Movement (MJP), 171, 172,
    173
youth unemployment, 75, 254

Zentrum (Germany), 66, 67
Zhivkov, Todor, 15
Zoli, Adone, 30